CAMPAIGNING FOR THE VOTE

CAMPAIGNING FOR THE VOTE

Kate Parry Frye's SUFFRAGE DIARY

Edited by

Elizabeth Crawford

First published by Francis Boutle Publishers
272 Alexandra Park Road
London N22 7BG
Tel/Fax: (020) 8889 7744
Email: info@francisboutle.co.uk
www.francisboutle.co.uk

ISBN 978 1 903427 75 0

Contents

List of Illustrations

Thursday May 21st 1914

To office. Attended Committee at 12.15 and had such a long list of fixtures and things to tell them that they all looked startled. The people I have roped in to help since I came on the scene.

Then in the afternoon I went to Buckingham Palace to see the Women's deputation – led by Mrs Pankhurst which went to try and see the King. It was simply awful – oh! those poor pathetic women – dresses half torn off – hair down hats off covered with mud and paint and some dragged along looking in the greatest agony – But the wonderful courage of it all. One man led along – collar torn off – face streaming with blood – he had gone to protect them. Fancy not arresting them until they got into that state. It is the most cruel & futile persecution because they know we have got to have 'Votes' – and others they have got us to this state – some women thinking it necessary and right to do the most awful things etc in order to bring the question forward – Oh what a farce to come to in a

A typical page from Kate's diary. On 21 May 1914 she watched as Mrs Pankhurst led women to the gates of Buckingham Palace in an attempt to see the King. Kate recorded that the resulting fracas was 'simply awful'.

Dramatis Personae

Family

Kate's father (*right*), Frederick Charlwood Frye (1845–1914), was one of the nine children of John and Cecilia Frye of Saffron Walden. John Frye was the town treasurer, a teacher of music and, after his appointment at the age of 8 in 1820, continued to be organist at Saffron Walden parish church until 1884. Frederick Frye was educated, until he was about 15, at Saffron Walden Grammar School and, after leaving, worked as a clerk to a solicitor.

Kate's mother, Jane Kezia Frye (1844–1925), was the youngest daughter of William and Kezia Crosbie of Winchester. William Crosbie was a Scots-born grocer with a shop in Winchester High Street.

Kate's sister, Agnes, was born in 1874 and died, unmarried, in 1937.

Kate's fiancé, later husband, John Robert Collins (1878–1958), was the son of Col John Robert Collins and his wife, Frances, of Kirkman Bank, Knaresborough, Yorkshire. He matriculated at Selwyn College, Cambridge, 1897, but did not take a degree. He joined the Cambridge University Rifle Volunteers, 1898, was transferred to the Volunteer Medical Staff Corps and served with the Yeomanry Field Hospital, Bearers Company during the South African War, 1900. He obtained a commission in the 26th Middlesex RVC, 1901, and transferred to the 3rd Middlesex Volunteer Artillery, 1906. He had begun his acting career by 1903 but maintained his interest in the Territorial Army. In 1910 he transferred to the Essex and Suffolk Royal Garrison Artillery in which unit he was serving, stationed at Shoeburyness, in August 1914. Here he commanded the 2nd line Company and temporarily held the appointments of adjutant RA and staff captain. He went to France in

1916 in Command of the 222 Siege Battery RGA and was awarded a Military Cross at the Battle of Arras in 1917. After the First World War, while remaining a member of the Territorial Army and becoming a special police constable, he returned to the theatre, working as an actor and as stage manager with the New Shakespeare and other companies, with varying degrees of lack of success. During the Second World War he was promoted lieutenant-colonel and worked with the Home Guard. In the 1950s he began a slow decline into dementia, Kate caring for him at home for as long as possible. With no money to provide for private care, John was certified and spent his final two years, much to Kate's distress, in St Bernard's Hospital, previously known as Middlesex County Asylum.

Kate's second cousin, Abbie Hargrave (c.1871–1936) was the relation to whom she felt the closest. Abbie was born Gertrude A. Frye, in India, the daughter of Charles Frye, a brother of Kate's grandfather. After she and her sister, Maggie, were orphaned when their father died in 1886 they were taken into the household of their father's elder sister, Caroline Hargrave. Aunt Caroline died in 1904 and on 2 August 1905 Abbie married her uncle-by-marriage, Basil Hargrave. The laws of consanguinity made it necessary for the couple to go abroad, to Brussels, to marry. Their son, Basil Truscott Hargrave, was born on 3 August 1911. Abbie had worked for a time as a governess and began her career as a writer of magazine stories in the 1890s. Later, using the pseudonym 'L. Parry Truscott', she published a number of novels, the first in 1902. On general election day in January 1910 Kate took Abbie round the North Kensington committee rooms and polling stations, 'showing her some of an election for copy'. [17 January 1910]. Abbie's 1913 novel, *Hilary's Career*, has a suffrage theme.

New Constitutional Society for Women's Suffrage – in order of appearance

Alexandra Wright (1879–1942) and [Frances] Gladys Wright (1884–1950) daughters of Lewis Thomson Wright, a scientific chemist, and his wife, Mary. Kate may not have been entirely correct in saying that the sisters 'had both taken degrees from Cambridge'. Alexandra had attended Notting Hill High School and then Newnham College, 1898–1900. She finally graduated from Bedford College, London, with a chemistry degree and undertook microscopic work for a research project with Karl Pearson, published as 'A Cooperative Study of Queens, Drones and Workers in Vespa vulgaris' in the journal 'Bio-metrika', 1907. However, she does not appear to have pursued a research career any further, but, rather, to have devoted herself to the suffrage movement from then until the vote was won. In 1933 she married Crescenzo Gambardella, the owner of a magnificent hotel on the Amalfi coast and eventually died in Italy.

Gladys Wright (second left) and Alexandra Wright (right) photographed at The Plat, summer 1906, together with Mrs Frye (left), Kate (third from left) and Agnes, somewhat obscured, as ever, in the background

Gladys Wright (1884–1950) had a BA degree, probably from the University of London. In 1908 she had been honorary secretary of the London Society for Women's Suffrage North Kensington branch, but resigned from the LSWS and was, from 1912, secretary of the New Constitutional Society for Women's Suffrage. She married Geoffrey Larpent Simmons in 1915 and had a son in 1925.

Helen Ogston (1883–?), daughter of the professor of forensic medicine at Aberdeen University. She had a science degree from Aberdeen and had trained in London as a sanitary inspector. She joined the WSPU in 1908 and became notorious for wielding a dogwhip against a steward at a Liberal Women's Federation meeting in the Albert Hall, at which Lloyd George was a speaker. She presumably left the WSPU in 1910 when she was appointed an organiser for the New Constitutional Society for Women's Suffrage. She shared a flat at 70 Albany Mansions, Battersea Park, London.

Adeline Chapman (1847–1931) president of the New Constitutional Society for Women's Suffrage. The widow of Arthur Guest, a Liberal MP, in 1899 she married Cecil Chapman.

Cecil Chapman (1852–1938) husband of the president of the NCS, a London police magistrate and member of the executive committee of the Men's League for Women's Suffrage. He was the author of *Marriage and Divorce*, 1911, in which he stressed the necessity for gender equality in marriage law.

Jessie Georgina Green (1862–1954) an active suffragist at whose house, 14 Warwick Crescent, Kate had attended suffrage drawing-room meetings. Miss Green's 1911 census return, completed by the enumerator, gives her age as 'about 50', living on private means. She has written across it 'No Vote No Census. I have conscientious objections to giving information to any Government which legislates for women without their consent'. By 1915 she was the honorary treasurer of the NCS.

Jean Forsyth (1879–1933) later Mrs Todhunter, grand-daughter of William Forsyth, the MP who had introduced women's suffrage bills in the House of Commons in the 1870s. She lived with her mother at 59 Carlisle Mansions, Westminster. A month earlier, when the census was taken, their caretaker wrote on the form that the family consisted only of women and that, therefore, they did not count as citizens. Jean Forsyth was at this time, with Gladys Wright, joint honorary secretary of the NCS.

Beatrice Hartley (1859–1940) adopted as a child, after the death of her parents, by the novelist Eliza Lynn Linton. She had left the London NUWSS to help found the NCS and was organiser of the Hampstead branch. 168 Adelaide Road, Hampstead.

Rose Lightman (1879–1912) born in Whitechapel, daughter of immigrants from Austria, by 1901 was a teacher, living with her mother and sisters in Walthamstow. Her younger sister, Nancy, was a speaker for the WSPU when Kate was campaigning for the NCS at the Reading by-election in autumn 1913.

Myra Sadd Brown (1872–1938) suffrage activist and mother of four. Imprisoned in 1912, she went on hunger strike. Crossways, Spring Elms Lane, Little Baddow; 34 Woodberry Down, Finsbury Park, London N.

Rev. Hugh Boswell Chapman (1853–1933) incumbent of the Savoy Chapel, brother to Cecil Chapman. Despite the flutterings he was to cause in Kate's heart – and apparently to others – he never married.

M. Slieve McGowan, Irish graduate with an interest in the theatre. In 1911, writing in *The Vote*, she urged suffragists to support the revival of Ibsen's *The Doll's House* at the Royal Court Theatre. Her play, *Trimmings*, was first performed in April 1911 and then again, produced by Madeleine Lucette Ryley, during the 1911 WSPU Christmas Fair.

Margaret Alice Simeon (1886–1961) later became secretary to the NCS. She was a cousin of Vere Awdry, author of *Thomas the Tank Engine*, and had previously been secretary to a Bath city councillor.

Clara K. Merivale Mayer [or Meyer] (b.c.1863) a professional suffrage speaker with a colourful and rather mysterious past. Known professionally as Miss Clara Merivale, she had received opera training in Paris, appeared briefly with the Carl Rosa Opera Company in Liverpool and London and, in 1880, had joined the D'Oyly Carte. She later worked in Australia, where she set up her own operatic company but, in Melbourne in 1891, with her husband, Gustave Mayer, she was declared bankrupt. The couple had been married in Australia in 1890, but separated in 1902 and she returned to England. In 1908 a divorce petition brought against her for desertion was dismissed on the grounds that her husband was living with another woman. Her operatic career over, Mrs Mayer opted for a public speaking role, spreading her services among the suffrage societies. She spoke for the NUWSS at Barnsley in 1911, for the Australian and New Zealand Women Voters at the Hyde Park demonstration in July 1912 and for the WFL in May and August 1912. She was hired as a speaker for the NCS in January 1913. Based in London, she lived for a time in a ladies' residential club in South Kensington.

Editor's note

Faced with an overwhelming amount of material, I have taken the editorial decision to limit this 'suffrage' edition of Kate Frye's voluminous diary to her activities, from early 1911, as a paid organiser for the New Constitutional Society for Women's Suffrage. It has, therefore, been necessary to omit many splendid descriptions of suffrage meetings and suffrage-related activities from the days when she had the luxury of giving her services freely to the suffrage cause.

In addition, with the intention of producing a version of Kate's diary that will capture the imagination of the general reader, I have taken the decision not to use elision points to indicate where material has been omitted, whether whole entries or sentences within an entry. To do so, while more correct, would have been seriously to interfere with the reader's enjoyment. The material omitted in no way alters the sense of the entries or of the whole text.

The illustrations are either of items that Kate herself collected and laid in her diary or photographs from her archive.

My thanks go to Anna Kisby, formerly of the Women's Library, who drew my attention to Kate Frye's archive, to my husband, Grant Crawford, for taking a real and practical interest in this project, and to Agnes and Massimo, to Edmund, Jackie and Lily, and to Beatrice for all their kindnesses.

All possible effort has been made to trace the copyright holder of Kate's estate.

Kate as a writer. Photograph taken at Berghers Hill by John Collins, probably in the 1930s

Introduction

Kate Parry Frye was a diarist. She was also a girl, a young woman, a middle-aged woman, an old woman, a daughter, a sister, a cousin, a niece, a fiancée, a wife, an actress, a suffragist, a playwright, an annuitant, a letter writer, a Liberal, a valetudinarian, a playgoer, and a shopper. She was a rail traveller, a bus traveller, a tube traveller, a reader, a *flâneuse*, a friend, and a political canvasser. She was a diner – in her parents' homes, in digs, in hotels, in restaurants, in cafés and later, of reluctant necessity, of her self-cooked meals. She was an enthusiast for clothes, a keeper of accounts, a reader of palms, a dancer, a holidaymaker, a visitor to the dentist, to the doctor, an observer of the weather, a worker of toy theatres, a needleworker, an animal lover – indeed dog worshipper – a close observer of the First World War and then of the Second. She was a radio listener, a television viewer, a neighbour and, finally, a carer, recording in detail the effect on her husband of the remorseless onset of dementia and the disintegration of his body and mind. Every one of these roles is played out in minute detail in the diaries she kept for 71 years, from 1887, when she was 9 years old, until October 1958, barely four months before her death in February 1959.

From this daily record of an entire life it is the diarist's involvement with the Edwardian suffrage movement that is highlighted in this drastically abridged edition of her diary. This is not because she played in any way a prominent part in that campaign; quite the reverse. It is because Kate was a mere suffrage foot soldier that her account is worth reliving. No other source allows us to experience in such detail and over such a length of time the day-to-day existence of a working suffragist. Although other 'suffrage diaries' survive in the public domain, most were written primarily because that involvement represented a singular experience, a highpoint in the diarist's life.[1] Kate's diary is valuable because, writing without the benefit of hindsight, she records the inconsequential daily details of, say, finding a chairman for a suffrage meeting in Maldon or dealing with an imperious speaker in Dover, as well as the rather more momentous suffrage occasions, such as waiting on the platform at King's Cross station as the train carrying Emily Wilding Davison's coffin is about to leave for Morpeth. No organiser from any other suffrage society has left such a

Kate with 'Joey', 31 March 1896

full account of the day-to-day struggle to convert the men and women of Edwardian England to the cause of women's suffrage. In *Women of the Right Spirit – paid organisers of the Women's Social and Political Union (WSPU)*, Krista Cowman draws material from a wide range of interesting sources in order to analyse the working life of Kate Frye's WSPU equivalents. Kate's diary adds another dimension, allowing us not only to observe her work but to share her experience.

Moreover, because the society that employed her – the New Constitutional Society for Women's Suffrage (NCS) – has otherwise left very little trace of its existence, Kate's diary increases immeasurably our knowledge of its rationale and personnel.[2] We can observe first-hand how a society campaigning in a constitutional manner to raise awareness of the necessity for 'votes for women', backing in particular the Conciliation Bills that were before parliament for much of the time that Kate was organising in the country, was affected by the activities of the militants, and how it became increasingly difficult to make and keep members appalled by the methods of the WSPU, or to hire halls in which to hold meetings, or even to find lodgings.

Although Kate's diary contains much of interest for those to whom the quotidian detail of life a hundred years ago appeals, allowing us to trace her train, bus and tube routes, to trudge with her on the hunt for digs, to accompany her to Westbourne Grove and West End shops, to the theatre and to tea shops, above all it allows us to accompany her in London and in Norfolk, Kent, Berkshire and Sussex as she knocks on doors, arranges meetings, trembles on platforms, speaks from carts in market squares and deals with the egos and foibles of her fellow suffragists. It was not a way of life to which she was born.

That event occurred on 9 January 1878 at the family home, 19 All Saints Road, North Kensington in London. This address, then and today, covers a building on the corner of All Saints Road and Lancaster Road. Then, as today, the ground floor of the building is a shop. In fact, then, as today, All Saints Road was a road of shops. In 1878 number 19 was a grocery, one of a chain of stores, trading under the name of 'Leverett and Frye', owned by Kate's father, who described himself as 'Grocer' on her birth certificate. It would appear that the Fryes and their two servants were the only residents of the building in a street where virtually every other dwelling was in multiple occupation, packed with a medley of greengrocers, cheesemongers, monthly nurses, needlewomen, painters, carmen, dressmakers, drapers and staymakers. Moreover, opening onto Lancaster Road, 19 All Saints Road has its own front door, giving it an entrance separate from the shop. This proximity, but disjunction, between the family home and the source of income was to characterise Kate Frye's view of the world. Her direct connection with 'trade' was not an aspect of life that, from the evidence of her diary, concerned her.

In 1878 Kate's parents were relative newcomers to Kensington, the prospect of commercial advancement having drawn her father, Frederick Charlwood Frye, to London from his home town of Saffron Walden. Indeed it was probably a commercial connection that had drawn him to his wife, Jane Kezia Crosbie. When they married in 1873 she was living with her elderly parents at Wooburn House, the Buckinghamshire estate of her married sister, Agnes Gilbey. Before his retirement, their father, William Crosbie, had been a grocer in Winchester and it may, again, have been through a trade connection that Agnes Crosbie met and, in 1858, married Alfred Gilbey, one of the brothers who had founded one of England's most successful wine and spirit importerships. Trading as W. & A. Gilbey, the firm dominated the wine and spirit market, owning vineyards in France, importing wine, and distilling gin and whisky. At her christening, held at St Michael's Church, Ladbroke Grove Road on 2 April 1878, Kate was named 'Parry' for her godfather, Henry Parry Gilbey, one of the original partners in W. & A. Gilbey. This family connection was to prove of great importance in her life.

Top: Kate was a keen – and early – radio listener.

Below: Kate in the foreground, with , left to right, her cousin, Abbie Frye, her mother and her sister Agnes. Photographed at The Plat, July 1899

Two years before his marriage Frederick Frye had set up a grocery business, as the junior partner of Frederick Leverett, the husband of one of his sisters. Although grocery was a competitive trade, the *Warehouseman and Drapers Trade Journal* recording 2500 retail grocers in London in 1872, Leverett & Frye had, from small beginnings – one shop in Church Street, Greenwich – expanded rapidly. It was one of the first firms to open a series of shops – a 'chain' of stores. The shop at 19 All Saints Road had opened in 1873/4, one of the first in the Leverett & Frye chain which, by the time of Frederick Leverett's early death in 1880, comprised around 13 branches. Under Frederick Frye's sole command the firm had then expanded, opening over 40 more stores, employing around 180 people and spreading over to Ireland.[3]

Frederick Leverett (1838–1880) was a member of a long-established Saffron Walden family. He was an accountant whose father had been a draper and grocer and mayor of the town.

The Gilbey connection proved invaluable. According to Alec Waugh,

'Gilbeys financed the company, feeling that it would provide a useful market for their wines, and, when Frye became MP for North Kensington, took over the entire business'.[4] Certainly Leverett and Frye were agents for W. & A. Gilbey, whose rapid expansion had been based on selling liquor in such 'off-licensed' premises as grocery stores, and in 1894, by which time Frederick Frye was an MP, the firm was formed into a private limited company, with W. & A. Gilbey as the major shareholder.[5] Frederick Frye was, however, expected to continue to manage the firm as he had when it was his own company. He was at this time an important figure in the grocery world, by 1891 chairman of the Metropolitan Grocers' Association.

However Frederick Frye's ambitions exceeded the world of grocery. In 1889, as a member of the Progressive party, which included both Liberals and members of the Labour movement, he was elected to the Kensington North seat on the London County Council and then, on 7 July 1892, as a Liberal, to the constituency's parliamentary seat, which he held until1895. Of the day of his election 14-year-old Kate confided to her diary that it was 'the most exciting and pleasing day I have ever gone through'.

In November 1893 the Fryes moved from All Saints Road to 25 Arundel Gardens, a six-storey house built in the 1860s as part of the rapid development around Ladbroke Grove. This solidly middle-class area, a definite step up in the world from All Saints Road, suited the Fryes very well. Westbourne Grove provided all the delights of a modern shopping street and Paddington Station was nearby, convenient for the train to Bourne End. For it was in this Buckinghamshire village that the Fryes leased their country house, The Plat, the fortunes of which had paralleled those of the family. The original small house, wonderfully positioned on the banks of the Thames, had acquired new, expanded, facades, transforming it from a modest dwelling into a home to which any late-19th-century small-time entrepreneur might aspire. Here, at The Plat, Kate and her elder sister, Agnes, spent idyllic youthful days, canoeing, punting and bicycling. For a few days in the summer the very popular Bourne End Regatta took place on the stretch of river alongside the house, giving the Fryes the opportunity to exercise patronage by offering hospitality to Regatta subscribers. In return the Frye daughters had the privilege of an introduction to whichever scion of an aristocratic family was that year presenting the prizes. For, as a local justice of the peace, Frederick Frye held a certain posi-

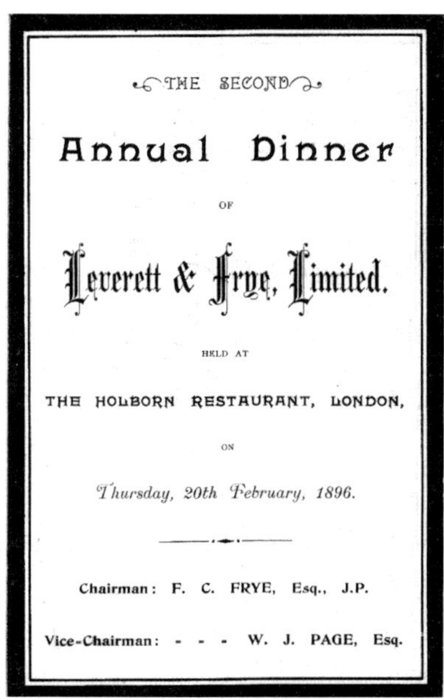
THE SECOND

Annual Dinner

OF

Leverett & Frye, Limited.

HELD AT

THE HOLBORN RESTAURANT, LONDON,

ON

Thursday, 20th February, 1896.

Chairman: F. C. FRYE, Esq., J.P.

Vice-Chairman: - - - W. J. PAGE, Esq.

Leverett & Frye, for a time, a successful grocery chain

tion in Buckinghamshire society, as he did, as a politician, in Kensington.

But even more important to the Fryes than Bourne End's pleasures as a fashionable resort was its proximity to Wooburn House and Kate's Aunt Agnes, whose husband, Alfred Gilbey, had died in 1879 leaving her a wealthy widow. She and her daughters, particularly Constance, were to prove generous benefactors to Kate, her mother and sister in the years after the collapse of Frederick Frye's finances. It was ironic that it was because Agnes Gilbey's sons had called in monies owed them by Frederick Frye that, in the summer of 1913, the final collapse occurred.[6] But both before and after this catastrophe Kate was an intimate of Wooburn House, entirely used to staying in a grand 18th-century mansion, a point to bear in mind when we accompany her canvassing, as a paid employee, at the doors of lesser establishments.

In Kate's diary we can trace, in daily detail, the interconnected circles of family and trade – the grocerage and the beerage – in which the Fryes moved. At the end of the 19th century the Gilbey firm was expanding and family connections were multiplying as sons grew up and new sons-in-law were settled in a range of associated enterprises. However, although the Fryes attended the parties and weddings of the Watney, Blyth, Gold and Gilbey families, it is clear that Kate appreciated the social – and financial – dis-

Top: Bourne End Regatta in its heyday. Tea was served on the lawn of The Plat

Left: Admission card for Bourne End Regatta

tinctions that existed – and over the years increased – between the various elements. In the late 1890s, when attending elaborate functions at the glamorous houses in Portland Place owned by Sir James Blyth and Henry Blyth, she noted what she perceived as snubs from girls of her own generation – for instance, a refusal to shake her hand – and wondered 'yet we go to their parties – it's no use not to really and I do enjoy seeing all their celebrated friends'. [17 February 1898] For a star-struck young woman such parties were indeed a delight. In 1896, at a previous Blyth 'At Home', Kate recorded that she spoke to the author Anthony Hope and observed in the room not only Beerbohm Tree but also the theatrical couples Henry Esmond and Eva Moore and Winifred Emery and Cyril Maude.

Outside the family, but still inside the trade, William Whiteley, the 'Universal Provider', was a close family friend and his store, which dominated Westbourne Grove, or 'the Grove', as Kate refers to it, was the Fryes' favoured destination for the purchase of clothes and all manner of articles for the home. When in London, Kate, her sister and her mother made daily outings to Whiteleys, augmented by frequent visits to Regent Street and Bond Street. William Whiteley's presents were generous, although Kate lamented his lack of taste. In 1907 the Fryes were, naturally, shocked by Whiteley's murder, shot in his store by a man claiming to be his illegitimate son. Although Kate's own attitude to Whiteley is somewhat condescending – hinting that he was not quite a gentleman – she gives no indication of knowing anything untoward in his private life. Although the Fryes must have known that he was divorced, Whiteley was a welcome guest at The Plat, joining them on summer expeditions on the Thames in their launch, the 'Loosestrife'.

Apart from shopping, Kate's main occupation was the theatre. She and her family were devotees, seeing several plays a week and in 1901 she took the bold step of deciding that she would put herself on the stage. Over the years she and her sister had received music, singing and recitation lessons. Neither had attended school, but had received lessons at home from a daily governess, the last being a Miss Cox, who lived in Maidenhead and travelled into London to teach them. However after she left at the end of 1893, when Kate was barely 15, there seems to have been little formal education, other than a visiting French governess and a music teacher. Throughout her life Kate lamented her lack of education, writing, for instance, on 4 September 1914, 'Neither do I understand why I was born if I wasn't to be educated'. She was a keen reader and in

Above: Kate and Agnes canoeing in the flooded garden of The Plat. This image was used on the Frye's 1903 Christmas card.

her youth filled volumes with analyses of books she had read. She had literary ambition, her interest in writing evident in the enthusiasm she maintained in recording the daily entries in her diary. In later life she wrote numerous plays, only one of which, co-written with her husband, was published.[7]

31 Porchester Terrace
Hyde Park. W
January 9th 1899.

Dear Kate,
I wish you very sincerely "Many Happy returns of the day" May Heavens richest blessings rest upon you throughout a long and happy life – is the sincere wish of
Yours most sincerely
William Whiteley

Kate took acting seriously, in 1902 becoming a pupil at the Ben Greet Academy as did, a year later, another would-be actress, Sybil Thorndike.[8] Kate suffered no opposition from her parents, although she felt that her father might have been more actively encouraging. There was certainly no suggestion that to be an actress was to flout any standards of propriety. Using the stage names 'Kate Parry' or 'Katharine Parry', she did receive some acting engagements, for instance touring in England and Ireland with the production of J.M. Barrie's *Quality Street* produced by the A. and S. Gatti and Charles Frohman Company. However around 1908 she came to the conclusion that acting did not pay and, although on some later occasions was sufficiently desperate for employment to think she might have to try the theatre again, in the event employment as a suffrage organiser saved her from a return to the boards.

Above: The letter from William Whiteley that accompanied Kate's 21st birthday present

Left: On 7 October 1903, three days before Mrs Pankhurst founded the Women's Social and Political Union, Kate was in Dublin, being photographed in her Quality Street *costume*

The *Quality Street* tour, however, was to have a fateful impact on her life as it was while playing in Blackpool, in September 1903, that she first mentions John Collins, a fellow member of the company, to whom a year later she became engaged. Although in her diary Kate makes it all too clear, both then and, indeed, through the rest of her life, that the romance was somewhat one-sided, that she was fond of him because he was so very much in love with her, close proximity during a subsequent theatrical tour had led her into a situation which she later described as 'infatuation'. At the time she wrote, 'I ought to have fought against loving him – but instead I have just given in to my senses'. This same entry, written on the evening of the engagement, continues, 'I must not ever let him guess I am not quite satisfied – having put my hand to the plough'.[9] The toiler in the field is not the most romantic of images and reflected Kate's clear-sighted view of the situation. The entry goes on, 'And what do I get – will John turn out ever a satisfactory husband. He seems doomed to failure not success'. John had no family money and little prospect of earning enough to keep Kate in the style that convention thought necessary. The engagement, therefore, continued for over 10 years until, in late 1914, Kate, now homeless, decided that, with the prospect before her of living alone in a succession of digs, what pre-war society had deemed necessary no longer applied in wartime. Moreover John was now in receipt of an officer's pay – and looked rather handsome in khaki. They were married on Kate's 37th birthday, 9 January 1915.

Messrs. A. & S. GATTI
AND
Mr. CHARLES FROHMAN'S
TOUR
"Quality Street"

Aug. 31st	P. of W. Theatre	Birmingham
Sept. 7th	O. H. and W. G.	Blackpool
" 14th	Alexandra Theatre	Stoke Newington
" 21st	Fulham Theatre	S.W.
" 28th	Shakespeare Theatre	Liverpool
Oct. 5th	Theatre Royal	Dublin
" 12th	Opera House	Belfast
" 19th	Theatre Royal	Newcastle
" 26th	Opera House	Croydon
Nov 2nd	Borough Theatre	Stratford
" 9th	Coronet Theatre	W.
" 16th	Camden Theatre	N.W.

DAVID ALLEN & SONS, LTD., LONDON, HARROW, BELFAST &C.

Calendar for the Quality Street *tour, 1903*

In the early years of her engagement Kate worked as a volunteer for the constitutional women's suffrage campaign, her growing interest in this cause reflecting its growing popularity in the country. Politics, naturally, were of great interest to the Fryes. On several occasions in the 1890s, when her father was an MP, Kate had accompanied him to the House of Commons, even, on 24 March 1893, sitting in the Ladies' Gallery through an all-night session. Of this she wrote 'It was a most interesting and extraordinary debate first on the payment of members of Parliament then on something to do with army "rations" – with the Conservative party obstructing everything all through the night and morning and using up the time.' For much of the 1890s her mother was president of the North Kensington Women's Liberal Association, hosting drawing-room meetings that Kate and her sister were expected to attend. Although there are a few mentions in the 1890s of NKWLA meetings devoted to suffrage concerns, from 1906 Kate's diary records her growing involvement in the suffrage campaign, first as a volunteer and then as a paid organiser for the New Constitutional Society for Women's Suffrage (NCS). It is this period of professional engagement, from early 1911 until mid-1915, which is the subject of *Campaigning for the Vote*.

The New Constitutional Society, formed in early 1910, had among its founding members Alexandra and Gladys Wright, whom Kate had known since January 1906, when she met Alexandra while they were both campaigning at the general election for the North Kensington Liberal candidate, H.Y. Stanger. The Wrights were then living at Linden Gardens, near Notting Hill tube station, but moved, in 1910, to the detached, stucco splendour of 27 Pembridge Crescent. Commenting, on 28 March 1906, on her first formal afternoon visit to Linden Gardens, Kate wrote 'The girls have both taken degrees at Cambridge so must be very clever. It doesn't show much but they are very bright – and I like Alexandra very much'. As leading members of the NCS the Wrights were in a position to offer employment to Kate, for which patronage the diary shows she was on occasions both grateful and resentful. From once occupying a secure position in society as daughter of the local MP she was now reliant on the goodwill – and took orders from – women whom she found, now that the trappings of her middle-class security had vanished, difficult to count as friends.

For the offer of paid employment by the New Constitutional Society had proved fortuitous, coinciding as it did with the complete collapse in the Frye family fortunes. It is clear that Frederick Frye had for some time mismanaged his affairs. In April 1906 Kate noted that they were letting The Plat for the Season, commenting on how very different it felt to be compelled for financial reasons to do so rather than, as in the past, renting it out while enjoying a splendid holiday on the continent. In November 1908 the Arundel Road house was exchanged for a North Kensington flat which, in turn, was given up in January 1911. The Fryes then retreated to Bourne End, until, on 12 September 1913, even that became beyond their means and Kate records the final leaving of The Plat. Her mother, father and sister moved into rented rooms in Worthing. Kate was now to all intents homeless, living in a succession of digs or, if working in London, often being obliged to stay with the Wrights.

Top: John Collins photographed while on tour with Kate in Quality Street, *1903*

Left: Kate and John were engaged on 20 September 1904, touring with Thoroughbred, *a play by Ralph Lumley*

Kate took up her employment in March 1911 and, even after war was declared in August 1914, continued working for the New Constitutional Society in its London office, now committed to 'war work' rather than to suffrage. A few months after her marriage in 1915 she succumbed to an illness that is never fully explained, and never returned to the NCS office, finally resigning in 1916. She did not work again, apart from a brief return to the stage in 1932/3 touring, with her husband, in the play, *The Miracle*.[10] For after distinguished service in the First World War John Collins resumed his career as actor and stage manager, which was, as Kate predicted, dogged by failure. The couple remained childless, perhaps not entirely from choice. In 1920/21 they, with Kate's mother and sister, bought from their Gilbey cousins a group of properties in the hamlet of Berghers Hill, on the ridge above Wooburn House. They knocked two cottages together and named the resulting house 'The Old Cottage'; the other was 'Hill Top'. Here they lived for the rest of their lives.[11] Although these properties are now eminently desirable, for much of the time that the Collinses and Fryes lived there they had few facilities. When they first moved in, Old Cottage's pump was not even in the kitchen, but out in the yard and, to Kate's horror, the water in the well was condemned as typhoid bearing. Although matters did improve, life was a constant struggle which, together with a lack of any meaningful occupation, manifested itself in an increasing concern with health. For a time in the 1920s, when the Collinses still maintained a small London flat, Kate was a patient of Dr Ethel Bentham, a senior member of the Labour party whose LCC election meetings she had attended in 1910. Dr Bentham, a progressive physician, does not appear to have been entirely sympathetic to Kate's medical concerns. After a visit to the surgery on 3 March 1921 Kate wrote, 'She was in a most peculiar mood and so vented it on me telling me I really must be more sensible. Female doctors are touchy.' Dr Bentham was also consulted by Agnes Frye, who was already well into a long decline that culminated in her death in 1937. On 8 April 1922 Kate wrote: 'Just finishing tea at 5.30 when Dr Bentham arrived, had not been expecting her – I don't know

Kate outside The Heights, Berghers Hill, c. 1918. The Old Cottage, where her mother and Agnes lived, is to the left.

which of us she had come to see or both. She had a long talk and she is a nice old thing. But she rather frightened me about Agnes says her condition may become serious unless she has occupation. I feel very disquieted'. From Kate's references to her sister's life it is all too likely that Dr Bentham's diagnosis was entirely correct. Agnes, who never worked and had few interests, appears, after the loss of the family's money, status and all hope of marriage, to have given up on life, spending much of her later years in bed, drifting towards death.

Despite her valetudinarian concerns, Kate lived to be 81. She wrote her final diary entry on 1 October, five months after John's death, her handwriting as steady as ever. It is likely that soon afterwards she suffered a stroke, dying on the following 16 February in a Buckinghamshire nursing home. Her will reveals that the diaries, together with the 'zinc-lined double doored double locked bookcase' in which they were kept, were in effect her main bequest.[12] Although the bookcase has been lost, Kate's diaries, long separated from anybody who knew anything of her, survive, albeit in an outwardly damaged condition, along with a copious archive of photographs and ephemera that illustrate her life. Although she never intended her diary for publication, Kate occasionally refers to a future reader of what she termed 'the Chronicles of myself'.[13] Writing in her diary on 10 February 1918 of the passing of the Equal Representation Act, which gave votes to women over 30, she noted her surprise that 'someone hasn't thought of me in connection with the work'. She might well, therefore, be gratified to discover that, nearly a century later, that omission has been rectified and the 'myself' that is chronicled in this version of her diary is that of Kate Parry Frye – suffrage organiser.

OCTOBER 1958

Wednesday **1**
(274-91)

And a pouring wet day. Some of the showers so heavy one could hardly hear oneself think - and at 1 o.c. in the torrential downpour heavy thunder and I eat my dinner with the Electric light switched on. I did rush out just before getting tea to get rid of the rubbish. Was awake early - B'fast at 8 - and up and dressed before 10. Expected Mrs B. but no sign of her and I was glad as there wasn't much I wanted her to do and I could do it. And do the veg. for dinner still off the Chicken and enjoyed a nice meal. Some other jobs then a rest and nap. Just washing up tea when Mrs L. arrived she has been busy with visitors I had not seen her since Friday. And then a few jobs and to my desk. Woke up feeling much better quite different and am thankful. Tried to speak to Dr Edwards but he was not in Surgery.

Kate's final diary entry

Prologue

The women's suffrage campaign was launched in 1866 with the aim of giving women the same right to a parliamentary vote as that enjoyed by men. Through the 19th century campaigners lobbied steadily, if unsuccessfully, using all the constitutional methods at their disposal and forming a succession of societies which developed on an ad hoc basis, dynamic, interactive and reactive. Most of the members of these societies were committed, in varying degrees, to the Liberal party. The Frye family's politics, as shown in the following entry from Kate Frye's diary, was at the radical end of the Liberal spectrum; Mrs Fawcett's was at the conservative.

'Friday 20 March 1896 [London: 25 Arundel Gardens]

Mother and I went to a Drawing-Room Meeting held at Mrs McGrath's at 32 Colville Terrace of the NKWLA [North Kensington Women's Liberal Association] to hear Mrs Henry Fawcett lecture on 'Woman's Suffrage'. Mother took the Chair. We had to go in a cab as it was such a dreadfully wet evening but walked home in the rain. Mrs Fawcett speaks well but she did not seem to go down very well at the Meeting. She is very much a Conservative except on the one subject which with her way of looking at it isn't very Liberal either, only the Lady house holders to have Votes – you see that won't quite do for us – if they have it at all – they ought to have them as the men do. Altogether I did not care for the evening.'

At the time of the 1896 meeting the two Liberal extremes – as exemplified in the views of Kate Frye and Mrs Fawcett – were represented by two different suffrage societies, formed after a split in 1888. In 1897, however, they agreed to harness their resources in order to work together more effectively within the newly-created National Union of Women's Suffrage Societies (NUWSS). Six years later, with little progress made, the NUWSS resolved to bring greater energy to their campaign. It may have been a coincidence that it was a week before this October 1903 meeting that Mrs Emmeline Pankhurst, who had worked for many years as a member of various suffrage societies, took matters into her own hands and founded the Women's Social and Political Union (WSPU). On the Saturday night that she summoned the first meeting of this

Millicent Garrett Fawcett (1847–1929) widow of a Liberal MP, had been involved in the suffrage movement since its beginnings in 1866 and was soon to become president of the National Union of Women's Suffrage Societies.

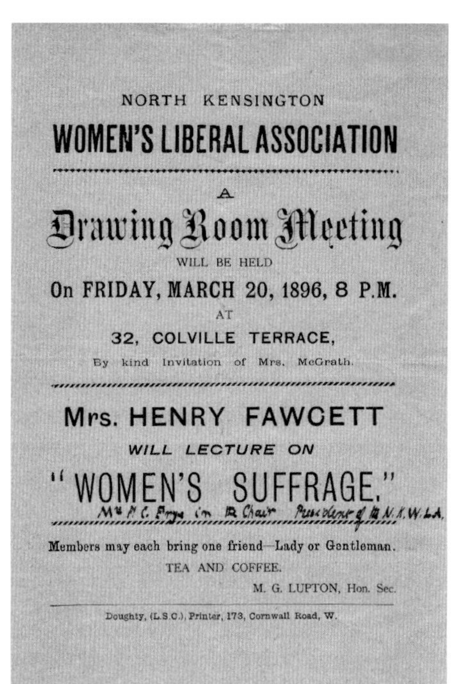

NORTH KENSINGTON

WOMEN'S LIBERAL ASSOCIATION

A

Drawing Room Meeting

WILL BE HELD

On FRIDAY, MARCH 20, 1896, 8 P.M.

AT

32, COLVILLE TERRACE,

By kind Invitation of Mrs. McGrath.

Mrs. HENRY FAWCETT

WILL LECTURE ON

"WOMEN'S SUFFRAGE."

Mrs H. C. Frye in the Chair President of the N.K.W.L.A.

Members may each bring one friend—Lady or Gentleman.

TEA AND COFFEE.

M. G. LUPTON, Hon. Sec.

Doughty, (L.S.C.), Printer, 173, Cornwall Road, W.

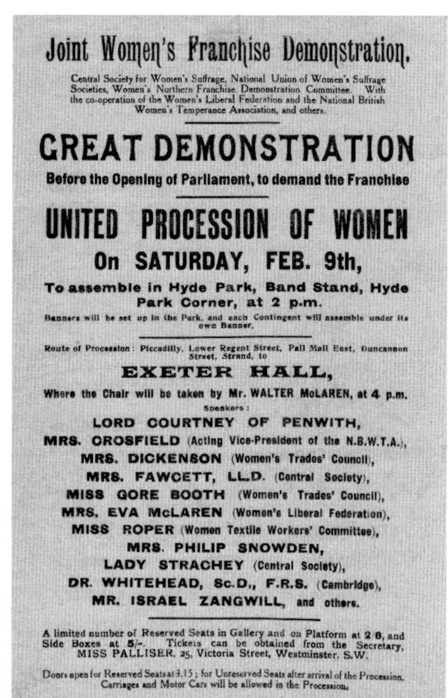

Joint Women's Franchise Demonstration.

Central Society for Women's Suffrage, National Union of Women's Suffrage Societies, Women's Northern Franchise Demonstration Committee. With the co-operation of the Women's Liberal Federation and the National British Women's Temperance Association, and others.

GREAT DEMONSTRATION

Before the Opening of Parliament, to demand the Franchise

UNITED PROCESSION OF WOMEN

On SATURDAY, FEB. 9th,

To assemble in Hyde Park, Band Stand, Hyde Park Corner, at 2 p.m.

Banners will be set up in the Park, and each Contingent will assemble under its own Banner.

Route of Procession: Piccadilly, Lower Regent Street, Pall Mall East, Duncannon Street, Strand, to

EXETER HALL,

Where the Chair will be taken by Mr. WALTER McLAREN, at 4 p.m.

Speakers:

LORD COURTNEY OF PENWITH,
MRS. CROSFIELD (Acting Vice-President of the N.B.W.T.A.),
MRS. DICKENSON (Women's Trades' Council),
MRS. FAWCETT, LL.D. (Central Society),
MISS GORE BOOTH (Women's Trades' Council),
MRS. EVA McLAREN (Women's Liberal Federation),
MISS ROPER (Women Textile Workers' Committee),
MRS. PHILIP SNOWDEN,
LADY STRACHEY (Central Society),
DR. WHITEHEAD, Sc.D., F.R.S. (Cambridge),
MR. ISRAEL ZANGWILL, and others.

A limited number of Reserved Seats in Gallery and on Platform at 2/6, and Side Boxes at 5/-. Tickets can be obtained from the Secretary, MISS PALLISER, 25, Victoria Street, Westminster, S.W.

Doors open for Reserved Seats at 3.15; for Unreserved Seats after arrival of the Procession. Carriages and Motor Cars will be allowed in the Procession.

new society to meet around her kitchen table in Manchester, Kate Frye was in Dublin, on tour with a theatrical company.

Two years later, in October 1905, when Mrs Pankhurst's daughter, Christabel, brought the WSPU to newspaper prominence after being imprisoned, with Annie Kenney, for their behaviour at a Liberal party meeting, Kate was living at home at Bourne End and made no reference in her diary to this new entry on the suffrage scene. A few months later, during the January 1906 general election, while still 'resting' between theatrical engagements, she worked for the successful North Kensington Liberal candidate, H.Y. Stanger. She was elated by the Liberal landslide, but made no mention of the prospects for women's suffrage, more interested in the 'Free Trade' aspect of the campaign.

However on 26 April 1906, during a Social Evening given by Mrs Frye for the NKWLA, Kate noted that 'there was a little discussion of what took place in the House last night – the disgraceful disturbance kicked up by some women during the Woman Suffrage debate. Mrs Stanger had a letter from her husband on the matter – and the Misses Wright who came as our guests spoke. It really was awfully comical and no one showed any sense of humour.' From now on it is likely that Kate did take notice of the increasingly newsworthy suffrage campaign. In October, although she made no comment, she cut out and laid into her diary a newspaper cutting reporting the imprisonment of Mrs Cobden Sanderson and other members of the WSPU after their arrest outside the House of Commons.

By the end of the year, interested in the subject, but probably not convinced by the WSPU's militant tactics, Kate had joined the Central Society for Women's Suffrage, which operated under the umbrella of the NUWSS. The Central Society was a descendant of the society of which Mrs Fawcett had in 1896 been the representative. In 1907, for greater clarity, it was renamed 'The London Society for Women's Suffrage'.

As the women's suffrage campaign became more public, Kate's interest grew. In February 1907 she took part in the first public procession staged by the NUWSS through muddy London streets, writing, 'We were an imposing spectacle all with badges – each section under its own banners. Ours got broken, poor thing, unfortunately, and caused remarks. I felt like a martyr of old and walked proudly along. I would not jest with the crowd – though we had some jokes with ourselves. It did seem an extraordinary walk and it took some time as we went very slowly occasionally when we got congested – but we went in one long unbroken procession.' [9 February 1907]

In the following months she attended drawing-room meetings, acted as steward at large public meetings, read palms at fund-raising bazaars, followed the progress of suffrage bills, including one introduced by H.Y. Stanger, and on occasion delivered leaflets to houses and flats in North Kensington. In April 1907 her growing interest in suffrage coincided with her devotion to the theatre and she was delighted to be taken by Alexandra and Gladys Wright to see 'Votes for Women!', a play by the American actress and WSPU supporter Elizabeth Robins. Of the event she wrote, 'Needless to say the acting was perfection as it generally is at the Court Theatre and the second act – the meeting in Trafalgar Square – ought to draw the whole of London. I was besides myself with excitement over it – so were the Wrights – we all loved it.' [16 April 1907]

In August and September 1907 Kate was on tour with the company of Arthur A. Horner, playing, for £2 weekly, in a J.M. Barrie farce, *Walker, London*. On her return she stewarded at the annual meeting of the London Society for Women's Suffrage on 6 November and at a particularly disorderly meeting held at Paddington Baths on 5 December. Of this she noted, 'It was Bedlam let loose'.

Although a member of the constitutional London Society for Women's Suffrage, Kate was very happy to attend a meeting organised by the militant WSPU. She found 'It was all just a little too theatrical but very wonderful. Miss Annie Kenney interested me the most – she seems so "inspired" quite a second Joan of Arc. I was very pleased not to be missing so wonderful an evening'. [19 March 1908]

Miss Katharine Parry,
Palmist.
At Homes, Bazaars, etc.
14 Colville Mansions,
Powis Terrace,
Bayswater, W.

As a palmist, Kate used her stage name. By this time the Frye family had been obliged to move from their London house into a flat

In June 1908 when the NUWSS staged a spectacular summer proces-

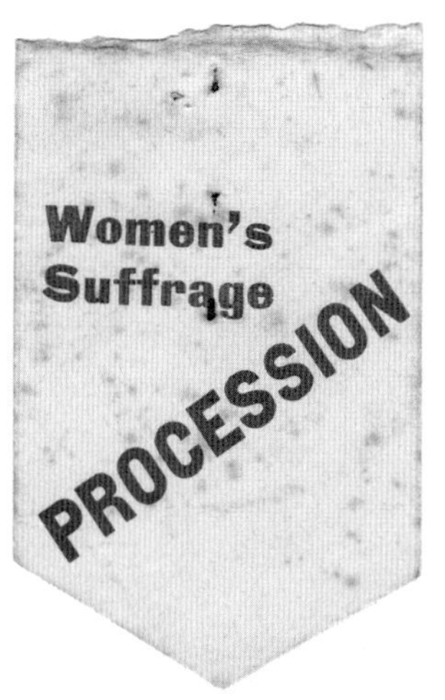

sion of which magnificent banners, designed by the Artists' Suffrage League, were a feature, Kate was proud to carry that for North Kensington, even though it was tiring work.[14] After the long march from the Embankment she described how 'I got in the [Albert] hall about 5.10 and they started the meeting just as I sank down. I must own to feeling completely done when I left the Banner. I got cramp in both feet at once and felt 1,000 but I dashed into the hall found the seat in my box with the Wrights and Alexandra, like an angel, got me a cup of tea. She, Gladys and another girl looking most awfully charming in cap and gown.' [13 June 1908]

The following year Kate was, naturally, interested in the new suffrage society, the Actresses' Franchise League (AFL) that had been formed to represent women in the theatrical profession, first attending one of its meetings in March 1909. There she was introduced to the actress Eva Moore, of whom she wrote, 'She didn't seem to like me much but I am used to treating all Suffrage women as merely women not little Queens'. [23 March 1909] In the same month she had spent a morning standing outside Chancery Lane tube station with Alexandra Wright, handing out London Society for Women's Suffrage leaflets. Of this experience she wrote 'It was curious work and a bitter wind blew on us but the men were really quite nice and we had no unpleasant experience. I suppose people are getting used to "Suffragettes"'. [8 March 1909]

In November 1909, while at Bourne End, Kate refused to help the Liberal candidate campaign at the forthcoming general election. 'I had to explain that as a keen Suffragist I could not do anything to help the present member, Mr Herbert – he is so very Anti.'[6 November 1909] A couple of months later her suffragism was made manifest on the tea table when, for her 32nd birthday on Sunday 9 January 1910, 'Annie [the cook] had made me a birthday cake with "Votes for Women" around it'. In the same month, during the general election campaign, Kate canvassed North Kensington and Islington for signatures for a petition organised by the NUWSS. It was signed by 280,000 male voters and presented to the House of Commons in March 1910, but did nothing to change government policy.

On 5 January 1910, as campaigning for the general election was underway, the New Constitutional Society for Women's Suffrage was founded by former members of the London Society for Women's Suffrage, including the Wright sisters. The founders explained that 'the powerlessness of the private member in the House of Commons to pass any Bill into law which has not been accepted by the Government of the day renders it absolutely necessary to direct all available force to the conversion or coercion of the Government only, and for this reason the NCS has adopted what is known as the anti-Government policy. The definite character of this policy has already met with a large response from Constitutional Suffragists who, while disquieted by the pronounced tactics of the more forward-going Societies on the one hand, have felt dispirited by the half-hearted and perplexing counsels on the other'.[15] The intention was 'to unite all suffragists who believe in the anti-Government election policy, who desire to work by constitutional means, and to abstain from public criticism of other suffragists whose conscience leads them to adopt different methods'. The NCS was, thus, carrying out the election policy of the WSPU, but eschewing the WSPU's other weapon, militancy. By resolving to work against government (Liberal) candidates it was going further than the current NUWSS policy, which was only to do so when the candidate did not include support for women's suffrage in his election address.

In April 1910 the NCS opened a London office at 8 Park Mansions Arcade, which ran between Knightsbridge and Brompton Road, underneath a newish block of flats. On 13 April Kate noted in her diary: 'After tea I did up a large box of flowers and sent off to Alexandra Wright at the Offices of the New Constitutional Society at Knightsbridge as they are having an "opening" there tomorrow'.

Then, as now, Knightsbridge was a distinctly 'shopping' area of London and not one favoured by any of the other national suffrage societies, all of which were now positioned in 'business' areas. The NCS's choice of Knightsbridge could be seen as reflecting the upper-middle-class worldview of its founding members. This was peculiarly exemplified in one campaign it devised that required members and sympathisers to send tradespeople, when paying bills, a pledge card declaring that they had resolved to

London Society for Women's Suffrage.
Hitherto known as
The Central Society for Women's Suffrage.

Telephone: 3119 Victoria.
Central Office:
25, Victoria Street,
Westminster, London, S.W.
President:—
The Lady Frances Balfour.
Secretary:—
Miss P. Strachey.

Please reply to:—
100. Westbourne Grove
W.

Local Hon. Secretary for:—
N. Kensington.

June 11th 1908.

Dear Kate,
It seems that I must send in the name & address of my Banner Bearer in chief to the Artists League in order that the men's League who is to hang on to it till you take charge may know who is the authorised person.
As time is getting short

Above: Gladys Wright invited Kate to carry the North Kensington banner in the June 1908 NUWSS Procession

The New Constitutional Society for Women's Suffrage.

Shop and Office - 8, PARK MANSIONS ARCADE, KNIGHTSBRIDGE.
OFFICE HOURS 11–6. SATURDAYS 11–1.

Hon. Sec.—Miss F. GLADYS WRIGHT, B.A.

Special Fixtures.

Entertainment.

Saturday, April 9th, 8 p.m.
Entertainment in aid of the funds of the Society arranged by Mrs. Nesbit at 6, Wentworth Studios, Manresa Road, Chelsea.
Cicely Hamilton's Waxworks.
Recitation of Olive Schreiner's Dream by Miss Winifred Mayo.
Miss Maddeline Roberts in a duologue, and others.
The Rev. Hugh Chapman will speak.
Refreshments will be provided at a moderate charge.
Tickets, **2/6** and **1/-** each, can be obtained from:—
Miss Edith Craig, 31, Bedford Street, Strand,
Miss Cicely Hamilton, 28, Glebe Place, Chelsea.
Mrs. Nesbit, 2, Trafalgar Square, Chelsea.

Opening of Shop and Office.

Thursday, April 14th, 3.30–6 p.m.
The President and Committee invite members and their friends to rally round them and make the opening of the office an enthusiastic and inspiring occasion.
Tea will be served, 6d each.

April 19th and every Tuesday, 3.30–6 p.m.
"At Homes" for members and friends. Tea 6d.
From 7 p.m.—"At Homes" for shop assistants and others.

Friday, April 22nd, 8.30 p.m.
Mrs. Rhuvon Guest "At Home" to members and their friends at 14, Bedford Square, W.C. The Rev. Dr. Cobb will speak.
Other "At Homes" will be announced later.

On and after Tuesday, April 19th.

The Committee will be glad to receive presents of Cakes, Sweets, Flowers, etc., for the "At Homes," or for sale in the shop. These should reach the shop not later than 12 o'clock on Tuesdays.

SPEAKERS, WORKERS, and CANVASSERS URGENTLY NEEDED

spend as little as possible until the vote was won. It was hoped that in this way women could be seen to be capable of exerting economic pressure. The NCS also tried to break down what they perceived as a press boycott on women's suffrage by encouraging its members to support, over any other newspapers, the *Manchester Guardian*, which had always been sympathetic, and the *Standard*, which had introduced a 'Woman's Platform' page. Over the years the NCS expanded its offices, in 1911 acquiring a shop at 9 Park Mansions Arcade, and by 1916 occupied a mezzanine floor above Farrows Bank at 143 Knightsbridge, as well as a shop and mezzanine floor and basement at 8 Park Mansions Arcade. The NCS never opened branch offices around the country, as did the larger suffrage societies; all local NCS branches operated from the homes of its members – or the digs of its organisers.

In February 1910 members of the House of Commons formed what was termed the 'Conciliation Committee' to prepare a private member's 'Conciliation Bill' acceptable to all parties. The bill passed its first reading on 14 June and, in order to give the campaign maximum publicity, the WSPU and another militant society, the Women's Freedom League (WFL), joined together with other societies, including the AFL, to mount a spectacular procession through London. This time Kate, to her delight, marched with the actresses. 'Everyone was interested in us and sympathisers to the cause called out "Well done, Actresses."' [18 June 1910] The NCS invited members of the NUWSS, which had refused to take any official part in the procession, to walk with them under their 'green, white and silver banner and so help to show the strength of the constitutional demand'.

In November the hopes of suffrage campaigners were dashed when, at a meeting in Caxton Hall, members of the WSPU and sympathisers, such as Kate, heard the news that, with the two houses locked in a battle for supremacy, parliament was to be dissolved. This meant that the Conciliation Bill would be killed. In retaliation the WSPU immediately ended the truce it had maintained during the summer and autumn and prepared to resume militant tactics. A deputation of 300 women, divided into groups of 10, set out from Caxton Hall for Parliament and in

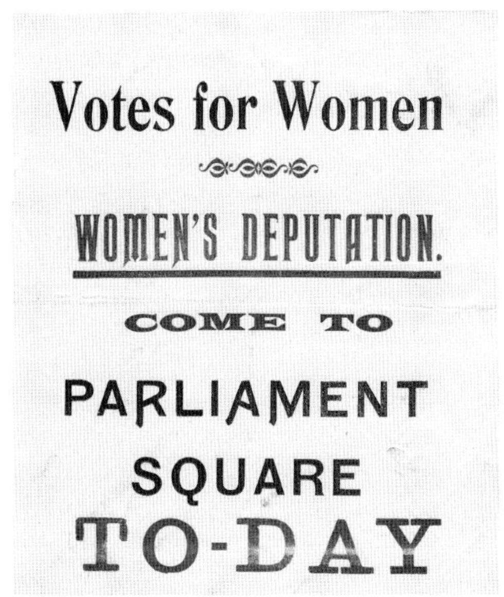

Parliament Square met with violence such as they had never previously encountered. This day has gone down in suffrage history as 'Black Friday'. As Kate reported, 'I was almost struck dumb and I felt sick for hours. It was a most horrible experience. I have rarely been in anything more unpleasant – it was ghastly and the loud laughter & hideous remarks of the men – so-called gentlemen – even of the correctly attired top-hatted kind – was truly awful.' [18 November 1910]

As a result of what she witnessed Kate resigned from the NUWSS and joined the WSPU. She remained, however, a WSPU sympathiser, not an activist, and in the campaign leading up to the second general election of the year volunteered to work for the NCS, which had opened up committee rooms in Hoxton, Battersea and Kennington.

The Frye family finances were now so parlous that it was necessary to give up the London flat and retreat to the country. On 21 December Kate wrote in her diary, 'Finished my packing. Sad work – as this is good-bye to the flat and London. We go to Bourne End now to reside but goodness alone knows how long we shall be there, or what sword is hanging over our heads now ready to fall. I feel very depressed. Of course I haven't tried very hard for work, but it seems out of the question to get any.' A very early entry in her 1911 diary made the position quite clear.

'Monday 2 January 1911 [Bourne End: The Plat]

The Women's Social and Political Union,
4, CLEMENT'S INN, STRAND, W.C.

MEMBERSHIP CARD.

THIS HALF TO BE RETAINED BY THE MEMBER. . . . . . .

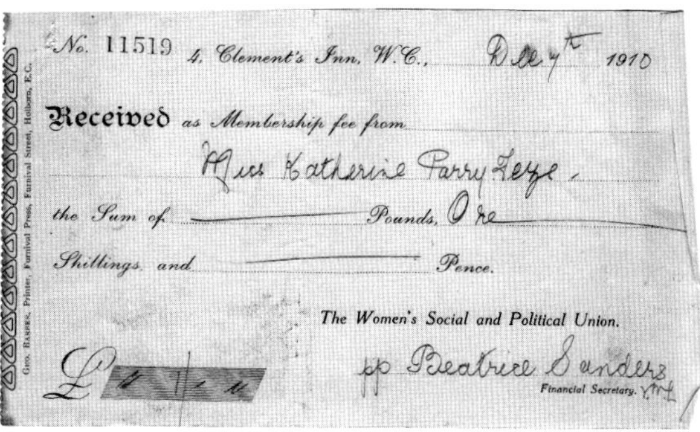
No. 11519 4, Clement's Inn, W.C., Dec 7th 1910

Received as Membership fee from Miss Katherine Parry Frye

the Sum of ——— Pounds, One Shillings, and ——— Pence.

The Women's Social and Political Union.

£ [illegible]

pp Beatrice Sanders Financial Secretary.

Top: WSPU 'Black Friday' flyer, 18 November 1910

Bottom: Kate's WSPU membership card and the receipt for her subscription

It was a real Black Monday we discussed & discussed our affairs for hours and we seem in a more terrible way than even I thought. A most hapless muddle – debts, debts, debts and only about £400 a year for us all to live on. It seems hardly possible. But it isn't possible to live on here – with rent and rates and I fear it will never be anything but an inglorious muddle for the rest of his [that is, her father's] life – and after he has gone – simply nothing whatever for us three women. I can hardly write any of the horrors that came to light. And Mother will be quite ill – she is never at rest and her nerves are all so unstrung. Oh! We are in a terrible way – and I feel so hard and miserable about it – as if it ought not to have happened. '

Frederick Frye, who had resigned as a director of Leverett and Frye Ltd on 11 January, was making desperate attempts to raise money. A sale of 'antique furniture etc belonging to Alderman Frye' was advertised in *The Times*, 7 February 1911, by Knight, Frank and Rutley. The furniture included most of the contents of the London flat as well as some items from The Plat. Kate trailed round theatres and agencies seeking stage work, all to no avail and in early March was much relieved to be offered employment by the NCS. She now embarked on a new professional career, as a suffrage organiser.

CAMPAIGNING FOR THE VOTE

Kate Parry Frye's SUFFRAGE DIARY

SUNDAY, MARCH 5TH 1911 – BOURNE END: THE PLAT

I have heard I am to go Suffrage campaigning in Mid Norfolk and start next week some time.

Kate makes no mention of receiving any specific training but she was well accustomed to canvassing at elections and her experience of theatrical touring had prepared her for the itinerant aspect of the new employment. The salary of £2 a week, the amount she had received as an actress, was the rate paid to their organisers by other suffrage societies.[16] *It is never explained, either in Kate's diary or in an NCS Annual Report, why the NCS thought the small, albeit thriving, market town of East Dereham in Norfolk should be the centre of their propaganda efforts. The society did not appear to have any influential supporter in the district, nor was there anything remarkable about Dereham's demographic; in 1911 it had a population of 5729, evenly divided between men and women. One can only surmise that it was chosen for its good transport links within the Mid-Norfolk parliamentary seat.*

MONDAY, MARCH 13TH 1911 – BOURNE END: THE PLAT

Had a letter from Alexandra Wright by the evening post saying she and Miss Ogston were just off to East Dereham and would I follow on Wednesday – they would Telegraph the address as soon as they had settled on rooms. So I at once began my preparations. Got out clothes for airing etc and thought out what I should want to take.

In East Dereham Kate lodged at first with Mrs Alice West (b. 1874) a widow with a young daughter, Hilda. Mrs West's friend, Parisian-born Elise Emery, whom Kate later mentions, appears to have been a semi-permanent visitor.

THURSDAY, MARCH 16TH 1911 – BOURNE END: THE PLAT/ EAST DEREHAM: 65 COMMERCIAL ROAD

Changed into the fast train at M'head [Maidenhead]– came underground to Liverpool St and then the 3.20 to Dereham. Travelled comfortably till just past Ipswich when some Cable People got in the train and were awful. Alexandra & Miss Ogston were at Wymondham and we came along together. The Hotel man brought the box which had come on by my train and bag to my rooms and I went to the Hotel [King's Arms] where we all had a dinner meal. Sat till about 9 – then the two girls walked me round to my rooms for the time being. So nice – comfortable and so clean and a fire in my bedroom to unpack by. I came upstairs in a few minutes – unpacked – wrote diary etc – then bed. We seem to be eyed with the greatest interest. It is a funny cross between being on a visit and a theatrical tour. I have nervousness for tomorrow's work but it is not so bad as a first night.

SATURDAY, MARCH 18TH 1911 – EAST DEREHAM: 65 COMMERCIAL ROAD

A most bitterly cold day – a lot of wind – no sun but hardly any rain. To the Hotel by 10 – then till 12 o'clock canvassing the shops again. Then an hour's waiting while the others were out – back to lunch at 1. Roast chicken, stuffing & sausages – new potatoes, greens, gravy, bread sauce, rice pudding, stewed prunes, Camembert cheese, standard bread. The lady is being very kind to me. I think she likes me and is sorry I am going. I shall feel strange at the Hotel alone and shall miss Alexandra – but she is going on Monday. My landlady is a sad little widow – come down in the world. Went back to the Hotel soon after two o'clock. It was crowded with football players. Alexandra & I went out paying calls – so amusing – some people quite nice. The Minister nice but so quaint – the district nurse quaint – but with us – and the Minister's wife most annoyed with us – and the doctor's wife shaking with rage. It was funny – she did so want to be rude – but we weren't quite the sort. I came in to tea – then back to the Hotel to find a Mrs Caley having tea in the Coffee Rooms while her husband & brother or cousin were with the defeated Cup Tie folk next door having a frilled ham tea. It seems they are the chocolate people who live at Wymondham, where we go after here to get up a meeting. She is a most sweet little woman and has promised us introductions and help and her husband too was nice. I came back at 7.30 for dinner – wrote letters and diary after, though I felt very tired, more indeed to enjoy the cosy room and nice warm fire but I have only sent post cards home so far. Mrs West came in to know if I would join in a card game. The message came from Mr Moon, the teacher who is a permanent lodger here. I have noticed he has kept his door open to have an eye on me.

Sunday, March 19th 1911 – East Dereham: 65 Commercial Road

Went round to the King's Arms at 10.45 and Alexandra and I went to Church. We were all in our best and were conscious that the eye of everyone was upon us. A bitterly cold dull day. I had a very nice lunch and sat a while looking out names in the directory then at 3.30 to the King's Arms again. We sat for an hour talking, then Alexandra went off to tea with a Mr and Mrs Hewitt and Miss Ogston and I to Mr Pearse. He and his wife gave us tea and were very nice but I didn't like them. He is a brewer and told me he has lost £1,000 under Lloyd George's Budget. He certainly looked very ill and worried. Of course he is a bitter Unionist. I do hope he won't make it too 'party' when he takes the chair. She was impossible to interest in Suffrage, so I played with the dog and let her tell me all about her family. I had to admit I was a Liberal to Mr Pearse. I don't think he liked it. They frankly bored Miss Ogston but, as types, they interested me very much, though as people they were very uninteresting. I came into the Hotel with Miss Ogston and Alexandra was some time after us so we all sat & discussed social problems till 7.30 when I went back to the Rooms – had a very nice supper – a good salad and to bed at 10.30.

The King's Arms is now demolished, but was in Dereham's Market Place.

Monday, March 20th 1911 – East Dereham: King's Arms

Very cold again – a bitter wind but sunshiny, such a welcome change. I started off on my round and worked the shops and houses in Quebec St and Norwich Rd – higher up until 11.45. Then Miss Ogston and I went to see the master of the LCC School. He was no good – but the Mistress was interested. Came in and saw Alexandra then back to lunch. Then to the station to see her off to London at 1.50. I am very sorry she has gone. I liked Miss Ogston in a way but she is not so nice to work with and Alexandra is really very nice – the more I see of her the more I like her. Then back to the rooms and

Ethel Caley (1875–1945) wife of a chocolate manufacturer. The firm A.J. Caley was eventually bought by Mackintosh, a larger chocolate manufacturer, but is still in business in Norwich. The Caleys lived at Northfield Cottage, Wymondham.

Percy Moon (1879–1938) later moved, still a teacher, to Derbyshire and was a conscientious objector during the First World War.

George Hewitt, the local Unionist political agent. 26 Quebec Road, East Dereham.

Charles Pearse (1868–1936) brewer, and his wife, Eleanor (b. 1880), lived at Mount Pleasant, East Dereham. He was a member of the Urban District Council.

packed. I am sorry to leave them but the Hotel will be amusing I dare say and as I shall be odd man out it is cheaper to have me at the Hotel and let Miss Ogston and her friend share the rooms. Was round to the Hotel in my best calling things by 3.30. Sorted some Literature for Miss Ogston then went out calling. Met with no luck at first – then found a mother & daughter by name Crick. In to tea, then out calling again and met some charming people. The doctor's wife, a Mrs Belding, was quite fascinating and so nice. It is difficult though to get people enthusiastic. Not in till 7.15 – just in time to unpack and then go and have my meal at 7.30. The young men who I imagined to be working on the land valuation came in and had their dinner. I settled down to writing – making out lists of people, straightening the Literature – then writing diary & letters and they had the other table cleared and also wrote. Quite nice young men.

After the bother of exchanging rooms, Miss Ogston's friend was ill and did not come to East Dereham, but Kate remained in the King's Arms. The attractive Assembly Rooms were built in the mid-18th century.

WEDNESDAY, MARCH 22ND 1911 – EAST DEREHAM: KING'S ARMS

Round to Miss Ogston's the first thing and we spent the greater part of the morning preparing & making arrangement for the evening. She went back about 12 and I told her to leave the rest to me and have a quiet hour or so and I stayed in the Assembly Rooms arranging chairs and putting leaflets till 1. Came in, had my lunch in company with four motorists. It is funny the way men come in here and, seeing me, shoot out again and I hear whispered conversations outside on the landing with the waitress. Then they come in very subdued and make conversation one to another and try not to look at me. Awfully funny – they might never have seen a woman before – but I suppose it does seem a strange place to find one. Miss Ogston met Mrs Chapman at 4.7 and brought her here. I have given her my room and have moved to 11 as it has no fireplace. Mrs Chapman is quite charming. We were supposed to have a tea party of 14 but only 2 turned up – Mrs Crick and Miss Beck – very brave of them but so disappointing about the others. Mrs Chapman was so nice and we had a nice tea – such a spread of cakes – 3/3 worth without tea. They stayed about an hour. I was over at the hall at 7. We opened the doors at 7.20 and in very little time the place was full. I had to stand at the door and kept the youths and maidens out till the police officer arrived and then went up to sell Literature. I could have sold no end, had it

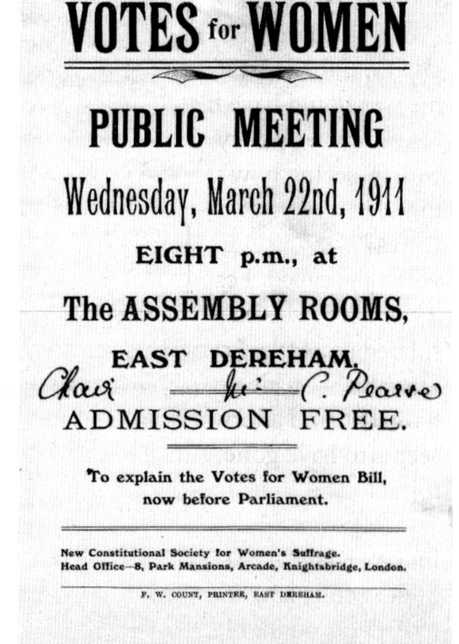

Mary Ann Crick, wife of an auctioneer's clerk. 23 Crown Road, East Dereham.

Bessie Beck (1882–1955) lived with her parents, Frederick Beck, auctioneer and estate agent, and his wife, Alice, at The Priory, Church St, East Dereham.

been suitable. All the suitable things were gone in no time. Such a splendid meeting – hundreds turned away – packed hall & 90 people the right sort – only of course mostly Unionist. Mr Pearse made a splendid chairman and was really most helpful and kind and kept beautifully clear of party and Miss Ogston pleased very much. She spoke very well and looked so handsome – impressed the people very well. Mrs Chapman spoke nicely and warmed the people by her fervour. Miss Ogston is a very cold speaker – it isn't that I mind in her, only I did want her to talk more of the Ideal Usefulness of the Vote to woman instead of all the time proving, most eloquently and logically & charmingly as she did, that we were fitted and suited to have the Vote. That is her Suffrage of course. I am so keen on the Social Reforms and so is Mrs Chapman so I appreciated her really more. I got £1-13 odd by the collection. They all thought it good. Nearly everyone I called on seemed there. I was meeting friends all the time, and the people do seem to like us. Miss Ogston came back to the Hotel and we had a chat then Mrs Chapman had coffee and I had cocoa and we talked. She wants me to go on to the Maldon division of Essex and spoke so kindly of my work. She says she is sure I could speak but if they think my work valuable without that of course I shall be pleased to go on. It pays for all but wear and tear of clothes and personal expenses – I wish it brought money but it is something even to keep oneself. To bed at 11 o'clock.

THURSDAY, 23RD MARCH 1911 – EAST DEREHAM: KING'S ARMS

Mrs Chapman came in to me at 8 o'clock to be 'done up'. A most drenching day – a perfect torrent. To Miss Ogston's at 1.15 as we were going to Wymondham but she had heard from Mrs Cayley and has put it off – such an awful day. We sat getting out a report – then I came back to the shops for her and had some interesting conversations – she had delighted all who heard her. Then back again and bought rubbers for myself and had a long talk with Mr Skoyles, the Liberal Agent. He is very chastened – a nice man and I am glad of it – I do hope I have done good. He likes me. At our interview he said I was the most sensible suffragette he had ever talked to and if they had all been like me we should have had our bill passed before now – and he is not an Irishman. I told him it wasn't policy to let the Unionists have it entirely their own way and now, of course, seeing how popular we are and hearing of our success has brought it home to him. He is a very nice man to talk to – and I have been absolutely given a gift with him. I am so glad – as Alexandra was so anxious we should get at him and he was always out when she called. I cannot think what has come over the Liberals to be so near sighted. They have Asquith to thank for it. He agreed with me about Churchill so he has considered us a little. I came in, took my wet things off. Had tea – wrote letters – sorted my Literature – made notes – changed my dress at 7 – dined at 7.30 – wrote letters, diary etc 8 till 9.30 and afterwards read a little. Am here alone. My Land Surveying gentleman seems to have gone. Am glad of an evening to myself but, though not really so comfortable, I find the Hotel much better fun than the rooms and much more of a change.

FRIDAY, MARCH 24TH 1911 – EAST DEREHAM: KING'S ARMS

I felt awfully lazy and was late up – had quite a rush to get fixed to go by the 10.50 train to Attleborough. Had to change at Wymondham and went that far with Miss Ogston

Robert Skoyles (1856–1940). The Limes, Wymondham, Norfolk.

who went to arrange about the meeting there for next week and have lunch with Mrs Caley and got back to Dereham in the afternoon. I travelled to Attleborough with two most interesting women – they seemed Suffrage – one was an Artist from Norwich and knew the Colmans. Miss Gaymer met me at the station – a nice person but she made me feel rather depressed – she seems so miserable – as if she has missed the 'bus'. We went round her tradespeople, leaving Bills for the meeting. Back to her home for lunch where I met her father, mother, and brother – did not care for them. Started off on my own account about 2.30 armed with introductions – most of the people were out – so I did the shops etc. Then met Miss Gaymer at 4 – and we went to see the Church which is beautiful – then to tea with the doctor's wife – a Mrs Rose – a nice little woman. Did not see her husband but another doctor was there who looked terrified of me and was struck dumb. Back to say good-bye to the Gaymers. Got to Dereham 7.15, called in on Miss Ogston to report myself – and back here to my meal about 8 o'clock.

SATURDAY, MARCH 25TH 1911 – EAST DEREHAM: KING'S ARMS

A most awful day – bitterly cold – terrific wind and snow and hail storms at intervals all day. At 4 o'clock Miss Ogston came round and we went to call on Mrs Pearse. Mr Pearse came home early from golf on purpose to see us as he thought there was a chance of our going. He admired Miss Ogston tremendously and seems to think us both good fun. I should say he is a handful himself. I wouldn't care to be Mrs Pearse unless I were a very clever woman. Had my dinner and at 8.30 went round to Miss Ogston's as she had asked me to and we had a chat. She seemed nervy and moped and she told me her life's history – a love affair, a crisis just past. She is very wrought up about it. I wish I had been better suited to give her advice – but I did what I could and, perhaps, talking did her good. She is a very passionate person and self willed but I don't know that she is quite as likely to be reckless as she thinks she is – but it has evidently been a big 'blow up'. Poor soul. Was not home till 11 – and then could not sleep.

Katherine (Kate) Gaymer (1876–1964) lived at home with her parents and younger brother at The Pleasaunce, Attleborough. Her father, William, was a cider manufacturer and the business survives, although the cider-making has moved to Somerset. Two of Kate's sisters had worked as commercial clerks, presumably in the family business. It would appear that Kate had been left, unmarried, as the 'daughter- at-home' having, as Kate Frye put it, 'missed the bus'.

SUNDAY, MARCH 26TH 1911 – EAST DEREHAM: KING'S ARMS

At 4.30 to the Becks in Church St to tea. Mr & Mrs & Miss Beck. I didn't like Mother and Miss is very ordinary and Pa isn't so bad. I talked hard and made them roar with laughter. The girl yelled – even Miss Ogston laughed and declared afterwards I had been telling 'risky' stories. She was very quiet – I don't know that she quite liked it.

WEDNESDAY, MARCH 29TH 1911 – EAST DEREHAM: KING'S ARMS/ATTLEBOROUGH

Did my packing – went round to Miss Ogston for cheque for my Bill, helped her settle account – took her books back, went to post etc. Paid bill – finished packing, back at 12.30 – I walked to station and the box came by bus. Miss Ogston and I together to Attleborough. Had to change at Wymondham and there got in the train with Miss Gaymer, who was going back from Norwich. Went to our Hotel – left our things – walked to the hall. Then back to the Hotel for Literature and over to hall to put it out. Miss Gaymer joined us there and we went to the Hotel and she had tea with us. Then to unpack a dress and be at the Gaymers' house at 6 o'clock. Mrs, Mr & Master Gaymer. I did not enjoy my dinner. I don't like the atmosphere of the house and do so dislike

Ma! Miss Gaymer and I drove first to the Hall at 7 – the others came later. Miss Gaymer was in the Chair and spoke very nicely – only it was so pathetic – I do feel sorry for her – and Miss Ogston made a very long speech. The place was very full and a most interested audience. The collection was 31/- odd. Literature sold 3/8 and I had 2 girls to help Steward. We all walked back to the Gaymers' as there was a letter for me. Then Master saw us as far as the Hotel again – a misty night – like a sea fog. Miss Ogston and I then had bread & butter – she milk – I cocoa and sat talking and got quite hysterical and howled with laughter. Then to bed – oh, the bitter cold of my room – wound myself up in a shawl but it was past 2 before I slept and I never got warm all night – the sheets struck like ice. I was unhappy and became conscious of a pricking in my throat. Miss Ogston ran in a dozen times before finally getting off to bed. She & I have become great chums these last few days. I shall miss her.

Carted Luggage was a method of sending baggage unaccompanied on the railway. Kate presumably sent her box home ahead of her to Bourne End.

THURSDAY, MARCH 30TH 1911 – ATTLEBOROUGH/THE PLAT: BOURNE END

Miss Ogston goes to Wymondham to-day for the meeting to-night – stays at Mrs Collyer – and Miss Gaymer is going to take the chair. Was waiting for my train [at Attleborough station] when Master Gaymer came along and very kindly saw me off. A most miserable day quite a fog all down the line & grey fog in London. John met me at L'pool St – nearly 3 months since I saw him – he looks very well & happy. I got my luggage to the underground and he came as far as Baker St and then went off to a rehearsal. He is playing in some performances of 'Atalanta' – then at Easter going on tour in 'Princess Priscilla Runs Away'. I left my bag at Paddington – sent my box off to Carted Luggage – train to High St Kensington – bus to Sloane Street & to the NCS Office 8 Park Mansions Arcade. Came in for a Committee meeting. Gave my report and allowed myself to be persuaded to go to Maldon tomorrow, Friday, instead of Monday as arranged. I am very disappointed – I wanted the weekend at home & I feel so seedy I know I must be going to have a cold. Gladys took me back to lunch with her. I did not enjoy it. Mrs Wright was very nervy – Alexandra has had a cold. I left just before 2 – apologising for rushing off. Train to Sloane Square from Notting Hill Gate. John had got stalls for Ibsen's 'A Doll's House'. Third row – splendid – I did enjoy it. Lydia Yavorska was the Nora and, in spite of her very broken English, excellent and so fascinating – she is a pretty creature. Ben Webster played very cleverly as the husband – his love making was very real – poor Miss Whitty. John & I had tea together in the King's Road. [Then] to Praed St and I got my bag & caught the 6.45 train [to Bourne End]. Got home to find Daddie seedy as usual – Agnes sunk in melancholy – Mother about the same and 'dear love' [her dog] delighted to see me.

Mrs Helen Collyer's husband was vicar of Wymondham.

Lydia Yavorska (1874–1921) Russian actress who had arrived in London in 1909 to some acclaim.

Ben Webster (1864–1947) and May Whitty (1865–1948) were a well-established theatrical couple. Kate had toured with May Whitty in a production of J.M. Barrie's *Quality Street* in 1903.

The Swan Hotel is still at 73 High Street, Maldon.

FRIDAY, MARCH 31ST 1911 – BOURNE END: THE PLAT/MALDON: SWAN HOTEL

Pratt took my box to the station and Agnes walked up to see me off by the 3 o'clock train. As luck would have it I had to travel up with Mrs Lehmann. She was very nice and interested to hear about my work. I got my box across by Metropolitan to Liverpool St. The 5.25 train to Maldon – had to change at Woodham Ferrers. No one to meet me at the station – took a bus to the Swan Hotel and Miss Harden there and the Landlady, Mrs Conn, did not seem pleased about me. However she said she could let me have a bed-room – a nice little place – it made me feel miserable. I unpacked a little – washed & tidied and sat down to dinner at 8 – feeling insanely miserable. Miss Harden came in about 8.20 – a very vigorous person – but not attractive to me. She had been to Braintree. I finished dinner then we went to a NU [National Union of Women's Suffrage Societies] meeting being held in a small hall. A Miss Cook [sic] was speaking – it seemed so tame – hardly as if they wanted the Vote. The Liberal men who got up and spoke for it I am sure didn't. A miserable lot. Two nearly lost their temper with me afterwards.

SATURDAY, APRIL 1ST 1911 – MALDON: SWAN HOTEL
I got my names together then went out calling from 2.45 till 6.15. One old lady kindly gave me tea. I disliked most of the people intensely – she was the only nice one and she was very deaf and a Liberal. They are all Liberal here and say they are Suffrage but you cannot move them to do anything to further the cause and when they are men they are all Anti Suffrage while all the time they tell you they are in favour – a poor lot. I came in absolutely done.

Suffragettes of the WSPU, WFL and other smaller societies, such as the Women's Tax Resistance League and the New Constitutional Society for Women's Suffrage, organised a campaign to boycott the 2 April 1911 decennial census. The slogan was 'No Vote, No Census'. Although we can see from her diary entry that Kate thought she had succeeded in boycotting, she was in fact entered on the Swan Hotel's census return, probably by the enumerator. Her details, given as 'Kate Parry Frye, actress, single, aged 32', are close enough to the truth to suggest that during her talk with her landlady Kate mentioned something of her history.

SUNDAY, APRIL 2ND 1911 CENSUS DAY – MALDON: SWAN HOTEL
It poured with rain all day – and I stayed in bed in my little room, 6ft square. Not a happy day but my cold was so violent and I ached all over. I was thankful even to lay on the bumps of wool rather than walk about. But I did feel miserable. Bread & butter & tea for breakfast – washed – had a talk to the landlady – read – rice pudding, bread & butter for dinner – read – bread & butter & tea for Tea – read – Bread & butter & cocoa for supper. 10 or rather before Lights out. I did <u>not</u> go down in the Census

TUESDAY, APRIL 4TH 1911 – MALDON: THE SWAN
Alas, my voice has forsaken me. Could only speak in a croaky whisper. I do feel a rotter. Had a card from Miss Harden telling me to go to Braintree but had to Telegraph that I had lost my voice and it would be useless to go. So then I had to pack up and send off all kind of things to her. Wrote a lot of letters and went out from about 12 to 1 to the shops about getting the large Bills up – fortunately met with success because I could

Alice Lehmann (c. 1874–1956) American wife of Rudolf Lehmann, Liberal MP for Market Harborough, 1906–10. Parents of Rosamond, John and Beatrix, the Lehmanns lived at 'Fieldhead', a house they had built on the river at Bourne End.

Jessie Harden, aged 25, gave her occupation on the census return as 'canvasser, New Constitutional Society for Women's Suffrage'.

[Alice] Geraldine Cooke (1868–1955) the daughter of a Birmingham haberdasher, educated at Somerville College, Oxford, by 1910 was a NUWSS organiser.

only whisper. Bought a lot of stamps – a paper and some books and did not go out again. It did not seem worth the risk – was most bitterly cold. So I made up a big fire – wrote letters all the afternoon and again after tea. It doesn't seem much good for me to try and work – I had better starve in a lady-like way. Fancy if I had to act or speak to-night. I simply couldn't. Private Life is the only thing I shall be any good at. I do feel so disappointed to start this sort of thing all over again in my new work. It takes the heart out of one. The landlady here, Mrs Conn, has been very kind to me – I feel very grateful – and it is such a beautiful old house – hundreds of years old.

WEDNESDAY, APRIL 5TH 1911 – MALDON: THE SWAN

Woke up to heavy snow. The old roofs looked very pretty opposite. I was told it was freezing hard in the shade. My voice has somewhat returned – I can croak – but I had a good bit of pain in my chest and back. I ought to be out but really am afraid and a very kind letter from Alexandra telling me to be careful made me feel I am not in such disgrace as I might be. I have tried to do what I can but, of course, I have had to neglect the canvassing and that is my special work. At 12.30 a tremendous snow storm again. I expected Miss Harden & Miss Stafford early in the day but they did not arrive till after 4 o'clock. They would not hear of my going out. After tea they went out, then Miss Stafford came in and she and I wrote letters while Miss Harden remained out till 8 o'clock. Miss Stafford is an Irish BA – very clever and quite nice.

THURSDAY, APRIL 6TH 1911 – MALDON: THE SWAN

A little snow and bitter cold still – a biting wind. My cold seemed better but I felt very queer in myself. Miss Harden and Miss Stafford were out most of the morning – working on my lists of people, while I sat doing the Literature and writing. Lunch at 1 and they went off again at 1.45 to give Bills at the Iron Works. Miss Stafford came in for a rest about 3 and Miss Harden and I went to the Hall to get it ready – put Bills up – Literature etc. It was most shockingly cold – Back to tea – then a little rest – and I was very untidy when Mr Reginald Pott of the Men's League arrived so I flew off to change my dress. He went off to the King's Arms or some other Hotel as Mrs Conn could not put him up. I went off at 7 to the Public Hall to be first there for the meeting. Miss Harden & Miss Stafford followed. Mr Pott and the Rector, the Rev. Kevill-Davies, were in good time and Miss Ogston arrived about 8.20. We had a packed meeting – and heaps of boys – it was rather touch and go with them but they behaved like lambs. I couldn't hear the speeches as I stood by the door all the evening – did not like to leave the youths. The

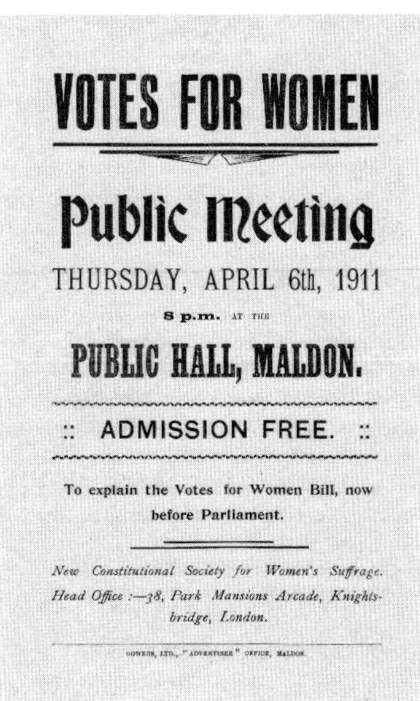
VOTES FOR WOMEN

Public Meeting

THURSDAY, APRIL 6th, 1911

8 p.m. AT THE

PUBLIC HALL, MALDON.

:: ADMISSION FREE. ::

To explain the Votes for Women Bill, now before Parliament.

New Constitutional Society for Women's Suffrage. Head Office :—38, Park Mansions Arcade, Knightsbridge, London.

Brighid Stafford (c1884–?) graduate of Trinity College, Dublin, pioneer member of the Irish Federation of University Women, later became chief secretary of factories in the Irish Department of Industry and Commerce. At this time she was living at 21 Abinger Mansions, Kensington.

Reginald Pott (1870 - 1957) treasurer of Men's League for Women's Suffrage, member of the Men's Political Union, stockbroker, member of the Fabian Society and author of the words of a suffragette song, 'The Purple, White and Green March'.

resolution was carried. I thought we should have a good meeting but this was really a packed one so we have every reason to be satisfied. I had a fit of coughing at the end which I am afraid upset the collection – I only got 13/-. When I could, I managed to go up to Mr Kevill-Davies and thank him as I was instrumental in getting him to take the Chair. We quickly collected our things and Mr Pott came back to The Swan with us and entertained us till after midnight – talking – singing and playing. Mr Pott is quite a character – a most extraordinary man. Alexandra had written telling me to fuss him so I was glad he seemed pleased with us and enjoyed the evening. We four women were all dreadfully tired but played up to him in a truly courageous fashion.

The ancient White Hart in Newland Street is still in business.

FRIDAY, APRIL 7TH 1911 – MALDON: THE SWAN/WITHAM: THE WHITE HART

All left soon after 2 in the bus for the station for Witham. Miss Stafford changed there for the London train and went off – and goes to her home tomorrow at Waterford, Ireland. We three drove to The White Hart – arranged about rooms. I unpacked the Literature & saw the luggage while Miss Harden and Miss Ogston went off and engaged the Small Public Hall and got Bills printed. We had already written a lot. [After tea] I tidied myself and went out canvassing until 7.15 when I flew into the Hotel and quickly changed my dress. I had some cocoa & bread & butter and we flew off to the Hall, getting there about 10 minutes to 8. Only 2 people – but by a little after 8 the hall was practically full – something under 50 people as it is only a small hall but it was an excellent meeting for a couple of hours work. Hard work, of course, but we felt very well repaid. Miss Harden took the Chair Miss Ogston spoke till just after 9 o'clock and I got 9s 7½d in the collection – wonderful. Miss Ogston flew off to catch the 9.25 train to London – two kind gentlemen seeing her to the station. Miss Harden and I cleared up then back to the Hotel. More cocoa and bread & butter and we sat over the fire till 11. Then to bed. A nice room but I was most miserably cold all night.

SATURDAY, APRIL 8TH 1911 – MALDON: THE WHITE HART/BOURNE END: THE PLAT

I went to Miss Harden just after 9. She was not up – so urging haste I returned to my room – packed my things – and the literature – labelled them got them brought down and breakfast on the table at 10 to 10. Miss Harden had to rush out and pay a bill and as our train went at 10.15 we only just managed it. Quite a lot of people recognised us and took their hats off. We had to change at Chelmsford – then got an Express to London. We saw the Literature off by Carter Paterson – then Miss Harden & I came on the underground together as far as Praed St. I sent my trunk off by Carted Luggage – put my bag in the cloak room – then to Pembridge Crescent. Mrs Wright came in first, then the girls. We had lunch and a long talk. Some tangled matters need straightening but I could not wholly smooth matters – they are very worried about some of the happenings. Then Notting Hill Gate to Praed St. Got my bag, met John and we came home to Bourne End by the 4.50 train. Daddie seems better than usual and Mother is alright. John seems very well and happy.

Kate spent the Easter holiday at Bourne End before returning to the NCS campaign. This time it was the area on the south coast around Rye that was to be targeted.

WEDNESDAY, APRIL 19TH 1911 – BOURNE END: THE PLAT /RYE: 13 MARKET STREET
Up to breakfast and finished my box. To the station and by the 1 o'clock train to London. A tremendous wind but also a lot of sunshine and it was beautiful in London. Got my luggage across from Paddington to Praed St and Charing Cross – then to the Main Line. They weighed the box and excessed it – it is a rotten line. So I took a second class ticket and, as the trains were very full, travelled in luxury. Did not stop before Ashford and changed there for Rye. Got a porter to bring up my Trunk and walked to Mrs Harvey, 13 Market St. What will happen to me with such a number? Real lodgings – but nice and clean and two nice large bed-rooms – much larger than the sitting-rooms. Had supper at 7.30 – then my box and arrived so I went up and unpacked that – then wrote letters & diary till 10 o'clock. Felt rather tired – and very on Tour – the Sunday night feeling in a strange town being intensified by the Church Bells being practised.

THURSDAY, APRIL 20TH 1911 – RYE: 13 MARKET STREET
Wrote a little then out the shops – and then back to fetch Bills, which had been sent in last night – and to start my canvassing. Did all up and down the High St and Mint as a beginning. Didn't feel very impressed with my work but suppose it is alright. At 2.30 out to Playden where I had some addresses and found a lot more. It was a good way so I stuck to that district. No real success – so many people out. In to tea at 5.30. A little more Bill distributing – then to the station to meet Alexandra, who arrived at 6.30. Talked till 11 o'clock, then to bed. A lovely day.

FRIDAY, APRIL 21ST 1911 – RYE: 13 MARKET STREET
I went paying calls. Met with some success. Got in the Nonconformist set and kept on till 1 o'clock. Alexandra went out again from 2.30 till 3.30 – then came back and a Miss Harris, Winchelsea, and Miss Spalding, the nurse here came to tea. Out at 5.30 till 7 again – more calls. A lot of people out but we got hold of the Vicar who promised to come. It was very windy all day and rather cold but the view was nice.

WEDNESDAY, APRIL 26TH 1911 – RYE: 13 MARKET STREET
Alexandra was very nervous all the evening as to the result of the meeting but I felt sure it would be alright. Showers in the morning but the day was fine. Alexandra & I went out, bought dinner, paid Bills etc and did some jobs. After lunch Alexandra lay down on her bed and went to sleep and I did some of my packing up etc. To the Hall at 4 o'clock to get it settled to our taste – a long job – to put out Literature etc. Back at 5.30. Miss Ogston had arrived and we began on the arrangements. She had had some tea – so we had ours – an egg. Then to change – leaving Miss Ogston to have some dinner at 7. Alexandra and I went to meet the Rev. Llewellyn Smith at 6.30 and take him to the Mermaid Inn. A chubby, cheerful young clergyman who seemed quite ridiculous when he spoke, as he constantly did, of 'my wife'. Leaving him to dine, we went on to the hall

Jane Harvey, a 48-year-old widow, lived with her 23-year old daughter, a clerk, at 13 Market Street, across the street from Rye Town Hall.

Margaret Spalding (1875–1968) district nurse, Queen Victoria Jubilee Institute of Nurses. She became a member of the NCS. Church Cottage, Rye.

Rev. Llewellyn Smith, honorary propaganda secretary of the Church League for Women's Suffrage, founded in 1909. His wife was the society's organiser. 7a Lyric Road, Barnes, London, W

soon after 7. A Mrs Harrison and a Miss MacMunn had arrived from Hastings so Alexandra took them back to Market St to have a rest – while I waited. I received the Stewards – two Miss Harrisons of Winchelsea, Miss Spalding and Miss Clements. They sold Literature and the Misses Harrison and I took the collection – £1-3-7. Lady Brassey took the Chair and her daughter came with her in a lovely car – they had to drive 50 miles so it was awfully decent of her, but she is very keen. A Lieut Col A. Savile came to assist Lady Brassey take the Chair and spoke after her. Then Miss Ogston – then Mr Smith. I didn't hear the speeches as I was outside with the boys – then in amongst some rather troublesome youths. But nothing happened and we had an excellent meeting – quite full and overflowing. The Vicar came, bringing Miss Proctor, who had vowed she would not come. I was very glad when it was over. Every one congratulated us and seemed to think it was a record for Rye. Miss Ogston went off with the Harrisons of Winchelsea. Mr Smith and Miss Spalding walked up with us – then went on to their respective houses. Alexandra and I had an egg each and some bread & butter. Then I went through the Literature and collection and we did accounts til midnight. Then to bed.

THURSDAY, APRIL 27TH 1911 – RYE: 13 MARKET STREET/BOURNE END: THE PLAT

We woke to a pouring wet day and it kept on till after 12. The Rev. Mr Smith appeared before breakfast was over – buoyant as ever. Then Miss Spalding came in and we all talked. She did not wait long, but he did not go till 11.30 or after and then we had to drive him forth. Then to the station for the 12.55 train – after parting with Mrs Harvey, our most kind and moderate landlady. Alexandra and I came together as far as Ashford. She went out to Hythe to see about a house there and we met Miss MacMunn, who was going to Margate for the afternoon. I left first for Cannon St. The train was miserably slow and very late. I tore on the underground to Paddington, but just lost the 4.50 train by 3 minutes. I was annoyed. [Back at The Plat] Had nothing to unpack, so sat and made plans for the meeting I have decided on here for Thursday, after telephoning Mrs Haden Tebb to definitely engage the hall for that day. It will be a tremendous task. Bourne End, I am sure, will prove difficult.

Isabella Darent Harrison (1856–1943), founder of Hastings and St Leonards Women's Suffrage Propaganda League. 1 St Paul's Place.

Miss Clements: either Kitty, a music teacher, or Edith, 6 High Street, Rye.

Lady Brassey (1858–1934) wife of Liberal politician and president of Hastings NUWSS.

Beatrice Haden Tebb (c1866–1954) wife of one the entrepreneurs who developed Bourne End's Abbotsbrook Estate.

FRIDAY, APRIL 28TH 1911 – BOURNE END: THE PLAT

At 10.45 to call on Mrs Lehmann. Found her very kind and helpful, but she will probably not be able to go to the meeting. Then to Marlow to arrange the printing – and to try and see Mrs Dickson, the doctor's wife, but she was out. I waited some time then caught the 12.50 train home. After lunch at 2.20 Agnes and I started off. First to Lady Thomas – just caught her and bawled in her ear, but she did not seem to hear much. Then to the Vicar – in – very nice with us but never attends public meetings, but he gave me a very nice letter for the Chairman to read. Then down to Cores End to pay a call on Mr Dickson, the Minister, who has promised to come. Also to find a Bill Poster. Home to tea.

SATURDAY, APRIL 29TH 1911 – BOURNE END: THE PLAT

I went at 11 o'clock to Mrs Tebb and had a long talk to her. She is being very nice over the meeting. Then to call on Mrs Tudor – a most comical interview. Then to the station to get the printing – quite good. 500 handbills – 50 poster Bills. Out at 2.30 to all the shops to get the Bills put up and distribute the others. I really think it is the most awful place one could attempt anything in. After tea Agnes and I went in to Mrs Matthews and down to Mrs Grantham Lunnon. Both got such long calls that we had not time for anything else.

WEDNESDAY, MAY 3RD 1911 – BOURNE END: THE PLAT

A bright morning but a terrific wind again. We had a lot of letters to write – Alexandra [who had arrived the previous day] and I – the first thing after breakfast. We got ready and went out about 11.30 till 1 o'clock. Hadn't much luck – nearly everyone was out. Again at 3 till 4.30 – people nearly all out though it had clouded over a good deal. Still we got into some of the houses on Abbotsbrook and it was very amusing. We meant to have done Upper Bourne End after tea but the rain started and came on a perfect deluge so we had to give it up.

THURSDAY, MAY 4TH 1911 – BOURNE END: THE PLAT

I was glad to have the day of the meeting at last but still gladder when the day was over. I felt most responsible and so, of course, was disappointed. A gorgeous day – and quite hot in the sun. Alexandra and I went out about 10.30 – first to the hall – then to put Bills all along the way and in Furlong Road and have a talk to the schoolmaster. Agnes had gone to meet Miss Ogston at 12.15. Alexandra and I were not in till 1 o'clock. It seemed quite natural to see Miss Ogston strolling about. She was very 'charmed', of course, and quite happy here. Of course the old man was delighted with her. Our new Cook came in on Tuesday so we were fearful as to the lunch – but it was quite alright. Saw Alexandra, Miss Ogston, and Agnes off soon after 2.30 for the hall with a few last things. I waited about feeling very nervous. Then to the station to meet Mrs Chapman at 3 o'clock from London – and Mrs Scott from Wycombe (Godstowe School) and a Mrs Peachall – and we all drove to the hall in a fly. Oh my heart. Not so bad really as far as numbers went – but only 50 all told – and none of the people who had promised – at least very few. So I was really most awfully disappointed – though considering what uphill work it has been all along it might have been much worse. Everyone said it was good to get even such a little meeting, but I thought of all the miserable women who had stopped away and I felt miserable. Was outside most of the time and only heard part of Mrs Chapman's speech. Miss Ogston, as usual, seemed the favourite. I sent Alexandra back in the fly with Mrs Chapman, Mrs Peachall and Mrs Scott. Daddie had walked off with Miss Ogston and, after waiting to clear up, Agnes, and I followed on foot – and we all had tea in the drawing-room. Daddie was so frantic he would hardly let me have a word with Mrs Chapman when she left. Agnes and Alexandra saw her round to her niece at Abbotsbrook and I saw Mrs Scott and Mrs Peachall off in the fly for the station and the 5.40 train. Then came back to Miss Ogston. She and Alexandra had some dinner at 7.30 and Daddie and I saw them both off at 8.14. Mrs Chapman joined them at the station. I came home feeling very tired.

Margaret Tudor (1857–1933). Brookfield, Bourne End.

Amelia Matthews (1850–1925) widow, lived with her son, a C. of E. clergyman. St Davids, Bourne End.

Enid Grantham Lunnon (1864–1946) wife of Thomas Grantham Lunnon, paper manufacturer. Bourne Bank, Bourne End.

May Scott (c1870–1958), assistant mistress at Wycombe Abbey School before founding England's first all-girls preparatory school – Godstowe School, Amersham Road, Wycombe in 1900. Strong supporter of tax resistance, speaking on the subject at a WFL meeting at Marlow on 17 March 1911.

The magnificently-decorated Criterion Restaurant at Piccadilly Circus was the favoured venue for AFL meetings.

VOTES FOR WOMEN!

. . A . .

MEETING

WILL BE HELD AT THE

VILLAGE HALL,

BOURNE END,

Thursday, May 4th,

At 3.15 p.m.

Speakers:

Mrs. CECIL CHAPMAN,

Miss HELEN OGSTON, B.Sc

Admission Free.

The New Constitutional Society for Women's Suffrage. Head Office—8, Park Mansions Arcade, Knightsbridge, London.

Welbourne & Simpson, Ltd., High Street, Marlow.

FRIDAY, MAY 5TH 1911 – BOURNE END: THE PLAT

Off by the 11.10 train to London. Then at 2 o'clock to the Criterion to Steward for the Actresses' Franchise Meeting. It was simply packed and there were some very good speeches. Miss Adeline Bourne in the Chair – Ella Wheeler Wilcox was guest of the afternoon. Her song 'The Awakening' was sung by Miss Muriel Terry, accompanied by the composer, Miss Teresa del Riego and someone recited some EWW. I had a long talk with some Kensington Anti Suffrage Ladies – their views shocked me. One was a horrid woman, the other looked nice but she must have been very hard. They said I was 'too charming' and 'too gentle' to be a Suffragette.

Kate followed the passage of the Conciliation Bill through its second reading in the House of Commons on 6 May, laying in to her diary relevant newspaper cuttings.

TUESDAY, MAY 16TH 1911 – BOURNE END: THE PLAT

Another sultry day outside – real summer. Up late – did my room then sat down to letters and wrote till lunch time. Heard from Gladys Wright that they want me in London on Thursday for work – so began to make plans at once.

Slaters' was a restaurant chain. Miss Ogston would have been lunching at the 13 Brompton Road branch, just across from the NCS office. The premises of the Actors' Association, a society of which both Kate and John were members, were at 10 King Street, Covent Garden.

THURSDAY, MAY 18TH 1911 – BOURNE END: THE PLAT

Quite a change in the weather – chilly and very dull early. To the station for the 8.40 to London. To the New Constitutional office. Miss Ogston was there. We had a talk about my work. Then I went out to get a directory and then went out to spy the land and find some suitable streets to start canvassing in. Back in a bus at 1 o'clock. Miss O. went off for her lunch left me to change my dress – and lock the office and take the key to her at Slaters. I left my other things behind. Took 10 minutes – scrambled by bus to the A[ctors'] A[ssociation] and didn't get there till after 1.30. Agnes had been waiting since 1 o'clock. We had lunch together and got to the Criterion at 2 o'clock. I had promised to Steward and Agnes bought a 1/- ticket for the meeting on the 'Inequality of the Marriage Laws'. Sir A. Conan Doyle in the Chair – Mr Cecil Chapman, Dr Vicary and

Adeline Bourne (1873–1965) actress, a co-founder of the AFL.

Ella Wheeler Wilcox (1850–1919) American author and poet.

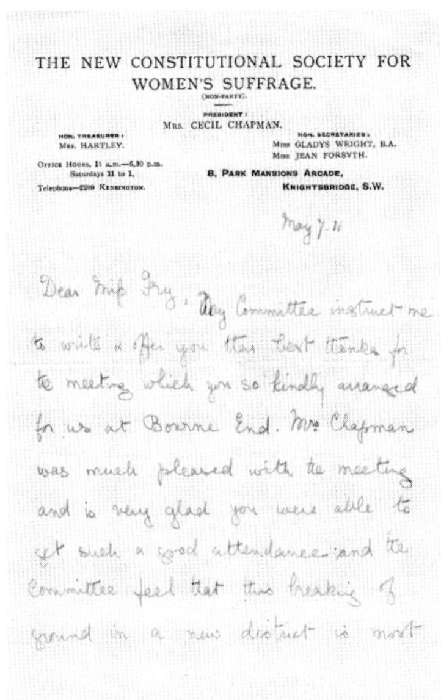
THE NEW CONSTITUTIONAL SOCIETY FOR WOMEN'S SUFFRAGE.
(NON-PARTY).

PRESIDENT: Mrs. CECIL CHAPMAN.

HON. TREASURER: Mrs. HARTLEY.

HON. SECRETARIES: Miss GLADYS WRIGHT, B.A. Miss JEAN FORSYTH.

Office Hours, 11 a.m.—5.30 p.m. Saturdays 11 to 1.

Telephone—2289 Kensington.

8, Park Mansions Arcade, Knightsbridge, S.W.

May 7. 11

Dear Miss Fry, My Committee instruct me to write & offer you their best thanks for the meeting which you so kindly arranged for us at Bourne End. Mrs Chapman was much pleased with the meeting and is very glad you were able to get such a good attendance and the Committee feel that this breaking of ground in a new district is most

Mrs Hugh Ames were speaking. Most interesting. I enjoyed the afternoon and my work and the little chats I had. Miss Mayo has asked me to be a Group Captain in the Procession and I shall quite like it. I went to N[otting] H[ill] G[ate] and to the Wrights' 'At Home'. People were thinning but still a good many. Miss Green I know – Mrs & Miss Graham, Miss Mayo, Mrs Chapman etc and I stayed till the end when Gladys gave me some tea and we all had a talk about my work. I did not want to stay too long but I couldn't catch the 6.45 – so had an hour more at Paddington for the 8.30 – felt awfully tired and sat in the waiting room but I knew the Wrights were tired too – so had not wanted to wait there. A very nice 'At Home' but they are dull things at best.

Flora Ames, author of *The Book of Divorce: its use and abuse*. Earlier in the year she and Hugh Ames had gone through a marriage ceremony in Idaho, after he had obtained an Idaho divorce from his English wife. In April 1912 they were both sentenced to six months' imprisonment for bigamy, his divorce being deemed invalid.

Kaiser Wilhelm of Germany was paying a short visit to London. On this Friday afternoon he and the Empress had visited the Naval and Military Tournament at Olympia, their royal progress somewhat inconveniencing Kate.

Friday, May 19th 1911 – Bourne End: The Plat

Got to the office at 10.10. The Boy let me in and Miss Ogston arrived at 10.30. I started to compile a list of people and started off at 11. Started Walpole St – very little result all the morning. About 4.30 I called at a house where they made me have some tea – such a dear old lady – a nice daughter but a soldier son hated me – 'Suffrage indeed' was writ large. When I politely refused cake the old lady with a knowing look got up, cut a slice, put it on a plate and handed it to me, saying 'Eat that'. I did quite joyfully. But it is terrible work for the most part. They look very suspicious – and no wonder – and, at best, it is very difficult to pass the servants. However I saw about 10 likely people and I suppose that wasn't too bad. Back to the Office at 5.30 for my dress box from yesterday – bus to High St Kensington – such a fight to get along – the Kaiser had not long since passed – train to Praed St and home by the 6.45.

Winifred Mayo, adopted name of Winifred Monck-Mason (c1870–1967), founder member of the Actresses' Franchise League.

No. 79.

VOTES FOR WOMEN.

The Conciliation Bill Explained.

What is the Conciliation Bill?

Will it give Votes to all Women?

What Women will get the vote?

Why are these Women chosen?

What about Married Women?

How many Women will get the Vote?

About One Million in the three Kingdoms.

Will it stop there?

Saturday, May 20th 1911 – Bourne End: The Plat

Woke up at 7 – breakfast 8 – leave 8.30 and catch the 8.40 train to London. That will be my programme for a bit, especially as I have decided to

Top: Letter to Miss Fry [sic] from Jean Forsyth of the NCS.

Bottom: WSPU pamphlet explains the Conciliation Bill, which was supported by all the suffrage societies.

have a fortnight's season ticket. Wrote letters, made a list for calling and started about 12. Not a lot of success in St Leonard's Terrace – and Mrs Bram Stoker – who[se] name I had found out – was out. But in Wellington Square I had excitements. No 15 a Miss Robertson going out, but I went back at 1.15 to see her. Waited some time. Then she came in with a Miss Limond and I talked Suffrage. Found them WSPU and also keeping a Hostel and Workrooms as a 'Rescue' for girls. They were such nice women and I talked on and on. Then they made me stay to lunch at 2 o'clock and I met the poor girls. We all had lunch together including the cook-housekeeper and some other ladies – a simple but good meal – then tea upstairs afterwards. I left about 3 – and, as I had promised to get someone to speak on Suffrage to an 'At Home' they are giving tomorrow, I went straight from Sloane Square station to Notting Hill Gate and saw Alexandra and she rang up Mrs Chapman who promised to go. So that was good. I had tea with Mrs Wright and Gladys – then to Paddington and down by the 4.50.

TUESDAY, MAY 23RD 1911 – BOURNE END: THE PLAT

Out canvassing. Lunch 1.30 till 2.30 in Chelsea, as I was down by the river at work. Then more canvassing till 4. Bus up Sloane St and to the At Home in the office. Mrs Brownlow speaking on the 'Woman and the Law'. At 7.30 to the Council Hall, Kensington Town Hall. There was such a crowd to see the Suffrage and the Anti-Suffrage Deputation. 10 of each. Miss Sterling & Mrs Eates spoke 'For' – A Mrs Colquhoun against. All spoke well, but Miss Sterling was a delight. The Motion was lost – the petition will not be sent to Parliament as asked, demanding that facilities should be given for the Conciliation Bill. A fearfully exciting time.

John Collins had a rented room at 19 Delamere Terrace, Paddington, in which, as he was away on tour, Kate stayed during this overnight visit to London. The performance she attended was the first English production of The Cherry Orchard, *of which her opinion was very much more positive than that of many professional critics.*

SUNDAY, MAY 28TH 1911 – BOURNE END: THE PLAT/LONDON: DELAMERE TERRACE

A most glorious day – but I was very tired. Not up till 11 – then housework. Thoroughly cleaned and tided my room. Hilda is either very lazy or incompetent. I show her things each evening but the next day they are just the same. Tea at 4.15, packed my supper and breakfast. Then Agnes walked with me to the station and I went up by the 5.5 train. At Maidenhead Mr Percy Harris joined me and we talked Suffrage all the way up to Westbourne Park, where he got out. He was very amusing and in a very 'coming on' disposition. The train was very late and I hurried to Delamere Terrace with my bag and got very hot. Was not in till 6.40. Fortunately my box had arrived and I just scrambled into my dress and off to the Aldwych Theatre for the Stage Society performance of 'The Cherry Orchard' (Dress Circle Row C nos 6 & 7). Mrs Carter joined me there as arranged but she did not enjoy it and left after the second act – when I saw her into a Taxi. She didn't seem happy so I was glad when she had gone and enjoyed it better. But it was a most extraordinary play – Russian – no plot in particular – each act like another. I found it interesting as a picture of Russian life and nature and some of

Mrs Stoker, wife of the author of *Dracula*.

Marion Robertson (b 1881) honorary superintendant of the hostel at 15 Wellington Square. Miss Beatrix Limond (1876–1949) was a 'visitor', when the census was taken. There were five dressmakers boarding.

Jane Brownlow (1854/5–1928) author of *Women's Work in Local Government*, 1911.

Louise Eates (1857–1944) one of the founders of the Kensington WSPU.

Ethel Colquhoun (1874–1950) leading member of the Women's National Anti-Suffrage League.

Percy Harris (1876–1952), later a Liberal MP.

the parts were well acted. Back in a bus from top of Kingsway to Bishops Rd. Then to Delamere Terrace at 11.45 –The rooms with the awful muddle and so many dusty things about were a complete nightmare. Oh will it never end.

THURSDAY, MAY 30TH 1911 – BOURNE END: THE PLAT

To the Office. In the afternoon there was the weekly 'At Home' in the Office – Laurence Housman came to speak on 'The Womanly Woman'. Quite a number of people there. Tea afterwards and talk – and I tried to collect people to canvass for the meetings on the 8th and 12th.

Kate was not exaggerating the ferocity of the storm on 31 May. There were deaths from lightening strikes and south of London a railway line was blocked by a landslide.

WEDNESDAY, MAY 31ST 1911 – BOURNE END: THE PLAT

Very dull when I left for London as usual at 8.30. First train to South Kensington to see the neighbourhood of the hall – then to see Miss Robertson. Then a bus to the Office. Miss Forsyth came in at 3.30 until I left – there wasn't a lot for me to do – but I had arranged to stay there. It thundered most of the afternoon. I went by bus to Cromwell Rd – left a parcel – and ought to have gone on to the High St Kensington but it was so awful I posted the parcel and took train from Gloucester Rd to Praed St and had half an hour to wait for the 6.45. At 7.30 we had got to Acton – were ploughing through feet of water almost to the carriage floor and to finish it a most terrific thunderstorm was raging and the atmosphere was so weird and perfectly terrifying really I felt dazed with it. We did not get in to Bourne End till nearly 8.30. Daddie was waiting with my coat and galoshes so I donned them and hurried home – the storm had passed over here but had been tremendous.

Monna Vanna, *a 1902 play by Maeterlinck, was banned by the censor but given this private performance – the first in England – at the Royal Court on 1 and 2 June 1911. It was staged, for members and their friends, by the Women's Aerial League of the British Empire. This society had been founded in 1909 for women interested in flying and ballooning, with the patriotic intent that Britain should not lag behind Germany in aviation matters.*

THURSDAY, JUNE 1ST 1911 – BOURNE END: THE PLAT

Dreadful to read of the disasters by the storm and floods yesterday. Acton and thereabouts, also the Derby, seemed to come in for the heaviest share of it. Bus to Sydney Street where I started canvassing for the meeting on June 8th – and went on till 1 o'clock – met with fair success. A bus to Sloane Square to the Court Theatre. Waited outside 20 minutes for the gallery then got a seat in the front row to see 'Monna Vanna'. I had joined the Women's Aerial League to be present as, of course, it cannot be performed publicly. It is a wonderful play – so modern in trend of thought, though written of the centuries long past. Adeline Bourne played 'Vanna' and was both good and bad. She received many floral tributes. Fisher White was very intense – James Hearn very good. Herbert Waring is no favourite of mine but I thought him distinctly good today. The crowd was the weakest part – so very amateur.

Laurence Housman (1865–1959) author, artist and ardent supporter of women's suffrage. His pamphlet, *What is Womanly?*, was published in 1914 by the WFL, the society with which he was particularly associated.

FRIDAY, JUNE 2ND 1911 – BOURNE END: THE PLAT

A most beautiful day again and very hot. Off as usual – taking dress for the afternoon in a box. To the Office. I changed upstairs & Miss Ogston did my frock up and I went off at 1 o'clock bus to Piccadilly. At 2 o'clock to the Criterion Grand Hall to Steward at the Actresses' Franchise League At Home. I was right up in the front and had a busy time and the place was so packed – the most crowded meeting we had ever had. Miss Decima Moore took the chair. Mrs Pankhurst, of course, was the attraction – Mr Forbes Robertson – Mr Jerome K Jerome – Miss Horniman. Miss Lena Ashwell was Hostess.

THURSDAY, JUNE 8TH 1911 – BOURNE END: THE PLAT

Off at 11 o'clock by two buses to Westminster to canvass. The people seem quite nice in the dwellings about and much easier than Chelsea. Back to the Office at 1.15 – just saw Alexandra and Gladys. I cleared up and got ready the Literature and packed up the things for the afternoon – and left about 4 for Chelsea. Got the hall all ready then went canvassing for an hour and a half and gave the rest of the bills away. Back to the hall in good time. Mrs Forbes, Miss Phillips and Miss Rawles came to Steward. Mrs Chapman, Miss Ogston and Miss Marsden to speak. Mrs Everitt to sing. Alexandra and Gladys came and five or at most seven other people. It was hopeless. I was disappointed after my week's canvass and Miss Ogston, Mrs Forbes and Miss Phillips have all helped. I stood outside trying to get people in – no good wandering about in the summer night or going to and from the Pub but I was so vexed. I had to leave at 9.15 as arranged for my train at 10. I was dead tired.

Decima Moore (1871–1964) actress, younger sister of Ada and Eva Moore, all popular actresses and active suffragettes.

Lena Ashwell (1862–1957) actress and, by 1907, manager of the Kingsway Theatre, later a vice-president of the AFL and a tax resister.

Kate and John were in the audience for the first performance of The Married Woman, *a play by C.B. Fernald. St Andrew's Parish Room was in Palace Street, Westminster.*

MONDAY, JUNE 11TH 1911 – BOURNE END: THE PLAT

John met me at Paddington and went to the Office with me. He looks very well. He left me there and went off to look for work. Then to Westminster – some canvassing and I felt it would be quite fruitless. So, as I had said, took an afternoon off. Walked to the Aldwych Theatre. John joined me there and we had stalls and saw *The Married Woman* – very clever and very enjoyable – quite out of the way good – I was glad not to have missed it. We walked back to Westminster – had tea – then to the Hall, St Andrew's Parish Room, and I got it ready for the evening and then John and I went and we gave away the last of the Bills. A Mrs Lynch and a Miss F. Wright came to Steward and Miss Robertson, Miss Limond and Miss Herr. It was really Miss Robertson's meeting – but for her it would have been nearly as bad as Chelsea – but the hall quite filled up. Mrs Chapman in the Chair. Dr Flora Murray and Miss Dora Marsden [as speakers]. I had to leave at 9.15. John came to Paddington with me and saw me off at 10. London is a most wonderful sight with coronation preparations.

Flora Murray (1869–1923) member of the WSPU and doctor to Mrs Pankhurst and other hunger-striking militants.

Dora Marsden (1882–1960) a teacher and early member of the WSPU in Manchester, took part in militant action and was imprisoned. For a time a paid organiser for the WSPU but in January 1911 resigned, moving to London to found a paper to provide a radical feminist platform. A couple of months earlier, when the census was taken, she was living in Edith Road, West Kensington.

In the summer of 1911 the WSPU called a truce on its militant activity, hoping they could trust Lloyd George's assurance that the government would allot further time in the next parliamentary session to the current Conciliation Bill. To give further publicity to their cause all the suffrage societies co-operated in planning a spectacular procession to take place on 17 June, when the streets of London would be decorated in preparation for King George's coronation. The New Constitutional Society's banner was made to be carried in this procession and, although it does not appear to have survived, it can be seen in the photograph accompanying the entry for 19 September 1914.

TUESDAY, JUNE 13TH 1911 – BOURNE END: THE PLAT
Straight to the Office. Miss Ogston had not turned up. Alexandra in a great state there alone. I had arranged to come late so was not blamed. Buckled to and presently several others arrived and we got the place ready for the Sale. Alexandra took me back to lunch and change at Pembridge Crescent and we got back to the Sale about 3. I began to Palmist at once and had a small interval for tea and to watch the presentation of the Banner – a beauty from Mrs Graham. Then on till I realised I just couldn't catch the 6.45. So vexing. Was a great success as a Palmist. Everyone liked me and I was so popular.

THURSDAY, JUNE 15TH 1911 – BOURNE END: THE PLAT
My month in London is out but as I have had some half holidays I went up to give a day's work and make up the time. As usual off at 8.30. John met me at Paddington and we went together to the Office. I had the key so could let myself in. Worked at getting the Banner poles unpacked. They had been packed hot and the paper was all sticking to them so it was a great work. When the Committee arrived I went off to Westminster and back to fetch the Literature left there from Monday. Until the Committee had finished, I gave away Procession notices. Then I was fetched in as Mrs Chapman wanted to speak to me. She has offered me the Post of Organiser for the summer campaign – Miss Ogston's work really but she does not seem any good at it. I feel very awkward but of course I accepted, though I said I was very nervous that I should be capable. Fortunately Miss Ogston didn't seem hurt with me though she was very hurt with the Committee and we went and had lunch together. Then back to the Office – and Mrs Hartley, Miss Forsyth, Alexandra and a Mrs Roland Hall came to practise the Banner. It was a great business and took all the afternoon. I got away just in time to catch the 5.50 train home. John was at Paddington to see me off.

By 'Adelphi House Terrace' Kate is referring to the office of the Actresses' Franchise League at 2 Robert Street, next door to the Women's Freedom League office at no 1. The Adelphi development was then still intact, as developed by the Adam brothers, an imposing and elegant complex of neo-classical terraces lying between the Strand and the Thames, close to Charing Cross. The Adam brothers had given 2 Robert Street, which still stands, ornamental ceilings and fireplaces in the style they had made their own. The AFL had decorated their office in the society's colours of pink and green, very much a combination favoured by the Adams, and had added blinds embroidered with the League's badge and name. The ribbons bought by Kate would have been in the AFL's colours.

FRIDAY, JUNE 16TH 1911 – BOURNE END: THE PLAT
Went by train to High St and went to Pontings and purchased a fur-lined coat for £4 14-

6. Quite a beauty for the money – I saw it in the window some days ago. Then train to the Temple. Walked along the Embankment to find the exact position for to-morrow – then to Adelphi House Terrace to purchase scarves – ribbons for tomorrow – then I walked along to Hyde Park Corner – along tomorrow's route – it is very wonderful to see London as it is now.

'The March' that Kate was delighted to hear herself singing in the Albert Hall was Ethel Smyth's 'March of the Women', with words by Cicely Hamilton, first performed in January 1911.

SATURDAY, JUNE 17TH 1911 – BOURNE END: THE PLAT

I woke at intervals listening to the rain – could hardly believe it wasn't raining when my breakfast was brought up – but the grey clouds were hovering and it looked most threatening. It looked like that all day – most frightening – but the wind kept the rain off and, though terrifically black, the clouds were always high. Agnes and I had lunch together and up by the 1 o'clock train. John met us at Paddington and I decided to leave my umbrella in the cloakroom but Agnes and I kept our mackintoshes. We went by train to Charing Cross. First to Adelphi House Terrace [AFL] to get my ribbons and decorate my pole with roses and green I had brought up. John went off before 4 to take up his position as banner carrier to one of the local WSPU contingents at Westminster. Agnes and I tidied ourselves in the cloakroom then leisurely walked to the Temple. Got there about 4.15. No-one at the New Constitutional Pitch – so she came on to my spot which was all agog – we were just behind and I could see the banners all the time. I was a Group Captain and had the announcement round my arm and much enjoyed the dignity. Was not with any very interesting people but it didn't matter as I was so taken up with myself. Lena Ashwell, all the Moores etc were up in front. I was the 3rd section behind the third Floral Arch – very pretty it all looked but some of the walkers of the AFL looked very dowdy. But it was all simply magnificent – 70,000 of us, five abreast, and some of the Sections were just wonderful – a real pageant and I enjoyed myself tremendously. It started at 5.30 and it was not much after 6 when we were off – we were in a splendid position. The end had not left the Embankment before we started the meeting at 8.30 – 7 miles 1,000 banners 70 bands. We were just behind one and it was quite lovely marching to it. We all kept time to it and at least walked well. Several of the onlookers I heard say that ours was the Smartest Section. We went along at a good steady pace – not nearly so much stopping about as usual and it was lovely to be moving, though I had not found the wait long. Such crowds – perfectly wonderful – there couldn't have been many more and they must have waited hours for a good view. The Stands were crowded too and one could see the men lurking in the Clubs – some of them looking very disagreeably. I wonder they stayed to look if they disliked it. The crowd was so quiet – hardly a rude remark and constant applause all the way for us. Then in St James's St Mrs Wolstenholme Elmy – the dear old Suffragette of over 40 years work – to be saluted by us all in turn. She must have been very proud and she stayed till right to the end of the procession. It was simply magnificent that the rain left off and it was a beautiful evening really for it. I was so sorry to be nearly at the end and, for me, we were all too soon there. Agnes was waiting and we enjoyed ourselves out-

Elizabeth Wolstenholme Elmy (1833–1918) had been an instigator of the women's suffrage campaign in Manchester in 1866 and, since 1903, a supporter of the WSPU.

side for a little and ate our sandwiches and chocolate and hoped to see John. But the whole of the National Union had to come first and they turned off at Exhibition Road, so there was a long gap of an hour. So just before 8.30 we went in to the hall – John did not come till past nine. As chance willed it our seats were just underneath the New Constitutional Society Box and I spoke to Mrs Chapman, Mrs Cope, Mrs Hartley & Miss Forsyth but did not see the Wrights and Agnes said something appeared to be very wrong with them. The meeting was magnificent. Mrs Pankhurst in the Chair – Christabel Pankhurst, Mrs Pethick Lawrence, Vida Goldstein, Mrs Annie Besant – the last named absolutely magnificent. First we sang the March – I was delighted at the sound of my voice in the Albert Hall and, for the moment, thought seriously about having it trained. We waited till the end and it was all too short. Agnes and I weren't a bit over tired. We ran all round the hall and just by chance met John. Then we walked, singing to High Street – train to Praed St and drank Lemonade with ice in the Bar – and came by the 11.15 train home. Mrs & Miss Graham came in our carriage and went on to Henley in it. We had to change at Maidenhead of course. Mrs Graham told me of a great kick up between her and Mrs Wright – so I should not think it was a happy procession for the NCS. John was almost dead and had a huge bruise on his neck with his banner. Supper – bed about 3 in the broad day light.

Emmeline Pethick-Lawrence (1867–1954) joint leader, with her husband and with Mrs Pankhurst, of the WSPU.

Vida Goldstein (1869–1949) Australian suffrage activist who, when she visited Britain for eight months in 1911, did much to encourage the WSPU. She represented Australia in this procession.

Annie Besant (1847–1933) renowned orator, political activist and president of the Theosophical Society.

Monday, June 19th 1911 – Bourne End: The Plat

I went by train to N[otting[H[ill]G[ate] and to Pembridge Crescent and Alexandra and I talked all the morning about the summer campaigns. Went to Knightsbridge to have a look at the new Secretary, Miss Rose Oh! dear she is plain. Miss Ogston was also there. Then a bus to Piccadilly, but it took so long I jumped out at Bond St and got another to Oxford Circus and walked to the Queen's Hall. Got there at 4 and had an hour of the meeting. Mrs Pankhurst in the Chair, Mrs Pethick Lawrence, the Rev. Percy Dearmer. Madame Yvette Guilbert's speech was over. The place was packed and, after collecting over £4,000 on Saturday, they got over £50 this afternoon.

GREAT PROCESSION OF WOMEN,
SATURDAY, JUNE 17th, 1911.

ACTRESSES FRANCHISE LEAGUE SECTION.

HOW TO GET TO THE STARTING POINT.

DRESS.

COLOURS.

STAVES.

SHOES.

HINTS FOR THE PROCESSION.

CHIEF MARSHAL

On 22 June Kate and John thoroughly enjoyed mingling with the crowds lining the London streets on George V's Coronation Day. 'I saw the King in his golden crown and could see him bowing. I was most wildly excited and yelled.' Back at Bourne End she returned to the business of setting up local NCS suffrage societies.

Women's Social & Political Union
WOMEN'S DEMONSTRATION
K 1077 STALL
JUNE 17th, 1911. TO BE RETAINED

WEDNESDAY, JULY 12TH 1911 – BOURNE END: THE PLAT

Went to meet Miss Ogston at 12.15. She came down, feeling very poorly with a feverish cold. She lay down after lunch and slept till I called her at 3.30. At four Mrs Lehmann, Mrs Bleek-Leech, Mrs Tucker, Miss Deacon and Miss Guinness came to tea. Mrs Bloxam came in to say she could not come. Then afterwards we had an address from Miss Ogston and resolved ourselves into a Local Propaganda Society for Women's Suffrage afterwards, which was most successful. Miss Ogston felt so queer she went straight to bed – but made a good dinner and was very lively and talkative. I left her about 10.

Rev. Percy Dearmer (1876-1936) Anglican priest and supporter of women's suffrage.

Yvette Guilbert (1865–1944) renowned French singer, actress and writer.

Sarah Bleek-Leech (b.c.1866) widow. Lindenhurst, Bourne End.

Alice Mompesson Deacon (c 1854–1936) was living with her sister, Mrs Tudor, at Brookfield, Bourne End.

Jessie Bloxam (1851–1926) wife of a noted surgeon. Vineleigh House, Bourne End.

Olave Snow (1879–1931) 'lady gardener' and wife of a solicitor's clerk. Carngray, Beaconsfield.

*In the summer of 1911 England languished in a heatwave that lasted from early July to early September. The Beaconsfield and District Women's Suffrage Association, founded at this meeting, was still in existence in 1919, by which time it was known as the Beaconsfield Society for Equal Citizenship. In 1913, 'feeling that our isolation was a weakness' (*South Bucks Free Press*, 3 October 1913) it had, despite its origin, affiliated to the NUWSS rather than the NCS.*

THURSDAY, JULY 13TH 1911 – BOURNE END: THE PLAT

Hotter than ever – a brilliant day. I was up to breakfast and spent some time waiting on Miss Ogston. Miss Ogston and I had some lunch at a quarter to one then to the station for the 1.40 train to Wycombe and 2.17 to Beaconsfield. Went to Mrs Snow, where Mrs

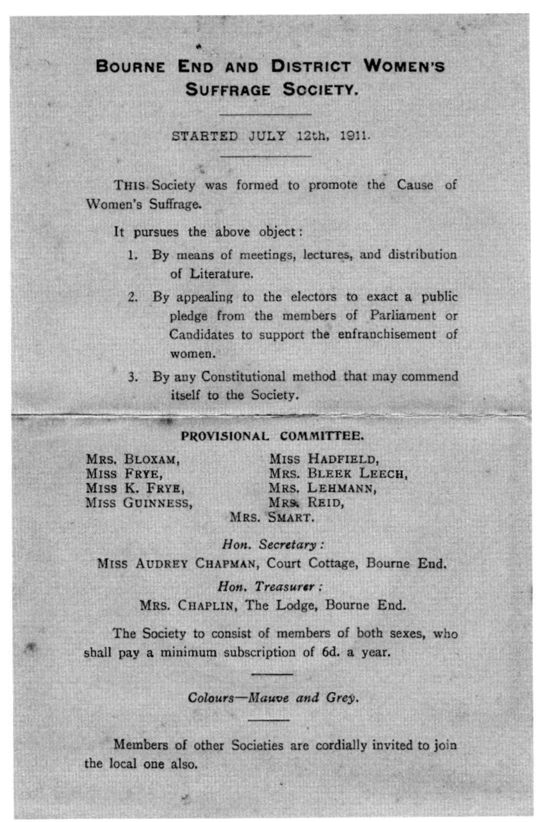

Bourne End and District Women's Suffrage Society.

Started July 12th, 1911.

This Society was formed to promote the Cause of Women's Suffrage.

It pursues the above object:

1. By means of meetings, lectures, and distribution of Literature.
2. By appealing to the electors to exact a public pledge from the members of Parliament or Candidates to support the enfranchisement of women.
3. By any Constitutional method that may commend itself to the Society.

PROVISIONAL COMMITTEE.

Mrs. Bloxam, Miss Frye, Miss K. Frye, Miss Guinness, Miss Hadfield, Mrs. Bleek Leech, Mrs. Lehmann, Mrs. Reid, Mrs. Smart.

Hon. Secretary:
Miss Audrey Chapman, Court Cottage, Bourne End.

Hon. Treasurer:
Mrs. Chaplin, The Lodge, Bourne End.

The Society to consist of members of both sexes, who shall pay a minimum subscription of 6d. a year.

Colours—Mauve and Grey.

Members of other Societies are cordially invited to join the local one also.

Dixon Davies joined us and we discussed the meeting. Then a little before 4 we all went to a Mrs Whitfield at 'Redlands' for the drawing-room meeting. Quite a good gathering and Miss Ogston again spoke well and a local Society was started there and all went very smoothly.

Kate was now sent by the NCS to campaign in rural Essex. Here she could count on the support of some influential suffragists.

MONDAY, JULY 17TH 1911 – BOURNE END: THE PLAT/LITTLE BADDOW: CROSSWAYS, SPRING ELMS LANE

To Liverpool St from Paddington, where John met me and, after seeing my box labelled, off to have some tea and the 5.30 train to Chelmsford. Sent my box from there to Witham and there found Mr E. Brown who motored me to Little Baddow, where Mrs Sadd Brown gave me a most kind welcome. Changed my blouse in their room and had dinner. Went outside for a little – such a glorious evening and a most sweet spot. I had no idea Essex could be so pretty – real rural England. Then discussed the campaign and at 10.30 Mr Brown carried my bag for me to the cottage where I more or less slept. It was so very hot and, though a clean room, so stuffy. I was very tired and I always get a worked-up feeling the day I start off for work.

TUESDAY, JULY 18TH 1911 – LITTLE BADDOW: CROSSWAYS, SPRING ELMS LANE/WITHAM: TEMPERANCE HOTEL, ALBERT ROAD

Put my things together & got up to 'Crossways' just after 8 o'clock. I played in the gardens with the baby then Mrs S. Brown took me to call on Mrs Ayrton Gould, who was seedy and not up. We saw Mr Gould and he promised to take our message. Then I was motored to Hatfield Peveril where we paid calls and to Witham – calls and the Printer. Then off to the Temperance Hotel where I am to stay. My box & the Literature had arrived. I tidied myself – then more calls by motor. Mrs S. Brown did some on her own account and so did I and she went off to Hatfield again. I had some tea at 5. Then the Printing was done so I took the Bills to the shops – then got back at 7.30. Some supper after unpacking and writing till 11.30 – then had not much sleep. The noise of the

Alice Davies (b. 1859) wife of a solicitor, in 1915 was a member of the International League for Peace and Freedom. Witheridge, Beaconsfield.

Margaret Whitfield (b. 1874) American wife of a doctor and mother of three, Redlands, Curzon Ave, Beaconsfield.

Barbara Ayrton Gould (1886–1950) daughter of the eminent scientist, Hertha Ayrton, she worked as an organiser for the WSPU before her marriage in 1910.

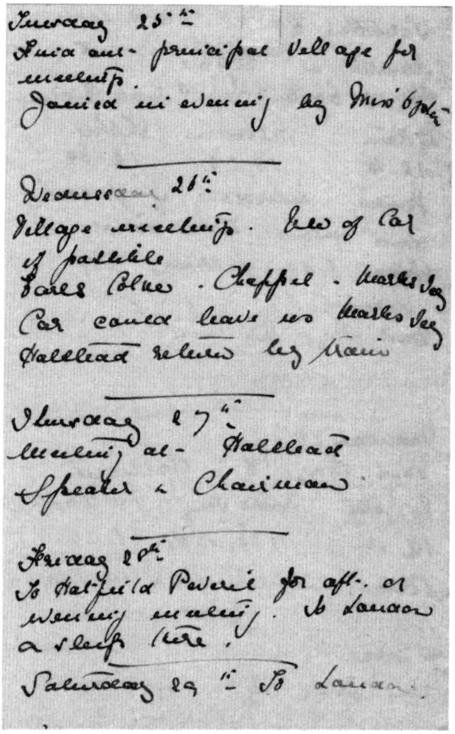

Tuesday 25th
Find out principal village for meetings.
Garden in evening by Mrs [illegible]

Wednesday 26th
Village meetings. Use of Car if possible
Earls Colne. Chappel. Wakes Colne
Car could leave us Wakes Colne
Halstead return by train

Thursday 27th
Meeting at Halstead
Speaker & Chairman

Friday 28th
To Hatfield Peverel for aft. or evening meeting. To London & sleep there.
Saturday 29th To London.

trains was so awful and oh! dear the heat. Then I was over excited and anxious after a strenuous day and so much talking and planning.

WEDNESDAY, JULY 19TH 1911 – WITHAM: TEMPERANCE HOTEL, ALBERT ROAD

By the 9.22 train to Felsted. Had to walk from the station. Very hot & dusty. Had only one name to rely upon but he – Mr Hicks – cycle agent – turned out a great help. Took the School Rooms for me – found a chairman – gave me names of people – and got a girl at the Post Office to write the Bills out. I paid calls, had some lunch at 1 and sat writing Bills, which I gave away to the good folks going to the Vicarage garden for a tea and garden party arranged by the British Women's Temperance. A bit of luck for me. I had met the workers by chance after I had called and the Vicar, who was a great trial, gave away bills. More calls – then, feeling very tired, I found a stile to sit on for an hour-and-a-half and wrote home to John. Then in one of Mr Hicks' Taxi cabs to the station.

THURSDAY, JULY 20TH 1911 – WITHAM: TEMPERANCE HOTEL, ALBERT ROAD

Another very hot day but quite a lot of wind. After lunch came up to my room – packed Literature for evening etc – did some mending – cut my nails – wrote my diary and at 3.15 lay down for a rest. At 4.30 I went off paying calls and canvassing. Only got back to the station in time to meet Miss Ogston at 6.45. She arrived very limp with the heat. We went across to the Hotel and had some dinner – then off rather before 7.30 to the large Public Hall. I had been there earlier to arrange it. Mrs Sadd Brown drove up with Mrs Ayrton Gould rather before 8 o'clock with Mademoiselle, who made herself very busy selling 'Votes for Women'. Mrs Sadd Brown took the chair and Miss Ogston and Mrs Ayrton Gould gave addresses. Rather disappointing – only 50 people, but it was such a tremendously hot night.

The 21 July edition of the WSPU paper, Votes for Women, *carried a notice from the NCS: 'In order to carry on this summer campaign the sum of £100 is absolutely necessary; £19 has been promised'. The appeal ran through the summer; it is not clear how successful it was. The Chequers is still a pub, but no longer a hotel.*

Ernest Hicks (1878–1944) cycle and sports dealer, operated from what had been Felsted's Bell Inn. He eventually expanded his business into car repairs and, later, buses.

Above: Kate's plan for the Essex campaign.

FRIDAY, JULY 21ST 1911 – WITHAM: TEMPERANCE HOTEL, ALBERT ROAD/FELSTED: THE CHEQUERS HOTEL, BRAINTREE ROAD

I took Miss Ogston's breakfast to her and she did not rise until lunch time. This hot weather is making her full of complaints but no doubt she does feel limp. I did my packing, some writing and then went into the town to pay bills etc. The heat was almost unbearable but really very wonderful. What a summer. The like of it I do not remember for many years. Lunch early, then at 1.22 Miss Ogston and I went to Felsted. Had a taxi from the station to the Chequers Hotel which was very comfortable. Then out to call on Mr Hicks and to see the Schoolroom. Back to the Hotel and had some tea. Miss Ogston went to bed and I called her at 6.30. We had a nice little dinner at 7, and, still panting with the heat, repaired to the Schoolroom. At 8 o'clock there were only 5 people, the place was suffocating. Mr Quibell the Chairman had arrived and he and Mr Hicks decided we had better turn it out of doors. So we did. Mr Hicks, a most wonderful man, let us have a car and the Chairman and Miss Ogston spoke from it. She spoke for over an hour and we had a good gathering round us, and a lot of questions asked. No one would second the resolution. I did so in a few feeble and high-pitched words, but not a hand raised for it – so we decided afterwards to have no more resolutions out of doors. However I felt the meeting had been quite a success and was very grateful to Mr Hicks & Mr Quibell. The latter took Miss Ogston back to the Hotel, with a Miss Madge Barker who had bicycled from Stebbing and I went in to the Schools to collect my things, attended by Mr Hicks and a half a dozen or so ladies. And we had a little impromptu meeting and I heard myself talking quite well to them. But conversational speaking is so different. Then I went to the Hotel and Mr Quibell insisted upon me having lemonade and we talked for a long time – an interesting man. Miss Barker was there, too, and they rode together. Then the flagging Miss Ogston & I to bed. I could not sleep for hours. Tried sitting by the window – then reading – the heat was terrific.

VOTES FOR WOMEN

A

MEETING

WILL BE HELD IN THE

PUBLIC HALL,

WITHAM,

ON

Thursday, July 20th.

SPEAKERS:

Miss HELEN OGSTON, B.Sc.

Mrs. SADD-BROWN

SUBJECT:

"THE CONCILIATION BILL."

CHAIR TO BE TAKEN AT 8 P.M.

ADMISSION FREE.

THE NEW CONSTITUTIONAL SOCIETY FOR WOMEN'S SUFFRAGE.
8, PARK MANSIONS,
ARCADE, KNIGHTSBRIDGE.

B. C. AFFORD, PRINTER, WITHAM.

SATURDAY, JULY 22ND 1911 – FELSTED: THE CHEQUERS/LITTLE BADDOW: CROSSWAYS, SPRING ELMS LANE

Only finished our breakfast in time to pop into the taxi, stop at Mr Hicks to say goodbye and catch the 9.19 train from Felsted back to Witham. The parched & bare Temperance Hotel did not seem tempting. Miss Ogston repaired to bed. We had lunch and waited till 3 o'clock, when Mrs Sadd Brown and Mademoiselle arrived in the car,

Probably Madeline Barker, 27, dressmaker, High Street, Stebbing.

'Mademoiselle' probably Angelique Larelli, governess to the Brown children.

and off we went to Tollesbury. The wind was so hot it positively scorched my face – yesterday and to-day are about the hottest days I ever remember. However I enjoyed the ride – but when we went between 50 & 60 miles an hour I was a little dizzy. Some of the country was charming. Rushing into the town I set them to write notices while I rushed and bought paper, borrowed gum and a brush and made a poster over one of the 'Votes for Women' notices. Then did a little canvassing till the notices were ready – when Mrs Sadd Brown and I went off in the car. I had borrowed a Bell and acted as Town Crier. People were curious but so shy. The first meeting that had been held there. They lingered on the outskirts and really only about 2 grownups came to listen and the children were so noisy. I hired a cart. Mrs Sadd Brown spoke first then Miss Ogston – while I went about hunting people up and distributing papers. We had finished soon after 7 – cleared up our things and departed in the car back to Witham. The ride was glorious. We left Miss Ogston at the Hotel to have supper and get the last train to London, and I got my suit case and Mrs S.B. brought me to Little Baddow. We had supper and a chat, then at 10.30 Mr Brown, such a kind man, saw me down to the cottage, and I tried to sleep. Oh the heat.

MONDAY, JULY 24TH 1911 – LITTLE BADDOW: CROSSWAYS, SPRING ELMS LANE/ HALSTEAD: BULL HOTEL, BRIDGE STREET

Left at 8.20 in the car with Mr Brown also Mrs Ayrton Gould, who asked for a lift into Chelmsford. I did not reach Halstead until about 12. Left my bag in the cloakroom and went first to Mr Barry, who was the printer and whose wife turned out most kind. Miss Courtauld, who I had arranged to meet at 12.45 at the station, had tracked me and we three had a talk. Then she took me off to the Temperance Hotel. It looked a miserable place and they would not have me and I went to see some wretched rooms. Then Miss Courtauld drove me to 'Cut Hedge' – her father's place – and I was plumped down to lunch with the family. Old Mr Courtauld over 80 – his 3rd wife, a great invalid, and his young son, quite a young man – a soldier – and 2 miserable looking daughters belonging to the second family. A most beautiful home. Something like Wooburn House. Miss Courtauld is quite like a man, a most extraordinary person, but very nice and a beautiful face. Young Mr Courtauld – Herbert – motored us in to Gosfield after a little rest and we paid calls and settled about the meeting. Then Miss Courtauld drove me back into Halstead and I went in to Mrs Barry to order the Printing for Gosfield and around Halstead and she took me round to see some

Thomas Barry, aged 52, newspaper editor and proprietor lived with his wife, Lavinia (both were Scottish) and their daughter, Mary, an art student, at 21 High Street, Halstead.

Sydney Renée Courtauld (1873–1962) member of the family that made its fortune from textiles, with mills in Halstead and the surrounding area, sister of Samuel Courtauld (founder of the Courtauld Institute and Gallery). She was an active member of the NUWSS.

people and to the Bull Hotel. I arranged to stop there and went to the station and got my luggage sent round. Then, exhausted with the heat, I had some tea then straight way started to write. I had called at the Post Office and got letters. Miss Barry very kindly came to the Hotel with the Printing and I got it all off to Gosfield and went to the post before 8 o'clock. The Hotel is a great improvement on Witham – a beautiful old building – and such a kind little waitress, Gertie who is most attentive.

WEDNESDAY, JULY 26TH 1911 – HALSTEAD: THE BULL, BRIDGE STREET

Distributed the bills at 12.45 to the women and girls coming out of Courtaulds, the weaving place. Had a rest after lunch and lay down on my bed after getting the Literature ready for the evening. Went to the station and met Miss Ogston at 4.30. We had some tea, then I changed and at 6 o'clock Miss Courtauld came in her motor from Colne Engaine to take us to 'Cut Hedge'. We were early so the sisters and she took us round the grounds. Most beautiful. Then dinner at 6.30, all the family again. Master Herbert rather enjoying the joke – especially when Miss Ogston let out about me being with the Actresses in the Procession. The two sisters went with us to Gosfield and at 8 the meeting started. Miss Courtauld took the Chair – or the motor seat – and spoke for a few minutes and Miss Ogston spoke for an hour. About 100 people assembled and listened very quietly. Then there were questions and Miss Courtauld motored us off – the two sisters to their gate and Miss Ogston and myself to the Bull. She has been most awfully kind about it all. A great National Union person – very Anti-Militant but she knew about Miss Ogston.

Letitia Dixon (c 1850 – 1916) had lived for many years in Leatherhead, where her father was noted as a philanthropist.

Alice Vaizey, a 64-year-old widow, living with her farmer son at Bentalls, Halstead.

THURSDAY, JULY 27TH 1911 – HALSTEAD: THE BULL, BRIDGE STREET

Paid more calls and did more canvassing and caught the weavers again. Miss Ogston went to bed after lunch. I went to my room and unpacked and re-packed & got the Literature ready for night. By that time it was time to change and go to the station at 4.30 to meet Miss Dixon. She is quite elderly and was quite done up with the heat which was tremendous. After tea she retired to rest. I took Miss Ogston up to call on Mrs Barry as she knew of her family in Aberdeen. Dinner at 7 – and it was a great 'to do' getting Miss Dixon up to the Market Hill by 7.45. Mrs Barry supplied the chairs and Mrs Vaizey, Miss Dixon & Miss Ogston spoke from the fountain. Mrs Vaizey only said a few words. Miss Dixon kept at it for half an hour but I am afraid was not heard. I couldn't hear her, and then Miss Ogston. Quite a number of people gathered together and it was a good meeting. But I had much ado to keep the children quiet and a young Mr Clover assisted me. Miss Barry and a Miss Goody assisted by giving Literature, selling & collecting. Miss Ogston brought the old lady back. I waited to thank Mrs Vaizey & walk back with the Barrys. Then to the Hotel – my charges had a light supper and I

Votes for Women!

AN

OPEN AIR MEETING

Will be held on

THE MARKET HILL,

ON

THURSDAY NEXT, JULY 27th.

Chair to be taken at 7.45 p.m. by

MRS. VAIZEY.

Miss Helen Ogston,

B. Sc. and

MISS LETITIA DIXON

Will speak on the

CONCILIATION BILL.

The New Constitutional Society for Women's Suffrage,
8 Park Mansions Arcade,
Knightsbridge, S.W.

BARRY & CO., PRINTERS, HALSTEAD.

got them to bed. I knew when Mrs Chapman suggested Miss Dixon she would not 'go down' and, of course, speaking in the open air is something quite different to ordinary speaking. Miss Ogston is indistinct because she speaks too quickly. I was glad to get to bed – but this heat prevents me from resting quietly.

FRIDAY, JULY 28TH 1911 – HALSTEAD: THE BULL, BRIDGE STREET/LITTLE BADDOW: CROSSWAYS, SPRING ELMS LANE

Left Halstead at 10.22. I saw my trunk off by Advance, the Literature by Goods, and took my suit case. We had to change at Marks Tey and Miss Ogston and I at Witham for Hatfield Peveril. Miss Dixon went straight on to London. Mrs Sadd Brown had sent Thomas in the motor for us. Miss Ogston put her case in the cloakroom & I bought her ticket to London for her, then to Little Baddow. It was so nice to get to 'Crossways' again and have such a hearty greeting from Mrs Sadd Brown and the babes – Bubbles, Emily & Jean – and the eldest girl, Myra (Honey) is at home now from School. We took off our hats and rested till lunch, had a Lobster salad – so cool – and sat in the garden until it was time to get ready to go in the car to Boreham (Chelmsford division) where a village meeting was held at 3.30. Mrs Maud came to take the Chair and there were about 25 people present. Mrs Sadd Brown spoke most beautifully to them. Miss Ogston was very languid. Then we had a chat to the women and gave some 'Votes' away and Mrs S.B. motored us to Hatfield Peveril to a Mrs Chappelow who had helped to get up the evening meeting. She and her daughter are very Militant. Miss Chappelow has a decoration for valour and forcible feeding in prison. Mrs Sadd Brown left us there, motoring back to Little Baddow for dinner and Miss Ogston & I really had a very unhappy time. Good kind people but so peculiar and so unwashed. Very emancipated – no servant and lots of animals not very fresh and all kinds of weird theories. A man staying there was most peculiar and would afterwards show us new nests and terrify us. Miss Ogston behaved like a child and I got quite hysterical, and when we were left alone we laughed till we cried. The most peculiar people I have ever come across. It was so nice to see Mrs Sadd Brown and the motor and she took us off to the Parish room – a queer little place with only about 10 chairs. I was so hysterical by that time I could only laugh, but it was serious. So off I flew to the caretaker – she knew nothing – so, collecting 4 strong boys, off I went to the Vicarage. They hadn't them there and the Vicar came in and was most peculiar so it ended by getting as many from the cottages as possible. But very few people came – greatly to the Chappelows' disappointment – but another boiling night – we should have done better out of doors. Miss Ogston took the Chair and spoke first – then Mrs Sadd Brown. Miss Ogston went off at 9.15 to catch her train and after the meeting Mrs Sadd Brown motored me back with her and Mademoiselle to 'Crossways'. A wonderful ride through the hot night. I had some supper and Mr Brown then saw me to my cottage. He really is a kind and long-suffering man. The room seemed hotter than ever. I did not unpack much, but got everything ready for the morning.

Grace Chappelow (1890–1971) was imprisoned on several occasions and was forcibly fed, for which she received the WSPU 'Hunger-strike medal' to which Kate refers. In later life she became increasingly eccentric and reclusive, as recounted in an interview with a long-time companion, Mrs Konter, in a recording held by the Women's Library (8SUF/B/108). Chelmsford Museum holds several items associated with her suffrage militancy.

On Saturday 29 July Kate returned to Bourne End for a couple of weeks, her diary full of the heat

and news of strikes and riots. In mid-August she was sent by the NCS to Suffolk to conduct a summer seaside campaign. The Triangle is a market place in the centre of Lowestoft.

TUESDAY, AUGUST 15TH 1911 – BOURNE END: THE PLAT/LOWESTOFT: 5 DENE ROAD
[From Bourne End to London] Paddington seemed very quiet and I got through to Liverpool St very comfortably and to the 3.24 train to Lowestoft. John came to see me off there from rehearsal. It was a very comfortable journey. We reached Lowestoft at 6.24 and got a fly to 5 Dene Place [Road], Gunton Cliff & Miss Lightman had arrived and greeted me and our rooms seem quite nice. Mrs Swann joined us for dinner at 7 and we went off at 7.45 to The Triangle for an open-air meeting which Mrs Clarkson Swann had arranged. She seems very energetic. It was quite a good meeting and the two speakers did their best. We got back about 9.15 and I soon went up to bed as I had my unpacking, and spent some time getting to bed. It was cooler when I left home this morning but here such a change seemed bitter – was glad to sleep in a dressing gown and then my feet were miserably cold.

THURSDAY, AUGUST 17TH 1911 – LOWESTOFT: 5 DENE ROAD
Mrs Clarkson Swann went off by herself – Miss Lightman and I went out advertising the meeting & shopping then to the North Beach and held a meeting there 12 till 12.45. Quite a good number of people collected. Home to lunch and Mrs C.S.'s son had arrived. She has a room for him at No 9 and he is to share our sitting-room and meals. Quite a nice lad of 17. Dinner, then the two went out. Miss Lightman rested and I wrote. Tea at 4, then I went out and tried to pay calls. At 7.30 Miss Lightman and I to The Triangle. Met Mrs Swann and we had our open-air meeting 8 to 9. Quite a good crowd collected. Miss Lightman spoke very well.

SATURDAY, AUGUST 19TH 1911 – LOWESTOFT: 5 DENE ROAD
A most beautiful day again. Miss Lightman and I went out and did the shopping, and gave Bills for the evening meeting. At 11.30 to the Beach where I gave papers and chatted to people about the meeting, which we had at 12.15, but very few people came to listen and it was not worth the bother. Another meeting at The Triangle at 8.45 and had to wait till the Salvation Army had done and we got a large crowd. Miss Lightman spoke excellently. She is improving every day and quite holds the people. Mrs Clarkson Swann is no good for open air and her delivery is bad – sometimes she talks the greatest nonsense.

Maria Clarkson Swann (1859–1937) wife of Howard Swann, an insurance broker, mother of four sons, 14 Homefield Road, Bromley, Kent. She was a member of the Women's Tax Resistance League, in 1910 was an active member of the WSPU, and appears to have evaded the 1911 census. The son accompanying her to Lowestoft was her youngest, Pelham.

MONDAY, AUGUST 21ST 1911 – LOWESTOFT: 5 DENE ROAD
Had a very heavy day. Wrote letters, then out canvassing and seeing about the hall for the meeting. Out till lunch time and again in the afternoon and evening, and a meeting at The Triangle at 8 o'clock. The air is beautiful here and suiting me but I do get a bit done and have not a moment to myself, and beside all the organising I have to do the housekeeping, keep the accounts and am generally responsible for everything. Mrs Clarkson Swann is a very worrying sort of woman. She gets on my nerves dreadfully and on Miss Lightman's worse so I have to be very careful to avoid friction, and she is a

trial to us both, so fearfully important and such a talker, her tongue is never still. She is very good on canvassing so I let her do a lot of it. The boy isn't bad – rather uncouth, a lazy sort of individual but, with training, might turn out very average. He is quite at home with us now and I really feel changes the atmosphere. Miss Lightman generally feels so ill that I do not ask her to do anything besides speak and days when we have the meeting she chalks the pavements, writes the bills and gives them out. By bed time I am generally done.

TUESDAY, AUGUST 22ND 1911 – LOWESTOFT: 5 DENE ROAD

Took a tram to the station and train to Oulton Broad at 12.48 and walked to Waldo Cottage to a Mr and Mrs Ponder where I had lunch. They are Socialists, Atheists, Vegetarians and Teetotallers. She is very nice. He is a great talker and talks well, really very beautiful are his ideas and I found them fearfully interesting, but he rather made me shudder. I went out canvassing and kept at it till 5 o'clock. Back to tea when Mrs C.S. & Miss Lightman had arrived. Then I went forward to the Free Quay and we had a meeting there at 7 o'clock. Mr Ponder took the Chair and about 50 people were present and it was quite a success. We took the train back from Carlton Colville at 9.15 and reached home very tired to have supper than came to bed.

Baker's Score is the cliff top at Corton. Kate had at least one other encounter with Mr Sisman, whom she clearly found simpatico.

THURSDAY, AUGUST 24TH 1911 – LOWESTOFT: 5 DENE ROAD

Mrs Clarkson Swann had a holiday and went off somewhere in the afternoon with her boy and to the Theatre in the evening. I canvassed round in the morning to get help with stewarding. Paid bills etc – and got the printing. Miss Lightman and I went to Corton at 5.25. Went down the town to catch an earlier train that didn't run – so went and sat on the esplanade after having had some tea. We had meant to have the meeting, but were persuaded to canvass for it – and arrange it for Saturday. One Mr Sisman of the Coast-guard Station was simply sweet and let us wait in his house and took us to see Baker's Score.

The 'Large Double Cross Bills' to which Kate refers were probably the cartoon posters depicting 'The Right Dishonourable Double-Face Asquith' issued by the WSPU during a 1910 general election. They advised the electorate to 'Vote against the Government and Keep the Liberal Out'.

WEDNESDAY, AUGUST 30TH 1911 – LOWESTOFT: 5 DENE ROAD

Mrs Clarkson Swann, Miss Lightman and myself donned our Posters & very trim and nice we looked – two in green linen and one in cream linen with the Large Double Cross Bills sewn on to stiff Brown Paper and tied round our necks with green ribbon. My heart beat horribly at first but it was really alright – and not bad when we got started. I went first, Mrs CS next and Miss Lightman 3rd. We walked all down the Main Road to the Pier – stood there while the people were coming off – then along South Parade and back up the Main Rd. Took a tram at The Triangle and got in at 1.45.

Horace Ponder (1849–1934) retired piano tuner. In April Mrs Ponder had attempted to boycott the census, spending the night with other suffragettes in a Lowestoft boarding-house.

Charles Sisman (1873–1944) Coast Guard Station, Corton, Lowestoft.

After lunch I had to pack up things for the hall and took a large tram load down. Got the key from Mr Pamphilon's office and had a good haul in there – re-arranging the chairs and putting the place in order. Got back about 5. Miss Ogston had arrived, looking very blooming and pleased with life. I left them at dinner when I started off at 7. I got to the hall early as 4 ladies had promised to steward. We opened the doors at 8 – and the meeting started at 8.30. The hall was quite full and I suppose it was a very satisfactory meeting, but I always want better than the best. I wanted hundreds turned away. Not half the people who had promised turned up. The Mayor took the Chair. Miss Lightman, Mrs Clarkson Swann & Miss Ogston spoke. Two terrible men from the theatre who came after Mr Pamphilon worried me. I don't know whether they thought they knew me or what. I was in my best and looking unusually nice, but I did not want their kind of attention. The bevy of young men round us in the morning had been enough. Evidently undergraduates thought they were going to have a lark. By a gift I was able to freeze them and they spoke quite nicely afterwards. But of course they had expected a 'rag' – what one does have to put up with. Well I suppose it is bracing. Dodging in and out Mr Pamphilon's office has been trial enough. I always felt I might blush. The sort of man who cannot get away from Sex. He has tried to be good with me and I think his interest in Suffrage is aroused, but I do happen to look particularly blooming down here. The East Coast always suits me and I am a person who varies very much. I can see it for myself – my face is as different as chalk from cheese some days and some places. I suppose it helps the Suffrage, but it shouldn't. But it is hard to live up to Suffrage. In some moods I could flirt with a Broomstick. One or two days even the boy [Pelham Clarkson Swann] had it and thrilled under it, though in his heart of hearts he prefers Miss Lightman. Well Mr Pamphilon doesn't and there it is plain. He always speaks of his wife, but there is attraction written in every line of his face. A peculiar predicament. So I generally manage to take Mrs Clarkson Swann or Miss Lightman in his office with me. These wretched arrangements have necessitated so many journeys. I wonder what he told these wretched theatrical men, boon companions, I suppose. I suppose they came out of curiosity to see me. He must have spoken of me. They asked me all sorts of questions – even my name. When I went to tell Mr Pamphilon he was wanted he looked very uncomfortable and would not stir from his seat. So they went off without him. The meeting ended with a collection of £1-1-6½ and a resolution carried unanimously.

VOTES FOR WOMEN

A MEETING

Will be held in

The East Anglian Hall,

MILTON ROAD, NORTH LOWESTOFT,

ON

WEDNESDAY, AUGUST 30th,

At 8.30 p.m.

CHAIRMAN:

THE MAYOR OF LOWESTOFT,

(Thomas E. Thirtle, Esq., J.P.)

SPEAKERS:

Mrs. CLARKSON SWANN, Miss ROSE LIGHTMAN,

MISS HELEN OGSTON, B.Sc.

Subject:—"The Conciliation Bill."

ADMISSION FREE. (A few Reserved Seats).

The New Constitutional Society for Women's Suffrage, 8, Park Mansions Arcade, Knightsbridge, London, S.W.

Thomas Hake, Printer and Stationer, Old Nelson Street, Lowestoft.

Sidney Pamphilon (1876–1958) auctioneer, surveyor and valuer. In 1912 he emigrated with his family to California.

Then I cleared up and we walked home. The boy and I had supper while the others had a slight meal.

Miss Ogston and Mrs Clarkson – with Pelham – left Lowestoft on 31 August.

FRIDAY, SEPTEMBER 1ST 1911 – LOWESTOFT: 5 DENE ROAD

A few jobs, then out in good time to do the shopping and pay the bills. Took Miss Lightman into Mr Pamphilon's office. He was quite nice. We had a long talk and he got the paper for us to read the notice from. I find he is a very keen Amateur Actor – he should be good with his temperament. In at 12 and started my letters – some important ones.Wrote all the afternoon while Miss Lightman rested. Tea at 4.30 then the two of us off to Pakefield by train. Consulting the Vicar's wife and the Police, fixed time & spot wrote our notices, canvassed and held a meeting at Florence Terrace at 7.30. Got a kitchen chair and I uprose on it and spoke for a few minutes to collect a crowd. I did not do well – felt very stumped for things to say and felt more than ever that I should never be a speaker. The only thing that sounded right was my voice and I liked hearing that again. Miss Lightman spoke for some time and though only a few people were present we had a most interesting chat afterwards with such a nice family. The son – 32 and a Soldier and quite Suffrage – besides being most awfully good looking. We had a long chat he and I. Back by train both very tired. I did not enjoy the night as I did without a night-light for Miss Lightman's sake and oh I was unhappy. All the time till dawn kept waking up and feeling I simply couldn't bear the dark.

Kate now returned to East Dereham, to continue the Norfolk campaign.

SATURDAY, SEPTEMBER 2ND 1911 – LOWESTOFT: 5 DENE ROAD/EAST DEREHAM: 65 COMMERCIAL ROAD

I had done most of my packing yesterday, so only had to finish and then Miss Lightman and I went out. Went down the town and to the station to hire a cab, then sat by the sea until 12 o'clock. I saw Miss Lightman off in her London train at 1.58 and then I had to hang about for an hour for my train, but I was glad to see her off. She is a nervous sort of being and the crush frightened her. So many people travelling. I did not enjoy my journey and at Norwich, where I had to change, it was quite a pandemonium, and so hot. The train was half an hour late in getting here and I did not reach Commercial Road [Dereham] till 5.30. Mrs West is away but Miss Emery, her companion, is here and such a nice woman and these rooms are so clean and dainty and really I do not feel sorry to be alone.

SUNDAY, SEPTEMBER 3RD 1911 – EAST DEREHAM: 65 COMMERCIAL ROAD

A beautiful day again. Went to Church in my best and was glad I did, though it was a bit of an effort, but heard a sermon about the necessity of a healthy public opinion and I feel it will help me in Dereham. When I first got in the Church and saw the rows of respectable & conventional backs my heart misgave me. Wrote till lunch time, again after. Reports for the 3 papers and to Miss Lightman and posted them when I went out to tea with the Becks in Church St. They gave me a very kind reception and after tea I sat in the garden till after 6. Not bad people and I got on better with them without Miss Ogston. Mr Beck gave me some useful information.

MONDAY, SEPTEMBER 4TH 1911 – EAST DEREHAM: 65 COMMERCIAL ROAD

About 10 o'clock it started to rain and kept on till 4. Tidied myself and went in to tea with Miss Elwin. She is quite nice but has a very quaint manner. Then to pay calls – the Curate's wife and Mrs Pearse. Waited till he [Mr Pearse] came in and we arranged about the meetings. She was very nice. He looks a spoilt person. I have no interest for him, but he enquired several times about the other one – meaning Miss Ogston. I cannot think what had made him even interested in the Question unless he firmly thinks all women are Unionists. And she is like a child – after 12 years of married life has nothing more in her than a doll. Very good and kind, I am sure. Too good to him I have no doubt. Oh it was hot and some thunder before it cleared up.

THURSDAY, SEPTEMBER 7TH 1911 – EAST DEREHAM: 65 COMMERCIAL ROAD

I really think it is the hottest day we have had this summer – a wind that scorched one – a blazing sun. I was up a bit earlier than usual, first to the High St then by the 10.8 train to Hardingham. Found it a very long hot walk to the village and when there met with so little success it took me a long time to make up my mind what to do. But I fixed a meeting – bought ink and sat outside the Post Office writing the Notices. Bought biscuits and chocolate at the shop – then went canvassing.

FRIDAY, SEPTEMBER 8TH 1911 – EAST DEREHAM: 65 COMMERCIAL ROAD

Felt most wickedly tired all day. Mr Count the Printer came round in a dreadful state of flurry to say Mr Pearse had been in the shop in a dreadful temper saying the date of the meeting must be altered. I could only apologise to Mr Count that my affairs should have caused Mr Pearse to be upset with him and said I would wait to hear from Mr Pearse before sending the cards out. All the envelopes were just ready. I guessed from Mr Count it was serious. Was too tired. I retired to my room about 3 and slept. When I came down at 4.30 a note waiting me, brought by Mr Pearse's groom beginning 'dear madam' and ending 'yours truly' saying, as he should be out Tuesday and Thursday, we had better arrange to get a garden elsewhere. What an-ill bred creature. And what a hole to put me in – 6/- of cards printed and ready to go out, some gone through the post. I feel very sorry for the wretched wife but she must be a fool. From all accounts I hear Mr Pearse is a thorough bad lot. I guessed as much, but as they are the Social Centre of the Town it is making it very awkward for our work his turning off like this. The whole place seems rotten to the core – all the people of any account stupid, bad and narrow and the others of no social consequence. I buckled on my things and went forth. To the Becks to say good-bye as they are going tomorrow. Really Mrs & Miss seem about the decentest people here – I wouldn't trust him, but I should say there isn't a man in this town whose morals one could trust. I saw Mr Hewitt and Mr Barnaby. To the former I told the troubles and he was quite nice about it. He is so nice I wonder if he can possibly be sincere. A thunder storm at 7 drove me in. It was the threatening of a terrific one

Catherine Elwin (1872–1955) district nurse, lodging at 89 Commercial Road.

Frederick Count (1851–1919) printer, bookseller, stationer and newsagent, two of whose daughters worked with him in the Market Place shop.

Henry Barnaby (1857–1949) schoolmaster and organist, whose wife, Ellen, became a member of the New Constitutional Society. Theatre St, East Dereham.

– but not much happened though the lightning was very vivid. It was getting on 10 o'clock when Mr & Mrs Hewitt came in to pay me a visit. We had a most interesting talk, they are both very advanced. If what he says of Dereham is true it must be a filthy little town.

SATURDAY, SEPTEMBER 9TH 1911 – EAST DEREHAM: 65 COMMERCIAL ROAD

Woke to the feeling of a very disturbed day. Could not make up my mind what to do for the best. Started out early, did a lot of canvassing for Tuesday, paid more calls and tried to get a garden or a lady to play hostess. The largest Social leader is a Col Hyde, who, I am told, is a most wicked old man. I saw his daughter, Mrs Butler, who looked a real old Harpy but was very girlish. Oh no she didn't like the Suffragettes, she was very sorry but she must confess it but she was a man's woman never had been a woman's woman etc. The Butler stood by all the time to protect his mistress in case the Suffragette threw anything because, of course, they always do throw things. The whole scene turned me sick. She was a most detestable female – coarse minded – feeble, shallow and yet old and haggard. It was impossible to argue with her. I was on the door step and she kept shutting the door by inches and was very kittenish withal. I went goosy all down the spine she had such an unpleasant effect. Yet I was told if I could get her all the town would flock. It seems inconceivable. The only decent people I have met are the Bank manager's wife and daughter – the Corys – they are true Suffragists but dare not take any part. So I settled, after calling on Mr Barnaby, to try and raise a meeting on our own but I am dreading a most dismal failure. Oh I shall be disappointed and shamed with Mrs Cecil Chapman here. To bed dead tired. I would [not] go through another week like this for anything.

SUNDAY, SEPTEMBER 10TH 1911 – EAST DEREHAM: 65 COMMERCIAL ROAD

Woke up feeling so tired and miserable – made up my mind not to go to Church. I had arranged to go out to tea with Mrs Pearse but after the way they have behaved, though I wrote very politely to her, I said I was afraid we should not meet again till I came to Dereham next time. I met her out yesterday and instead of avoiding me she came and chatted. Didn't seem to know of Mr Pearse's letter but hoped it wouldn't matter. Would any other day do? – so I put her off. She has the mind of a child. Mr Pearse, it seems, wants to play in a tennis Tournament on Thursday and it is her day at the Workhouse. I suppose it is what Workhouses are for – to give such people as she occupation. Ye gods!!! It is my aim to keep people from getting into Workhouses not to go and read to the poor tragical wrecks of humanity when there. Oh Dereham, Dereham, could I paint you in your true colours and hang you up for the world to see and to cleanse.

Col Henry Elwin Hyde (1837–1916) Moorgate House, South Green, East Dereham. His daughter, Mrs Beatrix Butler (1861–1948) was a widow.

Charles Cory had his position to maintain as manager of the Dereham branch of the London and Provincial Bank and treasurer of East Dereham Urban District Council. He lived with his wife Emily, daughter, Violet (1892–1969) and son, Carl, above the bank, 38 Market Place, East Dereham.

MONDAY, SEPTEMBER 11TH 1911 – EAST DEREHAM: 65 COMMERCIAL ROAD

Felt most seedy and had the rat so badly I determined to end it with a bottle of medicine. But I had to stick at my writing and worked against time to get the invitation cards filled in for the 'At Home' and just managed to get them in their envelopes by lunch time. Changed my dress after, went to the post with some and to buy more stamps and order my medicine. Went by the 4.17 train to Hardingham. Miss Ogston had come

VOTES FOR WOMEN!

MEETING

IN THE

MARKET PLACE, DEREHAM,

TUESDAY, SEPT. 12th,

Chair to be taken at 7.30 p.m.

SPEAKERS—

MRS. CECIL CHAPMAM,

MISS HELEN OGSTON, B.Sc.

Subject---The Conciliation Bill.

The New Constitutional Society for Women's Suffrage, 8, Park Mansions Arcade, Knightsbridge, London, W.

F. W. COUNT, TYP., DEREHAM.

from London and reached Hardingham at 4 and met me on the platform. We went to the Railway Hotel but could not be supplied with tea there. The lady was all in a fluster and had 'real ladies' for whom she was preparing a seven-course dinner. So, hoping for the best, we trudged on hoping to get tea at the post office. On the way we called at the School House to see if Mr Redford would take the Chair and, though he could not, he received us most kindly and gave us pleasant welcome and he and his wife entertained us to tea. A Miss Smith was there who I had spoken to in the village before – such a nice girl. Mr & Mrs Redford were going out to supper at the Vicarage so could not come to the meeting. Miss Smith took us a walk to find another possible Chairman but he was out. Then at 7 o'clock we repaired to High Common and in the gloaming held our meeting. Mr Pratt, the curate, first introduced Miss Ogston with a few words and she spoke about 40 minutes. We had a most excellent audience and quite a good crowd – they must have come from the neighbouring hamlets. Then Miss Smith took us to her Aunt and Uncle's where she is staying at the Hall Farm and we had cake and coffee then the Uncle drove us to the station for the 8.42 train. Miss Ogston was glad of her supper and to go straight up to bed. She is looking radiant with happiness. And in this very room in the winter she was calling the gods to witness how heartbroken she was with love over – another man.

TUESDAY, SEPTEMBER 12TH 1911 – EAST DEREHAM: 65 COMMERCIAL ROAD

Called on the Vicar's wife – Mrs Macnaughton-Jones – found her no good. Then I went to meet Mrs Chapman. The bus man brought her luggage up and she walked, and we had lunch. She has come from Hunstanton, where she and Mr Chapman have been staying. After lunch she went up to unpack and rest. I moved this morning from my nice room into a little wee room beyond Hilda's – a Box room so low one cannot stretch one's arms right out without touching the ceiling and most burning hot. Packed the Literature for the meeting, did a little writing and then to Market Place at 7.15 to get the waggonette in place, and Mrs Chapman and Miss Ogston followed me. Although we had no good local Chairman we had a most excellent meeting and a most orderly crowd, who were as quiet as quiet and listened most attentively and though I am afraid all could not have heard, those who did must have enjoyed the speeches, both of them

Thomas (1850–1926) and Elizabeth Redford (1850–1923) head and assistant teacher of the county council school, Hardingham.

Ethel Barker Smith (b.1879) a postmistress

spoke excellently. We sold a good many papers and made a collection – and returned home to supper quite content with the evening. I sat up with Mrs Chapman until she was ready about 11. She is very charming and quite satisfied with everything. It had been another boiling hot day and the night was stifling. I am sure we should not have got people indoors on such a night.

WEDNESDAY, SEPTEMBER 13TH 1911 – EAST DEREHAM: 65 COMMERCIAL ROAD

We woke to a grey and showery morning and much cooler – a most sudden break in the weather. It cleared up about 12 o'clock. I had a great many letters to write then went out for an hour with Miss Ogston to pay some bills and to exercise ourselves. I let her talk of Himself all the time. Changed my dress after lunch and at 2.15 a carriage came to drive us to Honingham. It kept fine till we got there about 3.30 but we were glad of coats to drive in. We went to the Buck Inn, where I had arranged accommodation for Mrs Chapman and Miss Ogston, and I went out to canvass. Went to Mr Rowbottom, the Steward of Honingham Hall, and got him to promise to take the Chair for us. I sent Miss Ogston in as it came on to rain so fast and I went on paying calls. Found most of the cottage women never stirred out and the men very unresponsive. 'Well I don't go so far as that, in my opinion a woman was made to be a help and a convenience to a man' said one of the men – quite amiably – to me. We had tea at 5. I could not go out after as it just poured with rain and I was very afraid for our meeting, but, wonderfully enough, the people came through the rain and we had our hall quite filled. The Vicar and his wife came, Miss Rowbottom and Mrs Boyle, the wife of the Member. Mrs Chapman and Miss Ogston spoke most excellently and I think altogether the meeting was a great success. We drove back in the pouring rain, very glad to find supper and a fire.

THURSDAY, SEPTEMBER 14TH 1911 – EAST DEREHAM: 65 COMMERCIAL ROAD

I went off to Wymondham by the 10.8 train. Went to the Vicarage and saw Mrs Collyer and then went about planning the meeting for the next day. Went in to tell Mrs Collyer what I had arranged, then to fix up a Local Chairman. Dr Lowe, who knew Miss Ogston's father, promised to preside. Caught the 1.20, and got in [at East Dereham] at 2 o'clock. Ate a hasty lunch, changed my dress, packed the Literature, then to the Masonic Hall with Mrs Chapman and Miss Ogston for our meeting there at 3 o'clock. Many more people came than I had dared to hope by an invitation meeting – just upon 40 – and Mrs Chapman and Miss Ogston spoke most exceedingly well – and we ended by making 5 members. I think it was simply splendid. We had left something behind us in Dereham – and I have made 3

The New Constitutional Society for Women's Suffrage.
8, Park Mansions Arcade, London, S.W.

The pleasure of your Company is requested to meet
Mrs. CECIL CHAPMAN,
Miss HELEN OGSTON, B.Sc.,
At the Freemasons' Hall, Dereham,
On Thursday, September 14th, 1911, at 3 p.m.

Speeches. Subject—"The Conciliation Bill."

R.S.V.P. to
Miss Katharine Parry Frye,
65, Commercial Road,
Dereham.

Francis Rowbottom (1857–1943) estate agent. 'Miss Rowbottom' was his 22-year-old daughter, Constance.

Charlotte Boyle (1860–1946) wife of William Boyle, elected Unionist MP for Mid Norfolk in 1910. Tuddenham Lodge, Horningham.

Dr George Lowe (1854–1914) had been born, like Helen Ogston, in Aberdeenshire.

people promise to take 'Votes'. So we returned to tea quite cheered. I went out afterwards to pay some bills and some good-bye calls – then up to my room to tidy it up and get the Literature right. We sold a lot during the afternoon.

FRIDAY, SEPTEMBER 15TH 1911 – EAST DEREHAM: 65 COMMERCIAL ROAD
I went off to Wymondham by the 10.8. Did some canvassing on my way to the Vicarage. Mrs Collyer's two daughters, Mrs Philip Connaught and Miss Mildred Collyer, are staying there and the latter took me out canvassing and calling till 1 o'clock. I had a very jolly lunch with them and sat awhile then at 2.30 out again till 4.30. Came in and wrote some Bills in the dining room as they were entertaining friends in the drawing-room and then I had my tea when Mrs Chapman and Miss Ogston arrived about 5 o'clock. Then I was taken out with Mrs Chapman by Miss Collyer to see the Church. Such a magnificent old place – absolutely thrilling – most glorious. To the hall about 6.20 to get it lit up and opened – people came in slowly – 7 o'clock was early for a meeting and anyway it was a bad night for the town. Rather disappointing but only about 40 people there and Mrs Chapman and Miss Ogston said they were very heavy to talk to. We left in a taxi considerably after 8 – and just caught the 8.17 train by the skin of our teeth. It was a non-stop so we got home very quickly. Had to do my packing when I went up to bed.

SATURDAY, SEPTEMBER 16TH 1911 – EAST DEREHAM: 65 COMMERCIAL ROAD/BOURNE END: THE PLAT
Miss Emery called me at 6.30 and I got up at once. The Hotel Bus came for the luggage and we walked to the station. Quite sorry to leave such a comfortable little house – they are both so nice and Mrs West seemed to me to look a lot more cheerful than she did in the winter. We all travelled together as far as Kings Lynn. There Mr Chapman met Mrs Chapman and they went off together for a holiday to Harrogate. Miss Ogston and I changed into the London train and came through Ely and Cambridge. We were due at 12.44 but not in till past 1. Miss Ogston all blooming and smiles as her Dr Townroe – 'Tod' – was meeting her. John met me but I felt tuned for tragedy and it happened. I lost my luggage. Two porters were very rude, I lost my temper and so thrilled the man at the lost property office that he had to stir himself. Then John and I went out and had some lunch in Lyons. I hated it and was miserable. Jealous, I suppose, of the air of romantic glamour and correct procedure of the really engaged ones, who I pictured lunching in cleanliness, off delicacies. What it is to be so stirred through one's imagination. But I seem to get a shock afresh each time John meets me. I don't know what is wrong but I criticise his legs away in the distance along the platform and I always hate the way he walks. Miss Ogston is the correct heroine of a really conventional novel, and I always feel like an Ibsen woman in comparison. I felt better after food, and there was my luggage when we got back. To Paddington by the underground, then we had to hang about for the 3.38 and John was not allowed to see me off. I lost my temper again and told an official that I had been travelling since the early morning and had come to the conclusion that the Railway companies made it as difficult as possible for people.

Mildred Collyer (1872–1955) an artist.

Kate spent a rather idyllic couple of weeks at Bourne End, punting on the river and listening to John rehearse lines for his part in a production of Romeo and Juliet *opening at the New Theatre in London at the end of September. She did not, however, desert her suffrage commitments.*

TUESDAY, OCTOBER 3RD 1911 – BOURNE END: THE PLAT

Felt in a great state of excitement over my committee meeting. Changed my dress – wore my new hat – and appeared at Mr Lehmann's at 3 o'clock and we were sworn in as committee. Mrs Lehmann, Miss Chapman, Mrs Chaplin, Mrs Bleek-Leech, Mrs Bloxam, Miss Reid, Miss Deacon, Mrs Smart and myself. Miss Chapman was appointed Secretary and Mrs Chaplin Treasurer and the whole thing was arranged most swimmingly and I was awfully proud of it. Then we had a most excellent tea and all came away in a group soon after five. I came home to write Alexandra a note. Took it out to post and walked as far as Wooburn Church & back.

THURSDAY, OCTOBER 19TH 1911 – BOURNE END: THE PLAT

So hot – very foggy and dull, some rain but fortunately it didn't keep on. Agnes and I walked up to Mrs Bleek-Leech's at Lindenhurst as she was most kindly having the first meeting of the Bourne End and District Women's Suffrage Society. It was such a success – about 50 people present. Miss Dove was going to take the Chair but in her absence Daddie did so. Mrs Cecil Chapman came to speak. She spoke for an hour and was most stirring. Mrs Graham from Henley also somehow got there and spoke for a few minutes on the sweated workers at Reading. Mrs Smart proposed a Vote of Thanks all round. Then tea. Mrs Leech had arranged it all most beautifully and was quite charming about it. I was as busy as a bee, of course. A good bit rested on me but I was delighted at the success. Mrs Chapman must have touched her hearers' hearts and although we only made 10 or so members people asked [?] that they had never heard suffrage before but were so interested they promised to come on Dec 15th. Every one was pleased. We stayed last finishing up things. Then after supper accounts for the 3 Suffrage Papers and the 'Standard'.

Nothing in Kate's diary indicates why the Folkestone area was selected as her next organising assignment for the NCS. From being a small port, Folkestone had developed during the second half of the 19th century as a seaside resort. The Leas, a wide grassy sward along the cliff top, provided visitors, Kate included, with a civilised promenade. The Grand Hotel, one of several that faced onto The Leas, had opened in 1905 and it was here that Kate booked in her more prominent speakers, such as Mr Baillie Weaver. Folkestone had a reputation for comparative exclusiveness, supporting a number of small private boarding schools and attracting the more monied holidaymaker. But, as it was well into autumn when Kate was directed there, it was more the support of the local townspeople that she was charged with winning, rather than that of visitors. Shorncliffe Camp, close to where Kate had lodgings, accounted for the military presence in Folkestone but, much as this supply of young men might have added to the jollity of social life, they were hardly the intended target for the NCS campaign. Nor did the town have any radical leanings, having voted for a Liberal Unionist candidate, Sir Philip Sassoon, since 1899. One can only assume that the NCS sought to target the area because it was to such seaside resorts that women of independent means tended to be attracted; in

Audrey Chapman, a niece of Mrs Cecil Chapman. The White Cottage, Bourne End.

Mildred Chaplin (b. 1872) wife of Nugent Chaplin, solicitor. The Lodge, Bourne End.

Frances Dove was headmistress of Wycombe Abbey School.

Folkestone women substantially outnumbered men (1911 19,592 women: 13,910 men). Kate may have been sent to this area simply because it was one the Wrights knew well. As Kate mentions in an entry, they had holidayed there recently and, in fact, it was at nearby Hythe that Mrs Wright was to die in 1922.

Folkestone had presented its first suffrage petition in 1868 and occasional meetings had been held in the town during the remainder of the 19th century. The NUWSS had had a Folkestone society since 1909 and the WSPU had had a presence in the area for some time. In August 1909 WSPU members there on holiday had sold copies of Votes for Women *in the streets and one had paid for a copy to be left in the reading-rooms of Folkestone hotels. A WSPU organiser, Florence Macaulay, was working in the area – Canterbury and South Kent – from February 1910 until late 1912. She lived as a lodger at 'Trevarra', 30 Bouverie Road West, across the road from the Kennys, so it is surprising that Kate makes no mention of her, or of WSPU activity, during her extended visits. However, it may be taken as a measure of the success of the local suffrage campaign that by the end of 1911 a Folkestone branch of the Anti Suffrage League had been formed.*

Shorncliffe Station, now Folkestone West, was a good way out of central Folkestone.

FRIDAY, OCTOBER 20TH 1911 – BOURNE END: THE PLAT/FOLKESTONE: 4 SALISBURY VILLAS

Up in good time – finished my packing and off by the 10.15 train. It came down a deluge while I was getting to the station. John met me at Paddington and came with me to Charing Cross where I left my luggage. Had lunch at Pembridge Crescent with the Wrights. Heard all Alexandra's woes. Mrs Wright seems to have gone utterly funny. It is hard on the girls. Got my orders, left about 3.30 back to Charing Cross where John met me at 4 – and I came to Shorncliffe. Mrs Hill was at the station to meet me. Her house was only 3 minutes walk – 4 Salisbury Villas. I had time to unpack and change and we had dinner about 7.30. She is a widow – has one girl at home. We sat and talked – went to bed at 10. She is very kind – gave me a hot water bottle and talked all the time. She is quite 'coming on' in Suffrage and I am supposed to be turning the last screw.

Bouverie Road West is a wide boulevard running westwards from the town centre. The entrance to the Kennys' large, red-brick house faces onto a private footpath, giving it a sense of greater seclusion and, hence, exclusivity. John Stuart Mill's The Subjection of Women *had first been published in 1869.*

Hilda Hill (1872–?1935) widow of Henry Ainslie Hill, a solicitor, had one daughter, 12-year-old Winifred.

SATURDAY, OCTOBER 21ST 1911 – FOLKESTONE: 4 SALISBURY VILLAS

Quite a mild day and needed no fire till evening but inclined to shower. I wrote letters – then at 11 to Mrs Kenny's – 63 Bouverie Road, Folkestone. She had asked me to lunch but Mrs Hill wanted me back again so, as there wasn't much I could do, I just had a chat with her and Mrs Chapman, who is staying there, and came back again. Changed and got back to Mrs Kenny's at 2.30 for her party at 4. Miss Lewis of Hythe took the Chair and Mrs Chapman spoke. There were between 70 and 80 people – mostly very smart – a military set. Mrs Kenny is very nice and Colonel Kenny is quite sweet. Some of the men were very amusing. I got a golf ball from one and sold it for 2/6. And got one young officer to buy *The Subjection of Women*. There was a most gorgeous tea, which no-

Col Henry Torrens Kenny (1858–1941) served in the Indian Army and became departmental secretary to the government of India. His wife, Zoe (c1868–1934), was born in Canada, daughter of the Agent-General for New Brunswick.

one hardly touched. Mrs Hill and I walked home together – got in about 6.30. Another evening of gabbling chat and to bed about 10 o'clock. She is very nice but so intellectual. I feel sorry for the child. A most terrific gale raged all night. I thought the house must be blown in.

Kate's territory included Hythe, one of the original cinque ports which, by the early 20th century, had, from its small, ancient centre, spread out along the coast. Seabrook Road, where Kate's contacts, Miss Cheffins and Miss Lewis, lived at 'Dunedin', linked Hythe to Folkestone. Most of of the large, detached houses that lined it had been recently built and were unnumbered, each with its own name. It has proved difficult to locate the precise position of 'Dunedin'. Kate's Hythe digs were in Mill Road, a narrow, twisting back road near the station. Mrs Beatrice Gravener's husband was a groom and they had two children.

WEDNESDAY, OCTOBER 23RD 1911 – FOLKESTONE: 4 SALISBURY VILLAS/HYTHE: 5 GLENLEIGH TERRACE

I got off to the station and caught the 10.20 to Hythe, changing at Sandling – a porter came for my things. Miss Lewis met me at the Station and brought me to my rooms – Mrs Gravener, 5 Glenleigh Terrace, Mill Rd. Cottagey but quite comfortable and beautifully clean and a very nice woman. We [Miss Lewis & Kate] had a long talk while the 2 pugs she brought with her snored and the half-bred pom collie made friends with me. Miss Lewis is another great talker. Then my luggage came. I unpacked, tidied myself – then out – ordered some stores, found my way about and to Seabrook Road to lunch with Miss Lewis and Miss Cheffins at 1. We chatted after – then armed with a directory I returned home – did some writing. Had a cup of cocoa at 4 then out to begin calls.

TUESDAY, OCTOBER 24TH 1911 – HYTHE: 5 GLENLEIGH TERRACE

The rain stopped about 11 and after some writing I went out, did my shopping then started the canvassing up Hill Crest Rd. Had heavy showers but I was prepared for it. Found people very nice but very uninterested. Out at 3 canvassing Seabrook Rd. In to tea at Miss Cheffins – then more calls till the rain came down in torrents again. I have never been out in such rain. I couldn't help laughing but I was frightened – it was so awful. Fortunately I had my Aquascutum, rubbers, umbrella but the rain was nearly ankle deep and I couldn't keep my skirts out of it.

Eva (Evangeline) Lewis (1863–1928), daughter of Bishop of Ontario. Lived with Georgina Cheffins from some time before 1901 until her death.

Georgina Fanny Cheffins (1863–1932) in 1912 sentenced to 4 months' imprisonment for taking part in a WSPU window-smashing raid in London. Kate kept in touch with Miss Cheffins and Miss Lewis well into the 1920s.

WEDNESDAY, OCTOBER 25TH 1911 – HYTHE: 5 GLENLEIGH TERRACE

Dull in the morning but much cooler and it turned out a glorious day. I was out from 11 till 1 – shopping and getting Bills of the meeting up in the shops. Miss Lewis brought them round to me early. Then I put on my best and called again from 3 till 6. Paid 26 calls in all. Found only one interested person. Some very, very nice – none nasty – but quite uninterested. Had some funny experiences in the way of being shown into family gatherings etc.

SATURDAY, OCTOBER 28TH 1911 – HYTHE: 5 GLENLEIGH TERRACE

Started my canvass early so as to catch some important people. Saw the Brewer's wife,

Mrs Mackeson. Out again 3 – down by the sea. It was bright and cold and kept fine. Not in till 7. Felt very tired. I had walked and talked tremendously.

SUNDAY, OCTOBER 29TH 1911 – HYTHE: 5 GLENLEIGH TERRACE

A glorious day. Went to Church and then saw the Church Parade after having enjoyed the officers' profile all the service. For a walk on the Parade till 1. To lunch with Miss Cheffins at 1.30. At 2.45 motor to Folkestone. Went to the Grand Hotel and ordered a room for Mr Baillie Weaver. For a little walk on The Leas, then to Mrs Hill's for tea at 4.30. She had a Mr & Mrs Greenwood and daughter there. He is a KC and it was my gentle task to convert him to Suffrage. His wife joined and I don't think he was so anti by the time they left, I worked very hard. He was an interesting man of the 'disappointed' sort.

The Hythe Institute, Prospect Road, had been built c. 1891 and the hall on its upper floor could hold 350 people.

WEDNESDAY, NOVEMBER 1ST 1911 – HYTHE: 5 GLENLEIGH TERRACE

Felt awfully seedy – such a pain inside and shivery. Up very late – Miss Lewis came in before I had had breakfast. Then at 12 – such a blow. A Telegram from Mrs Chapman to say neither the Brasseys could come to the meeting (Lady Brassey was to have taken the Chair) and could I find a good local Chairman. I dragged myself out to Miss Cheffins, where we decided I should call upon Mrs Congreve, wife of the Commandant. I found her very nice – but she had to consult her husband. So I went back at 2 – when she told me she would take the Chair and I had coffee with her and [was] introduced to her husband. Oh dear it was all a strain and I felt so plain. Changed – to Miss C[heffins] for high tea at 6 – then we three to the Institute at 7. We had help with the stewarding – and Mrs Hill amongst them. I received Mr Baillie Weaver, Mrs Chapman, the Kennys and Mrs Congreve and all went well. It was a very good meeting – though the hall wasn't full. Mr B.W. spoke excellently. The resolution was passed unanimously. Back for cocoa & bread & butter with Mrs C. Not in till 11.45. Wrote report before going to bed. Mrs Hill was full of my conver-

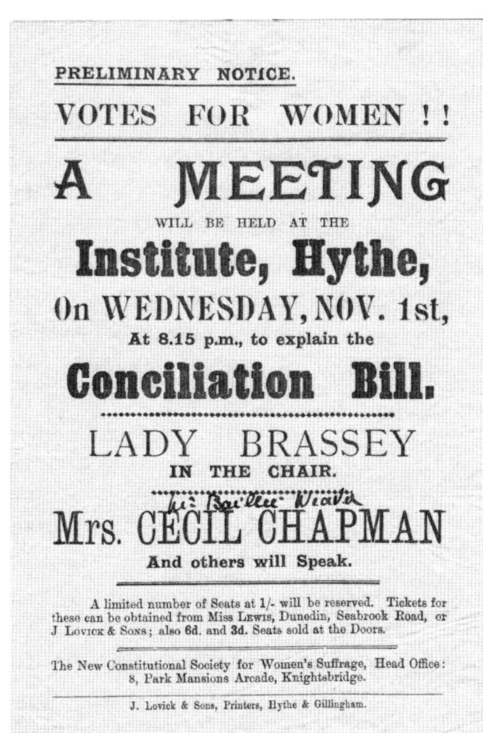

PRELIMINARY NOTICE.

VOTES FOR WOMEN ! !

A MEETING

WILL BE HELD AT THE

Institute, Hythe,

On WEDNESDAY, NOV. 1st,

At 8.15 p.m., to explain the

Conciliation Bill.

LADY BRASSEY

IN THE CHAIR.

Mr Baillie Weaver

MRS. CECIL CHAPMAN

And others will Speak.

A limited number of Seats at 1/- will be reserved. Tickets for these can be obtained from Miss LEWIS, Dunedin, Seabrook Road, or J LOVICK & SONS; also 6d. and 3d. Seats sold at the Doors.

The New Constitutional Society for Women's Suffrage, Head Office: 8, Park Mansions Arcade, Knightsbridge.

J. Lovick & Sons, Printers, Hythe & Gillingham.

Left: Lady Brassey was unable to take the Chair.

Ella Mackeson (1867–1933) wife of Henry Mackeson, brewer, The Dene, Hythe.

Harold Baillie-Weaver (1860–1926), active member of the Men's League for Women's Suffrage. His wife, Gertrude (1855–1926), was a novelist, member of the Women Writers' Suffrage League and supporter of the WSPU.

William (b. 1868) and Elvira Greenwood (1872–1931). 54 Radnor Park Road, Folkestone.

Col Walter Congreve (1862–1927) and his wife Cecilia (b. 1868) lived at the Commandant's House, Hythe. Congreve won the VC during the Boer War.

sion of Mr Greenwood – though I don't think one can convert a hoary old gentleman quite so easily. She says I am wasted as an organiser. I ought to be a speaker. Mrs Chapman was delighted with the success of the meeting and most affable.

SATURDAY, NOVEMBER 4TH 1911 – HYTHE: 5 GLENLEIGH TERRACE/RYE: 7 RICHMOND VILLAS

Paid some calls then to the station in a cab and the 11 train to Folkestone. Put my baggage in the cloakroom and walked to Mrs Kenny's, Bouverie Road West, for the Committee meeting – where we started the Hythe and Folkestone Branch. It went off alright but not so well as it might have done. However we did our best. It was over soon after 1 o'clock and I said good-bye to Miss Cheffins and Miss Lewis and I remained to lunch with Mrs Kenny, which we had with her little boy Ronald, and Miss Cook, the governess. [Arrived] Rye 4.16. I left my luggage and went up to the old rooms in Market St but Mrs Harvey could not have me but sent me to a Miss Neeves at 7 Richmond Villas, Rope Walk – stuffy rooms, but I wanted to settle so did so and went back to the Station and arranged for my luggage to be brought up. Then I did some shopping – called on Miss Spalding, who very kindly gave me tea. In at 6. No luggage – consequently could not get to much writing. Supper at 8 then the old Landlady went to the station to see about my luggage – it had come on a fearful night. The baggage had been forgotten and they did not send it up till after 10.

MONDAY, NOVEMBER 6TH 1911 – RYE: 7 RICHMOND VILLAS

A night of most awful wind again and a wet morning – then cleared up and turned very cold in the afternoon. Miss White, who is going to work Rye and district for members for 10 weeks, came over from Winchelsea where she lives at 11 o'clock and had an hour's talk with me. I explained my methods. She is a nice quiet intelligent sort of girl but not prepossessing. To call on Miss Clements and one or two other people. I wrote all the afternoon. Out 5.30 to 7.30 calling – with very good success. Supper. Then out at 9 o'clock to see Mrs Clements, who had only just returned home from a visit. She gave her permission for us to have the use of her room for a meeting – very kind of her.

Kate's mention of Asquith's 'Bombshell' refers to the Prime Minister's statement on 7 November that the government intended to introduce its own reform bill – a 'manhood suffrage' bill – that is, one giving votes to all men – that might, if the House of Commons desired, be amended to include women. This bill would replace the Conciliation Bill, on which the suffrage societies had placed their hopes. On 11 November the NCS issued a statement in The Times*: 'Women by this scheme will be relegated to a lower position than they have ever before held under the British Constitution'. On 17 November the NCS took part in a joint deputation of all the suffrage societies to the prime minister.*

Maud Letitia White (1882–1941), lived at Magazine House, Castle Street, Winchelsea. She remained connected to the women's movement, secretary of the Hastings branch of the WFL in the late 1920s.

WEDNESDAY, NOVEMBER 8TH 1911 – RYE: 7 RICHMOND VILLAS

A night of most awful wind again. Miss White came in at 11. She had a talk then went off to her canvassing. Miss Spalding came in at 2 o'clock to be introduced to her and have a talk. I went out canvassing. Got on well but had some experiences. This

Bombshell of Mr Asquith's in to-day's paper of Manhood Suffrage with no mention of Votes for Women has come as a knock-down blow. I feel really stunned. It is going to make our work enormously difficult. Here of course the ordinary people are not realising – but of course they will – the Conciliation Bill is child's play to what Universal Suffrage will be. I feel quite off my Balance. I suppose I shall recover it in a few days. I can only write letters of the deepest woe to everyone and I have to watch every word in canvassing lest I should say too much or the wrong thing. I had one great battle with a schoolmaster here, who ended by calling me a 'Barrow Scallywag'. We do live in stirring times.

THURSDAY, NOVEMBER 9TH 1911 – RYE: 7 RICHMOND VILLAS
Did my shopping and met Miss White. We were just against the Guildhall and saw the Mayor & Corporation come forth. It was so funny. I laughed till I cried – such frock coats and top hats on such heads. Then we watched the ancient custom of throwing pennies from the Hotel Balcony to the crowds below – such a scramble as good many got hard bumped. A good many pounds must have been thrown away like that – some of the coppers were thrown out hot on a shovel. Then out 3 till 5.30 to Playden. Met two very violent ladies – one good Christian woman, entertaining a working party for the Church, pushed me out.

SATURDAY, NOVEMBER 11TH 1911 – RYE: 7 RICHMOND VILLAS
I am beginning to be glad my visit here is nearing the end – these rooms and the poor old landlady gets on my nerves a bit. Was just changing when Miss Ogston came round, looking very blooming. Her Dr Townroe, who had come down with her, came about our plans and was allowed in and introduced to me. He seems rather nice – but not pretty. They went off to tea together to the Mermaid Inn and I went to have tea with Miss Clarke who is a newcomer here – quite a Suffrage friend. We went over to Mrs Clements' together – and Miss Ogston came in good time for the meeting at 5.30. It was a great success, but of course the weather must have kept a good many away. Still we started our Society and got about 12 members. The Vicar was there – and one of the Non Con[formist] Ministers – otherwise we were all females – about 18. I took Miss Ogston to the station and handed her over to Dr Townroe and they went up at 7.40.

SUNDAY, NOVEMBER 12TH 1911 – RYE: 7 RICHMOND VILLAS
Feel very satisfied with my work but glad it is over.

After leaving Rye, Kate paid a visit to her cousin, Abbie Hargrave, and her new baby, at Ditchling. She then returned to Bourne End on 16 November for a few days, before going to London on NCS business.

MONDAY, NOVEMBER 20TH 1911 – BOURNE END: THE PLAT/LONDON: 59 CARLISLE MANSIONS
To Paddington by the 3 o'clock train. To Carlisle Mansions. I went in and had tea with Mrs & Miss Forsyth, who are so kindly putting me up and paying my expenses to

London. Mrs Forsyth has gout in her ankles and could not go to the meeting, so Miss Forsyth and I went and got there about 8.15 for the meeting at 8.30. It was a special meeting of members of the New Constitutional Society to pass a resolution to the government after this great set back occasioned by the announcement of a new reform bill – votes for men – and none for women. Mrs Chapman was in the Chair and made a long and very strong speech – she was one of those present at the deputation to Mr Asquith and it was very interesting to hear her report of it. Then the Rev. Hugh Chapman spoke a very intense address. Miss Grace Jean Crocker gave some recitations to start. We had a collection and handed round promise cards and collected about £22 odd. Miss Lightman and I were there to do that and make ourselves generally useful. The Wrights were very grand in full rig – some were and some weren't. I was one of the wasn'ts. Mrs Pertwee & Miss Ada Moore were there. Miss Moore is going to be one of the demonstrators tomorrow night. It might have been for all the world a militant meeting so militant we all were, and the whole atmosphere was charged with it. Mrs Chapman introduced me to Captain Gonne who was there. She is very sweet to me and to Mr Hugh Chapman. He is to come & speak at the meeting I am to go to Folkestone and organise on December 5th. He is an interesting person too. We had nice refreshments – Miss Forsyth, Miss Lightman & I came back to Victoria together and we got in at 12. The Forsyths are wonderfully kind.

Grace Jean Crocker was an American performer.

This demonstration, by suffragettes who smashed the windows of government offices and business premises, was the WSPU's retaliation for what it perceived as the government's perfidy over the lost Conciliation Bill. The International Suffrage Shop, which advertised itself as 'The Only Feminist Bookshop', was at 15 Adam Street, just off the Strand and close to the WFL and AFL offices in the Adelphi.

Emily Pertwee (1857–1938) sister to Eva, Decima and Ada Moore. On tour in 1903, Kate met Mrs Pertwee's son, a member of another acting company. The Pertwee family's connection with the stage has descended through subsequent generations.

TUESDAY, NOVEMBER 21ST 1911 – LONDON: 59 CARLISLE MANSIONS/27 PEMBRIDGE CRESCENT

From a very mild day yesterday it has turned bitterly cold. Miss Forsyth had been willing to keep me for another night and I had arranged to stay but they heard that Miss Cheffins from Folkestone wanted to be put up as she is going to demonstrate. Of course, there was nothing to be done but pack up, which I did after breakfast – or rather the maid did – and depart soon after 10. The Forsyths had been most kind to have me. I was so keen to stay up that I decided not to take my bag to Paddington but see if anything turned up so I took it to the A[ctors'] A[ssociation] and left it there. Then I purchased boots – walked to the Office – rang up Alexandra and told her our plan of meeting was off as I should have to return to Bourne End. I invited her or Gladys to go to the theatre – Gladys accepted – had a chat to Miss Lightman who was genuinely delighted to see me. John met us and Alexandra but we had to wait for her so went in to the International Suffrage Shop. Then all had tea at the Cecil café. There it was decided that I should have a bed at Pembridge Crescent. I was given a latch key and told where to find my room and understood that the family would have retired to bed at 10 o'clock. [With John] then we went to Parliament Square – a cordon of Police were across it. John had to get back to the theatre for 'Romeo and Juliet' and I went in to

Ada Moore (1860–1932) eldest of the Moore sisters. In 1898 she visited the Fryes' Arundel Gardens house to give singing lessons to Agnes.

Capt Charles Melvill Gonne (1862–1926), Royal Artillery, author of *Hints on Horses*. Active suffragist, tax resister, cousin of Maud Gonne, the Irish nationalist heroine.

Lyons and had coffee and a sandwich. Who should I happen to sit next but Miss Ada Moore and 2 ladies – ready for the fray. I wonder I wasn't arrested as one – for I soon realised I was dressed for the part to the life. Long cloth ulster or coat, light hat and veil was the correct costume – no bag purse – umbrella or any extra. I only had enough money to get home with in my coat pocket – the rest I had put in the suit case – the latch key was slung round my neck. It was awfully exciting – one felt like a red revolutionist. Miss Moore & party left at 7.30 – her work lay in Whitehall, she told me – but she looked very white and strained and we did not talk much. I began to feel pretty green with all the force of strife in the air – I felt I too should only be in my rightful place when officially performing. I left Lyons at 7.45 and strolled about. At the stroke of eight there was smashing of glass at some government office – the War Office I took it for – and I saw several – 8 or 9 or more – ladies led off – all very quietly done – no rough usage – no struggling. I followed them down Whitehall to Canon Row. More arrests – more broken glass – more crowds, a little jostling – people being moved on this way or that way – for the most part silent crowds – growing bigger and bigger – a rush to see another arrest – a bigger crowd surging up the street following the policeman with the arrested women but oh! what a different scene from last year when the women were so brutally knocked about. I suppose the crowd was worse over the other side of Parliament Square but I was too timid to wander far, and I met Mrs Hartley, her daughter, 2 friends and Miss Green and we all kept together, and we shouted whenever a prisoner was led along 'Bravo' 'Well Done'. People took it up – but for the most part stood and watched silently. As far as I could see there no ill feeling whatever from the crowd to the women – the men stared solemnly at the proceedings. We met Mrs Chapman

VOTES FOR WOMEN

A

DEMONSTRATION

WILL BE MADE OUTSIDE THE

HOUSE OF COMMONS

ON

TUESDAY NEXT, AT 8 P.M.

To Protest

against the announced intention of the Government to carry a Bill next session giving the vote to every man and not including any woman.

To the Public!

I was present at the Women's Deputation to Mr. Asquith and Mr. Lloyd George, when they refused to grant our demand that the Government should substitute for the Manhood Suffrage Bill a measure giving equal franchise rights to men and women.

The Women's Social and Political Union will, therefore, make a Demonstration of Protest against the Government's unjust policy. As the leader of this Demonstration, I call upon men and women in their thousands to come to Parliament Square next Tuesday, November 21st, to see fair play, to protect women from being brutally victimized by police in uniform and in plain clothes as they were on **Black Friday** (November 18th, 1910), when, as a result of the ill-usage they received, one woman died and many were seriously injured; also, to take note of those constables who exceed their duty, and of hooligans obviously acting under their encouragement, so that they may be prepared to offer evidence, if necessary, in any subsequent police court proceedings.

4, CLEMENT'S INN, STRAND. (Mrs.) E. PETHICK LAWRENCE.

Geo. Barber, Furnival Press, Furnival Street, E.C.

WSPU flyer inviting women to demonstrate outside the House of Commons on 21 November 1911.

and Miss Forsyth. Mrs Chapman was anxious as her daughter, Mrs Mansel, was 'in' it. We stood talking and got a crowd round us so had to 'move on'. We saw Mrs Pethick Lawrence led into Canon Row. There was a good deal of excitement then a huge crowd pushing along with her and other ladies. It was awfully cold and it was all very dreadful but I have never seen work better done – nearly every window in Whitehall with a large round hole right in the centre. Downing St was guarded. No one was allowed near. Then people seemed drifting away so I made my way to Charing Cross – got my suit-case from the cloak room. Arrived [27 Pembridge Crescent] just about 11 o'clock. Took some time to fit the key – got in the hall – turned up the light – went in the dining-room – nothing to eat or drink – only a glow of fire so as I couldn't warm myself or feed there was nothing to wait for – so very cautiously I found my room – the light had been left on so I found it – but no hot water or any comforts and I had no night light. I was just getting drowsy – after 12 o'clock when a furious banging at the door. I guessed in a moment what had happened – I had locked someone out. Like a flash I jumped for my coat and the light – I flew downstairs. I heard Mrs Wright's door open – I called 'Alright I am going' and fled down stairs. Alexandra and Gladys in full ballroom rig. Alexandra had purposely kept it [the fact that they were going out] from me. Alexandra didn't want to go – Gladys had dragged her to a dance at the Grafton Galleries. They said all the Committee were taking the demonstration so seriously and they didn't want any one to know they were enjoying themselves. Alexandra had evidently not enjoyed herself. What rotten policy – one cannot do a thing and not be found out. They swore me to secrecy.

WEDNESDAY, NOVEMBER 22ND 1911 – LONDON: 27 PEMBRIDGE CRESCENT/BOURNE END: THE PLAT

There was only breakfast enough and coffee enough for three. I felt deadly uncomfortable but tried to look as if I did not notice. I had a chat to Alexandra but directly I could I went up to pack – got ready and departed about 10.30. I had been very glad of the opportunity of staying the second night in London, but it was the poorest hospitality conceivable, and only valuable as an experience 'what not to do'.

THURSDAY, NOVEMBER 23RD 1911 – BOURNE END: THE PLAT

Agnes and I went to tea with Mrs Lehmann at 5 o'clock. She came in with Miss Chapman and Mrs Goldie was staying there. We talked Suffrage but I did not feel brilliant. And she desires that Miss Evelyn Sharp shall not speak as she was one of the arrested on Tuesday. Oh dear I have the job of writing to her. The Vicar is to take the Chair and she thinks will not meet a militant. She is all wrong, but as she has had so much to do with getting up the meeting she must have her way. I came home and wrote the letter. It is a shame.

Mildred Mansel (1868–1942) an active member of the WSPU, daughter of Mrs Chapman's first marriage to Arthur Guest, and, therefore, a cousin of Ivor Guest, the Liberal Chief Whip.

Kate sent a box of flowers to welcome Evelyn Sharp on her release from Holloway. The letter of thanks that she eventually received appears to have been written in another hand and only signed by Evelyn Sharp. Kate had also written to Mrs Sadd Brown, who, too, was arrested on 21 November, and from her received a personal note of thanks.

Evelyn Sharp (1869–1955) journalist and novelist and one of the WSPU's most inspiring speakers.

TELEPHONE 7000 P.O. HAMPSTEAD.
HAMPSTEAD TUBE STATION.

2, CHESTERFORD GARDENS,
HAMPSTEAD, N.W.

10/12/11

My dear Miss Frye,

How nice & how kind of you to write me such a sweet letter on the small part I took in the doings of the last few weeks. I suppose to each one who takes part in such events it is more or less momentary occasion, and perhaps one of those when with Adelaide Procter "we should count time by heart-throbs, not by minutes

SATURDAY, NOVEMBER 25TH 1911 – BOURNE END: THE PLAT

A beautiful day, bright but cold. Alexandra, Gladys, Agnes and I went in to Marlow at 11.16. Mrs Lehmann journeyed in by our train and we all arrived at Mrs Dickson's together. Two Miss Wade Robinsons were the only other two. We expected to find a room full of Marlow Suffragettes. We had a sort of informal talk as to the best way of getting Suffrage into Marlow. Alexandra spoke very interestingly and we planned a meeting if speakers can be promised for Dec 5th the date the Folkestone meeting was to be – as I am not to go to Folkestone after all – greatly to my relief.

SUNDAY, NOVEMBER 26TH 1911 – BOURNE END: THE PLAT

I got dreadfully tired of talking to them [Alexandra and Gladys]. Gladys is a pig of a person. Two such greedy unresponsive people one could not find in a hurry. I did a little Palmistry and that entertained them. But Gladys wants all the virtues and has none so it is trying.

TUESDAY, NOVEMBER 28TH 1911 – BOURNE END: THE PLAT

To Marlow. Went first to Mrs Dickson's. I have heard both speakers can come, so, after seeing her, Miss Wade Robinson took me round to the Sec. for the Hall and I hired that. Then to try and find a Chairman. I couldn't – so went and ordered the printing. Paid calls till 1 o'clock. Had some lunch in the Confectioners then continued canvassing til 5.30. I am to put in a week's official work for the New Constitutional Society.

THURSDAY, NOVEMBER 30TH 1911 – BOURNE END: THE PLAT

Mother and I to London by the 11.11. I telephoned to Alexandra as I have had a telegram from our main speaker for the 15th, Mr Hinscliff, that he is ill and has had to cancel all engagements. She is going to try for Mr Chapman. Miss Broadhurst is coming instead of Miss Sharp. Alas !!! We went to Aunt Lena's who was giving a Suffrage afternoon 'At Home' and were the first arrivals. Miss Ogston was the speaker. She spoke well but I did not think gave quite the address to interest all her audience. Quite a party – about 30 to 40 people.

FRIDAY, DECEMBER 1ST 1911 – BOURNE END: THE PLAT

To Mrs Lehmann's at 11 till 12 to arrange canvass etc for Bourne End and distribute tickets and notices. I went round afterwards with some of the tickets and Bills. Then to Marlow by the 3 o'clock train. Canvassed the High St. Tea at Mrs Dickson's and most

Rev. Claude Hinscliff (1874–1964) founder, with his wife, of the Church League for Women's Suffrage.

Mary Adelaide Broadhurst (c1857–1928) a science graduate who had headed the science department in several girls' schools. She had been an organiser for the WFL in Liverpool and in 1911 was co-founder of the National Political League. This group saw the suffrage campaign as the first stage in its work of bringing about social and political reform – for men as well as for women.

Kate's Aunt Lena and Uncle Alfred Frye lived at 32 Castlebar Road, Ealing.

Above: Mrs Sadd Brown's response to Kate's 'kind and sympathetic letter' to her on her imprisonment

heated talk with Dr Dickson who now refuses to have anything to do with the meeting because I am a militant and working for it. Really these Liberals. I patiently stated my case while he raved. Cannot get a Chair for Marlow. I am so disappointed. Mrs Scott of Godstowe had promised and now finds she cannot.

SATURDAY, DECEMBER 2ND 1911 – BOURNE END: THE PLAT

All day at Marlow – to 6.30. A cold, damp miserable day and some heavy showers. Canvassed Station Rd etc. Lunch at the Pastry Cook, thereby making 4 men who were severally also lunching there exceedingly and morbidly uncomfortable. Why is it that a respectable woman has such an effect and that a common one is so enjoyed? Well I didn't worry myself and went placidly on. Went on canvassing till 3. Then to Mrs Dickson's where I met Miss Wade Robinson and Miss Hayes. I had hoped for a few others but there really seems no-one in Marlow – we were misled about it. I had tea and a talk – then Mrs Dickson went round to some of the shopkeepers with me, to implore their help. She is in a terrible state of fright because she has heard we are going to have a rowdy meeting. I have sworn it will be alright – so I trust that it will. Of course Marlow is a beastly place, but I feel sure it will be alright on Tuesday. However as she, Miss Hayes & Miss Robinson are all in such terror I had to do what I could so I went round soliciting Stewards. We found one or two who were willing to try and help us but who could not come till late. Last time they had a meeting I believe it was most awful, but we must see what we can do. I have so canvassed the place, they must feel differently about it.

TUESDAY, DECEMBER 5TH 1911 – BOURNE END: THE PLAT

Up in time to go to Marlow at 11.11. Agnes went with me. I feel simply deadly and was very sick again, but I had to go out. I had a good many things to see to – and a few calls to make. I felt most miserably weak. We met Mrs Dickson in a dreadful state of fright. She had heard all kinds of rumours and was white to the lips. Her husband was coming to protect her. Poor soul, but she made me a little impatient. Why talk about it. I dare say she frightened no end of people. [Went home] Changed my dress after tea and Daddie, Agnes and I went to Marlow at 6.46. Mr Chapman came down by that train and Daddie and he went to dine at the Dicksons' where Mr Chapman was to be put up. Agnes and I went to the Hall to get it ready. Miss Hayes came to Steward, also Mrs Lehmann and Miss Chapman. Everyone was very excited with the mob of boys waiting outside. It didn't look pleasant, certainly, and when they trooped in they started stamping and sitting in a herd – but it was even at the beginning rather a spasmodic noise. The place soon filled up, mostly poor people. I only left the door to receive the speakers. Miss Broadhurst was being put up by a Mrs Forrest, who brought her. I went to chat to them and warn them of our audience. The place was packed by eight and men kept on coming and standing at the back. We had a special constable and the Supt was present all the evening. It was a combination of causes that kept our meeting from being broken up. Daddie in the Chair, the policemen present, my canvassing, the fact that Agnes, Mrs Lehmann and I were at the bottom of the hall amongst the roughs all the evening. And I had sworn they should not break up my meeting and they didn't.

Edith C. Hayes (1860–1948) an artist, by 1913 secretary of the Marlow branch of the WFL and a member of the Tax Resistance League. Drift, Great Marlow.

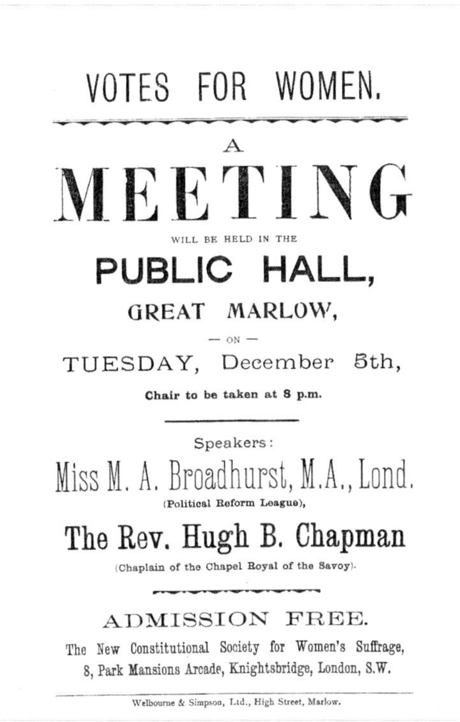
VOTES FOR WOMEN.

A

MEETING

WILL BE HELD IN THE

PUBLIC HALL,

GREAT MARLOW,

— ON —

TUESDAY, December 5th,

Chair to be taken at 8 p.m.

Speakers:

Miss M. A. Broadhurst, M.A., Lond.

(Political Reform League),

The Rev. Hugh B. Chapman

(Chaplain of the Chapel Royal of the Savoy).

ADMISSION FREE.

The New Constitutional Society for Women's Suffrage,
8, Park Mansions Arcade, Knightsbridge, London, S.W.

Welbourne & Simpson, Ltd., High Street, Marlow.

Then Miss Broadhurst was wonderfully tactful. She talked down to them but they listened patiently with a spurt of stamping & whistling now and again. But when the Rev. Hugh Chapman rose it was another matter. He was angry with them and sat down. They started ringing a bell and shouted and stamped. Miss Broadhurst got up again – then the old man [Frederick Frye] left the Chair and stalked down the room. 'Who is it?' – it was a youth in front of me with an awful squint – I had argued the matter with him, but no good. 'Turn him out'. He was seized from behind by the special constable and vanished. For a few minutes again Mr Chapman had some difficulty but when he got in to his stride one could have heard a pin drop and he gave it to them hot and strong. The young men looked sheepish but he had vanquished them – and the meeting ended in Triumph. The first unbroken Suffrage meeting ever held in Marlow. I was thankful. We carried the resolution and we had a collection – not a rich one – it was nearly all in pence – still the boys helped. It was over very early – by about 9.20 – too early really, but it had seemed like hours. I flew round collecting things, paying tips etc and then Mrs Lehmann brought us three back with her and Miss Chapman in the motor. Dr Dickson had appeared to shield his wife from mice or blows and had grown so excited he had made a speech at the end and all about me too – really funny after his annoyance at my views, but men are not logical.

SATURDAY, DECEMBER 9TH 1911 – BOURNE END: THE PLAT

Mrs Bloxam came in the morning. She is full of fears about the Bourne End meeting – hears of gentlemen supplying themselves with 'sacks of rats' etc.

Despite his experience at Marlow, the Rev. Hugh Chapman had agreed to speak for Kate again, this time at Bourne End.

FRIDAY, DECEMBER 15TH 1911 – BOURNE END: THE PLAT

John arrived at 4.30. After tea we changed and made ourselves look as nice as possible. Daddie went to meet Mr [Hugh] Chapman and brought him down in a fly by the 6.45 train. I just waited to speak to him, then John, Agnes and I went off to the County Council Schools and Mr Chapman dined here at 7 o'clock and Mother and Daddie drove with him to the meeting. Mrs Chaplin, Miss Chapman and Miss Beley came to Steward. Mrs Lehmann was very queer with a bad cold, but she came later with Miss Broadhurst, who she is entertaining, Mrs Scott and Mrs Dickson, and Mr Lehmann also came. I made him buy *Women and Economics* [by Charlotte Perkins Gilman]. I hope he will read it. I think he was interested in the meeting. Mr Unsworth arrived in good time, and the Rev. Dickson and Mrs Dickson to sit on the platform. Mr Unsworth was not a good chairman, in fact he quite offended Mr Chapman, who is really awfully quaint. Still Mr Unsworth did appear rude. He muddled up the Agenda and was pink in the face with excitement. But of course his name has been a draw. The place was packed, a lot only got round the doors, but everyone managed to hear, I think, and the meeting was a triumphant success. No attempt at rowdyism – no rats, and only a little Boorish laughter at Mr Chapman but he does rather 'ask for it'. Such a crowd of young girls – a most hopeful sign. Of course there were a lot of people one would liked there, but we shall get them in time and, after all, a public meeting is for the masses. John made himself useful and had two of Mrs Lehmann's men to help and I ran about and had a busy evening. The speeches were not long, the meeting was over by 9.30. Mrs Scott said a few words of thanks to the speakers at the end. The collection came to £1-10-9. Mr Chapman seemed to turn to me as a friend – and we chatted, then he came in while we had supper and he ate some sandwiches. Then we went back to the morning-room and we talked till 12. He told some amusing tales, but never for more than a few minutes got away from Suffrage. I am used to it, but the 'old man' was done. And the Rev. Hugh turned from him – I was the one chosen – I must say he had a fascination for me. But he was rather indiscreet – some of the things he spoke of, were best left alone in the bosom of a family party.

Rev. Reece Unsworth (1871–1938) vicar of Wooburn.

Votes for Women.

THE BOURNE END AND DISTRICT
WOMEN'S SUFFRAGE SOCIETY
WILL HOLD A

MEETING

IN THE
Bourne End Council Schools,
ON
FRIDAY, December 15th,
At 8 p.m.

CHAIR TO BE TAKEN BY THE
REV. REECE UNSWORTH.

SPEAKERS:
MISS M. A. BROADHURST, M.A.,
LOND.
Political Reform League.
AND THE
REV. C. HINSCLIFF,
Secretary of the Church League for Women's Suffrage.

A Collection will be made to defray expenses.

FREE ADMISSION BY TICKET.

Tickets may be had from the Hon. Sec., Miss Audrey Chapman, The White Cottage, Bourne End; Mrs. Turley, The Post Office; Mrs. Harold Wicks, Wooburn Green; and Messrs. Welbourne & Simpson, Ltd., Marlow.

Welbourne & Simpson, Ltd., High Street, Marlow

Flyers for the meeting had already been printed, bearing the Rev. Hinscliffe's name as a speaker, before the Bourne End Society learned he would be unable to attend

SATURDAY, DECEMBER 16TH 1911 – BOURNE END: THE PLAT

Breakfast at 8.30. I was down in good time. The Rev. Hugh was very late had slept on till we were at breakfast. Poor little man, he isn't for family life. And he talked so hard to me he didn't seem to know what he was eating and he talked on and on till Daddie drove him off to catch the 10.20 train. Fortunately Hilda had packed for him. He told Daddie last night that I was a 'fine girl' and 'very intelligent' so I knew I was a favourite. And then he took a fancy to John and when he heard of our theatrical endeavours 'well you are interesting people' and John has a 'real Terry face' and I am 'very highly developed' – so between it all I got in a fine flutter. The truth of it is, as I told him, – he is so very young and so makes me feel so old. He has only had Suffrage 18 months or so – it is all a new toy to him – he is quite crazed about it. 'You have got it badly' I said. 'I have got it very beautifully, I pray for it. I pray for it at Communion'. He is like a young man in love – and his love is Suffrage. But he is quite capable of being in love with a woman yet too, I feel sure. He is ridiculously young. John and I went to see him off and we panted out conversation all the way to the station and while he was seated in the train. He looked very dishevelled – we had not sent him off as sprucy as when he arrived. Unshaven, his hat crushed all the wrong way. He is going to think out plans to convert all his friends and he is going to make John's future with introductions. When we got home we sat and laughed and laughed. Daddie was very severe on him – quite 'made him blush' – and Mother and Agnes did not at all approve of some of his conversation. It was a good thing Agnes had not heard him at breakfast.

MONDAY, DECEMBER 18TH 1911 – BOURNE END: THE PLAT

Bed at 11 after reading Sir Edward Grey and Mr Lloyd George's speeches on Women's Suffrage in the Horticultural Hall on Saturday.

TUESDAY, DECEMBER 19TH 1911 – BOURNE END: THE PLAT

Agnes and I went round the village. Everyone seems pleased with the meeting. Mr Ford (the grocer), who is quite a character, was not present himself, but all his family returned home 'confirmed'.

TUESDAY, DECEMBER 26TH 1911 – BOURNE END: THE PLAT

I wonder what 1912 will bring. I do hope lots of work and pay for me, but as I hear they have a new organiser at the Office I suppose that means they will only want me for special jobs. I feel a bit worried about it.

SATURDAY, DECEMBER 31ST 1911 – BOURNE END: THE PLAT

[Writing of John's theatrical career] It is a heart breaking profession – one step forward and two back and he won't grow fat on £1-1 a week. Oh dear what a miserable state of things. I think I am in the worst state of depression that I ever remember. And I have money, money, money on the brain. Oh for a little so that one could feel free. One scrapes and saves every penny one gets – and in the Bank it goes. What result at the end of the year – a few beggarly pounds after all the work and all the saving. Then one adds one's accounts and finds instead of spending less one has been spending more with less result. And all the time on feels so shabby, one hates to go out, and every day something stares one in the face – wearing out – must be replaced. One spends all one's time making or mending, the result – a very inferior garment – and no time for reading, time for thought, oh yes and it comes to this, one finds one is giving all one's time to dreams, idle dreams, one discovers one does nothing but one is always dreaming. In my fancies I see myself everything in turn – everything but what I truly am. What am I after all? – I see myself left money. Making money. Spending money. How? As a great actress – a great playwright. A success. Enough money to dress on – to travel upon, to marry with. A home of my own – sometimes a house – sometimes a flat. I furnish it even to the details. I waste precious moments deciding even on saucepans. I people it with servants, visitors, I work in it myself. But always I am great, have done some work to make me proud and sought out. I cast my plays, sometimes I act in them. Mostly I act in others' plays, my success is violent. I map out tours – to America – I plan the people who I shall meet. John even is losing his spirits at last – a gloom is often on him – and who can wonder. What a failure he is. What a failure I am. What shall I do what shall I be when I am really old. And sometimes I feel so alive, so vital, so wonderful, it does seem a shame I should cease to exist. I don't want to be blotted out. The old year gone, and how it has slipped by. I cannot ever remember a year going so quickly. Work has done it, what a blessing my work has been. How I trust it will continue with this year. I cannot think how Agnes can stand her existence.

Kate looks back over the past year.

MONDAY, JANUARY 1ST 1912 – BOURNE END: THE PLAT

Then the first of the Suffrage for the New Constitutional Society – off to Dereham. Alexandra's exciting offer and ever since work, more or less. I do trust it will be more this year, the more I am at home the greater seems the need to do something definite. I worry all the time at home, when I am away I forget myself in my occupation.

WEDNESDAY, JANUARY 10TH 1912 – BOURNE END: THE PLAT

I had a letter from Alexandra Wright in the morning which surprised me very much. The girls have been anything but happy at home with their Mother latterly, and now I hear their father is taking them to Paris with him for some weeks and perhaps on to the south of France. She speaks of the arrangement for me to go to Folkestone about the 14th for a meeting on the 21st and says they may want me occasionally to help in any rush in London. Well that is rather surprising, except that, quite casually, in one of her letters Miss Rose Lightman mentioned that they were having a new organiser on trial. I think I can understand what has happened. Miss Helen Ogston was engaged as organiser and speaker. She was a success as a speaker – a failure as organiser, forgetful, offended people – so I was taken on to organise. Now Miss Ogston is going to be married, in her place they would naturally get someone to do the work she was first intended to do. I do not blame them. But what I do object to is that they should not have been honest with me over the affair and told me what arrangements had been made. I dare say the Committee left it to the Wrights to tell me and the Wrights feared to offend me etc. So here, instead of having a busy year as I was led to expect, Alexandra told me I was to go to Dorset and to Wales etc – I am only to have any odd work that can't be done by the Staff. I must say I am disappointed. Not that I wish to spend my life in organising for Suffrage, but it suited me so well now and they have all led me to understand – including Mrs Chapman with 'you must not think of leaving us till the Conciliation Bill has passed' 'Miss Frye is invaluable' etc – that they were pleased with my work and hoped I should go on. I don't believe mixing Friendship and Business – I never have. I am not in the least likely to be offended with the Wrights over business but I do expect friends to be honest over Business as they would over Friendship. But the Wrights really are not quite straight – they have a funny underhand way with things they do. But the whole substance of Alexandra's letter was about the Matinée they are having in aid of their funds on March 21st. Would I, as a favour to her, and as there is no one else she can trust to remember all details and as Miss Mayo may be in Prison again, 'offer to organise the matinee giving an average day a week or so in town for preliminary arrangements and then 2 or 3 weeks of hard work at the end for a small sum to cover wear and tear and expenses in addition'? This is to be my winter's work – 3 months and as a reward 'wear and tear' compensated only, and it is 'wear and tear'. I do not feel in the least little bit pleased. If it was sandwiched in between other work I should not mind in the very least – but for this to be asked of me as a personal favour makes it very awkward. Would I write to Mrs Chapman? So I have written saying I will do it if they wish me to. I thought some time and feel it is the best thing to do, but I must let them know after March I cannot be at their beck and call and I must make up my mind by then what I am going to do – go back to the Stage or seek some other work. But it does seem hard after nearly a year of work to be back again at this. I do not in the least blame the Committee, as I feel at a tremendous disadvantage living here – and I quite understand they want someone to combine speaking with organising. I have told them so myself but I do think considering how I have worked with them and for them they ought to have let me know – very likely I should have had a chance of getting something this winter. Still it is easy enough to talk of getting work another thing to get it, so I think I am wisest in accepting this till March. It will keep me alive and in touch with London, and perhaps I shall have opportunity for looking round and suiting myself. But it is rather a crusher. I have been expecting it ever since Miss Lightman's letter before Christmas.

The Coronation, *a play by Christopher St John and Charles Thursby, had an anti-armament, rather than suffrage, message. The Lord Chamberlain apparently objected to the representation of 'the King' figure. As Kate remarks, a society – 'The Coronation Society' – was formed so that the play could be performed as a private production. Kate's part was non-speaking. The performance was to be a fund-raiser for the International Suffrage Shop, with which Edith Craig and Cicely Hamilton were both closely involved. Always short of funds, the shop struggled on until 1918.*

THURSDAY, JANUARY 25TH 1912 – BOURNE END: THE PLAT

By the 6 o'clock post a letter from John telling me the Censor refused to license the play 'The Coronation' but that a Society was being formed and it would take place, then a call on the Telephone from Miss Craig's flat – they have had to postpone it as the Savoy will not let them have the theatre. I was just in the midst of packing up my things for the dress rehearsal tomorrow.

The Savoy Theatre authorities relented and the first performance of The Coronation *took place on 28 January. As Kate mentions – and the reason now seems unfathomable – her name and part was inked out in the printed programme. However with a magnifying glass it is still possible to pick out 'Miss Katharine Parry' through the heavy scoring.*[17] The Coronation *was followed by a staging of G.Bernard Shaw's* Man of Destiny. *John R. Collins is listed in the programme as one of the two stage managers for the event.*

SUNDAY, JANUARY 28TH 1912 – BOURNE END: THE PLAT

I nearly froze getting to the station with my basket and the train was so cold. Then to the Savoy Theatre. I was early of course but John was there before me, very busy appealing to everyone. It was some time before Miss Craig turned up with the dresses. I was given a room next to the Stage to dress in, No 4, which was also used for properties, so very gay. I unpacked and sat there talking to all and sundry, and then when the dress arrived I got into that and then waited and waited. At last I was ordered out – my cloak was on the stage, simply gorgeous, all gold – the front a mass of jewels and coloured pictures. Miss Craig had arranged my head piece and crown, only the veiling net was not forthcoming till night and then I had three crowns set one on top of each other and fastened together by jewels. I felt very fine, but the dress fascinated me most, the top, stockingette and the skirt blue green crepe which hung most beautifully. There was great agitation getting me enthroned, Miss Craig and her excitement being too funny. I could hardly keep my face straight though my life was in peril and in two ways hung in the balance. The effect was the thing, my life and happiness nothing. We tried this and that and the other, my knees would get in the way. At last two boxes with a rolled-up carpet on top did for my seat, and a few books would have done for a footstool could I have reached them. However good at climbing as I am I was thankful to escape with my life. Then the rehearsal started, all dressed more or less, but not made up, but a most prolonged affair. One principal not there, his part read by Mr Thursby, who is part author of the play. Godfrey Tearle was delightful in the part. I shouldn't have thought anyone could have done so much with it and he is such a nice man. Haidée Wright too was immensely clever, her voice made the tears come into the eye of the Statue of the Madonna which wouldn't have done at night. There had been a great row over my name on the programme and they had spent all last evening blotting it out with Indian Ink. There was no good in making a fuss but I must say I felt disappointed. If it had been put in the proper place at the start all would have been well, but as it was no one could have read it. Miss Craig soon came up and told me not to trouble to sit still as she did not want me to get tired for the evening. She just waited to see if I was capable of doing it but I could tell she was pleased with me. I heard her and Mr Thursby talking together and they liked my appearance. Then it was only to get an impersonal expression on my face and leave it at that. I suppose we started about 1 o'clock and I was not off my throne till about 3.30. My shoulders ached a bit with the weight of my robes but otherwise I felt alright. We had to wait to get photographed by the Daily Mirror. Then leaving my robes on high, I descended and changed. Miss Craig asked me into her box and I partook of ham roll and butter which saved my life. John also ate, and then to the light of day and the cold of the street to the Tube to Edgware Rd and to his rooms 23 Hawley Place where we partook of tea. It was soon 6.15 when we had to start off again as he had to be at the theatre by 7. So I got him to take me to his Club and leave me there till 7.30 and then I followed on to the Theatre. I could not dress till Miss Jean Sterling Mackinlay had finished. She opened the performance at 8 o'clock with Scotch songs which I should think were fearsome. It did not take me long to make up and dress and Miss Craig came and put on my headgear and did it beautifully. I was much improved by the white veiling. I felt a lot churned up but felt pretty sure of myself. Then the moment came and up I went on my rickety throne and got my cloak round me and soon all to attention and up went the curtain. I think the Stage must have been beautifully lighted and the Theatre not at all. I was very little conscious of the audience, and I kept my eyes down, and found it all very little of a strain. The performance took 37 minutes by the Staff time, without calls, and there were several. I knew from reading the play it would take longer than Miss Craig's 20 minutes. However the time did not seem so long as when doing it at home in a room alone, though I know without that practice and discipline the strain would have been awful. As it was I did enjoy it and everyone was so nice, and Miss Craig seemed quite pleased. Wanted me to go to Liverpool with her. I am sorry I cannot. Afterwards she told me a reporter had spoken to her about the Statue and asked if it was a real woman because he did not think anyone could have kept so still. And I didn't feel stiff either so I think I must have had the right look. I was very glad to have done well. Harcourt Williams was in my dressing-room when I came back and I had a word or two with him. He does look a highly strung individual. I should have liked to see 'A Man of Destiny' but thought I ought to get away, so dressed and packed and then, as John was done with, he and I departed. Miss Cecily [sic] Hamilton was in there with Miss Laurence and Miss Craig, who thanked me nicely, and we all parted good friends. I do love to see Miss Craig lose her temper it is too funny, once so soon over.

SAVOY THEATRE
SUNDAY, JANUARY 28th, at 8 p.m. sharp
A
Benefit Performance
BY THE
PIONEER PLAYERS
IN AID OF THE FUNDS OF THE
INTERNATIONAL SUFFRAGE SHOP,
15, ADAM STREET, STRAND.

MISS JEAN STERLING MACKINLAY
WILL APPEAR IN
OLD SONGS & BALLADS.

A NEW ONE ACT PLAY WILL BE PRODUCED ENTITLED
"THE CORONATION"
By CHRISTOPHER ST. JOHN & CHARLES THURSBY
&
"THE MAN OF DESTINY"
BY
GEORGE BERNARD SHAW.

THE CASTE INCLUDES

Miss MARGARET HALSTAN	Mr. HARCOURT WILLIAMS
Mr. DAWSON MILWARD	„ GODFREY TEARLE
„ MICHAEL SHERBROOKE	MISS HAIDÉE WRIGHT

Doors open 7.15. (The curtain will rise at 8 o'clock prompt, and visitors are earnestly requested to be seated early.)
TICKETS must be purchased before the day.
Boxes £3-3-0 and £2-2-0; Stalls 10/6; Balcony 7/6; Circle 5/- and 4/-; Pit 2/6; Gallery 1/-; from
The I.S.S., 15, ADAM STREET, ADELPHI—& at the Theatre.

MONDAY, JANUARY 29TH 1912 – HAMMERSMITH

[Kate had stayed the night with a friend near Hammersmith] A bus to Hammersmith station, train to Bishop's Road and to leave my basket at the cloak room Paddington and buy a Daily Mirror, but cruel disappointment only pictures of Miss Wright and

Jean Sterling Mackinlay (1882–1958), actress, was married to the actor Harcourt Williams (1880–1957), who was playing Napoleon in *Man of Destiny*.

Godfrey Tearle, such a shame. Then walked to the A[ctors'] A[ssociation] at 1 o'clock and met John. We read the accounts in the papers, full of praise and of course going into details because of the Censor, but not a word about the Madonna, 'tis a shame.

Kate was now sent again to Folkestone and Hythe to continue with the NCS campaign.

SATURDAY, FEBRUARY 10TH 1912 – BOURNE END: THE PLAT/HYTHE: SEABROOK ROAD
Mother and Agnes came to see me off and I came up to London by the 1 o'clock train. From Praed St to Charing Cross. [John] was able to see me off at 4.25. Miss Lewis and Miss Cheffins were at the station [Hythe] to meet me. I left my Trunk in the cloak room, having packed my bag for the week end. I had a very kind reception from the two kind ladies at 'Dunedin', Seabrook Road. There is a third inmate there now, a Miss Margaret Ormonde. Miss Lewis had turned out of her room for me. I unpacked and had a walk and then we had dinner and then sat talking of Suffrage and affairs till bed time. I had a lamp in my room and a hot water bottle and was cosyness itself, and fell asleep in clover.

SUNDAY, FEBRUARY 11TH 1912 – HYTHE: SEABROOK ROAD
About 11 we went to see 'Cravenhurst' [Napier Gardens], the house Miss Cheffins has bought and is having fitted up to her requirements – a nice little place. There is to be a room called 'The Prophet's Chamber', reserved for me and done up in Suffrage Colours. After lunch Miss Cheffins and I had a talk to our two selves, and then a Miss Nancy Smart, a WSPU and ex-prisoner came to tea. A big hoyden of a girl with a heart of gold, but very rough.

Nancy Smart may have been a daughter of Mrs Smart, a Folkestone WSPU activist. However, we cannot be sure because Mrs Smart had refused to fill up her census schedule in April 1911. The enumerator described her as a 'boarding house keeper' and it was at her home, 'Trevarra', 30 Bouverie Road West, that the WSPU organiser, Florence Macaulay, lodged. Nancy Smart was to be imprisoned after taking part in the London window-smashing campaign in March 1912 but, from Kate's remark, would appear to have already served at least one prison sentence.

MONDAY, FEBRUARY 12TH 1912 – HYTHE: SEABROOK ROAD/FOLKESTONE: 4 SALISBURY VILLAS
Packed up and away, calling on my road to the station on Mrs Gravener, my landlady, who was very pleased to see me. Then I booked my box and came by the 11 o'clock train to Folkestone, the box being put out at Shorncliffe and delivered. I left my bag and parcel of books in the cloak room at Folkestone and walked to Mrs Kenny's in Bouverie Road West and we had a long talk about arrangements for working the meeting. I just caught the 1 o'clock train from Folkestone Central to Shorncliffe and came with my bag to Mrs Ainslie Hill who is putting me up for the time I am here. [After lunch] I went out to start my work. Took a motor to Guildhall St and did some canvassing. To bed at 10.30 – a bath and to read 'The Suffragette' by Sylvia Pankhurst, so interesting, Miss Lewis has lent it to me.

FRIDAY, FEBRUARY 16TH 1912 – FOLKESTONE: 4 SALISBURY VILLAS
Writing as usual first, then out canvassing. Went with Mrs Hill out to tea at 4 o'clock to a Mrs Gore and talked Suffrage to a lot of old crows, and 'shocked them' but we parted on the best of terms so it was alright. We did not stay long, so off I went canvassing Radnor Pk West until 7.

Saturday, February 17th 1912 – Folkestone: 4 Salisbury Villas

I wrote some letters, then out canvassing the Cheriton Road, in at 1.30.Then changed my dress and in to Folkestone, then a motor to Hythe to tea with Miss Lewis and Miss Cheffins. I thought things seemed rather strained and unhappy there. I did my best to dispel it but there was a cloud. This silly rumpus with the WSPU, I expect.

Monday, February 19th 1912 – Folkestone: 4 Salisbury Villas

[Mrs Hill] took me out to the Vicarage for tea, a most impossible party with more to follow, and one of the few men there, I had canvassed, oh dear!!! I couldn't bring in Suffrage, it might have burst the party but as there were some of Mrs Gore's party there, and Mrs Gore herself I dare say they talked us over when we left which we did right early. We laughed all the way down the street. It had been one of the most comical things I was ever at. It tried to rain all the time but I went on down to Folkestone paying calls, and went in to see Mrs Kenny and was not in till 7.40

Tuesday, February 20th 1912 – Folkestone: 4 Salisbury Villas

It was a drizzling morning. I finished canvassing Cheriton Road. After lunch and a rest I went into Folkestone and paid some special calls and went in to tea with Miss Nancy Smart. At 8.30 Mrs Hill's guests arrived, a Mr Davison, Clergyman and Grammar School master, a Mr [Walters?], Bank Clerk, Colonel Benfold – Mayor of Folkestone, Mr & Mrs Hesketh, Mr & Mrs Temple. It came as a great surprise that I was not playing Bridge and that I was a Suffragette. Mrs Hesketh so disliked it all she would not even shake hands. I was eyed considerably by the male portion of the party. I had done the best I could with myself and wore my mauve velvet dress, a shape of years ago, but just now when every woman looks just like every other woman to my mind I was refreshing. I did my hair very plain and wore no ornaments and sat and read while they played. I suppose I did look pale, but I have a detached air and one has to introduce the subject in and out of season, if not in words, then in look. We retired to supper about 10, and then Mr [Walters?] would have it so I talked Suffrage while the other men pretended to chat but came and stood round listening. Mrs Hill told me afterwards, that Mrs Hesketh said afterwards 'Poor Mr [Walters?]'. I think myself he was not so much to be pitied. Soon after 11 I rose up and left saying I should return to my juvenile days and to bed – feeling deliciously young for once. Mrs Hesketh's face was a study. She likes to be the one, and for once I am afraid she wasn't.

'The Car' was the name given to the coaches – Pullman cars – run as public transport by the Folkestone Motors Company Ltd.

Wednesday, February 21st 1912 – Folkestone: 4 Salisbury Villas

The day at last. Bright in the morning, and I went off to town after letter writing, saw the Town Hall, made a few calls, and then gave away the rest of the hand bills. Tea at 5 – then I changed and made myself look as presentable as I could manage, though I haven't anything I fancy, then started off at 20 to 7 for the Town Hall. The first Car was packed so it ended by my walking all the way, and Mrs Hill and Winifred arrived at the

Probably Mrs Edith Gore, wife of a doctor, Beachborough Villas, Folkestone.

same time, two girls from Dover had arrived to Steward, and soon after Miss Lewis and Miss Cheffins arrived and more Stewards. The first people came early and I hoped we were going to have a packed hall, but we didn't. Ash Wednesday and the damp night together had been most unfortunate. Soon after 8 I went down to the door to receive the speakers. Countess Brassey as Chairman, Lady Meyer and Mr Hugh Chapman. I did not know I was going to be so pleased to see the latter, till I saw him. I had felt a little hurt, by a letter coming in answer to mine, address [sic] 'Miss Frie', he had given it to someone to answer, it wasn't his hand but it wasn't complimentary. So I said to him 'I am Miss Frye, do you remember me?' 'Remember you', he said 'I should think I do' with such a beam, so I smiled upon him. I wanted to throw etiquette to the winds and follow him, but I had to attend to Lady Brassey. Mrs Kenny turned up at the right moment and gave her and Lady Meyer a beautiful spray of roses, and with great difficulty I got them to attend to the Resolution and Agenda and got them on the platform. I nearly fainted with relief. The meeting went well – £3-7-3 in the collection, about £2 of seats sold and the Resolution carried unanimously. Lady Meyer was too long and I did not think good, but Hugh made a magnificent speech, really eloquent and beautiful, far away in front of anything I have heard him do before, unless I am getting prejudiced in his favour. The meeting was very late over and I had several things to see to, then we all went off to Mrs Kenny's, Mrs Hill and I went with the same man, I don't know his name. Army I suppose, a lot of her friends were there. Mr Chapman was staying there. I felt very hurt not to have him to myself all the time, but he was talking to some wretched rich woman in magnificent clothes, and a great feathered hat. It isn't fair, I wanted feathers. I had hardly spoken to him, and then I was only able to say good night. I didn't want supper but I did not starve all the same – soup, sandwiches, lobster in Aspic, chocolates etc. Mrs Kenny is a kind and delightful hostess and so generous in every way. Lady Meyer was there, though she had arranged from choice to put herself up at the Metropole, she was talking with her head in the air, a smart woman, clothes again. Oh Pish. I felt in the devil of a temper. Mrs Hill and I couldn't get a taxi so we had to walk home. I hoped to feel calmed but didn't. I went straight upstairs, tore my clothes off and howled. Excitement, fatigue, responsibility and 'seediness' and clothes all combined made me behave in the Tragic vein. One cannot canvass for a fortnight, screw oneself up to such a pitch, become a living mass of Suffrage, and be taken about to attract and then meet Hugh and have no reaction.

Lady Adele Meyer (1863–1930) honorary secretary of the Saffron Walden NUWSS society and co-author, with Clementina Black, of *Makers of Our Clothes*, 1909, a study of sweated workers. John Singer Sargent painted her flamboyant portrait; Kate could not be blamed for envying such an extravagance of costume.

THURSDAY, FEBRUARY 22ND 1912 – FOLKESTONE: 4 SALISBURY VILLAS

Breakfast brought a 'veneer' of calm, but I had got the mood on me all day. I was ready for anything and it was a good thing there was nothing. Mrs Hill to see me off and the 11.28 train from Shorncliffe. Fortunately a carriage to myself most of the way. I put my feet up and scowled into space. [At Waterloo] put my baggage in the cloak room meaning to have a walk, but it was pouring so I just sat in the station from 2.20 to 4.10 bought a Votes for Women and read. I did not want to see John, but I felt very hurt that he did not come to meet me, it was the last straw, though I should have been abominable if he had turned up I have no doubt, but I suppose he was rehearsing or something.

Kate travelled from Waterloo to Bournemouth to holiday there with her sister and her Aunt Agnes and Cousin Constance, returning to Bourne End on 8 March. She makes no mention of the dramatic window-smashing campaign carried out by members of the WSPU on 1 March, nor of Mrs Pankhurst's subsequent imprisonment and Christabel's escape to Paris. She returned to work at the NCS on 11 March. In February, while Kate was in Kent, Helen Ogston had resigned as organiser. The house in Claverton Street, Pimlico, where Kate found digs, has now been demolished, but was one of a tall, stucco terrace. The Misses Heffer – Georgina (1873–1953) and Edith (1874–1948) – occupied four rooms and the others were let to a transient population of actors, actresses and journalists. Kate remained friendly with the Heffers well into the 1920s.

MONDAY, MARCH 11TH 1912 – BOURNE END: THE PLAT

Up in good time and off to London by the 8.45 train. A couple of buses to Knightsbridge to the Office. I found a Miss Green installed there as temporary Secretary and Miss McGowan the new organiser not yet arrived, so I waited for her, then we had a talk together. She is working in Dulwich and I am to go there and help her, not work in the Office as I expected. It seems Miss Ogston has left altogether and they are trying for someone to fill her place, and I suppose Miss McGowan is in my place. I do not see only two months work in front of me, as poor little Miss Lightman is so ill, not expected to live and anyway never likely to come to the Office again, so her place must be filled. I don't feel the old pleasure in the place and really don't seem to care if they give me work or not. I am to have £3-3 and do for myself in London. That will be alright if I remain here, but if I am to be sent away travelling expenses will soon swamp it. There really seemed very little to do, but I kept on till 1 – then went out with Miss Green to lunch. From there, as I had bargained for the afternoon off, I walked Sloane St and to Markham Square to look for rooms, no good. Miss Heffer, 49 Claverton St, had a 9/6 back room and the house seemed much cleaner than usual. I went to see 21 Lupus St where Miss Lightman lodged but didn't like it so well, so came back and settled on the room. Then to Victoria and brought my basket and bag in a cab also my supper which I had bought on the way to Victoria after having some tea in Lyons. I had a complete unpack and settled in and then had my supper. An egg, sausage, bread butter and cheese.

TUESDAY, MARCH 12TH 1912 – LONDON: 49 CLAVERTON STREET

I was called at 7.45 – took a bath, warm if not hot. Walked to the Office and got there in ¾ of an hour. I found some clerical work to fill the morning at the Office, there was another helper there, and Miss Forsyth came in. We all went into an ABC for lunch. I could find nothing else eatable but poached egg & coffee. Then back to the Office, more work till time to clear up for the afternoon At Home. I did not enjoy it a bit. Miss Graham was there, Mrs Chapman, Mrs Hartley, Mrs Forsyth (who I took for someone else and made an awful blunder) and all the usuals and lots of people I did not know. After it was over Mrs Chapman wished me to go with a message to Miss Broadhurst at the Actresses' Franchise League. I felt sure they would be closed and so they were.

WEDNESDAY, MARCH 13TH 1912 – LONDON: 49 CLAVERTON STREET

Walked to Victoria and caught the 9.40 train to Crystal Palace High Level. Miss McGowan joined me at Honor Oak and I spent the day with her. First we went in to the Free Library and made out a list from the Directory for canvassing, and then we canvassed the Belvedere Rd till 1 o'clock. I saw a great many people but little success to come of it. We had a 1/- lunch – very good – in a Pastry Cook's then had a most tremendous walk to Dulwich Village. I thought we should never get there, and we steamed along at such a pace, I was about done when we got there. We arranged to hold a meeting just outside the Park gates, but it was hopeless, no one would come and listen and it had to be given up. We were both very disappointed. However we filled up the time with canvassing what shops there were.

The London Opera House had opened very recently, on 13 November 1911. It was in Kingsway, on the site of what is now the Peacock Theatre. Kate's allusion to 'Berners St' is probably to the Women Writers' Suffrage League, whose office was at no. 55, from where she collected their banner in the course of her busy day.

THURSDAY, MARCH 14TH 1912 – LONDON: 49 CLAVERTON ST

Started at 10, bus from Victoria to Charing Cross and to the AFL. Miss Broadhurst had not arrived so I went down to the London Opera House on an errand and did some canvassing round there. Then back and Miss Broadhurst commissioned me to collect the different banners. Miss McGowan was there, so we halved the job. She was to get the NCS, the Church League, and the Roman Catholic Society. I went off by bus to Oxford Circus to Madame Garrud who has the [Women's Social and] Political Union one. She was out, so I went and had lunch and went back at 1.45. I had to wait some time for her and watched a boxing lesson. When I had seen her, I walked to Berners St. I had arranged about the AFL. Then I had to go back to the AFL. Then to the Men's League and arrange for them to fetch a banner. I was so tired by then, I felt done, so went to the A[ctors'] A[ssociation] and ordered some tea.

The meeting that Kate was organising was advertised as a 'Suffragists' non-militant and non-party demonstration'. The hostel that she inspected at 92 Charlotte Street was the Theatrical Mission and Home 'for the temporal and spiritual benefit of theatrical employees'. She clearly decided against moving in there, whatever might have been the financial benefit.

Edith Garrud (1872–1971) taught ju-jitsu at her gymnasium at Argyll Place, Oxford Circus. A couple of weeks earlier suffragettes involved in the WSPU's window-breaking campaign had taken refuge there, claiming to the police that they were members of her class.

FRIDAY, MARCH 15TH 1912 – LONDON: 49 CLAVERTON STREET

Out at 10 to the AFL then to the London Opera House, where the office manager, Mr Boxall, who I also saw yesterday, was very kind and polite and promised his help. Then I got to the Writers' League and took their banner in a Taxi to the London Opera House. Left it in charge of the door keeper, then walked to the AFL. It was still raining hard. Got there at 1 o'clock. Miss McGowan was there so we went out to lunch together, calling for John who was waiting at the International Suffrage Shop and we went in to Lyons. We got rid of Miss McGowan. Then we went together on the Tube to Goodge St and to the Theatrical Homes in Charlotte St. I had an interview with the

Superintendant who was very nice and I saw the cubicles, drawing room, dining room etc. Not an ideal spot to reside in, but wonderfully cheap and if I do not funk it I mean to try it. The 'young ladies' are the worst of it, all of a pattern and so shoddy and rowdy. I made my way back to the AFL. Mrs Cavendish Bentick had arrived in her motor and asked what she could do, so I suggested she might take me, the banner and the collecting boxes to the Opera. So very sweetly she did and, as it was coming down in buckets, I was very thankful and she took me back again. I waited there till the tickets were ready at 4, then Miss Graham joined me and I took them to the Opera House and left them in the Box Office. Then to the Stage door where we found Miss McGowan and then there was a nice old fuss. First to get Mr Boxall to give us a room to unpack the Banners, then to get then unpacked and then to get them up. However by dint of much exertion the job was done and we could leave them and, filthy to the eye brows, I went with the others to a shop in Fleet St where we had tea and omelettes, a wash, and back to the Opera at 7. I began to feel frantically ill, the whole day had been a nightmare. I was put to Steward in the gallery, but, as I had a note to hand to Mrs Chapman, I waited on the Stage till she came and enjoyed that much more and there was no need of me to do anything in the Gallery as there were so few people and plenty of Stewards. I spoke to Eva Moore and Miss Whitty amongst those who came on the platform – and the usual lot were there, with two Members of Parliament and Sir Alfred Mond in the Chair. Mr Hugh Chapman was not there. I hear he is not in good health but he has promised to speak at Dulwich on the 22nd. I wondered if Miss Forsyth looked curiously at me when she mentioned his name. She did, only I suppose really it was not over him but something else. Anyway the Church League was not officially there as they did not approve of the resolution and we did not have their banner. The banners looked quite nice I thought. I heard most of the meeting from the gallery, but went down at the Collection and stood in the wings and heard Eva Moore, Miss Abadam, who was magnificent, and Mrs Cavendish Bentinck. Then I had to see all the Banners rolled up.

Kate continued working in the NCS office until she was sent once more to Kent, this time to Ashford. Fernley's Hotel (10 High Street), a fine early-18th-century building, was then a temperance establishment and is now, ironically, a J.D. Wetherspoon.

WEDNESDAY, MARCH 20TH 1912 – LONDON: 49 CLAVERTON STREET/ASHFORD: FERNLEY'S HOTEL

Up in good time, had my breakfast, finished my packing and then got a four wheeler and took it to Charing Cross station and put it in the cloak room – Basket, bag and Parcel of Literature. [Took] the 3.30 train to Ashford. I put my luggage in the cloak room and then set forth to find a lodging. It was early closing day and the place was deserted. The porters had directed me, but a lady in a greengrocer's, which was happily open, re-directed me, but I was most depressed by the appearance of the street and rooms. I felt rather desperate, and it began to rain. Catching the name of Dr Vernon on a door plate and remembering a doctor of that name was to take the Chair for us, I boldly rang and asked for Miss Vernon. She was such a nice girl and she brought in her

Ruth Cavendish Bentick (1867–1953), illegitimate daughter of a son of the Duke of Somerset. Joined the WSPU in 1909, Fabian, NCS executive committee member. In 1923 she gave a library of feminist books to the National Union of Societies for Equal Citizenship, later a founding collection of the Women's Library.

Eva Moore (1868–1955) one of the Moore sisters. Her husband wrote a suffrage sketch, *The Vote: a comedy in one act*, which the AFL found too light-hearted. Eva resigned in protest after she was asked not to perform it again.

Sir Alfred Mond MP seconded the Second Reading of the Conciliation Bill on 28 March 1912.

Dr Claude Vernon, Stoke House, 5 Church Road, Ashford.

Father who advised me to go to Fernley's Hotel. So off I went and, though the manager Mr Steadman had sent word that he did not approve of Suffragettes, I bargained with the manageress and concluded to stay for 35/- per week and the Hotel Porter went down to the station for my things.

THURSDAY, MARCH 21ST 1912 – ASHFORD: FERNLEY'S HOTEL

Arrived down to breakfast at 9 o'clock and clattered into the room to find a man at table eating. My heart sank. I saw a repetition of the sort of thing that used to go on at Dereham – dumb meals with men off their head with fright. Not a bit of it, my friend wished me a cheery good morning and we talked all through breakfast. Rather an interesting face, but long hair and an unkempt appearance but a very pleasing voice. I wondered if he were a School Inspector or something to do with the Non Con. [Nonconformist] Church. I had to do some writing afterwards – he walked about a bit then vanished – and I kept at my writing until the arrival of Miss White from Winchelsea, who has been organising in Rye and district ever since I left and who has arranged this meeting. She has been getting on so well and has 40 members in Rye. She came about 11.30 and I had a long talk to her. I had so much to say and she liked hearing the latest opinions and developments. We talked till my lunch came arranging details, then she went off to lunch. I had mine with my friend the gossip and I revealed my work and he his. He is a lecturer on The Insurance Bill – is doing the outskirts of Ashford and Ashford on Friday. We had an animated lunch and Miss White came in before we had finished. Leaving the two I flew off to get ready and Miss White and I had an afternoon canvassing together. We came in late to tea and my friend enjoyed the tales & experiences – some were so comical. One cannot help talking to him. Then Miss White went off home by train. I went upstairs and tidied myself and brought my writing downstairs. Mr Campbell Joseph was called for by the Sec. of the Liberal Association and they went off together to some village in a motor for a meeting. The little Temperance Hotel is very comfortable indeed and the food quite nice. So much more cheerful than rooms.

FRIDAY, MARCH 22ND 1912 – ASHFORD: FERNLEY'S HOTEL

Breakfast with my friend and gossip – though we were both late. Then I started off on my canvass quite early, beginning with the High St. Depressing work, I really had an awful day of it and kept at it hard. I did not feel human by the evening. Such arguments but I think I am getting my answers in well. But oh what work. Lunch with my friend and we discussed all kinds of things, book, plays etc. He is very companionable and has smartened up wonderfully already. His father is a Welsh Non Con Minister and he has sisters at Reading – keen WSPUs. He talks well and hasn't a scrap of self consciousness, most refreshing. I told him what most men were like to a stray Suffragette in a Hotel. He roared. He was in when I came in to a late tea and we had a long talk. Then I went up to my room with every determination of not going to the Temperance Meeting. Then, realising that I should get narrow if I heard nothing but Suffrage I put on my hat, after changing my dress, and went down to announce my determination to Mr Joseph. He said he was flattered. I let him go off, then I walked quietly to the hall. Very few peo-

David Campbell Joseph (1882–1959) born in Wales, the son of a Congregational minister. In 1911 his sisters, Madeline and Olive Joseph, were assistant mistresses at Wilton House School, Parkside Road, Reading, and, as Kate was to discover, members of the WSPU.

ple – not more than 50 at any time, and must have been disheartening for those interested. Mr Joseph talked well, his wit was cheap – and I told him so – and he really was very impartial and as honest as he could be over the Bill. I slipped out when he had done as some very prosy old gentleman began. I had nearly finished supper when Mr Joseph came in. He had some bread and mild and Miss Hardy the manageress came in and chatted. I felt dead tired so did not wait long, but I stood there by the fire sometime talking about the Bill while he ate. I think I was a little naughty, but he was an interesting man and I was tired of seeing him so unmoved, besides I knew he, in his turn, was interested and liked me well enough. And so to bed with a smile.

Saturday, March 23rd 1912 – Ashford: Fernley's Hotel

To my horror when I came down to breakfast I found two very shy and awkward men. Evidently the Commercial gets spring cleaned on Saturday and so they joined us. However I took it lightly, rang the bell for my breakfast, wished them good morning and we had some light chat. My how they did squirm. Then in came my friend and gossip. He looked at me and then down and I saw in a moment a change and set in – oh! such a change, he was as shy as the commercial travellers. I began to feel awkward too, but it was rather a game. The commercials soon fled but my friend was still somewhat diffident. I started out on my canvass about 10.30 and did Bank St. Oh dear, it came on to pour and was a miserable morning. Had to change boots etc before coming in to lunch. I found Mr Joseph and one of the others already at it and we had a chatty meal. Oh! the difference in ideas between the two men, it was laughable. The height of one to see 'The Quaker Girl' and my friend and I politely trying to keep our opinions to ourselves. An amusing meal. It was coming down a deluge, I could not venture out for a bit. I said I was going but I heard 'do sit down, you can't go out in this'. So we drew our chairs up and talked most intimately until it was time for him to go, he was to take a train journey for another meeting. He did bemoan it. I really don't know where we didn't get to in our talk, and we parted the best of friends. I am sure my manner was flawless. We both wondered if we should meet again, he hoped so and I cheerfully echoed his words. Then he went. I did miss him when he had gone. I had tea early and then went out canvassing as the rain had stopped. Came in tidied myself and came down for my supper with a book, knowing I should much miss the rubbing of my intellect with a brain of my own make. I thought over the result of the acquaintance and came to the conclusion that, much as I had been interested, I had taught him more than he had taught me. The only person I feel the other way round with is Mrs Cecil Chapman. Much as I love Hugh I feel he has very little to tell me of ideas, but of course he is brimming over with personality. I am longing to see him again. To my horror I was not alone at supper or during the evening – a most quaint little person in the shape of a woman who was returning home to Worthing but who, owing to the alteration of trains owing to the strikes, was unable to proceed further than here joined me and we chatted, it seemed so rude to read during dinner and so it was no good after to try it as I had felt it my duty to talk 'Votes' – she was eager to hear. She avowed her intention of going to bed at 10 but, alas, did not budge till I did. She was so quaint in asking me all the things it would be correct to do or leave undone and did my parents approve of my staying in a Hotel by myself etc etc.

WEDNESDAY, MARCH 27TH 1912 – ASHFORD: FERNLEY'S HOTEL

The day of the meeting at last. Miss White came over in the morning. Together we went to see the Hall and make final arrangements. She got some lunch out, and then came in to the Hotel while I had to go out again. Then I went upstairs, did the Literature and made plans, changed my dress and Miss White went up and tidied herself. Mr Joseph Clayton came at 5 o'clock and had some tea with us. Miss White went to meet Mrs Chapman, who arrived just before 6 o'clock, and I went down to the hall at 6 o'clock to meet the Stewards and make final arrangements there. It was a ticket meeting and we got a few of the people we wanted but the hall was not as well filled as I should have liked. Dr Vernon took the Chair, Mr Clayton spoke first, then went off to catch the 8.38 train and then Mrs Chapman spoke and we had the collection and the resolution was carried. Mrs Chapman waited for me and we walked up to the Hotel together. She has been given a nice room on the 1st floor. She had something to eat while I ate my supper then I saw her to bed. I was very late to bed as I did most of my packing, and had to sort my things as Mrs Chapman has suggested I shall stay the night and go to the Albert Hall meeting with her, as she may have a ticket to spare. It is most kind of her to suggest it.

The Albert Hall meeting was organised by the WSPU for the evening on which the latest Conciliation Bill was due to have its second reading in the House of Commons. With Mrs Pankhurst in prison, Christabel in Paris and the Pethick-Lawrences charged with conspiracy, the leadership of the WSPU had devolved onto Annie Kenney. As Kate mentions, the bill was defeated in part due to the voting tactics of the Irish parliamentary party who feared losing time for a Home Rule Bill if the Conciliation Bill continued its progress.

In the 29 March 1912 issue of Votes for Women *the Rev. Hugh Chapman published a 'Pen Portrait' of Mrs Pankhurst. In the same issue the report from the NCS mentioned that their organisers were now working in Ashford, Rye, and Dulwich and appealed for volunteers for outdoor speaking, bill-distributing and canvassing. Sir Almroth Wright, a British bacteriologist, had written a letter to* The Times, *28 March, claiming that women's physiology led them towards hysteria, making them unsuitable to be voters. He published a fuller exposition in* The Unexpurgated Case Against Women's Suffrage, *1913.*

THURSDAY, MARCH 28TH 1912 – ASHFORD: FERNLEY'S HOTEL/LONDON: 24 BUCKINGHAM GATE

Mrs Chapman and I had breakfast together at 8 o'clock and the bus came for her to take her to the station in time for the 9.5 train to London. I finished my packing putting things for the night into my bag then went out to pay for the Hall, Police etc. It was past three when I got to Paddington, from there I telephoned and found it was alright about the ticket, so feeling very excited I sent off my basket by Carted Luggage, the literature by Railway Delivery to the Office, then, bag in hand, went on 2 buses to Victoria and walked to Buckingham Gate. Mrs Chapman had told me she would be out so I just left my bag with the Butler and went out to enjoy London and get some tea. [Back at Buckingham Gate] very nervous I went in. Mrs Chapman greeted me and introduced Mrs Mansel, her daughter, who of course I have heard and read so much about. She is

Joseph Clayton (1868–1943) a writer interested in social reform.

most wonderfully young looking in spite of her grey hair and being a grandmother. She has certain little tricks that make her very like her mother. I was shown to a dear little bedroom, changed my blouse and made myself look as party as I could and at 7 Mrs Chapman, Mrs Mansel and I sat down to a delightful dinner table. The whole house is a delight, just what pleasure. The fourth place I vaguely imagined was for 'Cecil', though later I realised he was at the House, but all the time subconsciously I knew it was for Hugh called Boswell, and when he came in of course I realised that I had expected it from the first. In fact some days ago I had seen myself at a meeting with him and Mrs Chapman. As a family they do not go in for surprise and I sort of slid into the family. I was fairly quiet during the meal, it was so much nicer to hear them talk. But Boswell did make me smile once or twice, in fact I felt I was grinning, and I saw an answering grin on Mrs Mansel's face. We four went in a Taxi, I in a dream. Boswell shouting things at me or clasping at me as the occasion warranted, he was fearfully excited. So was I. The thing that struck me this time about him is his wonderful memory for details, and the most extraordinary thing how he has escaped matrimony – if he has. Arrived there, the fluster was tremendous. The first thing Boswell did was to buy me a Votes for Women as I had not seen it and there was something by him in it. We had delightful seats where we could hear and see to perfection. Mrs Chapman went in first, Mrs Mansel, myself, then Boswell throwing his hat down on my seat, he allowed me to sit on it all the evening. It was a soft green one, but the remarkable part was that he knew where to find his hat at the conclusion of the meeting, and as I had pushed it to one side I had done it no harm. The Forsyths were just in front of us. Miss Forsyth was very bright and animated with Boswell. My excitement during the evening was immense, having Boswell beside me, clutching at me, practically throwing his arms round me at intervals. The meeting was just about the most wonderful meeting possible to be held in the Albert Hall, and only the WSPU is capable of gathering together such throngs as filled it. And I was so delighted to see so many men, and hear them too as they called out 'Shame', 'Traitor', 'Cowards' etc with no uncertain voice. We were in just nice time, the organ was being played, then came a procession to the Platform and in the midst Mr and Mrs Pethick Lawrence, this day released from Holloway on bail to await their Trial for Treason. My, what a greeting, voices shrill & hoarse, handkerchief waving, general delighted, and those two dear things, smiling and looking so serene and happy. One feels ashamed to think of one's own horror when one read of their arrest. They did not speak, of course, but sat in the centre of the platform and looked so pleased, and the meeting spoke to its noble Treasurer through Miss Evelyn Sharp, who appeared in her place – over £10,000 was collected. Miss Annie Kenney took the Chair, Mrs Besant spoke most nobly, most gloriously, rising in her usual way right up out of the ordinary. Miss Elizabeth Robins with her magnificent voice and delightful argument – struck me very much. Then Zangwill – I turned to Mrs Mansel, just before he finished, saying 'Doesn't he make one think of – and isn't he like – Spring'. That word concluded his speech, and it was like the Spring in its freshness and gaiety, life and hope, and so deliciously witty. I have never heard a large audience laugh so quickly and as gladly as this audience, the response was almost before the spoken word, in fact there was not a dull flash of the eye all the evening. We came away in a hubbub of excitement

Israel Zangwill (1864–1926) Jewish novelist and very effective writer and speaker in support of women's suffrage.

and fixed up a four wheeler. To return in that seemed so comical to me. We came in and ate cake and cocoa, and talked, and then the tension began to wax and grow, and at last Cecil came in, dirty, excited, in fact off his head and full of bitterness. The Conciliation Bill had been defeated. He had been at the House all the afternoon and evening and we had all the details. The Irish Party had betrayed us, by arrangement with Mr Asquith just as Christabel – that Spirit of Fire and Air – foretold. If they get home rule it will come to them smirched with the doings of to-night. But I simply do not care about the Conciliation Bill. Mrs Chapman was deadly disappointed. I sat very quiet pondering. The more I thought and thought, the more I came to one conclusion, and at last I blurted it our. 'How dare they?' Mrs Mansel turned and looked at me and said 'Yes, how dare they?' It seemed to lift me miles beyond where I have ever been in Suffrage before, absolutely emancipated, and I do feel 'How dare they?' 'Who are these miserable men that they should try and stop our growth? How dare they?' Mr Cecil Chapman told us the trend of all the speeches, the dullness of most of the Suffragists and the intense excitement and jubilation of the Antis – he said they were in deadly earnest. These letters of Sir Almroth Wright in the Times are causing a hubbub, but I am glad of them, they are only shameful to him, these vile assertions, let him and his kind and the Anti Suffragists throw all the mud and filth they like at us, it will benefit. Decent people will see the real nature of the fight, will range on our side on the moral question and then see in the Vote the symbol of all we are fighting for. 'How dare these unclean men judge for the noble women who are fighting this battle for a decent humanity?' These thoughts kept crowding my brain. Mr Chapman went and took some supper, then Boswell left without saying good-night and saying he should come in in the morning and soon after I went to bed. I didn't want to sleep so I read Boswell's article and a good deal of 'Votes for Women'.

In the 5 April 1912 issue of Votes for Women *Mrs Chapman commented on the 'betrayal of our cause', stating 'how right we [the NCS] and the WSPU were to have no faith in a private member's bill', insisting that only a government measure in favour of women's suffrage would suffice.*

Kate returned to Bourne End for the Easter holiday. The Plat was to be let for the summer from 1 May and she spent a considerable amount of time travelling around looking at possible, cheaper, houses for the family to rent. After much searching, a house was eventually found at Gerrards Cross.

SATURDAY, MARCH 30TH 1912 – BOURNE END: THE PLAT

Had to sit down to my writing and wrote all day long finishing up the Ashford work – it always means a couple of days' work after a campaign but, although I noticed there was to have been a sort of retaining fee when I was working at home, I have never seen a penny of it, and Mrs Hartley has only given me a week's salary for Ashford, and one for London, that London one I was out of pocket with my cold and having to pay extra for a large room for 2 nights in the next week. And I told her, as I had not been able to be out on the Monday, I should not count that. She is close. I asked Miss Forsyth if there was likely to be more work for me else I should to look for something else. I also heard Gladys Wright was coming to fill the post of Secretary and is to start after Easter as they are returning to England.

Saturday, April 13th 1912 – Bourne End: The Plat

By the second post I had a letter from Gladys who has now taken up her duties as Secretary, putting me off from beginning work on the 17th. I was to have gone to Cromer, then it was altered to Bedford, now it seems I am to wait while particulars are found out about Essex. Considering I asked Miss Forsyth if there would be work, if not I would find something else (easier said than done) and that I have only had 4 weeks' work this year and am out of pocket by one of them, I feel a little hurt. However as it seems we may be going to be in London after all I shall try and do some theatrical work.

The report of this meeting in the South Bucks Free Press, *19 April, reveals that it was held in the Schoolroom in the grounds of the Lehmanns' house, Fieldhead. This was to be the last suffrage meeting organised by Kate in Bourne End. The resolution about 'Forcible Feeding at Aylesbury Gaol' refers to the situation of WSPU prisoners imprisoned after the March window-smashing campaign, some of whom, because of the overcrowding at Holloway, had been moved to Aylesbury. There they had gone on hunger strike and, as a result, were being forcibly fed.*

Monday, April 15th 1912 – Bourne End: The Plat

To the station. Miss Chapman was there also and we met Miss Abadam at 4.45. Brought her home to tea – then she came upstairs to rest. I got the Literature ready and did some jobs and then changed. Dinner at 7.15. I thought we should never be through. Agnes went off at a quarter to 8 and we did not leave till after 8. I was glad to get her there. Miss Eva Moore had motored over and dined with Mrs Lehmann and the hall was nearly full. Disappointingly few Bourne End people but Marlow, Cookham and Beaconsfield helped to fill our room and it was really a delightful party – everything of the best. Mrs Lehmann said a few words, then Miss Abadam made a magnificent speech and I got her to the station in time to catch the 8.35 train. We had expected her to stay the night, but though it was a rush it it was a great relief too, with Mother and Daddie like this. Miss Moore made a little speech and recited twice and Miss Chapman played the Cello. Then came the refreshments. Agnes and I were too busy to get any. We tried to talk to all we could. Then as everyone had gone, Miss Chapman's friend sat down and played a waltz and we danced. It was simply gorgeous. I did enjoy it – I wanted it to go on. So we came away. I am glad to have the party over but from all those invitations we sent out not to have had more people it did seem sad. Mrs Dixon Davies of Beaconsfield proposed a resolution about the Forcible Feeding going on in Aylesbury Gaol and Dr Dickson of Marlow got up and made a perfect ass of himself. Of course he is worse than an Anti. How can people be so foolish.

Realising that her family's finances were approaching yet another crisis and concerned, probably without reason, that the Wrights were keeping her on the NCS staff more or less out of charity, Kate had approached Edith Craig and other theatrical managements in an attempt to get theatrical work. When rebuffed she was 'dazed with disappointment'. The Wrights, who probably had not appreciated just how necessary it was for Kate to be assured of a steady income rather than, as in the past, episodic employment, did now offer her a permanent post.

SATURDAY, APRIL 20TH 1912 – BOURNE END: THE PLAT

I have written to Alexandra accepting and to Miss Craig apologising for troubling her.

From 25 April, in her new role as permanent staff member, Kate kept an 'Organiser's Report Book' in which she made brief daily entries, presumably for viewing by the NCS committee. Gladys Wright resigned as joint honorary secretary in order to become the NCS secretary in place of Rose Lightman, who died in May, not long after Kate's visit.

FRIDAY, 26TH APRIL 1912 – LONDON: 27 PEMBRIDGE CRESCENT/EAST DEREHAM: 65 COMMERCIAL ROAD

I packed my valise and started out about 10.30 with my bag for Liverpool St. Left it there in the cloak room and then by bus to Hackney and to St Joseph's Hostel, Mare St, to see Miss Lightman. The nurse went up to see if she would see me and she came down instantly. I nerved myself for the effort, and it was an effort. Poor little soul she is in the last stages of consumption, and I don't think she can last much longer, I can only pray she may die soon – she must suffer so terribly. If one could only remove her into luxurious surroundings for the little span of time yet to run. It is dreadful to think of her in that sordid little place, lying coughing her life away. She looked so dreadful – poor little creature, not wholly of the world now. She seemed so pleased to see me, and I feel so mean not to have gone before, but the only opportunity I had had was when I was in London, and that awful cold made it impossible. I stayed just upon an hour – as long as I could – she seemed to wish it – and I had an opportunity of seeing her doctor, Dr Wilks, such a nice woman. I tried to keep her from talking and just sat and talked to her, she seemed most terribly weak. I don't think she will ever be moved from that place. She cannot sleep at night now unless she takes a drug and cannot lie down. And the food is so impossible there – so untasty she was unable to manage a mouthful of her dinner and it didn't seem worth the effort. She kissed my hand at parting, and I kissed her brow, poor Miss Lightman, and so short a time ago she was atop an orange box working away her life in arguing with those louts for the cause. I sketched a plan for the summer, a campaign for us, urging her to get better for it. With a very dubious look 'Will they want me to speak?' I expect by the summer she will speaking with the angels. The Committee are most awfully good in keeping up her salary to keep her there, as it is a great drag on their pockets. I got a bus back to Liverpool St and to Dereham by the 2.35 train.Was not in till 7 o'clock. Walked to 65 Commercial Road to find a warm greeting from Mrs West, Hilda and Miss Emery. I felt most deadly tired and depressed and am very fearful about the work here.

Dr Elizabeth Wilks (c1866–1956) a keen supporter of women's suffrage, from 1910 treasurer of the Women's Tax Resistance League. Her husband, a teacher, was imprisoned for refusing to declare information about her income to the tax authorities. She lived in Hackney, not far from the St Joseph's Hospice.

TUESDAY, APRIL 30TH 1912 – EAST DEREHAM: 65 COMMERCIAL ROAD

Called on the Pearses and had tea with them both – most affable. He is an extraordinary creature. He is beginning to show what he is in his face. She, poor creature, is more limp than ever. I managed to make two members, the Misses Shellabear, such funny old ladies, so it was not a bad afternoon.

Misses Emma and Ellen Shellabear – the 'funny old ladies' – were then aged 54 and 51. 2 Quebec Road, East Dereham.

Wednesday, May 1st 1912 – East Dereham: 65 Commercial Road
Letters in the morning, and out at 2.30 and went to call on a Mrs Olley at Softwood, one of our members, and was just in time to save her from retiring owing to the Militants.

Saturday, May 4th 1912 – East Dereham: 65 Commercial Road/63 Norwich Street
Had dinner with Mrs West and then came to Mrs Cox, 63 Norwich St, as Mrs West is expecting a sister from America and she has not room for me. I am very sorry to leave, it is so nice there. Just left my bag and then went out and had a long afternoon canvassing and ended with about an hour with the Vicar, a great triumph as I have got him to take the Chair. Was not in till past 8. Mrs Cox is most awfully kind and nice.

Kate had encountered Mr Moon the previous year when he was lodging with Mrs West.

Sunday, May 5th 1912 – East Dereham: 63 Norwich Street
Breakfast at 9.30 by myself then to Church with Miss Cox. We all suppered together, including the male lodger, a Mr Moon, a schoolteacher, who goes in for the Higher Thought movement and who lent me a book over which I dozed all the afternoon.

Kate had previously visited King's Lynn in the course of a theatrical tour.

Tuesday, May 7th 1912 – East Dereham: 63 Norwich Street
To King's Lynn. I had a busy and successful day there finding out all I wanted to, but as the NU [National Union of Women's Suffrage Societies] has lately started a Branch I do not fancy we should go there. I do dislike Lynn, the remembrance of those unhappy days before, when I was in those awful rooms. I could not find any likely rooms all hopeless.

The books Kate read were Christian Larson, Thinking for Results, *1912, and Lida Churchill,* The Magnet, *1903, both published by L.N. Fowler, the phrenological publishing house.*

Wednesday, May 8th 1912 – East Dereham: 63 Norwich Street
Writing and canvassing again. I had got my courage up to promise to address a meeting of girls but it hadn't come off. Mr Moon, the Schoolmaster here, is highly diverting. I have read two of his books 'Thinking for Results' and 'The Magnet'.

From Kate's Organiser's Report Book, May 9th: 'It was decided to form into a branch to be called The Mid Norfolk Branch of the New Constitutional Society for Women's Suffrage. Miss Cory elected as Hon. Secretary; Miss Shellabear Hon. Treasurer and the 12 members to act as a Provisional Committee. It was decided to start a Library for Suffrage Books – each member to contribute a book or 6d or whatever they could towards a book. Miss Cory to be in charge of the books.'

Amelia Olley (1850–1924) wife of a farmer.

Martha Cox (b. c. 1856) widow, who lived with her 23-year-old daughter, Nora, a teacher.

The vicar was the Rev. W. H. Macnaughton-Jones, whose wife Kate had previously found 'no good'.

THURSDAY, MAY 9TH 1912 – EAST DEREHAM: 63 NORWICH STREET

I felt very nervous all day over the members' meeting I had to conduct at 3. An extraordinary hot day – like midsummer. I wrote in the morning, canvassed in the afternoon, in to tea, then to Miss Cory where the meeting was held. It went off splendidly. 6 besides myself, and we set the Branch going. I am really comfortable here, Mrs Cox is ever so good, too good and I hate to think of her at work all day long in this rotten old house. Miss Cox is teaching. It is a hard struggle for them.

MONDAY, MAY 13TH 1912 – EAST DEREHAM: 63 NORWICH STREET

The news in the morning paper of the death of Sir George White, member for the Northwestern Division of Norfolk, altered the outlook. I had a morning at writing then out at 12. Lunch and then to Fakenham at 1.52 to secure lodgings, which I did after some difficulty.

Kate now moved 12 miles north, to Fakenham, using the town as a base for two weeks while she conducted the NCS's by-election campaign. Her landlady at Carlton Villas was Mrs Thompson, who charged 12/6 per week for a bed-room and sitting-room.

TUESDAY, MAY 14TH 1912 – EAST DEREHAM: 63 NORWICH STREET/FAKENHAM: 1 CARLTON VILLAS

1.52 train to Fakenham. Came in the Hotel Bus to 1 Carlton Villas, Queen's Road, and found everything very comfortable and most spotlessly clean.

All that Kate 'found out' on her visit to Burnham Market is detailed in her Organiser's Book: notes on the town's hotel, policeman, a room in which a meeting could be held – with the cost – together with a list of sympathisers and possible chairmen.

THURSDAY, MAY 16TH 1912 – FAKENHAM: 1 CARLTON VILLAS

Off to catch the 9.33 train from here to Burnham Market via Wells. I found out all I wanted to in Burnham Market. Such a quaint pretty spot. Arrived in Fakenham 6.16. Bought fish for my dinner. Dinner 7.15 then to the Corn Hall to hear Mr Hemmerde KC the Liberal candidate. The place was packed and I got the very last seat. We had the usual tedious speeches while waiting for Mr Hemmerde, he was speaking at Burnham 7.30 – then Creake. Mr Costello, Liberal candidate for Brixton, a worm of a person, came after two 'Locals' then Mr Hemmerde – very blooming. A good looking youngish man – made a good speech from the party standpoint but his personality grated on me – something in his voice and in his conceit. I kept thinking 'Hot Stuff'. I don't know why. The usual pretty wife accompanied him but did not look particularly interested – and one felt it was all very business-like. He gave out he was for Votes for All Women. After the meeting I tackled him, my heart was beating, I expect my voice was all over the place and the crowd jostled me. I was quite hurt, but somehow I did it. 'Would you be willing to vote against a measure giving more Votes to Men unless it gave Votes to Women?' 'No' He tried to pretend I had been silly but the people round saw it, and he looked cross, he likes things his own way does Hemmerde KC. These political bounders, how I hate them and how they hate the Suffragettes. The National Union, one hears, satisfied with both candidates so merely Propaganda, the WSPU, as we, are Anti-Government. The NU's one very large plain horsey looking person in quite a state of fright, [and] one very small undersized person, but the WSPU girl quite sweet to look upon. Both those Societies have Committee Rooms. Oh it's a game, but I am glad I am not a man. Home very excited to eat cake and oranges then to bed.

FRIDAY, MAY 17TH 1912 – FAKENHAM: 1 CARLTON VILLAS

Lunch at 2 o'clock, writing till 4. To meet Miss McGowan, the London organiser, who has been sent up to speak and help me. We drove up to tea – sending her box on to Miss Eke in Oak St where I have arranged a bed-room. I went through the Literature. She has brought a large box of it.

For the by-election the WSPU fielded centres at Hunstanton (Olive Bartels), Fakenham (Miss Jarvis) and Kings Lynn (Miss West and Grace Roe). In Hunstanton, where its organisers were Miss Coyle and Miss St John, the NUWSS had a committee room in the High Street. The NUWSS had the great advantage of a car in which to motor around the constituency.

SATURDAY, MAY 14TH 1912 – FAKENHAM: 1 CARLTON VILLAS

Canvassed for a meeting in the market place. No news yet in the paper about Polling day but I have had a start fixing things or we shall all be left behind. The NU and the WSPU have centres in Hunstanton and in Lynn so, of course, are working more easily. I have to arrange for Hunstanton and Lynn and am beginning to feel the responsibility weigh heavily upon me. One person must do it and I don't believe Miss McGowan and I would really pull awfully well together. We are so utterly different. So I had a hard day. Such a cold day. We had to hold our meeting at 7.30 as the NU were holding one but fortunately our Trolly was in the right position – their's the wrong one. The police would not let them speak there and so we were first in the field. It gave the right impetus for, without thinking, up I climbed and started. I did not speak for many minutes but I did alright and my voice sounded fine – people came round and I had a good-tempered crowd to hand over to Miss McGowan who spoke for an hour or more. We got a huge pack of people. The NU got so mad they actually started but very few left us and I noticed she did not hold them. Miss McGowan was so furious it was as much as I could do to keep the peace – but it was simply no good to be on one's high horse these times – one had to laugh and look as if one liked it all. We were both pleased with the evening. Miss McGowan thought I had done very well and, for a wonder, I was satisfied with myself.

Although the Eastern Daily Press *account of the by-election mentioned both the NUWSS and the WSPU campaigners, it ignored the NCS, despite Miss McGowan's article and Kate's interview. On 21 May the paper set out the election policies of the NUWSS and the WSPU, declaring them puzzling. The NUWSS backed Hemmerde because he had agreed to support women's suffrage; the WSPU campaigned against him on the anti-government principle. Perhaps the paper found the existence of another, separate, 'Keep the Liberal Out' society just too confusing.*

Louisa Eke (1852–1936) kept a draper's shop and charged 6/- a week for Miss McGowan's room.

Sunday, May 19th 1912 – Fakenham: 1 Carlton Villas

Had a great scramble to get to Church by 11 but I did it. I always think Suffragettes look such heathens if no one goes. I was the only representative. Miss McGowan is an RC There are two jolly WSPU girls here – a Miss [Kathleen] Jarvis and a Miss Bartels – so nice looking too and, as both have been in prison, naturally they are the centre of interest. They have a Committee Room in Oak St as have also the NU. Miss McGowan turned up to lunch and spent the rest of the day on an article for the *Eastern Daily Press*. I had interviewed the reporter.

Monday, May 20th 1912 – Fakenham: 1 Carlton Villas

Miss McGowan I left to canvass after we had been to the printers together and I had ordered the handbills – and I went to Hunstanton by the 9.30 train. I had a great scramble in Hunstanton to do all I had to do, but found a great friend in one Mr Crown, a bill poster and a Salvationist. He most kindly assisted me round the town when seeking knowledge. I was most hard put to know what to do for the best – the Town Hall was not available for any evening – so I booked it for the afternoon and a small hall for the evening of the same day. Arranged printing and posting. [Back to Fakenham] I went down the town to the WSPU shop and the two girls [Kathleen Jarvis and Olive Bartels] gave me tea. Then at 9 down to the Town Hall to give away the bills of our meeting outside the WSPU meeting. They had a real packed hall – a huge success and were very delighted.

Tuesday, May 21st 1912 – Fakenham: 1 Carlton Villas

Had another busy day getting up Market Place meeting and had a lot of arrangements to make and letters of all kinds to write. Our Hon. Organising Sec. seems making a fine muddle about speakers for Thursday and Friday. I am receiving and sending off more telegrams than ever I have dealt with before. We had our rally in the Market Place again – it had to be at 7 this time as someone else was there at 8. So we did not get so good a crowd – I got up first and kept on some time. Miss McGowan said I spoke for quarter of an hour as 'to the manner born' but I don't think it was so long. Anyway I did do rather well. I was surprised at myself and Miss McGowan, who was strolling round the Market Place, said I could be heard at every quarter. I noticed when I asked the men to move nearer they said 'we can hear you', but they moved nearer for Miss McGowan. She spoke very well. She is an excellent open-air speaker of the Tub Thumping Style – no quarter – but I should have liked a bigger crowd. We stayed some time talking and I took the names of interested people. We made one member in a Miss Pollock – a teacher – and as she spends some of her time in Dereham she may be a help.

Olive Bartels (1889–1978) WSPU organiser in the eastern counties, in July 1912 based at Oak Cottage, Park Road, Chelmsford. In 1914 she became the WSPU's chief organiser in London, working 'underground' and receiving instructions from Christabel Pankhurst in Paris.

The 'Earl of Leicester', long since closed, was a pub in Burnham Street, Creake.

Wednesday, May 22nd 1912 – Fakenham: 1 Carlton Villas

[Early evening] To Creake. We went to the far end – canvassed. Back to the spot we had marked for our meeting outside the 'Earl of Leicester' and then commenced our meeting. I spoke first and did quite decently – any how the crowd gathered – and then Miss

McGowan spoke very well for over an hour and quite held the crowd. I don't suppose for a moment they took much of it in, but we drove off amidst a chorus of 'come again'. The drive back was lovely – so restful – but very cold and some of it was through a thick white mist. I partook of Brandy and made Miss McGowan have some for supper. She isn't a bit my sort and we really have nothing in common but we do find a good bit to laugh at and so long as I don't cross her we get along well.

THURSDAY, MAY 23RD 1912 – FAKENHAM: 1 CARLTON VILLAS

A day of tremendous hard work. I went off by the 9.30 train for Burnham Market leaving everything fixed up for Miss McGowan. I never had a moment all day. I worked like a slave – first in Burnham Market and I had lunch there in company with two Irish politicians – Anti Home Rulers – and we chatted all the time and I talked Suffrage. It was quite refreshing to be with some men again – and I think they enjoyed the joke and the repartée. At 2.30 I left in a dog cart and drove to Brancaster. I had permission to use the Inn to write my notices – then I canvassed till the last possible moment before returning by dog cart to Burnham Market. I was just finishing tea just before 7 when the Motor arrived from Fakenham with Miss McGowan, Miss Hessel and no Mr Clayton. Awful. I could see at once Miss Hessel was no good. Miss Pollock had come over with them – our new Fakenham member – a teacher and a very nice girl. They had some tea etc and then, though it was drizzling, we went down to the bottom of the Green and started. We were getting a nice crowd round us – though Mr Jodrell was to speak at 7.30 in the Schools – but, when Miss Hessel got up, they streamed off in a long procession. Oh the agony. She read poetry – very badly for the first 10 minutes and it settled the people. Miss McGowan, for some unknown reason, was not up to follow. We drove off to Brancaster and I had a heavy heart. Such a crowd there to greet us at 8.30 – and taking matters into my own hands – up I got and spoke. Of course I was given a gift but it was dark and I was excited and I knew everything hung on the first 10 minutes and I completely held the people. 'Let's give her a cheer' they said. I had announced Miss Hessel for 5 minutes only and she wasn't quite so bad. I had given her a hint. Then Miss McGowan spoke well for an hour and the whole thing was splendid and we drove off in great excitement with much cheering. I was glad of my heavy furlined coat and enjoyed the drive back.

Mary Dick Pollock, 24, Scottish, a teacher of cookery, who boarded with Miss Eke.

Kate Hessel (1856–1940) had been an active member and speaker for the NCS since at least May 1910. In 1891 she had been an assistant teacher at 'Queenswood' Wesleyan College for Girls, Clapham, and by 1901 was headmistress of a girls' boarding school in Southport. She appears to have evaded the 1911 census, but was living in London in 1914 when she was a visitor at Portsmouth conference of the International Federation of Abolition of State Regulation of Vice.

FRIDAY, MAY 24TH 1912 – FAKENHAM: 1 CARLTON VILLAS

A fearfully busy day over the meeting. Telegrams going and coming re the speakers – writing and canvassing. Down to the Hall to arrange it later in the day, after calling on Miss Hessel who had lunched at Miss Eke's. I tore back and had tea and changed there to meet the speakers – two men turned up – the Rev. Green and a Mr Lloyd – the latter from Australia and a rough diamond. I took them to the Hotel – and we had a talk and then Miss Hessel joined them for dinner and Miss McGowan and I went to the Hall. Oh dear – people came in very slowly and it was not really a good meeting – the truth is people are getting overdone with meetings – and Mr Hemmerde had a meeting in the Schools with Mrs Hemmerde in the Chair. Mr Lloyd is no speaker – Miss Hessel was very weak – the only one was Mr Green. I was pleased with him as he ended up on the right note. Afterwards the 3 went off to the Hotel. Miss McGowan waited and helped me clear up then came back to supper with me and though we were very tired and rather disappointed we managed to get some fun out of it.

SATURDAY, MAY 25TH 1912 – FAKENHAM: 1 CARLTON VILLAS/HUNSTANTON: PALACE HOUSE, WESTGATE

I was up early and down at the Hotel at 9.30. Mr Green had already gone but I settled up with Mr Lloyd and he is coming again next week. Then to Miss Hessel and arranged for her – and then paid bills and did jobs vigorously. Back about 11.30 and packed up. Miss McGowan saw Miss Hessel off then came up to lunch. Then the bus called at Carlton Villas for us – at Miss Eke's for Miss McGowan's luggage and we came by the 2.29 train to Hunstanton. Miss Rosalie Mansell, Miss McGowan's greatest friend, joined us from London. We all put our things in the cloak room while we hunted for Rooms. We found them – Palace House, Westgate. We had tea then I went out again to get the printing and make different arrangements.

MONDAY, MAY 27TH 1912 – HUNSTANTON: PALACE HOUSE, WESTGATE

I canvassed morning, afternoon and evening for the meetings on Wednesday. I am very nervous about them. Miss McGowan spoke on the sands at 3.30 at a joint meeting with the WSPU and ourselves. Joan Dugdale and Miss Bartels. Miss Mansell went with her to represent the NCS as I felt I could not spare the time. It wasn't a great success I heard – a real Bank Holiday crowd.

Rev. H.M. Green, whose wife was secretary of the Islington branch of the Church League for Women's Suffrage. St Marks Vicarage, Tollington Park, London.

Kate hired a motor for 22/- from Johnson's Garage in Hunstanton to take Miss McGowan, Mrs Chapman and Mr Lloyd to Burnham Market.

In 1902 Rosalie Mansell (c 1867–?), was superintendent nurse at the Lambeth workhouse infirmary, leaving after allegations about her 'moral character'. She won a libel case against a newspaper, granted a testimonial by the Lambeth Workhouse Guardians, one of whom was Charlotte Despard. She became a mainstay of Despard's Currie Street clinic.

Joan Dugdale (1892–1970) and sister, Una (1880 -1975), active supporters of the WSPU. Their father was a member of the Men's League for Women's Suffrage.

TUESDAY, MAY 28TH 1912 – HUNSTANTON: PALACE HOUSE, WESTGATE

Had a lot of writing to do in the morning and had to go out to make arrangements and then a great rush to get something to eat and off to Burnham Market at mid-day. I took the Literature to the Hotel, left it here and ordered tea – then I canvassed hard and walked all the way to Burnham Overy. Came [back to Burnham Market] to Hoste Arms Hotel – found one of my Irish friends still there – the younger married one – at least the other was married too – but I gathered he was separated from his wife. My friend greeted me quite tenderly – we met as old friends – there were two other Irishmen – Anti Home Rulers and two Liberals – a young coming-on Politician – quite nice looking – and an older man who, I was told afterwards, was Mr Ouithwaite – a candidate somewhere. We all had tea and eggs and Suffrage discussions – Mr Ouithwaite was quite violent – but I really had him every time – quite a roar went up at some of my answers – I enjoyed that tea party immensely. I think we all did – Mr Ouithwaite least of all, perhaps, but I felt I was scoring – and as only the two odd Irishmen were inclined for Votes for Women I had no help. No 1 Irish was not so rabid though. I only got to the Schools just in time to have the doors open and let the crowd in – no policeman there so the boys had to go – it looked like a rowdy meeting from the first. The place was pretty full when the car arrived – Miss McGowan with Mrs

Chapman and Mr Lloyd. Miss McGowan took the Chair – and they were fairly quiet while she spoke – but directly Mrs Chapman got up the trouble began. No one could hear her – she was feeling so dreadfully ill with a feverish cold – she must have had a miserable evening and I felt so sorry for her – and the people were so insolent. I went and stood right at the back amongst the rowdies and it was a lively evening – and so stuffy. Mr Lloyd (from Australia) stood on a Chair and bellowed – 'Oh men of England' over and over again – he tried his best and was cheery but not much of what he shouted could be heard. I took a collection – which was brave I think – but I felt I had to do something. I was so disappointed and we drove off amidst groans. A very Liberal place – but the boys were the mischief – once in they wouldn't quiet. We motored back to Hunstanton – left Mrs Chapman at the 'Golden Lion' – then Mr Lloyd at the Temperance Hotel in our road – then home. The WSPU had been holding a meeting in the Town Hall and Miss Mansell had been down to help Steward – but only about 100 people turned up – some said 50 – so they had an open air afterwards as Mrs Massy and Mrs Haverfield were there. That was just over so we three tramped off to Roberts Room where Mr Hemmerde was speaking – a small room but well filled. He was just answering questions put to him by our lively friend Mr Lloyd – so when the people came out we gave away our handbills.

WEDNESDAY, MAY 29TH 1912 – HUNSTANTON: PALACE HOUSE, WESTGATE

We went to enquire for Mrs Chapman who was still feeling very seedy, then Miss Mansell, Miss McGowan and myself Poster Paraded 11.30 to 1. Miss Mansell had very kindly made the Sandwiches [sandwich boards] yesterday. I think it was a success – certainly anyone to see looked at us. Flew off to the Town Hall at 2.30 – I had seen it was ready in the morning. I had expected 5 or 10 – so when something like 50 straggled in – some very late – some not to stay – I felt quite relieved – but it was a fiasco. However we got a decent collection and a new member. Saw Mrs Chapman to the Hotel and back to tea. Mr & Mrs Hemmerde are at the 'Golden Lion' and lots of their helpers. I managed to run up against the gentleman every day – we do not like one another. Meeting in Rays Rooms 8 pm. Oh my hat – worse than ever – melancholy wasn't the word and I felt it was rotten arrangement on my part. It is difficult going over to a place for a few hours. I imagined Hunstanton a much bigger and residential place. And poor Mrs Chapman was feeling so seedy and Mr Lloyd has got on all our nerves. He is an absolute terror – and I don't believe he is straight. Now I find that no-one knows anything of him – I am sure I am right. Miss McGowan walked back with Mrs Chapman while I cleared up – then we all three went for a walk by the sea – and being all tired were inclined to be cross with one another. At least, Miss McGowan and myself were. Back to supper and bed. Miss Mansell is a tremendous help over the catering – she buys tins of things and cooks over her stove and makes salads etc and she is so jolly and cheerful. She kept me in roars of laughter all day over those wretched meetings.

Rosamund Massy (1870–1947) wife of an army colonel, had twice been imprisoned as a result of her suffrage activities. The Hon Mrs Evelina Haverfield (1867–1920), while remaining an active worker for the WSPU, had given the NCS a donation in 1910. Both she and Mrs Massy were good public speakers and much in demand at by-elections.

THURSDAY, MAY 30TH 1912 – HUNSTANTON: PALACE HOUSE, WESTGATE

I went to call at the Hotel for Mrs Chapman. She was mercifully feeling better and she came and sat on the Green and talked to me and then I saw her off to London. The wretched Mr Lloyd turned up too – and then I marched him to our rooms and Miss McGowan and Miss Mansell absented themselves while I tried to go into his accounts with him. But they have given him so much money at the Office – £8 – about that I can't do anything with him unless they authorise him to settle up with me. I know he ought not to spend half that – the man is impossible. I have told him we do not want him – but he has decided to stay on till Saturday or Monday. We had a violent thunderstorm in the early afternoon which quite bowled me over. Miss Mansell was such a dear – bustled about and made tea and was so sympathetic. Miss McGowan is so harsh over these things. She is very sincere though – and I ought to like her better than I do. We went over to Snettisham – the rain leaving off in time – about 5 o'clock. We put a notice on the Tree and we canvassed and then the time being short we got up a Musical Parade – Miss Mansell purchasing Trumpets for about 24 children – then we borrowed a big bell – and like lunatics went round the Village. Oh, it was funny. I wasn't feeling quite in the right condition to appreciate it – back ache and all the rest of it – but it helped me to go through it gravely as if we were in for our everyday occurrence. The rehearsal was the funniest. One, two, three, off. Blow Blow Blow 'Votes for Women'. The Mothers were so proud – in more than one instance the children had been hurriedly stuffed into their Sunday frocks. Then the meeting 7 to 8.10 – all the time we had. I got up on the Chair and started off but did it very badly and didn't talk sense – but I held a sort of discussion meeting on my own – and quite converted a nice young man. We hurried to the station – some way off – and caught the last train.

FRIDAY, MAY 31ST 1912 – HUNSTANTON: PALACE HOUSE, WESTGATE

I slept late – was awakened by Miss McGowan dashing in – she had been summoned back by Alexandra as she will have to go to the Hythe by-election tomorrow. So she packed in a scramble while I got up – and I did up the Literature etc while I ate some breakfast and then I tore down to the station, after rapidly doing the accounts with Miss Mansell, and saw them both off at 11 am for London. I felt a bit homesick seeing them go – but really felt so tired and done up I was thankful to see them go. It simply poured with rain. I had to slop about in the wet – started paying accounts etc. I had received a Telegram from Alexandra asking me to verify Mr Lloyd's accounts, receive surplus etc, but as they hadn't wired him, too, I couldn't. However I sent a note asking him to come and see me – making as the excuse the wrong change he had sent me. He came in dripping and excited – very excited – he had just been having a drink with Mr Jodrell (the Unionist candidate) and was fetching people to the Poll in his cars. I made an appointment for him at 2pm on Monday with Alexandra – told him Mrs Hartley would want to see the Hotel Bills etc. He tried to flatter me up and ran down Miss McGowan – he had some project in mind for himself and me and threw out a feeler – he wanted to know if I was 'straight' or not. I was very business like with him. He said he should tell them at the Office what he thought of me and my organising etc couldn't speak highly enough etc. And naturally I have written to say what I think of him – they will get no change for their £8 – the man is a regular wrong one – I doubt if he is from Australia at all. A fearful wet day for the Election – but it cleared up in the evening. Cars were dashing about all day. Mr Jodrell looking quite mad with lucky emblems tied over the car –

black cats etc – and of course the pink and purple. The Hemmerde colours are Blue. I heard the crowds cheering when he got back here just before 8pm.

SATURDAY, JUNE 1ST 1912 – HUNSTANTON: PALACE HOUSE, WESTGATE
Outside the G[reat] E[astern] R[ailway] Hotel waited to hear the result. I knew it must be Hemmerde – and, though it is a greatly reduced majority, it is a bigger one that it ought to be. What it would have been without our efforts – the Poster Parade and the Trumpet Parade one does not like to think.

SUNDAY, JUNE 2ND 1912 – HUNSTANTON: PALACE HOUSE, WESTGATE
I really felt most dreadfully done up and seedy so did the wisest thing I could do – read a perfectly idiotic book *The Reason Why* by Eleanor Glynn most of the day. I did not attempt to go out till I was obliged to – at 6 o'clock as a WSPU member, a Miss Muriel Moore, who keeps the Greenaway Tea Rooms, had kindly asked me. She had a cousin there and we all went and sat on the Pier till 8 o'clock. It was quite lovely.

TUESDAY, JUNE 3RD 1912 – HUNSTANTON: PALACE HOUSE, WESTGATE/EAST DEREHAM: 65 COMMERCIAL ROAD
Back to Dereham via King's Lynn. I hear the Rev. Hugh cannot come – it is a shame but I don't believe him – and Gladys recommends I should write to him myself.

WEDNESDAY, JUNE 5TH 1912 – EAST DEREHAM: 65 COMMERCIAL ROAD
Writing and canvassing. Miss Cory came round and helped me get out tickets and notices to the different members – and she very kindly took them round for me. A sweet letter from the Rev. Hugh saying he will come – I thought he would for me – when he tried to wriggle out of it I expect he didn't know I was here.

The 'White Slave Trade' – the trafficking of young women – was much in the news in 1912. The Eastern Daily Press *reported that the Vicar, Mr Macnaughton-Jones, had discovered girls from East Dereham were being lured to Yorkshire with offers of work in domestic service but that the work was, in reality, of a different nature. Several girls had ended up in the York Home of Refuge. The Council was told that 'there were people living in the town who got their living by procuring girls'.*

THURSDAY, JUNE 6TH 1912 – EAST DEREHAM: 65 COMMERCIAL ROAD
Writing and canvassing. A special letter to the Members of the Council as there has been lately brought up by the Vicar a case of Traffic in Dereham girls. It was in to-day's *Eastern Daily Press* – so I have lost no time in sending them a pamphlet and asking them to come to our meeting.

Kate had spent the last few days in exhausting rounds of canvassing for this meeting between visits to Norwich hospital where Mrs West, her landlady – and now friend – was keeping vigil at the bed-side of her dying sister. After helping to arrange funeral details, Kate moved back to Mrs Cox's 'as obviously I cannot go on with the daily round in this house of mourning'. For Kate Wednesday 12 June was a very busy – and memorable – day. The funeral was held in the afternoon and the NCS meeting in the evening. The Vicar had booked the Assembly Rooms in the afternoon for a 'girls' tea', hence the problem Kate faced of ensuring that the hall was cleared and re-arranged in time. The Eastern Daily Press *report, 14 June, mentioned that Rev. Hugh Chapman 'in a forceful speech' declared that 'if womanhood had the vote there would be infinitely more freedom in the country' and that the resolution, '"that this meeting calls on the government to give votes to women in 1912"', was 'carried by a large majority, only four or five voting against.'*

WEDNESDAY, JUNE 12TH 1912 – EAST DEREHAM: 63 NORWICH STREET

The usual details to see to – arranging work and change for Stewards – and I have to collect the tickets, find out how many to reserve etc. Then to the station to meet Miss Bass at 4.17. A nice woman, very capable and sensible. We drove in the bus to the Miss Shellabears, who put her up, and we all had tea together. I left Miss Bass and got to the Assembly Rooms at 10 to 6. To my horror – but I had known it would be so – all the drivers sitting at tea and the tables just as everyone had got up. For 10 minutes I kept my patience and my temper but I saw that would not stand me in any stead at all – they merely promised to be quick – then to be out by 7 – but when I lashed out they got a move on then. Even [then] it had to be done in a great scramble – all the forms put right – the chairs carried up – reserved ones ticketed etc. About 5 to 7 I flew off in a great rush to the station. It came on a deluge of rain and I had to turn in to Norwich St and change my shoes and get rubbers – then to the station just in time to meet the 7.12. What I expected in the way of a greeting I don't quite know – I was excited, but I was in a dead calm to Mr Chapman. He had written me a very sweet letter a few days ago – but his greeting. No half measures – he just beamed, clasping me by the hand and arm telling me he had come for the pleasure of seeing me – the journey had been nothing with the reward of seeing me at the other end. It was pouring and we got into the 'King's Head' bus as in a whirlwind – his secular clothing – especially the upstanding collar and the green hat – gave him a most rakish appearance. I was delighted to see him. I can really talk to him. Going along in the bus he told me a piece of news that really upset me – Mrs Chapman appears is very bad, will have to have 3 months complete rest – heart after influenza. I told him about Dereham and the Vicar and gave him the cutting about the White Slave Traffic here to read and strolled him in to Mrs Carter and told her to look after him – give him a nice drink and send him down to the Hall at 8.15 – and then I returned in the bus. People poured in early – always a good sign – and the Stewards looked after things well. Miss Cory sold tickets downstairs and I was doorkeeper and spoke to everyone coming in. I must say I felt a bit light headed – the greeting had absolutely gone to my head. The Vicar and Miss Bass arrived in good time and we started off punctually. I did not hear the Vicar but he declared himself a strong Anti-Suffragist – rather irregular, but I was beyond anything – no doubt Miss Bass and the audience were startled – I felt nothing could surprise me. Miss Bass spoke next. I hovered up and down stairs until 8.30. A clergyman and party had driven up at 8 o'clock – a Mr Davidson from Stiffkey, a friend of Mr Chapman's, and they had gone off to fetch him. I lived on thorns until his arrival. They brought him in the Motor – then seizing his hat and umbrella – I led him boldly in – he rather jibbed at the procession up the room – but it had to be done and I found some seats for his friends in the front row

Miss E.S. Bass, 22 Willifield Way, Hampstead Garden Suburb

– a most frivolous clergyman with a frivolous wife and a beyond-all-whooping frivolous young lady – destined for the stage – the whole party seemed quite mad. Miss Bass made a good ending and then Mr Chapman started. Just as I was leading Dr & Mrs Howlett up to the front – I heard him telling the audience how he admired Miss Frye – how altogether admirable I was – and how he had come to speak for me – a woman of heart and brain and altogether the right sort – but nothing seemed to matter – the madder the better – I was only glad I could keep serious. But he spoke of his ideal Mother and the ideal woman as if he had at last found her – so no wonder people looked at me. But I was so proud of him. He went on to speak magnificently, as one inspired – I have never heard him half so fine – at Marlow and Bourne End he was quite bad – at Folkestone he was excellent but not so good as this. He absolutely held the audience spellbound – he fascinated them completely. It was a tremendous success. We had sold £1-19 in tickets and took £1 in collection and the hall was quite full – the people I had canvassed too – so it was the result of work. The Vicar, poor man, didn't know what to make of it – he seemed to shrink into nothingness besides Boswell – it was like a night-light to an Arc Lamp. Afterwards I had much ado to get Mr Chapman round to Mrs Davy who had kindly prepared sandwiches and coffee – but the Davidsons motored him and the Vicar and I walked and there were one or two other people there. I had tried to make some sense of the Vicar and Mr Chapman and I both had a go at him while eating – – and the atmosphere was so electric no one displayed much sense. Mrs Davy must have been astounded – and she is so very deaf, poor soul. I made a good meal. Then the Davidsons motored Boswell and I to the 'King's Head' amidst the greatest excitement – we were packed like sardines – then Boswell walked with me to Mrs Cox's. Going along I told him somewhat of her sad story – and on the spur of the moment I said when I got to the door 'Will you come in?' 'Oh for anything.' In we popped. Mrs and Miss Cox were up – and I was proud of Boswell – he did behave sweetly – absolutely charmed Mrs Cox. He asked them didn't they very much enjoy having Miss Frye – naturally they said they did. He talked to them so sweetly and ended by a long prayer – it nearly sent me off, but when I pulled myself together I realised it was very beautiful only it went off so suddenly, and it made Mrs Cox cry. I let her lead him down the steps and to the gate. I was afraid he would break himself and better her than me I thought. 'Man in woman's hands' he said. He is a marvellous mixture. To bed but not to sleep – oh! dear no.

THURSDAY, JUNE 13TH 1912 – EAST DEREHAM: 65 COMMERCIAL ROAD

Got round to the 'Kings Head' about twenty minutes to 9. I have never known so much packed into a mere 20 minutes before. Hearing he was at breakfast I went in to the Coffee room – he was alone and I sat down to wait till he had finished. Like a whirlwind he was telling me he loved me – I had a 'heart' and a 'brain' and if only I were a Christian I should be perfect. He had told Mrs Chapman he loved me and would do anything for me – I gather. Speak at my meetings, that he would attempt to surmount the mass of difficulties that would be in the path of a settlement. I cannot pretend to think that he has gone through all these years in the world looking for his Ideal woman, as he told me, he has to find her in me – and yet from the scene in the Coffee room it

Rev. Harold Davidson (1875–1937) rector of Stiffkey. Kate's description of this clergyman – and his party – and her summation of them as 'quite mad' – rather concurs with history's verdict. In 1932 Davidson was 'de-frocked' having been found guilty by a Consistory Court of charges of immorality; his interest in 'fallen women' may have been misinterpreted. Penniless, he took to the public entertainment circuit as 'Daniel in the Lions' Den'. The end came at Skegness when a lion turned on him.

'Mrs Davy' probably Mrs May Elizabeth Payne Davey, widow. 9 Withburga Lane, East Dereham.

did seem like it. I told him I hadn't attained all I was without a struggle – and he said 'No of course not – I understand my darling'. It is all the greatest muddle. I couldn't bear to see him go – but he went, planning a meeting at Stiffkey and saying he should join me in Norfolk next week. Knowing it would never come off, I did not attempt to reason with him – but it seemed to keep him happy. He left me in an absolute turmoil inside out. From what I said and did I should say I never appeared calmer or more collected outwardly. How I went through the morning I don't know – I was just given a gift – and I lived on knowing that Monday would come when I should get away from Dereham. Last night he was all excitement – that I should return home with him today. One other thing that struck me was, when speaking of my Stage career and that I must have been a 'rotter' never to get up to £10 per week, he asked me if I had ever been made love to on the Stage. Then, when I chaffed him about his being so afraid that the 'new woman' wouldn't be quite the woman that he liked, he was so meek but gave a very sly smile. I couldn't think of anything or anyone else, as I say, for a moment, but, as I say, I went through the morning without turning a hair – but I was conscious of the way people turned round to stare after me. Then to Misses Shellabear – and I walked with Miss Bass to the station and saw her off at 10.55. She seemed keenly amused – I didn't say much about Mr Chapman only that he had arrived in a state of excitement and I had seen him off in a state of excitement and she laughed. Then I came in and fought for the rest of the day. I kept at the accounts, letters to the Papers – Prime Minister – of thanks, checking tickets. I only did one silly thing but it had got to be done. I wrote to John telling him if he wanted me to keep on loving him he was to write to me every day for a week and not ask the reason. He is bound to know. I said to him a few days ago, with more or less truth, that Boswell was writing me nice letters and more often than he was. I wrote and told Agnes. I was obliged to tell someone, though I know it is silly. It makes no difference in what I feel for John but falling in love with him was always a bitter disappointment to me – it hurt my pride. I feel I love Boswell with my brain – it is his culture that fascinates and I seem so at home with him and it has done my pride good. I feel bitterly sorry it has happened too – because I cannot ask him to speak again – it would not be fair to him or to me – and, oh dear, the heavy weight to fight. I couldn't eat and I couldn't sleep. The day passed in a jumble of work and thought – I simply could not venture out again – and all I could wonder was – what would happen.

FRIDAY, JUNE 14TH 1912 – EAST DEREHAM: 65 COMMERCIAL ROAD

After a restless night I did not feel fresh. I called all day long making members wherever I went – it was wonderful. I tired myself out – the last one was not over till 8.30. When I came in at lunch I knew there would be a letter for me – I absolutely made for it. It was very sweet – typewritten – ending 'I am always your affectionate friend' – and saying 'Meanwhile, you have a friend who will do in anything in the world for you if it is in his power, which you know already without any words from me.' I answered it after lunch – talking friendship, saying I hoped I should be the sort of friend he would like to have but that I was afraid the path was not easy. I thanked him for his help, told him the good he had done here, that I was returning to duty in London and told him not to forget to bring a coat another time – and ended 'Yours'. So he could take it as he liked. I felt pretty miserable by evening and thoroughly tired out. But there is no doubt work is the thing at these times.

SUNDAY, JUNE 16TH 1912 – EAST DEREHAM: 65 COMMERCIAL ROAD

I had got Boswell very badly on the brain again. Oh dear what funny phases I do go through – this has certainly got to be fought down.

With The Plat let, the Fryes were renting a house at Gerrards Cross, Buckinghamshire. 'Innisfail' was a ten-minute walk from the station.

MONDAY, JUNE 17TH 1912 – EAST DEREHAM: 65 COMMERCIAL ROAD/GERRARDS CROSS: INNISFAIL, NORTH PARK

The 9.3 train to London. I travelled with two of the plainest females it has ever been my lot to be with – like horses and so got up and common and playful – they had a curious effect on me. I couldn't help considering Boswell's point of view and realizing how men must dislike the idea of a female growing away from their ideals. Had I been a man these women would have made me sick. It was so extraordinary to be so unfair. Men are hideous enough, goodness knows. John met me at Liverpool St and I couldn't help thinking of that other meeting last September when Dr Townroe was meeting with Miss Ogston. John had a new suit and looked very well but it didn't seem to matter – I seemed so apart – but no doubt I should have felt worse if his appearance had worried me. Of course he couldn't keep off questions but I was as nice as I could manage. I answered him truthfully, but I told him he must give me my head a bit and then it would come alright.

The pamphlet by Hugh Chapman to which Kate refers is Linked in Loss, *1912, a meditation on St Francis of Assisi and St Clare.*

TUESDAY, JUNE 18TH 1912 – GERRARDS CROSS: INNISFAIL

[Talked to Agnes] and of course we had to discuss the Boswell episode. I made it very funny – well it is funny – he is such a quaint being – and as I am beginning to recover my poise and feel more normal I can see the funniness – I am making myself do so. But I am beginning to understand it less. I can only turn to the pages of his pamphlet 'Linked in Loss' and try and believe that is his attitude to me. But it is a funny way of showing his. He was not calm last Wednesday. There has been no further letter at all – and, as I guessed, the visit to the Davidsons and the meeting at Stiffkey seems to have blown over.

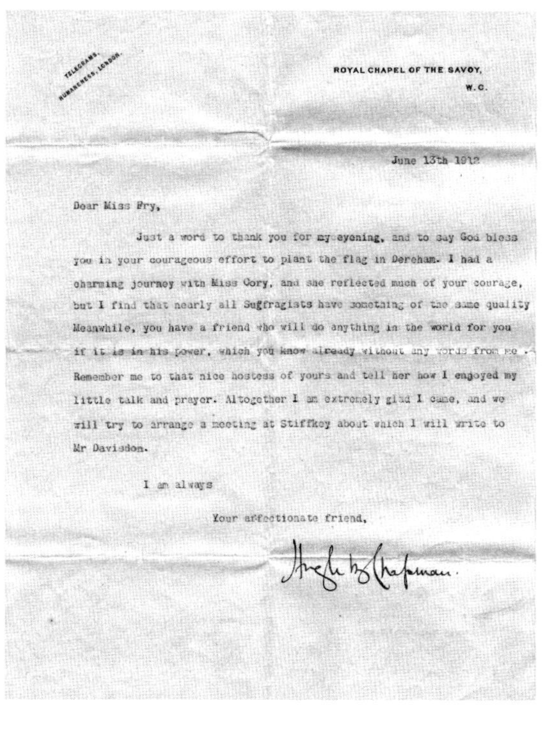

TELEGRAMS, HUMANENESS, LONDON.

ROYAL CHAPEL OF THE SAVOY,
W.C.

June 13th 1912

Dear Miss Fry,

Just a word to thank you for my evening, and to say God bless you in your courageous effort to plant the flag in Dereham. I had a charming journey with Miss Cory, and she reflected much of your courage, but I find that nearly all Suffragists have something of the same quality Meanwhile, you have a friend who will do anything in the world for you if it is in his power, which you know already without any words from me. Remember me to that nice hostess of yours and tell her how I enjoyed my little talk and prayer. Altogether I am extremely glad I came, and we will try to arrange a meeting at Stiffkey about which I will write to Mr Davisdon.

I am always

Your affectionate friend,

Hugh B Chapman.

The 'very sweet' letter from the Rev. Hugh Chapman. What a pity that there never was to be a Stiffkey suffrage meeting presided over by Mr Davidson, the 'frivolous clergyman'.

WEDNESDAY, JUNE 19TH 1912 – GERRARDS CROSS: INNISFAIL

8.47 train to Paddington. Then I walked across the park to 8 Park Mansions Arcade. Found Gladys installed and looking very well. I am to help with the Garden fête at Chiswick on the 29th. A Miss Greenwood – a WSPU organiser – (or one who used to be) has it in hand. I am to help her and Stage Manage on the day, under a Mrs Buchanan who is Forbes Robertson's sister – and who has taken it up because her friend, Mrs Geoffrey St Aubyn, who originated it has collapsed with the strain – so the whole thing has been very much muddled. I do not feel I shall be in the least good. It is always difficult to pick up the threads of other people's work and I am feeling absolutely rotten and in need of a real rest. I call it very short-sighted policy on their part not to give me one. Miss McGowan had a week after the Hythe campaign. [Miss Forsyth] has promised to write her thanks to Boswell for me – I said I couldn't say any more or mention expenses to him. She wanted to hear all about him. I am quite sure now that she did look curiously at me when his name came up at the Office before I went away. I daresay Mrs Chapman has said something – and then Miss Forsyth herself has been making attempts to speak at meetings Boswell has spoken at. She very nearly came up to Dereham. I wonder if he makes love and settles down to friendship with all his ladies!!! Such a mad world. Could he possibly be as sincere as he seems over Suffrage?

In May Mrs Pankhurst and Mr and Mrs Pethick-Lawrence had each been sentenced to nine months' imprisonment on a charge of conspiracy to commit damage. The procession to Holloway in which Kate took part was to support them and other suffragette prisoners who were on hunger strike and, except for Mrs Pankhurst, whom the authorities never dared abuse, being forcibly fed. 'Smiths' to which Kate refers was one of W.H. Smith's main stores, at the south-west side of Kingsway.

SATURDAY, JUNE 22ND 1912 – GERRARDS CROSS: INNISFAIL

By the 9.19 to Paddington, a bus to the Grove to see one or two people about advertisements [for the fête programme] – no good. Then to the Office. Then first to Albemarle St and to Dorset Square – fruitless errands and I had a great rush to get back – get the boy to let me in the Office as, of course, Gladys had gone and I had to get two of the Bannerettes. I had a hasty lunch in Lyons – then by Tube to Covent Garden and to Kingsway at 3 o'clock. No one turned up at the appointed place – outside Smiths – so I gave it up and went up to where the procession was being marshalled – it was mainly WSPU – just ourselves and a few Tax Resisters – but it was a good crowd. Alexandra turned up with Mrs Wright – no Gladys of course – she carried Hythe – I carried Dereham – Miss Forsyth and Mrs Hartley carried two others – Rye and Winchelsea. I must say it was a hot walk to Holloway – boiling and I had a coat and skirt instead of summer garb – and I had the Rat pain gnawing my inside something awful. I just went stolidly through it. Of course I was glad to do it. It was the very least one could do – for those tortured and starving beings in Holloway – and there was to be one at night – to Brixton for Mr [Pethick-] Lawrence. We seemed hours getting there. Such a crowd to line the route – and we looked a pack at the open-air meeting held outside the gates. Mrs Drummond, Miss Sylvia Pankhurst, Mrs Massy. It was so stuffy – I removed to the outskirt for a little air – so did not hear much. Then we formed up and processed round the prison cheering – the cheering was really very wonderful and we all went at it as if possessed. We had also sung the 'March' [of the Women'] at the beginning, conducted by Dr Ethel Smyth.

The Eustace Miles Restaurant was a popular vegetarian restaurant in Chandos Place, off Trafalgar Square. The London Pavilion is at Piccadilly Circus.

MONDAY, JUNE 24TH 1912 – GERRARDS CROSS: INNISFAIL
To the Office. Some writing then to Chiswick, but it came on to pour with rain and I could do very little but take shelter. Back at the Office at 1.10. Then with Miss Greenwood to the Eustace Miles Restaurant for lunch and to the Pavilion to give away our notices [about the fête] while the people were going in for the WSPU weekly meeting. I went in and heard Miss Kenney, in the Chair, describe how Mrs Pankhurst had her back to the wall defying the doctors last Saturday when our band struck up outside the gates. It was on the Posters as we went in that she had been released – but we were told she was very ill. Then came the news of Mrs [Pethick-] Lawrence's release and several more from Holloway and some from Birmingham – all too ill to be kept in any longer. Oh it is awful to think of the suffering still going on. It was a most exciting meeting – news kept coming from Clements Inn to the Chair. I heard the Rev. Ivory Cripps – then I went and stood downstairs and gave notices to the people as they were leaving and gleaned news about the prisoners.

TUESDAY, JUNE 25TH 1912 – GERRARDS CROSS: INNISFAIL
We had a wild morning preparing for the sale and Strawberry and Cream Tea. I stayed in the Office while Gladys had a leisurely lunch, then at 2.15 ran hastily to Lyons – ate mine quickly then back to change my dress upstairs and, before I had done, Miss Cory arrived and was told to come up – not very considerate – but however. She came to help and was quite a success. The Marchioness of Devonshire, who came to open the Sale, arrived very late. However she was very pretty and spent a lot of money. Mr [Cecil] Chapman was there and I had a chat with him. Mrs Chapman is better – no mention of Boswell. But in talking over the possibility of a three-cornered contest at Folkestone and our going there to support the Labour, Mr Chapman said 'Oh no – I don't think it would do to trust Tom Mann and Ramsay Macdonald with Miss Frye' – or some such words. So I suppose they take it as a joke. There was a dreadful rumour that Mrs Pankhurst was dreadfully ill. It appears that on Sunday night she was very seriously ill in Holloway – they were up all night with her – and when removed she had to go in an Ambulance. Mrs Lawrence was too weak to walk. I wonder how Miss Cheffins is getting on – she is being forcibly fed. It is enough to make anyone feel ill to hear of these horrors

The NCS fund-raising fête was held at Walpole House, The Mall, Chiswick. Barkers, the Kensington department store, were hired to provide the tea, the seating and the awnings. By 'Morris dances' Kate is probably referring to the troupe of children, an advertised feature of the fête, taught by a young Margaret Morris – rather than traditional Morris dancing.

SATURDAY, JUNE 29TH 1912 – GERRARDS CROSS: INNISFAIL

The fateful day at last. It opened by some of the most torrential rain possible. The marvel is it went of as well as it did and that so many people turned up, but it must have made a difference. John turned up at 11.30 and helped pack up the taxi and we drove to Walpole House. I was in a fever and it was pouring. No-one but Miss Porter – Barkers had not arrived – Miss Greenwood turned up later. Fortunately Mrs Goldman turned out to be extremely nice and most helpful. She threw the house open to us – entertained Miss Greenwood and John and I to lunch – let their servants fetch and carry – and were simply delightful. I cannot express how kind they were – and I had been so warned that they would not do much etc. I was in a turmoil. Stewards arriving – we were still at lunch. Once free, I flew about like mad and got things underway – but we were somewhat late. However by a miracle it went right. I didn't feel I had any grip of it till then. Then I had to. Lady Meyer was most difficult, and Mrs Buchanan did not do anything after the start. The start was the thing – at last I got Mrs Cavendish Bentinck to begin – then started the drenching rain – fortunately 'The Ribbon Counter' could begin in the dining room and the Morris dances could be put off – and so it had to go on through the afternoon working in as best we could. From one end of the lawn to the other I flew – in my Aquascutum and rubbers – no time to take them off. But I hated it all and the Wrights were appallingly beastly. Gladys did not turn up till 4 – then wouldn't do a thing. Miss Greenwood, after getting her Stewards to work, seemed to vanish. It was neck or nothing – so when I had worked into it I literally managed the thing. At last it was over. Then I could pack up – John went off for a taxi and Miss Greenwood, John, the luggage and I drove off. To the Office – the boy let us in and we left the things there.

MONDAY, JULY 1ST 1912 – GERRARDS CROSS: INNISFAIL

To Kensington to see Miss Sylvia Pankhurst about the decorations for the demonstration and to Barkers about the fete accounts and when I got back to the Office to my indescribable grief I found I had lost my Onoto pen – I felt sure it had gone – but I wrote to Miss Pankhurst on the chance I had left it there. Miss Geenwood came in and we did the accounts of the party. It has come out better than we thought – £40 odd to the good and considering the expenses not so bad – they were so very heavy and then the weather was so wretched.

WEDNESDAY, JULY 3RD 1912 – GERRARDS CROSS: INNISFAIL

To London 9.19. First to Studio at Kensington but no Onoto Pen and nothing from Bus Office or Scotland Yard. To the Office. Gladys was ill and did not appear all day. So I had to attend the Committee as Secretary and take notes for the letters.

SATURDAY, JULY 6TH 1912 – GERRARDS CROSS: INNISFAIL

Wrote all the afternoon – did my Dereham account for Mrs Hartley and list of members for Miss Cory and my diary after tea till bed time. It had been so neglected I was glad to get it up to date, but it was an effort.

Mrs Goldman was the wife of Sidney Goldman, a wealthy business man who had made his fortune in Africa and was now the Unionist MP for a Cornish constituency.

Sylvia Pankhurst (1882–1960), a younger daughter of Emmeline, was organising the 14 July demonstration in Hyde Park. The decorative scheme was based around a suitably revolutionary motif, the Red Cap of Liberty.

The fact that the Chapel Royal of the Savoy was the Rev. Hugh Chapman's church explains its attraction for Kate.

TUESDAY, JULY 9TH 1912 – GERRARDS CROSS: INNISFAIL

To the Office. Did some writing in the morning and then helped get the office ready for the weekly At Home. When Alexandra came she asked me to go to the opera in the evening – for a moment I thought of Agnes [who was ill] and refused and then I accepted – I have so wanted to see the Russian ballet. [After the At Home] I tidied myself, locked up, took a bus to Piccadilly – had some dinner in Slaters – then walked down the Strand to the Chapel Royal of the Savoy – feeling rather like a criminal – but what a delightful spot it is. I have never in my life seen it before – and for that I am rather grateful, it seemed like a fairy story seeing it now. Then to the Royal Opera Covent Garden. Fortunately I had gone up in my grey dress – so although not in evening dress I was respectable. I enjoyed it most immensely. As for M. Nijinsky, well words fail me – it is a thing I have done in dreams to dance like that, but never thought to see it in reality – what a dancer – he is too wonderful. Nijinska did a most beautiful bacchante dance – I don't think it could be surpassed. I was beside myself with joy. Then we had 'Le spectre de la Rose' – the beauty of the performance again passes all description – they trod the boards as if blown by the air.

WEDNESDAY, JULY 10TH 1912 – GERRARDS CROSS: INNISFAIL

To the Strand. I went for a little wander round and had another peep at the Savoy Chapel. I see he [the Rev. Hugh Chapman] is preaching twice on Sunday. To the Kensington Town Hall for the Women's Demonstration in support of the Criminal Law Amendment (White Slave Traffic Bill). I had one of the eight official NC Society tickets and sat with Mrs & Miss Forsyth, Mrs Wright, Gladys and Mrs Geoffrey St Aubyn (what a dear little person she is). Mrs Hartley was the representative on the Platform. It was a packed and excited meeting. To begin with the Chairman tried to bar Suffrage – but out it came – Mrs Philip Snowden sat down at first, refusing to speak. Mrs McKirdy introduced it in a roundabout way – nearly all the speakers – certainly those worth listening to – a Dr Wills and a member of the Committee – it really was funny – the Duchess of Bedford looked so cross – and there were a lot of Antis there – the Anti Suffrage Society was represented. At every mention such applause and excitement, how good it must have been for those wretched Antis to hear also the questions at the end. 'Wasn't it a fact that since the Women of Australia had had Votes the White Slave Traffic had been done away with?' etc. And surely they must learn by the fact that the Bill has been murdered in committee and is absolutely spoilt. Saw in the Marylebone Rd a wretched woman training another in her miserable trade. Oh! what a face that woman had. I saw the woman dodge and follow one man – he wasn't having anything to do with her, but he turned and followed me.

On 13 July 1912 The Plat, together with two neighbouring properties, was offered for sale by auction. An advertisement appeared in several issues of the South Bucks Free Press *up to and including that for 12 July and among Kate's papers is a catalogue, with photographs, prepared for the auction by Vernons of Bourne End. However, very surprisingly, Kate makes no mention of the auction and gives every indication of expecting that, whatever the family finances, they would be moving back to The Plat once the summer let had come to an end. In addition, advertisements in both* The Times *and the* South Bucks Free Press *reveal that the whole of the Gilbeys' Wooburn Estate, including the Manor House, the Kennels, the Manor Farm House and the Home Farm, was to be auctioned by Hampton & Sons on 30 July. No sale, for one reason or another, was made but, again, Kate makes no mention of what would have been another life-changing event.*

On 14 July, Bastille Day and Mrs Pankhurst's official birthday, Sylvia Pankhurst organised a WSPU suffrage demonstration in Hyde Park, in co-operation with other suffrage societies. Her mother, on her release from prison, had gone to Paris to confer with Christabel. The NCS took Platform 13 at the demonstration. Miss Slieve McGowan was the chairman and the other speakers for the NCS were W. L. George, Joseph Clayton, Mrs Cope, and Dr Weston. 'The dominant note from all platforms was: "The country doesn't want manhood suffrage alone, according to the Reform Bill now before Parliament, but Womanhood Suffrage also; this insult of leaving the womanhood of the nation unfranchised cannot be permitted"' The Vote, *20 July 1912.*

SUNDAY, JULY 14TH 1912 – GERRARDS CROSS: INNISFAIL

To London by the 10.47 train. I had half thought of going to the Royal Chapel of the Savoy but I thought better of it. It was a most gorgeous day – very hot really, but there was a thin veil of cloud so that the sun was not trying and there was a lot of wind. I walked to Marble Arch and was at the Banner carts at 1.30. Miss Wiskemann met me there and together we carried our Banners and Mrs Hartley's, Mrs Cavendish Bentinck's and Miss Simeon's. Miss Simeon went to the Office with Ethel and brought the Bannerettes. The others got their own. It was quite a task getting them to Platform 13 and a great business getting all in order. Miss Sylvia Pankhurst came round like a General – visiting the Platform Steward and seeing everyone in their place. It was a wonderful sight. 22 Platforms with 12 Banner holders to each with large glowing Banners or flags – all our ones made for the occasion with special devices and all with Red Caps of Liberty on the top of the 14-feet poles. There was a huge crowd of people, but somehow I was surprised there weren't more – in the centre, of course, there were many more but we only had a quite easy crowd round us. Miss McGowan took the Chair. Mrs Cope spoke, Mr George and Mr Joseph Clayton. It was over very punctually – the Bugle was sounded and the resolution put and then I helped put the Banners in the carts and was free. I wandered round and returned to some of the outside speakers. The strikers had marched up about 4 – and there was evidently some riot just as I was leaving the park. I saw policemen running in a perfectly idiotic way towards Park Lane.

Miss Wiskemann – possibly Eugenie Myra Wiskemann (1890–1979) daughter of Hugo Wiskemann, a German-born chemist, and elder sister of the future historian, Elizabeth Wiskemann.

Against a background of ever-increasing WSPU militancy, two unreconstructed anti-suffragists, J.A. Pease and Lewis Harcourt, were shepherding the second reading of the government's despised Franchise and Registration Bill (Manhood Suffrage Bill) through parliament. On 13 July Lewis Harcourt's Oxfordshire home was subjected to a suffragette arson attack.

THURSDAY, JULY 18TH 1912 – GERRARDS CROSS: INNISFAIL

[To Office] Went to find a policeman for the Jumble [sale on the 19th] first, then divided my time in writing and attending the Committee meeting. It is a very grave crisis – all these serious militant actions and the absurd criticism of all the other people and the Reform Bill going through in the autumn with no chance of an amendment passing. Then to Camberwell for our meeting at 3.30. I spoke better and we had Miss Fripp to help us, a pupil of Miss Leo's but she has no voice. Then Miss McGowan, quite a nice meeting and a better audience.

WEDNESDAY, JULY 24TH 1912 – GERRARDS CROSS: INNISFAIL

[To Office] I had the keys and Gladys did not come till 11.30 as she had been shopping. I had to leave at 12 o'clock for Hackney Wick. Met Miss McGowan and we had a lunch-hour meeting outside Clarnico's Chocolate place where 2,000 girls are employed – some nice, some very rough. I had about 10 minutes but it was very difficult to talk to them. Then Miss McGowan spoke till they went in at 2.

THURSDAY, JULY 25TH 1912 – GERRARDS CROSS: INNISFAIL

[To Office] Committee meeting. It was the breaking up meeting and everyone seemed in very good spirits – Miss McGowan was quite beside herself and we were both very frivolous. I had a cheque for £10-10 – it does seem a lot – last week's and this week's salary – the first week of work when we start on the 29th and two weeks of the holiday money. If I go on like this I shall soon go to Italy. We waited to say good-bye to Mrs Hartley and then Miss McGowan and I went across to Lyons and had lunch – then on top of a bus and a train to Camberwell for a meeting at 3.30. Miss Fripp met us there, she is very good but I do not think will ever make a speaker. I felt I wasn't much of a speaker – I had nothing but children so I gave them a special address, but when I turned to address the Adults I couldn't think of anything to say. Miss Fripp kept on some time but I couldn't hear a word. Then Miss McGowan gave it to them hot and strong. There were some perfectly awful people.

MONDAY, JULY 29TH 1912 – GERRARDS CROSS: INNISFAIL

[To Office] Gladys told me quite casually in the middle of the morning that the Rev. Hugh has had a breakdown – his heart is out of order. He has been ordered abroad for a cure and is now somewhere on the continent. It gave me a nasty fright. I had just been making a joke and laughing about it and it came like a thunder clap. Gladys roared with laughter when she said it was his heart. I told her she did not love him as I do or she would not have kept the news from me. But I do feel so awfully distressed. I do hope nothing that happened at Dereham has helped to upset him – but really a man who takes it out of himself as he does and with that emotional temperament is bound to live near the verge of breakdowns. I do wish he had written to tell me, but I suppose he does not do these things. I have been feeling quite sure he was not in London strangely enough. I went out to lunch feeling tragic and felt miserable for the rest of the day. Oh, what does it all mean? I would give so much to know. What did he mean at Dereham and why did he do it – or does he imagine he is a St Francis and that he can turn me into a St Clare?

Rosa Leo (1862–1948) had been a concert singer and in 1901 had given Kate a few lessons in recitation, proving an exacting teacher. A couple of years later, now a 'professional', Kate felt able to describe Rosa as 'a pushing young particle' (a Gilbert & Sullivan bon mot). Rosa Leo joined the WSPU and the Actresses' Franchise League and ran speakers' classes for a range of suffrage societies.

TUESDAY, JULY 30TH 1912 – GERRARDS CROSS: INNISFAIL

[To Office] I posted a little letter I had written to Boswell – just saying how sorry I was and that I felt I had to say 'I am very sorry that you are not well.' [To Vauxhall] met Miss McGowan at 1.30. I had to get up and begin and had quite an interested crowd of men and got on better than usual for my 10 minutes. Miss McGowan starts for Ireland Thursday so I said good-bye to her.

WEDNESDAY, JULY 31ST 1912 – GERRARDS CROSS: INNISFAIL

The great day arrived at last for shutting up for the holidays. [To Office] we had very busy day.

August was particularly wet, matching Kate's mood. 'I feel most completely miserable about everything – my future – his [John's] future – the future of the family – our prospects seem pretty awful.' [25 August] She did, however, manage to complete the writing of a play – 'Juniper's Way'. She returned to work at the NCS office on 29 August and on the 31st the Fyres moved back to The Plat, horrified by the state in which it had been left by the summer tenants.

THURSDAY, SEPTEMBER 12TH 1912 – BOURNE END: THE PLAT

To Camberwell outside the 'Red Cap' for meeting at 3.30. I took the Chair and spoke very badly and very madly for a few minutes – no-one seemed to come – then Mrs Wallace Atkins spoke – she has applied for post of speaker. She seems a nice woman but is unused to open-air speaking. We got a good crowd in the end and Miss McGowan spoke very well. [On train back home to Bourne End] travelled with a lady who entered into conversation about Votes For Women – she has come to live at Wooburn and ought to join our Society. My badge attracts the ladies but absolutely terrifies the men.

THURSDAY, SEPTEMBER 19TH 1912 – BOURNE END: THE PLAT

[To Office] It was the first Committee – only Mrs Hartley, Mrs Rawles, Alexandra and Miss McGowan but there was a lot to settle, and it was not over till 1.30. I am to have a week's holiday because I don't really feel awfully fit to go to Folkestone Wednesday or Thursday for 2 months. I am so frightened when I think of it.

Kate was to continue with the NCS campaign in Folkestone and Hythe that she had begun the previous autumn. Coolinge Road was a more central Folkestone address than Kate's previous digs with Mrs Hill. Her 60-year-old landlady, Eliza Smith, lived at no. 33 with her husband, George, and various of their nine surviving children.

WEDNESDAY, SEPTEMBER 26TH 1912 – BOURNE END: THE PLAT/ FOLKESTONE: 33 COOLINGE ROAD

[To Folkestone] Travelled Second Class – in comfort & luxury – a carriage to myself – and the train did not stop between London Bridge and Sandling Junction and arrived at 1.47 – so was a beautiful train. I was directed to Coolinge Rd. The first lady's lowest was 18/- and the second at no 33, Mrs Smith, said she would take me for 14/-. I liked the look of her – she seemed homely – though I must say the amount of china ornaments & the photographs in the sitting room are appalling – but I could see the place was clean and I really felt in anything like a street I should not get rooms much under – so I closed with her, feeling she would make me comfortable. I must be proud and glad to be a worker, and after all it is very peaceful to be alone. I am anxious about the work here – I do so hope it will go well.

FRIDAY, SEPTEMBER 27TH 1912 – FOLKESTONE: 33 COOLINGE ROAD
To Mrs Kenny's at 10.30. Had about half an hour with her, then to see Mrs Green, who is the Hon. Sec. for Folkestone. Back by Motor to the Town Hall. Got a Voters List, then in to do some writing. Lunch, changed, to Mrs Kenny's at 2.40 and she took me to the Debating Club at the Grand Hotel. No-one spoke well and it was great footle but I saw some of the Folkestone élite and was introduced to Mrs Kenny's sister, a Mrs Lambert, and went home to tea with her.

The horse tram ran between Sandgate and Hythe. The summer tram, known locally as the 'toast rack', resembled an open sledge pulled by one horse. The premises at 83 High Street rented for the Hythe Suffrage Shop-Club are quite large with, as Kate later described, a room at the rear.

SATURDAY, SEPTEMBER 28TH 1912 – FOLKESTONE: 33 COOLINGE ROAD
[Afternoon] Bus to Sandgate but on a fruitless quest. Then to Hythe by the old horse tram. To 83 High St to the new Suffrage Shop–Club run by Miss Lewis and Miss Cheffins. Miss Cheffins has had some 3 months in prison, with 10 days of forcible feeding, since I saw her. They both look thin and were very violent against the NCS. They are dear people but are always difficult to steer clear of trouble with. However, if we separate Hythe and Folkestone, we may get on – but I feel very low-spirited about the work.

TUESDAY, OCTOBER 1ST 1912 – FOLKESTONE: 33 COOLINGE ROAD
Out by 10.30 and started my calls. No good result but I have made a beginning. I am afraid Folkestone will be a very hard nut.

Bay House, previously known as Spade House, had been built by C.F.A. Voysey in 1901 for H.G. Wells, who lived there until 1909.

WEDNESDAY, OCTOBER 2ND 1912 – FOLKESTONE: 33 COOLINGE ROAD
A wet morning but I had an appointment with a Miss Bishop at Sandgate Hill at 11.30 so had to go out – got the Car and arrived fairly dry, then to a Mrs Burke who lives at Bay House, the house H.G. Wells used to live in – a glorious place. Returned by Car from Sandgate and more calls. No result – this is awful. Did some writing after lunch – changed and tidied – then waited for Miss Bomford from Dover to come at 5.30.

THURSDAY, OCTOBER 3RD 1912 – FOLKESTONE: 33 COOLINGE ROAD
To Hythe for the meeting in the Suffrage Shop at 4 pm. Went by Car. Not many people

there. Miss Lewis took the Chair. Mrs Green spoke very nervously and I said a few words. Miss Lewis says I am to be speaker at the next, but it will be awful. Got off the Car in Folkestone and paid more calls.

SATURDAY, OCTOBER 5TH 1912 – FOLKESTONE: 33 COOLINGE ROAD

In my morning of calls, I only found two people at home. At 12.30 I gave it up. I did feel depressed. More so when, having met Mrs Kenny at the Grand Hotel at 3.30, where she was attending a wedding reception of a Miss Cooper, and whose good-byes I just came in for, Mrs Kenny and I called together upon the manager's wife, Madame Gelardi, and to my horror I found that her husband would not contemplate for a moment letting us have a Suffrage At Home in the reception room. Well that does put the lid on things.The time is slipping away here – the days fly, I love the place and am very comfortable in my rooms but I cannot seem to work here and I feel utterly miserable about it.

MONDAY, OCTOBER 7TH 1912 – FOLKESTONE: 33 COOLINGE ROAD

To Dover 2.41 and by train to Miss Bomford to discuss matters. Then she took me to a Miss Falloon to tea and afterwards we had a committee meeting there to arrange the formation of the Dover Branch of the NCS. I was very nervous in the Chair, but it all went off well.

WEDNESDAY, OCTOBER 9TH 1912 – FOLKESTONE: 33 COOLINGE ROAD

Out calling and seeing Halls etc. At 4 o'clock to Mrs Green's by invitation to tea to meet her daughter – but she did not arrive in till past 5. She had an Anti friend with her so I led up very gradually to Suffrage. I think I did her good. The girl took me up in her bed-room to show me dresses etc. I suppose it is what that type of girl does, but it was most astonishing. She seems a nice girl and unusual, but I can't quite make out if she is genuine.

Miss Bomford, a daughter of Sir Gerald Bomford, retired surgeon Indian Medical Service. She was probably Lorna (1883–1962) who in 1919 became the first woman councillor in Dover. Hillesdon House, Godwyne Road, Dover.

Either Kathleen or Hilda Falloon, teachers, who lived with their parents at Christ Church Vicarage, Effingham Crescent, Dover.

THURSDAY, OCTOBER 10TH 1912 – FOLKESTONE: 33 COOLINGE ROAD

To Dover. Walked up in the town to get a directory then to Mrs Wilson's at Eastcliffe who, after much delay, took me out calling. In the morning we only saw one member and not many in the afternoon. Mrs Wilson is a charming woman and has a delightful house. Mrs Wilson left me with a Miss Clarkson and after a talk to her I left and got to the station to find no train for an hour, but I got permission to travel on the workman's train to the Junction at 5.30. It was a pack. It stopped at the Quarry stations for the miners and navvies. They were very good but it wasn't all joy. They did eye me but I looked blandly at them as if I were a daily traveller that way.

Susan Wilson (1860–1933) a widow. 5 East Cliff, Dover

MONDAY, OCTOBER 14TH 1912 – FOLKESTONE: 33 COOLINGE ROAD

To Dover 11.9. A very hard day. Paid some calls but it was a beautiful morning and the people were mostly out. To Mrs Clarkson's at 1 o'clock where I lunched, then afterwards to Mrs Rolleston's. Miss Clarkson called for me and we went to pay a call in Eastcliffe. Two really horribly Anti ladies nearly froze my blood. It was unhappy. Then

Alice Rolleston (c1855–1917). Her husband was 'guardian of a mental case', who boarded in their house. 11 Waterloo Crescent, Dover.

back to Mrs Clarkson's, where a member called on me, then to tea with another a long tram ride off. Afterwards Miss Clarkson left me and I went to see Miss Bomford, who seems to get dreadfully worried by it all.

Tuesday, October 15th 1912 – Folkestone: 33 Coolinge Road
Out early and up to Wear Bay Crescent where I called upon the Rev. N. E. Goddard and got him to promise to take the Chair on the 4th but he won't have his name on the Bills. Coward!!! It really was a funny interview. I laughed to myself for hours afterwards. I hope he won't back out at the last moment, but something weird is sure to happen. Then I went to the Printers, came in and wrote letters. Then a bus to Cheriton. Paid calls. To Mrs Hill's to lunch – out again at 2.30 more calls up that way, but I was so tired I gave it up about 4 o'clock and came back.

Wednesday, October 16th 1912 – Folkestone: 33 Coolinge Road
Started off about 3 o'clock [to Hythe Suffrage Shop] and Mrs Green got into my Motor at the Metropole Corner. She was more nervous than I was though she was only taking the Chair. She is very keen to but I don't think she will ever make a speaker, anyhow she would have to go through the mill. Oh dear, I thought tea would never be over. I handed it about and chatted but the pit of my stomach felt awful. At last Mrs Green – and then my turn. Well somehow I kept on for a half an hour and 10 minutes. I didn't really feel nervous badly once I was going, another most astounding thing was I sounded so cheerful even to myself. The result of early training I suppose and going through so many things that one has hated with a smiling face. And I didn't dry up, and I didn't look much at my notes, but they helped me just to get on again once or twice on a fresh tack. I did not get badly hung up for words though naturally I did not express myself as I should have liked. I began telling them amusing anecdotes about first speeches – started my speech proper on the Political Situation and then drifted here and there, it wasn't a neat well-constructed speech and Mrs Green told me afterwards I was too hard on the men, which was a pity as there was one poor wretched man present. Oh dear, I don't ever want to do it again and was thankful when it was over.

Rev. Nigel E. Goddard (1870–1950) C.of E. clergyman. 35 Wear Bay Crescent, Folkestone.

Above: Mrs Wilson's house – 5 East Cliff, Dover – photographed by John Collins on 25 May 1913. Kate stayed here for several weeks in December 1912.

Kate's mention of 'this split' refers to the announcement Mrs Pankhurst had made on 17 October at an Albert Hall meeting that the Pethick-Lawrences were no longer involved with the WSPU. The Pethick-Lawrences' departure had been unilateral.

TUESDAY, OCTOBER 22ND 1912 – FOLKESTONE: 33 COOLINGE ROAD
As for the work I am doing here I am clean off it – I am doing nothing towards 'Votes for Women' – what do the people of Folkestone care and what is the good of trying to make them care? Propaganda may have had its uses in the past, it may still please some people, but I don't want to go on talking about the Vote – I want to get it! And I am wondering more than ever what is the way to get it. This split, if split it is between the Pankhursts and Pethick-Lawrences is depressing, but I am not at all sure there it not more in it than meets the eye. Anyway here one feels so out of things – the Vote seems a very tiny speck in an ocean of talk and twaddle. Back to tea and to write letters, then at 8 o'clock I tidied myself and went off to call on Lady Irving by appointment at 8.30. I was interested and so much enjoyed the interview, and she joined us as a member. I had been told of her powdered face, how, like the cat, she always walked alone, that all Folkestone hates her. I liked her immensely, she seems the only real person I have met, the only understanding person. I am told her temper is abnormal, that may be, she was sweet to me, and, after all, these sweet-tempered creatures can be temper trying enough for anything. That she and Henry Irving could not get on together I can quite understand. 'No surrender' is writ large in her composition – and after all why should the woman always give way. I imagine she had very strong views as to what was fitting for a wife and probably he did not live up to these. I did not stay long but we got a lot in the time and I think she liked me. How wonderfully young she is. Suffrage to her finger tips, and Suffrage before it was passably comfortable to be Suffrage.

WEDNESDAY, OCTOBER 23RD 1912 – FOLKESTONE: 33 COOLINGE ROAD
[To Mrs Kenny's] We talked of the arrangements and then somehow our talk got round to Hugh Chapman – as it does so very often. I don't understand what made him say what he did at Dereham or go on in that way, and I do not think it was right. I cannot excuse him unless it was 'real' and why should it have been – and he must know (from years of experience) what a remarkably fascinating man he is. Surely if a woman can give up flirting for the sake of Suffrage, as he tells a tale, he can. Agnes says he is rather repulsive to her, and I always feel he ought to be so to me – but he isn't. I am fascinated instead, but though I have always felt him as something 'corrupt' underneath his peculiar mask of goodness it came as a great shock when Mrs Kenny told me how someone speaking of him said what a 'rake' he used to be, meaning immoral. Mrs Kenny excused him, saying he had repented etc and that from his passionate nature his temptations must have been tremendous. To Dover at 12.9. No time to pay calls, so feeling in an unearthly mood I just walked to Waterloo Crescent – left my parcel of Literature – back to the station to meet Miss Forsyth at 1.15 – who arrived palpitating with nerves. In a fly to Mrs Wilson's where Miss Forsyth was to stay and we both lunched – also Mrs Harvey the new member. [Then] arranged Agendas with Mrs Rolleston who took the Chair and got my literature out, and people began arriving soon after 3 for the meeting at 3.30. Miss Forsyth spoke very well, everyone was very pleased with her and Mrs

Lady Irving, widow of the actor, Sir Henry Irving. She had separated from Sir Henry long before his death and now, aged 68, lived at 6 Bouverie Court, Bouverie Place, Folkestone.

Rolleston trotted down the room for me to come and say a few words – so in a great state of excitement I did my best. I heard people laughing so I suppose I was funny and then I thanked Mr and Mrs Rolleston as well as I could and that sounded alright, so I was a great success, Miss Forsyth said afterwards. I know who has made her [Miss Forsyth] come out as a speaker – the Rev. Hugh – I always knew it, and she said that his words that one of the things we should most regret hereafter would be our lost opportunities. What an extraordinary influence that man has over people. I wish he could influence me to speak as well as Miss Forsyth but that is where the difference in me comes in – I can or I can't and no one can help. Even he with the mysterious fascination he has for me cannot make me different – the chances are that I should influence him more than he could me – I feel so much the stronger personality of the two – strange as that may sound. When I meet the being who can influence me – a stronger personality than myself – one who I feel I am learning from instead of teaching – then in that day shall I triumph indeed. Well, we made 3 members, had a nice tea and lots of talk. They are dear kind people and I quite love them.

THURSDAY, OCTOBER 24TH 1912 – FOLKESTONE: 33 COOLINGE ROAD

I was seized with a panic that no one would come to the meeting so instead of going on with the Dover Rd canvass I wrote letters round to a great many people who had been invited and went out at 11.30 to 1 paying calls and trying to get people to go with no result. I went by Motor and arrived soon after 3.30 to Mrs Hill's. All was in readiness, and at 4 o'clock Mrs Kenny, Mrs Green and Miss Forsyth arrived and we had a very nice tea. At 4.30 for the meeting 3 people, no more and that was the meeting, it was crushing. I felt so sorry for Mrs Hill. Miss Forsyth was very nice about it and gave us a most excellent speech and I got up and 'spoke' better than yesterday, and again made the people laugh.

FRIDAY, OCTOBER 25TH 1912 – FOLKESTONE: 33 COOLINGE ROAD

Out canvassing the High St for the Public meeting [to be held on 4 November]. To Mrs Kenny's at 3.30. There was nothing for me to do – but arranged the Literature. We only made one member, and it was rotten. I loathed it. I loathed Mrs Kenny's fine friends. I want to shock them. I believe the atmosphere of that house gets on my nerves – there isn't any air. Lady Irving was the only one I like of them all. Before people left they were given more food – they only come for the good things they get, they haven't the brains to take in Suffrage, and as she thinks her set is the only one and is afraid to ask any outside people to her house, we are never likely to thrive. I am clean off this campaign. Then home to my pic-nic existence with a mood on me one could have cut off in chunks. I suppose it's a mixture of fatigue and homesickness and disappointment. If the work would only go well I would not mind and it would help me put up with my lot. Why must I live in horrid rooms amongst other people's hideous possessions. What am I paying for, shall I ever have done paying – if only something would come out of it, if only I could justify my existence somehow!!!!

SUNDAY, OCTOBER 27TH 1912 – FOLKESTONE: 33 COOLINGE ROAD

Bus to Hythe, and went to Napier Gardens to enquire for Miss Lewis who is ill. Miss Cheffins was just going to have tea so made me have some. I hardly meant to go in, thinking she was so hard worked over Miss Lewis but evidently there has been a lot of 'Jar'. Of course the only way was to pretend not to see it. I don't know whether I have offended Miss Cheffins, whether she is upset about Miss Lewis being so ill and so unmanageable, or whether it is 3 months of Prison & Suffrage, but there is something unmistakably crazy. She is quite spoilt. She made me miserable. I longed to get away. It was the same the time I went over to see them at the shop when I first came. They both have bitter tongues, but I really cannot compete. I am very sorry and I like Miss Cheffins, and I don't understand what it is, but, as I say, I was miserable with her and she looked fearfully unhappy herself. I did not stay long because honestly I felt I ought not, the servant was out and I thought Miss Lewis must want her but she might well think she had driven me away. Oh dear – I don't think I am very happy just now. An organiser ought to be without feeling, but unfortunately in me they have picked one whose feelings can be intense, who is so like quicksilver to atmosphere and who cannot do good work unless she gets a lot of encouragement.

FRIDAY, NOVEMBER 1ST 1912 – FOLKESTONE: 33 COOLINGE ROAD

Came in to lunch to find a letter from Alexandra asking me to go to Rye and Ashford to speak. Mrs Pertwee was going but she has lost her husband so there is no-one to actually represent the Society. Mr Clayton and Mr Cameron Grant are the speakers. Oh what a moment. I feel I can't and yet I suppose I must. I have been nerving myself to do it here on Monday but am feeling awful about it.

The meeting that Kate organised was held in the Edward Husband Memorial Hall, Dover Road, Folkestone. In her official report Kate estimated that there was an audience of 200.

MONDAY, NOVEMBER 4TH 1912 – FOLKESTONE: 33 COOLINGE ROAD

Wake with heaviness and fright upon me – such a day – so much to do. To get Literature ready, which I took to the hall. Then Bill distributing till 1.30 – writing all the afternoon getting Agenda etc, tidied myself. To station at 6 as I had heard, after having had to telegraph, that the Rev. C. Llewellyn Smith would come at 6. Mrs Kenny was at the station but he did not turn up – we waited for the 6.47 by which he arrived. I saw him safely off with Mrs Kenny, then walked to the hall and had to see to getting it ready as there had been a meeting until 7. Then the Stewards arrived – Miss Cheffins, Miss Lewis, Mr and Mrs Green, Mrs Hill, Miss Gore and Miss Barker. The audience came early. Oh! Blessed sight – but in the end the hall was only full. With 3000 Hand Bills it ought to have been over flowing. Oh! the work of it. Mr Goddard was niceness itself about the Chair, came out as a strong supporter, and Mr Llewellyn Smith pleased by his speech – it was very clever but he is too National Union now-a-days, but a nice little man. Then came my turn. Oh ye Gods – I had refused to sit on the Platform but bounced up and got underway alright. Did not say much but the result was 35/- in the Collection, which was a record. I did not feel nervous once I started, but the game isn't worth the

John Cameron Grant, an engineer, was in 1909 responsible for erecting the sign for the new Kensington WSPU shop. He spoke at WFL meetings and *The Vote* reported, 19 March 1910, 'he had for many years been a strong believer in the economic and political equality of the sexes'. Albert Lodge, Albert Place, Kensington.

candle – makes me ill with anticipation. The resolution was carried with the exception of one hand against. £1 taken in tickets – quite good – 3/3 in Literature. The collection I handed straight over to Mrs Hill to count and send up.

It was decided by the Folkestone NCS committee that Kate should, from the following week, concentrate her campaigning on Dover.

WEDNESDAY, NOVEMBER 6TH 1912 – FOLKESTONE: 33 COOLINGE ROAD

To Dover at 11 o'clock. Started room-hunting. Had found nothing at 1 o'clock when I went to lunch at Mrs Clarkson's, who has very kindly asked to to stay there, but I refused, went on hunting from 2.30 and only at 4.30 found a place I could bear to contemplate at my price. I was dead tired so took a tram to the station and waited till the 5.30 workman's train to the Junction and walked from there.

The meeting was held in the former Austin Friars monastery on Conduit Hill, in Rye.

THURSDAY, NOVEMBER 7TH 1912 – FOLKESTONE: 33 COOLINGE ROAD/RYE: 6 HIGH STREET

By the 5 o'clock train to Ashford, where I changed for the 6 o'clock train to Rye. Looked out for Mr Clayton and travelled with him, he is a dear and we had a most interesting talk. Mrs Lambert, his hostess, met him and took him off in a fly. Miss White met me and took me up to Mrs Clements who kindly put me up. Miss White and I had tea together, then I went up to my room to unpack and change into my new Mole Coloured Velveteen. It is very pretty – looks alright, I am glad to say – then Mrs Clements and I walked to the Monastery where the meeting was held – there I saw Miss Clark and Miss Spalding and several people I knew. But it was very badly filled – a poor meeting – I should have been miserable had it been mine. Miss White doesn't understand the amount of work a hall meeting means, I think – of course she is very inexperienced. It was a most cold audience and Mr Clayton shocked them and they began streaming out. Really I did not think what he said was new, it was like the Rev. Hugh – only not his personality or idealism – and some of it was a pity – he did not describe what the White Slave Traffic is but just got on the 'all men are beasts' track. The Mayor, Mr Adams, the printer, was in the Chair. Oh dear, when my moment came I did not stutter or hesitate but I felt I was going so slowly, I did not please myself but the people seemed to like it. I thought I ought to have gone on longer. I did not speak for more than 5 minutes, I am sure, and I ought to have found more to say but it was an impossible audience – Mr Clayton was nearly in tears over it, and I felt miserable. It was over very early, no questions and no trimmings of any kind. I went back with Miss Edith Clements, who had come in late from London and waited for me. She has become a most fine person – the development is wonderful – the homely one, Kitty, was at home when we got there. I took my things off and we had supper.

Ashford's Newtown Road Drill Hall, echoing this evening to Kate's 'clear, cold voice', was demolished in 1996 to make way for the International Rail Terminal.

FRIDAY, NOVEMBER 8TH 1912 – RYE: 6 HIGH STREET/FOLKESTONE: 33 COOLINGE ROAD

Breakfast at 8.30. Miss Spalding came in before we had finished. She said I quite took off the bad effect caused by Mr Clayton and she congratulated me on my speaking. I told her not to mind people going out – it sometimes rouses so much comment that good comes of it. I packed my box – then got to some writing and had a long talk with the fashionable Clements, who put up at the Three Arts Club when in London. I hurried off to catch the 12.50 train to Ashford. Miss White was in it from Winchelsea. Mr Clayton had come over and hindered her – she had come off anyhow and forgotten the handbills. I felt sure the Ashford meeting was doomed to failure, but it seemed cruel to keep rubbing it in where she was at fault – of course 7 pm is an idiotic hour – neither one thing or the other. Only a few handbills had been given away – no posters – no systematic canvassing. We took our things to the Fernley – ordered tea – left our bags – then went out canvassing and kept at it till I own I was nearly dead and at 4 o'clock refused to go on – it was too much work without handbills and I felt we were doing no good. So we went to the Fernley – sat down in heaps, and waited for Mrs Darent Harrison and then had a meal. We were all inclined to be quarrelsome. Mrs Darent Harrison was painfully nervous about speaking and I could see had no trust in me and wouldn't let me have a thing to do. It was very funny really – so unlike me – I felt I was full of fire – the truth was I was so tired I didn't know what I was doing. Mr Cameron Grant arrived at 6 o'clock and we left him to have tea. Then Miss White and I to the Drill Hall – not a soul turned up until 7 – and then only about 30 or 40 people drifted in. It was too terrible – however I never felt so nervous in my life of facing an audience. As I sat on the Platform during Mr Grant's wonderful speech my heart was thumping as if it would choke me and my nerves were shivering up and down my body. He spoke intensely upon the White Slave Traffic – wonderful and awful. I could see the horror on the faces of the audience. I was immensely impressed by him he was so absolutely solid – no fireworks no sensational effects – all incontrovertible facts. I nearly died when my moment came but I heard my clear, cold voice ringing out. 'Madam Chairman, Ladies and Gentlemen. There is one sentence above every other which stands out to me in that wonderful and impressive address we have been listening to here to-night, and that sentence is "Pray that she died soon" – and it is because we women Suffragists refuse any longer to have to say that of one of our sisters, if we can possibly help one, that I am here tonight. I am not speaking of what I do not know' etc etc and so on for about 10 minutes. It was not altogether what I could have wished – I wanted to be absolutely convincing on Suffrage but I think it is the best I have done, and I heard dramatic effects in my voice and it went down. But it isn't worth it to me – I have never felt so dreadful before over anything. There is nothing to take it off while one is on a Platform just waiting. I came on to catch the 9 o'clock [back to Folkestone] but Mrs Harrison and Miss White appeared before I left – they were getting the 9.15. Mrs Harrison has asked if I will go and speak at Hastings. She said she liked my calm, cool way of speaking and that I took up the point very well and that no one could have guessed I was nervous.

SUNDAY, NOVEMBER 10TH 1912 – FOLKESTONE: 33 COOLINGE ROAD

I am making plans for a weekend next week but have just heard there is a possibility of a bye-election at Tower Hamlets – if so I shall be wanted. I shan't mind provided I feel well, but now I do feel rotten.

MONDAY, NOVEMBER 11TH 1912 – FOLKESTONE: 33 COOLINGE ROAD/DOVER: 16 NORMAN STREET

Finished my packing before 11 then had to go out to do a round paying bills and leaving parcels etc. [To Dover] Got a man to bring my things up to 16 Norman St (Mrs Hulks) and I came up by tram. The luggage was not long coming – then I had lunch. The rooms are really very nice. Drawing-room floor – and the sitting room is much larger than Folkestone. After lunch I unpacked – had to dust and repaper drawers but I have seen worse. Mrs Clarkson had called and asked me to tea but I went round to see Miss Falloon at 4.30 so could not go.

With encouragement from Emmeline and Christabel Pankhurst, George Lansbury had resigned his seat at Bromley and Bow in order to stand as an Independent Labour candidate, making his main platform the suffrage issue.

WEDNESDAY, NOVEMBER 13TH 1912 – DOVER: 16 NORMAN STREET

Bitterly cold again and rain all day long. I had a lot of writing to do and, as I received a parcel of food from Mother, I did not go out. I really am a little bit at a standstill. I dare not make any plans in case I am sent for – it seems now more a question of Bow & Bromley than Tower Hamlets, but I should certainly love to go up and help Lansbury. It must show we are getting on for a man to give up his party and stand for re-election. I have asked Alexandra to telegraph tomorrow if anything is settled so that I do not go making a lot of arrangements.

THURSDAY, NOVEMBER 14TH 1912 – DOVER: 16 NORMAN STREET

I felt so excited all the morning, wondering whether I should be summoned to London. I did some writing then went out to hunt up the Minute Book. I was just finishing lunch when a Telegram arrived saying I should be wanted for Bow and to await instructions. So, of course, I could not settle much at the Committee. But it is what I have wanted horribly so I suppose I ought to be glad. I got to Mrs Wilson's at 4.30 and we had a beautiful tea – only Mrs Foster, Miss Chambers, Mrs Rolleston and Mrs Wilson. Mrs Harvey was present but, of course, she oughtn't to have been. It was a most inconsequent gathering – no one suggested anything and all agreed with everything I said. We arranged ever so many things but I expect they will all fall through.

Kate's cousin, Maggie Frye, sister of Abbie Hargrave, had led an increasingly erratic life and had by now succumbed to alcoholism.

FRIDAY, NOVEMBER 15TH 1912 – DOVER: 16 NORMAN STREET

I had a lot of letters to answer the last thing. Abbie is trying to interest Mr [Hugh]

Lucy Foster (b. 1885) a widow, became treasurer in 1913 of the Dover branch of the NCS. 19 Guilford Lawn, Dover.

Chapman in Maggie who seems in terrible straights – as far as she knows in Canterbury Jail now. But I don't know. I haven't much faith in him. I may be doing him a wrong but whoever in my life has slipped out of his path to do a good turn for one of us? If Abbie's letters have reached him he is taking no trouble, but as the Secretary of this Normyl Treatment Association has always answered them it is possible they have not reached him. Now I have written to him but I did not like the job.

Saturday, November 16th 1912 – Dover: 16 Norman Street/Bourne End: The Plat

[To London] John was at Victoria to meet me. We had a cab to Paddington and I put my things in the cloak room then telephoned to Alexandra at the Office – and told I was expected to go right on to Bow then and there. That Miss McGowan had got me rooms somewhere and had arranged a meeting for the evening. I was really cross as I had expected a message all yesterday and even this morning but nothing at all after the telegram on Thursday. If I had been told before I would, of course, have cancelled my weekend, but I told Alexandra I could not possibly and that I would go off on Monday and rang off.

Kate went home to Bourne End but then became ill, missing most of the Bow campaign.

Monday, November 25th 1912 – Bourne End: The Plat

I wrote to Boswell – I had been waiting for the right moment as I felt I ought to thank him as he has already taken a lot of trouble and is to see Maggie with Abbie on Thursday. Already there seems like something stirring in Maggie – for Abbie has sent me a letter she received from her consenting to see Mr Chapman and saying if she did not give up drink it would give her up – meaning I suppose be the end of her. [Kate had met a new inspirational clergyman at Bourne End.] He had seen me with Agnes and asked if I was her sister and I said I had been ill and could not come to Church before. 'Oh, you don't look very strong' he said, but when I started talking 'Votes' he was not so pleased. I told him it was my life and I could not keep religion out of my life if it meant anything – therefore Votes and my religion were one, but he was disappointed in me I could see, though he said he should like to have had a long talk to me on the question. I came out to find my umbrella had been taken from the porch – it was raining hard and I had to tear home through the rain. Too bad as, of course, it must have been stolen – after such an address too – enough to made anyone feel 'Edgy'.

The 'Brown Ladies', so-called on account of their brown costume, had been led by Mrs Florence de Fonblanque on a march from Edinburgh to London. En route they collected signatures for a petition in yet another attempt to gain public support for the suffrage cause. They had arrived in London on 16 November, a contingent from the NCS joining them in the final stretch from Camden Town to Trafalgar Square. 26 November was polling day at the Bow by-election.

Tuesday, November 26th 1912 – Bourne End: The Plat

[Letter] from Gladys in answer to one from me saying I would go to Bow, telling me they would be glad of my help – so I got up and went off by the 9.45. I arrived in due course at 167 Roman Road [the Committee Rooms] – going via Liverpool St and Coburn Rd Station. Found Miss McGowan looking very fit and Miss Mansell, who I was delighted to see again, at the Committee Rooms and after a chat I went off to one of Lansbury's Committee Rooms and got some canvassing to do and worked till nearly 3 o'clock. Oh, such a street – such poor folks but all so nice – really wonderful people, not a cross word from any of them for being brought up or downstairs and worried. Went back to Roman Rd and had some lunch, all the Brown Ladies, who have walked from Edinburgh and who shared Mrs Chapman's reception, were there, very jolly folks. I felt awfully tired but better after some bread and cheese and cocoa – most beautifully provided by Miss Mansell, who is a good sort. Then out again on some special visits. Got a ride in somebody's lovely car and wandered back in the rain. Tea at Roman Rd, then out in the teeming rain for an hour – more canvassing and it was so wet at some moments that I had to take shelter. I did not dare go on, so gave up my card when I had done that sheet and went back to Roman Rd and dried my coat before venturing home. [Travelled back to Bourne End] I was tired, and I felt sure Lansbury would not get in. What a chance too for the men of Bow to stand up for Liberty.

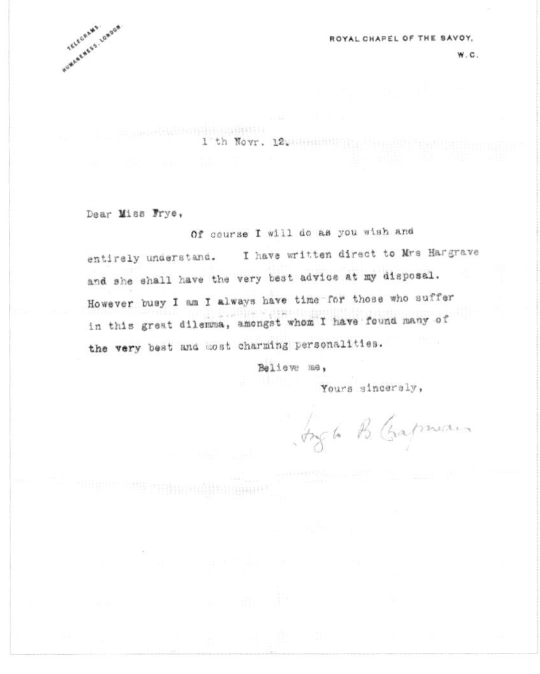

TELEGRAMS. HUMANENESS, LONDON.

ROYAL CHAPEL OF THE SAVOY,
W.C.

1 th Novr. 12.

Dear Miss Frye,

Of course I will do as you wish and entirely understand. I have written direct to Mrs Hargrave and she shall have the very best advice at my disposal. However busy I am I always have time for those who suffer in this great dilemma, amongst whom I have found many of the very best and most charming personalities.

Believe me,

Yours sincerely,

Hugh B. Chapman

WEDNESDAY, NOVEMBER 27TH 1912 – BOURNE END: THE PLAT

Lansbury defeated – well, one knew it must be so, but it is dreadfully saddening. However I suppose it is wonderful he got as many votes as he did – standing for Suffrage alone.

THURSDAY, NOVEMBER 28TH 1912 – BOURNE END: THE PLAT/LONDON: 27 PEMBRIDGE CRESCENT

I went up [to London] by the 3 [o'clock train] I left my heavy luggage at Paddington and went through on the underground to Notting Hill Gate – got an outside porter to carry my box to Pembridge Crescent. Mrs Wright was at home so I sat and chatted to her till Alexandra came in – then we had tea and about 6 o'clock I went upstairs to undo my things and dress. I had a beautiful fire in my room and was made as comfortable as it is possible to be in that atmosphere but, oh, it is an awful one – war, war. The girls had new frocks and looked very festive. I had my new one and felt it was very 'country' – however it did for the Palmist – and I was very keen to be Palmist and nothing else. We had dinner at 7.30. I should think it was as near a festive a meal as possible in that house. I made a tremendous effort and kept the conversation away from dangerous jars. Then

The helpful reply from the Rev. Hugh Chapman in answer to Kate's appeal for help for Maggie Frye.

we went off in a taxi, the three of us, to the dance at Mrs Kerr's, the Boltons, in aid of the NCS funds. The palmistry was a trial to see whether or not it would go and help the funds – so I was very anxious to make myself a success, and really it was less of an effort to me than usual, partly, I think, because I was made so comfortable and had such a beautiful warm cosy corner, just next to the fire in a sort of sitting and light refreshment room. I waited up there and did not go into the dancing rooms and really I had very good time though I worked from soon after 9 to about 2 am. I was a great success – about the best I have ever done and I had a lot of men, which was interesting. Mr and Mrs Chapman were there and he came for his shillingsworth. Mrs Hartley was there. Mrs Graham and several who were not dancing. But I did not move from my corner and had there been 3 of me I could have kept at work all the time. One lady came back for a second sitting. I went downstairs when they would not let me work any more and ate something – I had already been supplied with sandwiches and drink. Then we got a taxi home about 3.

Barbara Kerr (1862–1950). 2 The Boltons, Kensington. Her sister, Miss Raynsford Jackson, also spoke for NCS.

John Cameron Grant's pamphlet was The Heart of Hell: a note upon the White Slave Traffic, *the 3rd edition of which was published by the NCS in 1913.*

FRIDAY, NOVEMBER 29TH 1912 – LONDON: 27 PEMBRIDGE CRESCENT

Gladys went off to the Office. Alexandra and I sat talking. I felt absolutely certain I was not going to Dover, though I had received a sweet letter from Mrs Wilson saying she would put me up for a few nights, and I was not at all surprised when a telephone message came saying I was not to go to Dover but to the Office to help with a special piece of work. So I had lunch and then bustled off, telegraphing to Mrs Wilson on the way. Alexandra came later and there was a whole lot of people at work – a pamphlet of John Cameron Grant to be sent off to the House of Lords for Monday's debate on the Criminal Law Amendment Act. So we worked away till about 6.15 – then the three of us home together as Mrs Wright had kindly consented to put me up again.

SATURDAY, NOVEMBER 30TH 1912 – LONDON: 27 PEMBRIDGE CRESCENT/BOURNE END: THE PLAT

I put up my things, and Gladys very generously carried one of the parcels to the Notting Hill Gate and I put them in the cloak room then we went on to the Office together and I started off on my work again. Lots of people came in to help – Mrs and Miss Forsyth, Mrs Graham – lots of people I did not know – and Mr Grant himself. Alexandra and I had lunch with the Forsyths. I was very interested in meeting her because of a rumour circulated by the Wrights that Mrs Chapman is very anxious that she [Miss Forsyth] and the Rev. Hugh should marry. I have always felt on her part there was something – in fact I knew it from the first moment that I met her after I had met him – just about a year ago, I suppose, but I have never seen him with her. Alexandra says he looked upon her at the reception on Monday very kindly. Well it does not seem suitable to me – but, of course, she is rich. Just imagine her – only my age, 33 – it really doesn't seem possible to me. She is so staid. [Back to Bourne End] There was a most exciting letter from Abbie about Maggie. They got her to see Mr Chapman on

Thursday and she is now in a home. It all sounds very wonderful and he seems to have put himself about tremendously for me – for which Bless him and Abbie said he spoke of me so beautifully and that it was good hearing.

By 'letter box demonstrations' Kate is referring to damage caused by WSPU members. On 26 November they had destroyed thousands of pieces of mail by pouring acid, lampblack, ink and tar into post boxes in London and in provincial cities. In fact Kate's Organiser's book records that three Dover members resigned 'owing to Pillar Box Demonstrations'.

MONDAY, DECEMBER 2ND 1912 – BOURNE END: THE PLAT/DOVER: 5 EAST CLIFF

To Victoria from Praed St after getting my big luggage out of the cloak room and the 12.20 train to Dover. I took a cab up to 5 East Cliff and was shown my room. Mrs Wilson was out so I did some unpacking and then saw her second daughter, who was in, and sat and talked till Mrs Wilson arrived in about 5 o'clock. I went out to see Miss Robinson, whose uncle was going to give a Suffrage party and now won't owing to the letter box demonstrations.

TUESDAY, DECEMBER 3RD 1912 – DOVER: 5 EAST CLIFF

Miss Bomford has resigned the Treasureship so it will be a great task to pull the Society into working order. I went to see Miss Falloon at 12.30 and fixed up a meeting. I went out about 3 – met Miss Rolleston who asked me in to tea so, after some calls, I went back there at 4.30 and had tea.

Kate settled into a routine of making calls and canvassing, interspersed with drawing-room meetings.

TUESDAY, DECEMBER 10TH 1912 – DOVER: 5 EAST CLIFF

From early morning till late at night a pouring wet day – most disagreeable for my trip to Hastings and I felt so tired, and did not enjoy my day. I left at 10.30 and walked to the station for the 11.5 train. Everything was so dripping and I felt so superior that I afforded myself the second-class fare, making 2/- extra, but it was worth it. I travelled alone to Ashford and put my feet up. At Rye the two Miss Clements got in – one went as far as Hastings. I got a train to St Leonards. Found my way to 3 St Pauls Place to a Mrs Fryer Smith and got there soon after 2 o'clock and was given lunch – hot stewed Bunny – a thing I am not passionately attached to. Miss Fryer Smith sat and chatted and asked useless questions. Then I had a little rest while she went and changed. Then I was allowed to wash and tidy and then, over a cup of coffee, I met Mrs Fryer Smith – a nice old lady and some one else who was Anti. Then Mrs and Miss took me to Mrs Darent Harrison, (no 1 St Pauls Place) a few doors off, for the Sale at 4 o'clock. Miss White was there, of course, and I met a relation of Mrs Wilson's, who I was to look out for. The wetness of the day prevented the sale being the success it would have been. I only had 10 [palmistry] clients and my expenses were 9/- so I felt miserable. But that wasn't my fault as I did all there were. I wasn't the success I was at the dance but I did not like my room and my feet were cold. I had some tea afterwards and then I left with Miss White

Louisa Fryer Smith, a 72-year-old widow, who lived with her 42-year-old daughter, Constance.

and we got a train into Hastings – it was still pouring – and then had to wait some time and come on together, she getting out at Winchelsea and I came on to Ashford, where I had another hour to wait and there caught a quick train to Dover.

WEDNESDAY, DECEMBER 16TH 1912 – DOVER: 5 EAST CLIFF

To the station to meet the 5.26 train and Miss Sheppard. I found her very nice. Took her up in a tram to Miss Chambers who was putting her up – sat while she had tea. Then walked back to East Cliff. I had been very nervous of the meeting – and for the number of invitations sent out it was disappointing, but we got a room full and it was a nice audience. Miss Falloon took the Chair and spoke well, Miss Sheppard was very nice and I said a few words at the end about the Society and we had a collection. Lots of people who ought to have been were not there, and it does seem as if the Dover members are loath to take any responsibility.

WEDNESDAY, DECEMBER 18TH 1912 – DOVER: 5 EAST CLIFF

I went out until 7 o'clock. Then in to change – into my still elegant but somewhat old black velveteen dress. Looking at me she [Cissy, Mrs Wilson's daughter] said what a beautiful figure I could have. Why not say 'I have one' said I, and explained that I would rather be beautiful unclothed for my own pleasure than have a strapped-in figure to suit the fashion. I think I have given her many new thoughts if she is able to accommodate them.

FRIDAY, DECEMBER 20TH 1912 – DOVER: 5 EAST CLIFF

After lunch went out to seek a Chairman for the 27th. The Vicar was out, so I met Miss Burkitt who took me home and gave me tea. I met her sister. Then to Mr Elnor who I found nice but who refused to take the Chair. Coward – and I did my very best.

On 21 December Kate left Dover for Bourne End and a holiday, returning to work on 7 January.

TUESDAY, JANUARY 7TH 1913 – BOURNE END: THE PLAT/LONDON: 27 PEMBRIDGE CRESCENT

[To London] John met me at Paddington. I took my bag to Pembridge Crescent by train after sending my trunks by GWR cart. Saw Alexandra and her father, who seems to be at home and staying at home. I was somewhat startled but I suppose it is alright. I had understood, as Mrs Wright was away, that they would be alone. To the Office. I went off by bus to the Strand and on to Victoria St to different societies' offices for names of people.

Mina Sheppard (1847–1927) daughter of a wealthy Quaker corn factor. She had been a speaker for the WSPU earlier in 1912 and Kate was to meet her again in a couple of months' time.

THURSDAY, JANUARY 9TH 1913 – LONDON. 27 PEMBRIDGE CRESCENT

My birthday 35. The first Birthday I have ever spent away from home. Pembridge Crescent is not the spot for a jovial Birthday. I went off to the Office. The day was a horrible nightmare. I am certainly not suited for Office work on a Committee day and felt all at sea. However I did what I could and hoped for the best. Mrs Chapman was there and not looking well, I thought. [For a birthday treat she went with John to the theatre]

I felt really too tired and heavy with the air I had come from to enjoy it as I otherwise should. Then John saw me all the way home and I was glad he was there to battle with the latch key. We crept in all in darkness so he waited while I lit up – undid my dress at the back for me and then departed.

Returning to the NCS campaign in Dover, Kate was now to lodge with the Misses Burkitt.

SATURDAY, JANUARY 11TH 1913 – LONDON: 27 PEMBRIDGE CRESCENT/DOVER: 26 RANDOLPH GARDENS

[To Dover] I simply cannot bear these journeys and arrival in places. And such a pouring wet night and such a filthy station. Found my way to 26 Randolph Gardens – arrived about 10.30. Found the rooms I was to have had have been taken by a man, so I shall have no sitting room to myself and, as I was shown to a basement sitting-room, I suppose that will be the living room. I only saw one Miss Burkitt – the thin one, and I sat and ate biscuits and drank water – then upstairs to my room with a spare can of cool water to unpack, wash and go to bed. Everything felt wringing wet – so at last in agony and desperation I plucked off the sheets and slept in the blankets.

SUNDAY, JANUARY 12TH 1913 – DOVER: 26 RANDOLPH GARDENS

Woke up feeling very cold and miserable to have my breakfast brought up to me by Miss Burkitt. Bacon & sausage brimming in liquid and slices of bread and butter. Oh dear. However I managed what I could and then demanded water. A small jug arrived first and then after expostulation a small leaking can. Afterwards we came to the arrangement that for 2d per morning I could have a hot bath as the water is heated in a gas boiler and expensive. I jumped at the offer though the bath does not look fearfully tempting.

MONDAY, JANUARY 13TH 1913 – DOVER: 26 RANDOLPH GARDENS

To see Mr Jones about the printing and hunt up the Mayor. He was not at his works so I had to go again at 2.30. He refused to take the Chair, but I gave him 24 hours to think it over – I can see it is going to be difficult. Calls and jobs and writing all day long. I am very anxious for the success of the 27th. Everyone seems to think we shall not have a big meeting. These ladies do everything they can to make me comfortable and are most kind and a cheering hot bath in the morning certainly put me in a happier frame of mind. I don't see how people can be cheerful if they do not get opportunity of having enough hot water.

The Misses Burkitt – Emma Marie (1856–1941) and Minnie (Mary Ann b c 1859) were WSPU members, living at 26 Randolph Gardens, Dover. Kate was to get to know them well – and to remain friendly well into the 1920s. On several occasions Kate was to meet their niece, Hilda, a WSPU activist.

TUESDAY, JANUARY 14TH 1913 – DOVER: 26 RANDOLPH GARDENS

Out at 10.30 to see the Mayor, one Mr William Bramley, at the Town Hall. No good – would not take the Chair. Then started to hunt up a Mr Edward Chitty – he was not in so I did some canvassing and went back to his office. A very bigoted and irate Liberal. Wanted all particulars of the Society, which I sent him and gave him until the morning to let me know. Had a great many packages to do up as the printing has now come – and had to take the parcels round.

WEDNESDAY, JANUARY 15TH 1912 – DOVER: 26 RANDOLPH GARDENS
Note from Mr Chitty refusing the Chair. Wrote most of the morning, then out and did some canvassing. Left the question of the Chair for an inspiration.

THURSDAY, JANUARY 16TH 1913 – DOVER: 26 RANDOLPH GARDENS
Called upon Sir Montague Bradley the man who contested Dover in the Liberal interest – an astute interesting man – real Politician type – I should say he will get in and prosper in the House one day in the recognised manner. He refused the Chair. Out 3 to 4.30 again canvassing. In to tea as the Miss Burkitts had asked Mr and Mrs Ginever to tea to meet me. He is the Unitarian minister here and she my last hope as Chairman. A clever woman who lectures on many subjects – Hungarian by birth and and a nice little woman. I managed it very well – no mention of Chair for a long while, though we talked nothing else but Suffrage. Mr Ginever would have it – though he was most irate and furious about it. The typical Liberal – furious that we should have found the Liberals out etc. But, as I knew he managed all in the home, I went for him and really put my back into it – talk about Magnetism and when I mentioned the subject I knew I had won. She refused outright at the start but, again, I gave the night to think it over and felt sure he would order the doing of it or do it himself.

FRIDAY, JANUARY 17TH 1913 – DOVER: 26 RANDOLPH GARDENS
A note from Mrs Ginever in the morning saying she would take the Chair. Hurrah!!! At last – but what a waste of time it has all been. I wrote her as graceful a note of thanks as I could. A good lot of writing then out canvassing morning, afternoon and evening. Miss Burkitt's great friend came in the afternoon and I waited in until she had gone. They seem to like to show me off to their friends.

Charles (1871–1946) and Ilona Ginever (1869–1926) authors of several works on Hungarian language and history. St Ladislas, Castle Avenue, Dover.

SUNDAY, JANUARY 19TH 1913 – DOVER: 26 RANDOLPH GARDENS
After tea I went in to Mrs Capell – no 6 Randolph Gardens by request to talk Suffrage to two maidens there. They, Miss Janet Capell and the son, Wilfrid, went off to Chapel and I stayed on to talk to Mrs Capell, who, I hear, 'likes me so very much'. Then at 8 Miss Burkitt and I went off to hear Mrs Despard on 'theosophy'. A very interesting lecture but only the very first steps in theosophy. Nothing I did not know – or do I seem to know it all without being told? I spoke to Mrs Despard afterwards and did a little talking to others about the meeting. It is drawing near now and I felt anxious to do my best but quite sure really we are going to have a good meeting.

Clarissa Capell (1849–1929) widow, teacher of music, living with her daughter, Janet, a professional musician, and two sons.

Charlotte Despard (1844–1939) devotée of theosophy and leader of the Women's Freedom League, founded in 1907 as a breakaway group from the WSPU. Kate had heard her speaking in March 1909 at a meeting of the AFL and deemed her a little too emotional for her taste.

FRIDAY, JANUARY 24TH 1913 – DOVER: 26 RANDOLPH GARDENS
Breakfast in bed as the downstairs room was being spring cleaned. The house has got a lot cleaner since I came. It appears that they were so poorly off that they had to get rid of their servant for 3 months and she only came back the day of my arrival and so the house had got very dirty, but it has certainly improved.

SATURDAY, JANUARY 25TH 1913 – DOVER: 26 RANDOLPH GARDENS
Called upon the Ginevers by request. He has been ill and was in an awful mood – it

made me cross. I should think he is a 'difficult' gentleman. Out 3 to 8. Did the second half of the Folkestone Road. Had tea in the Café as I was really too late to come in and so very hungry. More work – then giving out of bills outside the Town Hall.

The government-sponsored Franchise and Registration Bill had passed its second reading in the House of Commons in July 1912. Although, as originally drafted, it had not included any mention of women, amendments had been formulated to include a measure of women's suffrage. Between July 1912 and January 1913 the NUWSS and other societies, such as the NCS, had been concentrating their campaign on raising public awareness on this possibility of achieving constitutional change. The WSPU's militant actions had been seen by the constitutional societies as likely only to prejudice their case. However, on 27 January the Speaker pre-empted any vote that might have been taken on the bill by ruling that the amendments so changed the measure that it would have to be withdrawn and re-introduced in another form. As a sop to the suffragists Asquith promised to give facilities for a private member's suffrage bill in the next session. But, from bitter experience, everyone knew that without government backing such a bill was unlikely to be successful.

MONDAY, JANUARY 27TH 1913 – DOVER: 26 RANDOLPH GARDENS

Great day of meeting arrived at last. I did not feel very grand – then I never do when I have responsibility – but I had not a moment to sit still and think from the time I was up. To Town Hall and Miss Burkitt went with me and we fixed that all up. Mr and Mrs Jones followed us to bring news that the Government Franchise Reform Bill has been withdrawn – the Speaker ruling it out of order to have the amendments. They came, both being in black as if to tell me of the death of a dear departed friend – and were astounded, I think, by my jubilation. I think as it is impossible that any one of the amendments should pass, that it is so very much better for us to have forced the Government to withdraw the bill. We start as it were with a clean slate – and Asquith is the one who will look sold – we have all along expected something of the kind – and I believe now they can never again introduce a reform bill without adding some women at least. Flew off to meet Mrs Pertwee at 5.26 and took her to Miss Chambers in a Taxi. Only just had time to see her in and introduce her and then flew off the the Town station to meet Mr Cameron Grant at 6.13 and take him to Mr and Miss Ritchie's. They have been most awfully kind and helpful about it all – and I left him very happy. His train was late so I had a great rush to get back to Randolph Gardens and then to the hall at 7.30. Most of the stewards were there before me and, oh dear, the fuss to get the work planned out by 7.45. We were short of stewards and only or or two were any good. However we managed somehow and Mr Ginever took charge of the Literature stall. Mrs Ginever and Mrs Pertwee were there at 8 and I introduced them – then began getting frantic about Mr Cameron Grant – he did not arrive until 8.15 so I had to hurry him on to the Platform as I did not want the meeting late. The hall, to my great relief, was fairly well filled – lots of seats to spare but, still, by no means empty and everyone was surprised and delighted. I was thankful when it was over. I packed up the takings and kept my eye everywhere until the collection. Mrs Ginever forgot to give it out so I had to trot up on the platform and remind her – it would have been fatal to me if it had been forgotten and then the stewards took it and handed it over to me – as I went out I heard a sort of murmur of applause. I am certainly popular in Dover – if nowhere else. Everyone seemed delighted with Mr Cameron Grant. I did not think Mrs Pertwee spoke very well. I saw everyone off – packed up the Literature and walked home with Miss Burkitt, Mrs Buckland, and Miss Clements as far as our roads went together. Miss Min [Burkitt] had stopped to cook kidneys for Mr Sapp and Ivan Phillipowski [the other lodgers] and then hurried away again back to them. It made me a little cross.

TUESDAY, JANUARY 28TH 1913 – DOVER: 26 RANDOLPH GARDENS

To the Harbour station to see Mrs Pertwee off on the 10.50. Oh I did feel homesick and Londonsick to see her go – and I want to be up and in the thick of all the excitement and enthusiasm of Votes for Women. Protest meetings and demonstrations everywhere. Mrs Chapman having a meeting at her house tonight. Then I went about paying bills and calling in money. Davisons very kindly refused to take any commission for tickets sold and they sold a good many – so that was very sweet of them.

WEDNESDAY, JANUARY 29TH 1913 – DOVER: 26 RANDOLPH GARDENS

The window smashing and pillar boxes have started again after a truce of a few weeks. Oh dear, the Militants are having a time of it. [To Folkestone] I found little fat Mrs Kenny bustling about as usual – a Colonel Curtis was there – Mrs Flora Annie Steele and her husband came to lunch and Mr Llewlleyn Smith arrived while we were eating. I got up as soon as I could and the little French governess and I, failing to get a Taxi, had to walk to the Town Hall – of course I arrived very late – too late to do any good really and that rather worried me – and the stewarding etc was not well arranged. Mrs Green had forgotten membership cards – had only the meanest collection of Literature and I was the only one there to sell it. I did what I could and talked to people as they came out and tried to make members. It was an excellent meeting the N[ew] C[onstitutional] and the N[ational] U[nion]. Mrs Flora Annie Steele took the Chair and Mr Llewellyn Smith spoke and there were a good many questions from a professional questioner – a most blatant woman who really got the worst of it – Mr Smith is excellent at repartée. It was really a most jolly meeting – rather happy-go-lucky but everyone enjoyed it and considering the awfulness of the weather quite wonderful and I saw several people who I called upon while there. Back to tea at Mrs Kenny's in the car and she had a large and very nice gathering and I ate immensely. I am beginning to enjoy my food out so much more – and the lunch had been simply delicious.

THURSDAY, JANUARY 30TH 1913 – DOVER: 26 RANDOLPH GARDENS

I wrote hard until 3.45 – changed – then flew off to catch the 4.45 train to Shorncliffe as Mrs Ainslie Hill had asked me to go over and dine and go to the Anti meeting. I had tea first – then dinner at 7 – after a long talk. Then Mrs Hill and I went off – having to stand up in the Motor to the Town Hall for the National League for Opposing Women's Suffrage meeting. It was most exciting – so many of us were there – Miss Stainer, the Miss Dillons, Mrs and Col Kenny with the Rev. L Smith, who had stayed down on purpose to ask questions, Mrs Steele and her daughter and lots of others. Mrs Colquhoun was to have spoken but Miss Gladys Pott spoke instead and I was delighted

Flora Annie Steele (1847–1929) novelist and president of the Women Writers' Suffrage League.

Gladys Pott (1867–1961) secretary of the National League for Opposing Women's Suffrage.

with her from our point of view – a most harsh, repellent and unpleasing woman. She began by saying we should not get sentiment from her and we did not. She spoke so carefully too – nothing really to impress her own side. The Countess Radnor was in the Chair and the platform was packed with good works but fearfully uninteresting men and women – with a very pretty and smartly dressed girl at each corner. If the show of hands had been counted they would have found that the resolution was only carried by a very small majority, if carried at all. We demanded a count – but it was no good they didn't mean to play fair. Question time was most amusing, but I must say it took a brave woman to question Miss Pott – she was positively cruel – snapped at them 'define your terms'.

SATURDAY, FEBRUARY 1ST 1913 – DOVER: 26 RANDOLPH GARDENS

Wrote till tea for the NCS. After tea my own accounts and diary. I do seem a success here. The Miss Burkitts seem so genuinely fond of me it is really wonderful – and we enjoy a great many jokes together. Really Miss Minn is very funny and witty and makes me howl sometimes – and Miss Burkitt is an awfully good sort.

For the next few days Kate followed the usual routine of calls, accounts and letter writing, including one to Sir Edward Grey, until she was directed to move her campaign to Wantage in Berkshire. She had enjoyed her stay in Dover, diverted by the congeniality of the Burkitt household and, in particular, the attention she received from a 17-year-old fellow lodger, Ivan Phillipowski (1896–1951), later to become an internationally-known pianist. When he bade her farewell she confided to her diary on 11 February, 'I tried to keep the tone light and to prevent him saying anything which he would regret when he is a famous and still young pianist and I am on crutches but it was rather pathetic and it hurt him for the moment'.

WEDNESDAY, FEBRUARY 12TH 1913 – DOVER: 26 RANDOLPH GARDENS/WANTAGE: REDLANDS, ORMOND ROAD

[Left Dover for Wantage] To Redlands, Ormond Rd, at last with Miss Barnes on the look-out for me – I have a large bed-sitting room and all board etc for 25/- and everything seems very nice – if very lonely. I just washed then went downstairs and had dinner – fish and meat, bread and cheese. The house seems overrun with curates – one strangely enough is a Mr Fry and I also heard a strong Irish brogue. Oh dear this constant moving on to fresh atmospheres and environments.

THURSDAY, 13 FEBRUARY 1913 – WANTAGE: REDLANDS, ORMOND ROAD

A Miss Stratton [sic, but probably Miss Stafford], a very plain old lady, seems to use the dining room to sit in but I don't know where she has her meals. Miss Crowhurst, a teacher at a school opposite, had dinner and supper with me. I came up to my room when I thought it would be warm and continued to write until lunch – there is a lot of Dover work to finish up. Then walked to Mrs Gurney Sheppard at The Ham – a most charming house. She is keen on Suffrage and that is why I have been sent to Wantage. She had a Mrs Birt, the doctor's wife, and a Mrs Riddelsdell, the curate's wife, to meet me – both are keen.

Catherine Barnes (1859–1947) monthly nurse.

Gertrude Birt, wife of Dr A. Cyril Birt, Newbury St, Wantage.

Ella Riddelsdell. Ormond Street, Wantage.

SATURDAY, FEBRUARY 15TH 1913 – WANTAGE: REDLANDS, ORMOND ROAD

Dover letters and writing and more calls. It is going to be heavy work in Wantage. But the people are very nice. Went to see the Vicar at 6pm but, though I went with an introduction from Archdeacon of Buckingham, he was very short and horrid with me. Oh I do dislike most of the Church.

Wantage was not on a railway line, and passengers relied on the Wantage Tramway, opened in 1875, to carry them between Wantage and Wantage Road Station on the Great Western Railway two miles north. It was the first tramway in Britain to use steam traction to operate a passenger service.

SUNDAY, FEBRUARY 16TH 1913 – WANTAGE: REDLANDS, ORMOND ROAD

I just sat down and hated and hated and hated Wantage at first – though I am really very comfortable here. Miss Barnes most nice and kind and attentive, the food excellent. But I have got such a feeling as if Wantage is a trap. I shall never get out of – it's because there is no railway here – and I haven't seen the little tramway yet.

TUESDAY, FEBRUARY 18TH 1913 – WANTAGE: REDLAND, ORMOND ROAD

Had a call from Mrs Sheppard in the morning while I was writing. A call from Miss Campbell in the afternoon. Had a lot of writing to do. The Report – list of meetings for the year and still a lot of Dover letters. Out again paying calls in the evening. Mr Fry was brought in and introduced and paid me a call until 11 pm. Oh dear, he does talk – doesn't give one a chance – but he is a real Anti – and a man without ideals.

WEDNESDAY, FEBRUARY 19TH 1913 – WANTAGE: REDLANDS, ORMOND ROAD

Writing and calls in the morning. Calls again 2.15 to 5.15. I had one funny adventure – called upon a very deaf old lady. The son wanted to be present at the interview but 'Ma' sent him off and I shouted the 'great message' down some yards of tubing. She was very Anti but quite pleasant. When I got in I found one Dr Macran of Childrey, as wild an Irishman as one could desire, had been waiting 2 hours to see me. So I walked a little way with him. He is quite an Anti but seems disposed to let us have the School Room at his village and is of course quite mad.

Eileen Gurney Sheppard (1884 -1955) wife of Samuel Gurney Sheppard, a wealthy stockbroker, descended from eminent Quaker families. She was nearly 20 years younger than her husband and was to be widowed in 1915 when he was killed fighting in France. Her husband's aunt, Mina Sheppard, stayed at The Ham later in the month while speaking for the NCS.

Charles Fry (b.c 1873) later became vicar of St Luke's, Maidenhead.

SATURDAY, FEBRUARY 22ND 1913 – WANTAGE: REDLANDS, ORMOND ROAD

Mrs Sheppard came at 11.30 and stayed till 12.30. I had to sort of hustle her out as Miss Stafford [fellow lodger] has dinner at 12.30 in the dining-room – and she has taken to looking at me very blackly whatever I do or say. In fact she is very difficult and quite dotty.

SUNDAY, FEBRUARY 23RD 1913 – WANTAGE: REDLAND, ORMOND ROAD

Miss Stafford was in an awful mood. I am afraid she will try and do me some injury. She seemed to like me at first but now seems to have become jealous because I talk and laugh with Miss Crowhurst. Well, Miss Crowhurst seems to appreciate my wit and my stories. Some of them shock her but I think she fancies she is seeing life and she is getting very keen on Suffrage.

Monday, February 24th 1913 – Wantage: Redlands, Ormond Road

Started for Childrey soon after 10 o'clock. It was quite exciting setting out on an adventure. At last I found my way to the Rectory and Dr Macran. A huge, great bare Rectory, most horribly furnished – real Irish in tone. I got the Rector to show me the Schools – then he took me to a Mrs Wicksteed – a possible 'Chair'. Then I started my canvass and went back to the Rectory at 1 and was introduced to Mrs Macran. A large lady in a Toque and lots of jet. Also Ma Macran – she so disliked me she was speechless – a weary old lady – a nasty old lady. Oh what a bunch, what an atmosphere with a small boy to wait, who had to be directed and who was most deeply interested in me. It was difficult to balance the conversation – it always is between husband and wife – but, of course, I was his – and I must say he is lovely, a large Irish heart. But what a face. I wrote out a lot more of my bills after lunch then, refusing their kind invitation to tea, I started off to canvass the village. It was most amusing – the more so that at every turn I met Dr Macran, who wanted to know how I was getting on. Our last encounter in the Post Office was too funny – when we got outside he leaned confidentially towards me and said 'I want you to tell me one thing'. 'Well' said I. 'Why did you choose Childrey?' I nearly collapsed, but it was lovely. I explained that he alone had given me any encouragement. I hope he does not think it was because we travelled by the tram from the station together on my arrival. I was tired when I started on my walk home but, oh, when I arrived in at 5.45 – having been on my feet since before 3 – I was tired. I could have wept. I just sank down coat, hat, & veil and remained where I was.

Friday, February 28th 1913 – Wantage: Redlands, Ormond Road

Busy all day. Out in the morning, canvassing Grove St. Met Dr Macran in a terrible state of fear. He had been 3 times to the Police station – was quite sure our meeting was going to rowdy and broken up. Everyone was advising him not to go etc. Such nonsense. Out to meet Miss Sheppard at 3.50 but the car had been sent to Wantage Rd so she did not turn up in the tram and I had to walk down to The Ham and leave her a message to tell her at what hour we would start. Back to The Ham starting at 5.20 – and the car came for us at 5.45 and took Miss Sheppard and I to Childrey. Went to the Rectory and I went off to hunt up a Chairman – and Dr Macran took Miss S. off to call upon the Dunns. Mrs Wicksteed would not take the Chair – neither would he [Philip Wicksteed] because of the policy. I must say I felt a bit worked up at the prospect – but I would not let on to anyone and walked back in the dark very feared of being mobbed or assaulted. I heard on every side – 'there goes the Suffragette'. It was very nervous work and it was quite dark while I walked back to the Rectory at about quarter to 7. The others weren't back so I got Mrs Macran to go over to the Schools – the policeman had arrived and, once there, I felt quite sure all would be well. The people began coming and I chatted and then went outside to tell the loiterers and at 7 we started. I took the Chair and made what I am sure was a blundering speech but it had the required effect – it kept the people in check. They were quite amiable and I handed them over to Miss Sheppard in good order. They were inclined to be a bit rowdy here or there, but nothing to count and the hall filled up and we had a splendid meeting – and when I got up at

Rev. Dr Frederick Macran (1865–1949) born in Dublin, a clergyman living with his wife and two children at Childrey Rectory, Wantage. C.S. Lewis in his autobiography, *Surprised by Joy*, described Macran as 'an old, gabbling, tragic, Irish parson'.

Mary Wicksteed (1845–1924) wife of Philip Wicksteed, an economist, member of a leading Unitarian family with a long association with women's suffrage.

the end I really slanged at them and they stood it splendidly. I was delighted but rather exhausted when it was over. Oh dear, what things one goes through.

WEDNESDAY, MARCH 5TH 1913 – WANTAGE: REDLANDS, ORMOND ROAD

Out at 11 to the Ham. I waited while Miss Sheppard got ready and she walked into the town with me to see the Town Hall etc. I went on with the canvassing. Met Mrs Merivale Mayer at 3.50 and took her to the Bear Hotel. Had a chat and then left her to have a rest. Went over to the Hall to put it all in order arrange, seats etc. [Back to the Hall] at 7pm. Miss Deare and Mrs Driscoll were my only helpers but they were splendid. When the doors were opened people rushed in and then they came thicker and faster. The free seats were filled in no time – people standing every where. Mrs Gurney Sheppard and party and Miss Sheppard arrived just as the people were streaming in. I made a way for them – then flew down and ordered the doors to be closed – that was 10 to 8. No Mr Crawfurd or Mrs Mayer – I was at my wits' end – rushing about – settling people answering questions etc – then I seized hold of my coat and was just flying off to 'the Bear' when they arrived. I am afraid I was very short with them, but if we had once got that audience stamping and shouting we should never have got it quiet. So I shoved them on the platform – having found Mr Crawfurd was prepared to address an overflow and got them started. It was a moment. Mr Crawfurd, who seems a nice young man, was up first and going carefully but I could not hear. I was up and down like a Jack-in-the-Box. Went and spoke to the crowd and told them if they liked to wait half an hour Mr Crawfurd would speak. Later the policeman sent and said he thought I had better not but I said I had promised and should at any rate make the attempt. When he had done I called him out and said he could either speak from a Balcony or from a stool in the Porch so he shouldered the stool and he and I and Miss Deare went below. I got up and said a few words by way of introduction and he spoke for about a quarter of an hour. But a drunken man was troublesome and it had to be taken rather lightly. However all went well and I got him back again on the platform for the questions. I hadn't heard a word of Mrs Mayer but I heard Miss Sheppard and did not think she was doing very well – it was so disconnected. Then came the collection – questions – & Miss Pott. Oh dear the meeting had already been long but I think the people stood it 2½ hours in all. The excitement raged. People either had their mouths hanging open or lip primly compressed. I hated it from the bottom of my soul and so did Mrs Gurney Sheppard, I could see. I did not think either questioner or questioned came off well, but Miss Pott I must say was vile – she was white with rage – I have never seen a more disagreeable display. She came so obviously not to further the Anti-Suffrage cause but to try and harass the speakers. Oh dear, if they had only kept their dignity but I suppose they couldn't and it is easy enough to criticise. Sometimes two, sometimes three got up and spoke together – nearly all stood. Mr Crawfurd was visibly trembling and his lips were drawn down in a petrified droop. Miss Sheppard quite lost her presence of mind – called her a 'tiresome person' and Mrs Mayer came out in her native veneer – and started giving back as 'good as she got'. I think Miss Pott deserved it and it is the way to tackle her and Mrs Mayer really gave some very clever hits but, oh, I would rather we had suffered and not hit back – I turned positively faint. I did not know what either of

Edith Katherine Deare (1872–1937) lived with her mother and several servants at King Alfred's Mead, Wantage. She joined the NCS after this meeting.

Horace E. Crawfurd (1881–1958) had recently become a speaker for the Men's League. In 1911 he was a lecturer in education at Liverpool University and on census night was staying as a member of a suffrage-sympathising house-party at the Sussex home of the former Liberal MP Charles Corbett. Crawfurd became Liberal MP for West Walthamstow, 1924–29.

the two ladies would say. I could see it worried Mr Crawfurd, who would have done better to answer all the questions himself. However they were questions on the speeches and such idiotic ones – most of them could have been ruled out of order. Oh it was funny – killing funny – as an experience – but I did not enjoy it at the time. I warned the speakers not to state anything that could not be proved by them as Miss Pott was expected and to keep away from votes and wages so there wasn't much they really said that she could get at so I think that made her angry. Mr Crawfurd tried to pretend he took it lightly to me afterwards but I know he was excited. I tried to make up to him for my harshness by hoping he was comfortable etc. I saw everyone off and cleared up.

THURSDAY, MARCH 6TH 1913 – WANTAGE: REDLANDS, ORMOND ROAD

To see Mrs Merivale Mayer off at 10.15 for Bristol. Mr Crawfurd had gone early. I don't – and feel sure I never shall – like her. Then to the shops and to find out the temper of the populace. All startled by the success of the meeting – there never has been anything like it in Wantage – and all delighted with it and especially Mr Crawfurd's speech. Many who really wanted to unable to get in and all most indignant with Miss Pott. So that is all right – quite a relief to me – no adverse criticism of our speakers. Miss Deare came to see me and buy her subscription. She had met one man who said if we wanted to have successful meetings always we had better get Miss Pott each time.

Lady Wantage (1837–1920), philanthropist and art collector, was extremely wealthy, having inherited the estate of her father, Baron Overstone. She was president of the North Berkshire Anti-Suffrage League, which had been formed in 1909 with Gladys Pott as its secretary. Because the county was considered to be under Lady Wantage's control, Berkshire was treated as strongly anti-suffrage territory. Lockinge House, built in the mid-18th century, was demolished in 1947.

SUNDAY, MARCH 9TH 1913 – WANTAGE: REDLANDS, ORMOND ROAD

Miss Barnes, Miss Crowhurst and myself started to walk to Lockinge to spend the day with Mr and Mrs Whittle. Mrs Whittle is his fourth wife and Miss Barnes' sister. A very nice woman. He was steward to Lady Wantage – now lives on a pension in the dearest little house in Lockinge House grounds. We met the Lady Housekeeper, Mrs Grant, a very grand person in black velvet and paste – and we went with her to the house. What a glorious place – ugly from the outside but built for comfort and really most beautiful inside – and a Museum of Art Treasures of all kinds. Such pictures some modern, some old. Turner, Corot, lots and lots of the old masters – a new picture by Frank Dicksee 'The Confession'. I remember it in the Academy 13 years ago. I came back and said to Mrs Grant who, of course, imagined herself a great Anti Suffragist 'I don't think a Vote could do Lady Wantage any good'. It is not surprising she is an Anti. An old woman in her position – what can she know of the women who do need the Vote for their protection. Mrs Grant said afterwards she couldn't understand me being a Suffragist – I seemed 'so nice'. I spoke very carefully to her about it and didn't go into it in too much but tried to be tactful. We had tea – I must confess the kind of conversation which that class of people go in for is very boring and irritating – so small – so vulgar – and so harmful.

Matthew Whittle (1838–1918) and his wife, Annie (1858–1938) lived at 4 Lockinge, Wantage.

Kate's campaign in Wantage had made 10 members for the NCS.

WEDNESDAY, MARCH 12TH 1913 – WANTAGE: REDLANDS, ORMOND ROAD/BOURNE END: THE PLAT

Mother's birthday – a nice day to return home on after about 9 weeks' absence.

MONDAY, MARCH 17TH 1913 – BOURNE END: THE PLAT

[To London] I went early to Pembridge Crescent. Alexandra and I had a long talk about business – then Miss Kerr & Miss Sheddon and Gladys arrived to discuss plans for a concert. I felt very dirty and untidy but had to do the best I could with myself. They all seemed so smart and so well dressed and so of a different life – the life really that we have left behind. Oh what a difference money makes.

Kate was now sent once again to East Dereham to continue the NCS Norfolk campaign.

TUESDAY, MARCH 18TH 1913 – BOURNE END: THE PLAT/EAST DEREHAM: 63 NORWICH STREET

My short holiday all too soon over. To Dereham. Mrs Cox was at the station to meet me. Came in to find everything very nice awaiting me and a most hearty greeting from Mrs Cox who has had the bedroom repapered and painted and spring cleaned for my visit.

Kate continued working in East Dereham over Easter, which was very early that year. On Good Friday she went to church for 'the 3 hour service', admiring the sermon and noting 'I must try and get [the Vicar, Mr Mcnaughton-Jones] for Suffrage'. The next day she happened to meet him in the Market Place and they 'stood for nearly an hour talking. I think he is much better on the great question, but very obstinate and so tied about by party prejudice that he cannot see the question fairly'.

TUESDAY, MARCH 25TH 1913 – EAST DEREHAM: 63 NORWICH STREET

Most of the day spent in hunting about for rooms for Mrs Mayer with no success – even the Kings Head refused to have her. Canvassing and bill distributing – beginning, as usual, to feel anxious about the success of next Monday's meeting. Changed and out at 4 to Miss Cory's to tea. I went to call on Mrs Pearse when I left there and saw Mr Pearse and asked him to take the Chair but he would none of it. We had all been so 'naughty' etc and of course the destruction of the golf links had been the last straw. He is a pasty-faced Villain. But I wish he would take the Chair for us because if he does not I don't know who will and I shall have to do it – the very idea curdles my blood.

Kate noted in her Organiser's book that she had eventually found rooms for Mrs Mayer with Mrs Harwood, 30 Crown Road, for 25/- a week.

FRIDAY, MARCH 28TH 1913 – EAST DEREHAM: 63 NORWICH STREET

To meet Mrs Mayer at 8.12. We went up in the omnibus to Crown Road and I saw her safely in the rooms. I am feeling very anxious about the week's work and shall be glad when it is over.

Miss Kerr, probably Madeleine, daughter of Mrs Barbara Kerr.

Saturday, March 29th 1913 – East Dereham: 63 Norwich Street

I did some writing and then went off to Mrs Mayer's to make arrangements. It was too wet for her to come out so I went on to the town alone. [In the afternoon] came in and helped to get the room ready, changed had tea at 4.30 and at 5.15 my meeting began to assemble. Mrs Mayer to address them. I had asked all the members – it was a very nice little meeting. Mrs Mayer spoke beautifully and we got promises of help and several of them stayed on chatting until nearly 8 o'clock. So we have made a good beginning.

Sunday, March 30th 1913 – East Dereham: 63 Norwich Street

Mrs Mayer came round for me at 4 o'clock and we went together to tea with Mrs Pearse. He came in to see us but had his most insolent friendly manner on – and nothing would move him to promise to take the Chair for us tomorrow. So then called upon the Becks, who were just about to have tea – so we had another. They were in the most flagrant mood – Miss Beck yelling with laughter – and all full of jokes as to how much Mr Beck admired me etc. Quite impossible. I do believe Mrs Mayer is one of those sort of personalities that bring out and accentuate people's weaknesses. She was awfully nice there really but begged me not to take her to any more houses like that. They had been two awful calls

Monday, March 31st 1913 – East Dereham: 63 Norwich Street

Some writing – then to call for Mrs Mayer about 11.30. To the Town – to post – to see the Assembly Rooms etc and then to call upon the Vicar. We found him in – I introduced Mrs Mayer and we were soon plunged into a heated talk. My real idea was to get him for the Chair, but, though he had promised to come to the meeting, he couldn't because he had to go to Norwich – so my last hope left me.We did not leave there till after 1.30 and we were awfully flushed and trembling all of us. I did not say very much and Mrs Mayer did not desire me to speak at all and negatived everything I said, but she and the Vicar had a real set to. I was most interested. I must say he came off badly. I had a lot of writing and arrangements to get through after lunch – the Agenda – work for Stewards etc and then get down to hall at 4.30. Miss Cory came down too but as they were only just bringing in the chairs, we could not do much. I came back to tea to make final arrangements and to dress. I was getting pleased with the effect when I found the lamp was smoking severely and covering me and everything with smuts. Did not get down until 7.30. However I had given Miss Cory charge of the Stewards and there were several there to do their best – which was pretty bad. However the hall soon began to fill and I began to feel deadly sick with dread and anticipation and Mrs Mayer arrived. We retired to the Ante room until 8 o'clock then made our way on to the Platform. There was nothing for it but for me to get up and do my best – but it was very bad best – quite the worst I have ever done – I knew it would be with Mrs Mayer. Mrs Mayer spoke beautifully and it a most quiet and attentive audience and the hall was quite full. I was thankful when it was over and I could mingle with the audience – and we made 4 members. Then to pack up – paid up and away. The collection amounted to 18/3. Ticket Money 1/6.

TUESDAY, APRIL 1ST 1913 – EAST DEREHAM: 63 NORWICH STREET
Always busy clearing up after a meeting. So I wrote solidly until 3.30. Then was out until 6 o'clock hunting up people for the evening meeting at Mrs Goddard's. Quite a nice little gathering and Mrs Mayer spoke beautifully. Three new members joined.

WEDNESDAY, APRIL 2ND 1913 – EAST DEREHAM: 63 NORWICH STREET
Found one Miss Cooper waiting for me – she had joined last night and then come to resign. She was quite absurd.

'Hobbies of Dereham' produced plans, kits and tools for making wooden models and toys.

THURSDAY, APRIL 3RD 1913 – EAST DEREHAM: 63 NORWICH STREET
Busy writing notices. Out 12 – in 1.15 – after having given notices to the workmen coming from Hobbies. Mrs Mayer here 2.45 and together to Mrs Barnaby's for a meeting at 3 o'clock – with tea after. A member made and several promises and a lot of people there had never been to a meeting before. [Evening] Mrs Mayer called in and together we went to the YMCA Room to the Literary and Debating Society special meeting to hear Mrs Mayer. There was no Negative. Mr Fisher was in the Chair and had to take the other side – and the Vote was carried 37 to 1 – and that one afterwards was converted in Private Chat and walked part of the way with us.

FRIDAY, APRIL 4TH 1913 – EAST DEREHAM: 63 NORWICH STREET
A card from Mrs Roots saying she could not have her At Home as arranged. I had to do some writing then Mrs Mayer came along and I gave her some bills to distribute and I flew off first to Mrs Roots then to as many people as I could get to in the time to get them to come to me instead. I flew about quite breathless with haste and then had to let Mrs Mayer know. We had quite a nice meeting – several new people – and we got 2 members. [Evening out-door meeting] It was not a bad crowd and most attentive. I got up and spoke a few flattering and idiotic words at the beginning – to try and collect the crowd but was thankful to hand them over and go about handing papers out. The best part of it was the thorough conversion of last night's Anti young man

SATURDAY, APRIL 5TH 1913 – EAST DEREHAM: 63 NORWICH STREET
To the station at 9 o'clock to see Mrs Mayer off. I was thankful to see her go because now I feel like going and the time gets beautifully near. [Afternoon] The Committee meeting here at 5.30. Present Miss Shellabear, Miss Cory, Mrs Hewitt, Mrs Barnaby and Mrs Teanby. We did quite a lot of discussing and settling and Miss Cory stayed behind and I gave her notes for the minutes.

TUESDAY, APRIL 8TH 1913 – EAST DEREHAM: 63 NORWICH STREET
A busy day clearing up my Dereham writing as I wanted to get it all done so as not to spread over my holiday. Several books to leave and calls to pay – upon the Misses Shellabear, Mrs Hewitt etc to say good-bye. Mrs Hewitt gave me a donation of 10/-. We have 23 new members since we came this time so I think have done really magnificently.

Mary St Swithin Goddard (1869–1923) widow, living with her mother and daughter at 35 Quebec Road, East Dereham.

Frances Roots (c 50), wife of an engineer and farmer. The Avenue, South Green, East Dereham.

Rosa Teanby (1868–1957) wife of an analytical chemist. She had joined the NCS in May 1912. Elvin Lodge, East Dereham.

WEDNESDAY, APRIL 9TH 1913 – EAST DEREHAM: 63 NORWICH STREET

1.52 train to Fakenham. I was met by a very high dog cart up into which I could not climb until I had lifted my dress to the knees – and was driven to West Barsham. I went to the abode of Mrs Thisleton-Smith, who got together a party of about 24 people – one man a clergyman, a Mr Whall of North Barsham, who took the Chair for me. I started about 3.15 and laboured on, not very pleased with myself, until about 3.45 there arrived one Mr Green and so I began to finish off and came to an end and asked Mr Green, who I had heard was of the Church League [for Women's Suffrage], to help me out. He spoke for about 20 minutes and did the trick. I made 4 members and had several promises and really it had turned out a very successful afternoon – but I was thankful it was over.

On 10 April the NCS concluded this three-week Norfolk campaign and Kate travelled home to Bourne End. She found the family 'fairly well but not cheery – and the old man looking very battered'.

PRELIMINARY NOTICE

Free Church League for Woman Suffrage

President - Rev. JOHN CLIFFORD, D.D.

To Raise Funds for the Educational Work of the League, A : : :

SPRING FAIR

WILL BE HELD AT

RECTORY ROAD HALL, Stoke Newington

(Rectory Road Station, G.E.R.).

On THURSDAY and FRIDAY, April 17 & 18

Band. Competitions. Entertainments.

The Committee earnestly appeals to all friends of the League for every kind of help to make their venture a success.

Enquiries and Contributions to be addressed to—
Bazaar Secretary, Mrs. TRAFFORD WILLIAMS,
218, Evering Road, Clapton; or
Mrs. FLEMING WILLIAMS,
2, Holmbury View, Springfield, Clapton, N.E.

Printed & Published by A. Storer & Co. (T.U.) 2 Walford Road, N.

THURSDAY, 17TH APRIL 1913 – BOURNE END: THE PLAT

[To London] Had lunch at Eustace Miles and sat till nearly 2 o'clock. To Rectory Road [Stoke Newington] and to the Congregational Church Schools for a Bazaar in aid of the Free Church League for WS where I Palmisted. It was opened at 3 o'clock by Mrs Heuffer. It was a very uninteresting afternoon. I worked as hard as I could but there were some very long gaps. Only did about 15 or 16 hands. Mrs Sadd Brown, who had asked me, was ill and unable to be there. I was disappointed. [On return] Up till 10 o'clock talking to Agnes. It appears that our affairs have come to a most awful crisis again – this seems the end. I don't know if the old man himself realises, but it seems that we shall probably be turned out of home in a few days without even furniture. The Mortgagee has died – the amount has been called in – Gilbeys had a large claim which they have also called in. I think it will be the death of Mother when she realises it. I don't even know if my own things, which I have bought myself, belong to me – or whether we just walk out of the house with what we stand up in. It makes me ache and ache – I feel all stretched. I could not sleep for my heart beating and bumping. And we don't seem to have a friend to help us.

FRIDAY, APRIL 18TH 1913 – BOURNE END: THE PLAT

I tried all day to feel as usual – not to show anything and not to mind. It is no use mind-

Elizabeth Smith (1875–1954) wife of John Thisleton Smith, farmer and estate agent. West Barsham, nr. Fakenham.

Edward Haversham Whall (1850–1922) widower, living with his two unmarried daughters at The Rectory, North Barsham.

ing. The only thing is to try and keep one's sanity and go on working. What a blessing I am in work.

Leaving the family sunk in depression, Kate returned to Dover on 25 April, lodging again with the Misses Burkitt, much to the pleasure of Ivan Phillipowski. Kate spent the following days canvassing for members and sending out invitations to meetings. By 'desperate doings in the [London] Suffrage world' she is referring to the proscribing of WSPU public meetings, the police raid on its headquarters and the government crackdown on its paper, The Suffragette, *which, until now, had carried reports of the work of the NCS. The issue that immediately pre-dated the raid was, however, the last to carry such a report. It is to be presumed that the NCS was wary of being seen to be too closely associated with a paper that the government was attempting to outlaw. In subsequent months reports of the NCS London meetings were included in the columns of the NUWSS paper,* The Common Cause, *and of* Votes for Women, *the paper of the 'Votes for Women Fellowship', the group that centred on the Pethick-Lawrences after their ejection from the WSPU. It is to be noted that the NCS gave little information about its activity – Kate's work – in the country.*

MONDAY, MAY 5TH 1913 – DOVER: 26 RANDOLPH GARDENS
To meet Mrs Mayer at 4.9 and the meeting was at 5pm. She arrived in a temper – wanted food not having had lunch – such nonsense – she should have got something on the train – she came by boat express.We had a nice gathering – made some members and Mrs M. ought to have been glad and helpful instead of full of grumbles. Why had she been sent to Dover? – such nonsense – etc etc. I could have slain her and she got on my nerves to a horrible extent. It is a most tremendously exciting moment in London – desperate doings in the Suffrage world and for Free Speech and for a Free Press, but if the Committee decide Mrs Mayer is to go into the country she ought to come and behave decently.

TUESDAY, MAY 6TH 1913 – DOVER: 26 RANDOLPH GARDENS
Waited for Mrs M. to finish some letters, over which she was very peevish. Took her to the Reading Room and showed her her bearings, then went off at 12 and met Miss Lynn who took me round to canvass her district [Dolphin Lane]. She went off when we had done the lot – it all seemed to me quite useless and I did some on my own. Canvassing all the afternoon. To meeting at Miss Falloon's Schoolroom at 8. Miss Lynn in the Chair. Mrs M. in a most disagreeable state. I did a little appeal afterwards for members. She was most rude to me on my way home. Nothing has gone right in the house since she was in it. She had supper upstairs alone and I went up about 10.30 and she made an awful scene because I asked her if she liked going to bed early and said I did. She was must insulting to me. I called Miss Burkitt into the room to end it. But Mrs M. was in an absolute fury – stamped about and departed to no 6 [to the Capells at 6 Randolph Gardens] in a real passion. She is making me feel so ill – putting the Burkitts about and I won't stand it. This is an insult to the Cause. How dare she preach the putting of other people's houses in order while she is so undisciplined herself. I always knew I could not get on with her but she is making me feel so ill.

WEDNESDAY, MAY 7TH 1913 – DOVER: 26 RANDOLPH GARDENS

Mrs Mayer did not put in an appearance. She has breakfast at No 6. I should think she was ashamed to face me. I avoided her all I could all day. I went out about 11.30 after some writing – and to the Stone Apron [at Dover harbour] at Noon for a WSPU meeting which Miss Ritchie was helping at. Did not much care for the speaker [Miss Billing, the WSPU organiser for the Canterbury area]. Mrs M. had gone off on her own account. She and I had to be down at the Stone Apron at 3 for our meeting. And a splendid meeting it was too. We had a crowd. There was no need for me to begin and Mrs M. would not let me anyhow – brushed me on one side and was most rude to me in front of some of the Committee. But she spoke magnificently and was most pleased with herself. Then she and I and Miss Ritchie went to tea with Mrs Wilson. [Later] Mrs Mayer had her supper of crab upstairs and we went below. I did not come up afterwards and left her severely alone. The Miss Burkitts loathe her – and so they do at No 6 – servant and all – so it isn't only me – but I do think she becomes worse when I come near her. So I suppose the dislike is mutual.

Kate reported in her Organiser's Book that at this meeting the resolution, 'That in the opinion of this meeting, the Government ought to introduce without further delay a measure giving Votes to Women', was carried, with two dissentients.

THURSDAY, MAY 8TH 1913 – DOVER: 26 RANDOLPH GARDENS

Very busy all day. Out canvassing but it was very showery. Out 3.30 to arrange Arthur Room, St James's St, for the meeting. Out at 7 to the Hall. Meeting at 8. Miss Falloon took the Chair until she had to go and then I filled it up. Very badly. Mrs Mayer does frighten me and she interrupted while I was speaking and said 'Ask for Questions'. I believe she is deadly jealous. She had as good as said that I had asked all wrong for the members and collection at Miss Falloon's meeting – so I left it for her to do to-night and she did it so badly I wished I had done it. About 65 people present – so it was not a bad little meeting – the hall was almost full. The Burkitts would not come to the meeting – they are so sick of the lady.

FRIDAY, MAY 9TH 1913 – DOVER: 26 RANDOLPH GARDENS

Mrs M. did not come in until 12 o'clock [mid-day]. I do not know whether she was only just up or what. Then she came in and grumbled all the time about the rain and Dover and the way she had to do things she didn't want. And she hoped there was fish for dinner as she was an RC. I mildly said she might have spoken of it before but that did not please her and then I said I would go for fish – that was worse. So dinner was very glum – she ate well of meat. To Miss Chambers at 3 o'clock, but hardly anyone turned up. Mrs Mayer gave a splendid little address and we had a beautiful tea. With Mrs Mayer at a little before 8 to the Market Place for the open-air meeting. It was a great success and we had a huge crowd. Some perfectly awful Market Loafers but, besides those, a really good crowd. Helped Mrs M. up and she commenced at once. She was very strung up about it and, of course, it might have been unpleasant. She was mobbed when she got down. There was no roughness – except that Mrs Buckland got struck by a drunken man. I got an invitation for a dance from a Petty Officer. It was to take place on the Pleasure Pier. I must have looked somewhat startled but he asked quite nicely and I replied politely that it was impossible. Funny things do happen. We came up home in a tram. I think Mrs M. was really rather done – but, oh, she is unpleasant. And there was such a scene because there was no Stout. I was really cross with Miss Burkitt. But she went out and procured some.

SATURDAY, MAY 10TH 1913 – DOVER: 26 RANDOLPH GARDENS
What a relief to wake up and realise that Mrs M. was leaving Dover. I don't think I can go on working with her. I dislike her so much.

SUNDAY, MAY 18TH 1913 – DOVER: 26 RANDOLPH GARDENS
I have my marching orders for London after Norfolk and am overjoyed.

WEDNESDAY, MAY 21ST 1913 – DOVER: 26 RANDOLPH GARDENS
To hall to see all in order – canvassing for meeting. To meet Mrs Cavendish Bentinck at 1.15 at the Harbour station. Took her in a taxi to East Cliff, where Mrs Wilson entertained her to lunch and was most nice. I went off to the Hall in good time – got there 2.30 and by 3 o'clock there were only 30 people. Oh! I did feel sick. I had to take the Chair and did it very nervously as usual but when I sat down Mrs CB, in her nice way, said 'well done Chairman'. She made a charming speech and chatted to the people afterwards. Then we walked back to Mrs Wilson's and had tea. A Taxi came and I saw her off by the Boat Train at the Town station. We made 2 members and had a collection of 19s 1½d. I always get a good bit when I appeal.

MONDAY, MAY 26TH 1913 – DOVER: 26 RANDOLPH GARDENS
At 12 to meet Mrs Rolleston about the printing. To meet Mrs Rolleston again at 4.45 at the Posters where at last we settled the business. Then we both walked up to Effingham Crescent [to the Falloons' Vicarage] for the Committee meeting at 5.30. The usual little party present and we had a lot to settle.

On Sunday 25 May John came to Dover for the day. He brought his camera. 'We went into the garden and John took snapshots of the group.' Then they 'walked along the front and took a photograph of Mrs Wilson's house and then back to tea'.

TUESDAY, MAY 27TH 1913 – DOVER: 26 RANDOLPH GARDENS
Was getting everything ready for the Hon. Treasurer and the new Hon. Sec., Mrs Buckland.

WEDNESDAY, MAY 28TH 1913 – DOVER: 26 RANDOLPH GARDENS
To meet 1.11 train at the Priory and Miss McGowan. Miss Burkitt is putting her up for the night. Miss Burkitt brought her to the Hall at 8 o'clock. I went off at 7.15 to look after the Stewards etc. It was not a bad little meeting about 40 people. I had to take the Chair and appeal for a collection. We got £1-0-3 and 3 members. Miss McGowan spoke very well, but I always think she is dry in a room. She agrees with me that Mrs Mayer is a most impossible person and it makes one's life a misery to have to try and work with her.

THURSDAY, MAY 29TH 1913 – DOVER: 26 RANDOLPH GARDENS
I had to pay some accounts and then we went hunting round for a permit to get on the Extension of the Admiralty Pier. I saw Miss McGowan off at 6 o'clock for London. I think she has thoroughly enjoyed herself here. I took a tram to Mrs Foster's to leave the account books instructions etc – then to Mrs Buckland to take her the minute book papers etc of the Dover Branch.

FRIDAY, MAY 30TH 1913 – DOVER: 26 RANDOLPH GARDENS/BOURNE END: THE PLAT
Went by tram to the Harbour station and I came to Victoria by the 10.50 train. [Then back to Bourne End] but the family affairs are troubled as ever. Oh dear.

Kate now returned to Norfolk, basing her campaign this time at Fakenham. Her landlady, Mrs Rush, charged her 28/- a week for full board.

MONDAY, JUNE 2ND 1913 – BOURNE END: THE PLAT/FAKENHAM: QUEEN'S ROAD
[To Fakenham] Mrs Warner had let me know of rooms as my old lady could not take me in – but I am quite near her – with Mrs Rush in Queen's Rd – and have the front bed-room and the furniture. [It] really is much nicer downstairs and everything is speckless and natty.

WEDNESDAY, JUNE 4TH 1913 – FAKENHAM: QUEEN'S ROAD
Called on Mrs Digby, who I want to take the Chair – saw the daughter who did not give me any hope. Out 6 to 7 canvassing. A salad supper – my landlady's lettuces are absolutely perfect. It is so very peaceful to be alone. My good landlady tells more than I need but she seems to like me and, as she has never had a lady lodger before, I must make a good impression.

Snapshot taken by John Collins of Kate, the two Misses Burkitt, Janet Capell, and an unknown woman in the garden of 26 Randolph Gardens, Dover.

FRIDAY, JUNE 6TH 1913 – FAKENHAM: QUEEN'S ROAD

Canvassing in the morning from 11.45 to 1.15 after the usual writing. Changed my things – dinner – then off by 2.40 train. It simply poured with rain. To Dereham. Miss Cory met me and we went together to Mrs Cox. Mrs Merivale Mayer had arrived at 1.40 and had some dinner as Mrs Cox was putting her up. I am so thankful she is some distance from me. She has lost a brother since she was at Dover so is in mourning. Mrs M, Miss C and I walked to Mrs Root's for a garden meeting at 3.30. It was a very small gathering. I was disappointed. However we made one new member. We had tea and it was a very nice party – only Mrs M. was very rough with one very Anti lady, who did everything wrong she could – even to spilling her tea – half on me and half on herself.

On Wednesday 4 June Emily Wilding Davison, a WSPU activist, ran onto the course of the Derby at Epsom, probably intending to grab the bridle of the King's horse, and was fatally injured. There is still a debate as to whether she really understood the danger of her action, done, one must assume, to obtain publicity for the Cause. She had, on several occasions, been imprisoned and forcibly fed and during one imprisonment had been badly injured after hurling herself over a barrier as a protest against the horrors of forcible feeding.

MONDAY, JUNE 9TH 1913 – FAKENHAM: QUEEN'S ROAD

The news of the death of Miss Emily Wilding Davison in to-day's paper – the woman who threw herself in front of the King's horse at the Derby as a WSPU protest. Poor soul – she never recovered consciousness. What a sacrifice of a life and she was a brilliantly clever woman. How long will this absurd and tragic struggle go on? To the station to meet Miss Ward, who came from London, and Mrs Mayer, who came from Dereham at 4.49. In the Hotel bus to 'the Crown' where I took a most awful dislike to Miss Ward and she and Mrs Mayer together turned me sick and they were so rude about everything. 'What awful waste of time and money etc to come to Fakenham' – 'whose mismanagement etc getting them both here etc?' I was furious. I left them getting their tea and went off to arrange the hall – feeling in about as black a mood as possible. The whole thing was hateful to me done in that spirit. If they are too good and too fine to come and speak at the country meeting, I wish to goodness they would send someone who is more suitable. Then to the hall soon after 7 for the meeting at 8. Mrs Thisleton-Smith came to help me and she was splendid and Mrs Stimpson who was no good. We could have done with many Stewards of the right sort. I had to sell tickets at the door – look after everything – greet the Chairman, the Rev. Anthony Fenn, Rector of Stibbard – introduce the speakers – get the meeting started – find seats for people – and soon – and then do what I could to stop the uproar. The hall was packed – but rows of the lowest type of men came in and stood at the back. They were noisy from the first – didn't give the Chairman a chance. They listened to Mrs Merivale Mayer alright, though, of course, she could not do herself justice – but Miss Ward could not get any attention. She was not a bit clever with them – talked a lot of nonsense quite unsuitable really, but, of course, it was an awful ordeal. How I longed for a tongue. I do believe they would have listened to me. They were so very friendly. I stood amongst them all the evening trying to get them to keep a passage way etc. The policeman was a nice man but quite useless. The people who wished to hear were quite nice and I was so sorry the meeting was spoilt for them. I can't think why some of the men did not get up and demand order – but I suppose there was no one there with sufficient authority. The feeling in the hall itself was certainly with us. What an argument for us that ignorant filthy roaring mob of men with no sense – knowing how much more important they are than the highest woman in the land. Miss Ward motored off with some relations to Hardingham. I cleared up and then went over to the Hotel to see if Mrs Merivale Mayer was alright and, as it was simply pouring with rain, to leave my parcel of books and banners.

TUESDAY, JUNE 10TH 1913 – FAKENHAM: QUEEN'S ROAD, EAST DEREHAM: 63 NORWICH STREET

To the Hotel to see Mrs Merivale Mayer off. I just stood and looked out of the window and turned my back on her while she ranted about the discomfort of the Hotel. Oh, she is a miserable woman. When she had gone I went round about and had chats with people in the shops. Found them all so nice and quite indignant that the meeting should have been so spoilt. To Dereham. Went straight to Mrs Cox and had tea with Mrs Mayer. Then to the Assembly Rooms to help Miss Cory get everything in order. Back to the hall soon after 7 for the meeting at 8. Mrs Merivale Mayer took the Chair and spoke and Miss Ward, who had been motored over. The hall was not well filled. I was very disappointed and so I am sure was Miss Cory, who had done it all. Still we made some members. The three of us went back to Mrs Cox to supper and the two dear ladies tore everyone to shreds and ate enormous suppers. I was very out of it, I am glad to say. I thought they were loathly. If they had been common theatrical people I could have understood it – but not Suffrage people. Mr Stimpson, the Butcher, was putting Miss Ward up so Mrs Merivale Mayer and I walked there with her.

Eva Ward, an imposing figure, had been a history teacher at Chatham County School for Girls, 1906–1908, NUWSS organiser in the Eastern Counties, 1911–12 and was a member of the National Political League. Three months after this meeting she was in the US and, in a letter to the *New York Times*, dismissed as ludicrous the views of Sir Almroth Wright on 'Militant Hysteria' and, despite the criticisms she voiced to Kate, declared her affiliation to the NCS.

Kate's mention of trying to buy a black hat indicates that she had already decided to go to London to participate in the public observance of Emily Wilding Davison's funeral.

THURSDAY, JUNE 12TH 1913 – FAKENHAM: QUEEN'S ROAD

Anniversary of the Boswell episode. It was at Dereham and he went away this day year and I have not seen him since. It has faded just as completely as if it had never been and, yet, I would not have had it for the world. And I should just adore to see him. Out to buy lunch and try and get a black hat. To Barsham. It was a gorgeous afternoon. I found Mrs [Thisleton] Smith and a nice young girl playing croquet. Several others were expected but did not turn up. However we had an informal chat and pronounced the North West Norfolk Branch formed and Mrs T Smith promised to be Hon. Sec. pro tem. And we played croquet and I enjoyed myself. I like her so much and she makes me feel nice.

Leila Stimpson (1867–1932) wife of Thomas Stimpson, family butcher. She became honorary treasurer of the North-West Norfolk Branch of the NCS. Norwich St, East Dereham.

During the few days after Emily Wilding Davison's death the WSPU conceived the plan for the spectacular funeral procession that, as Kate describes, made its way from Victoria Station, through Piccadilly Circus, to St George's Church, Bloomsbury, where a memorial ceremony was held.

Kate's allusion to 'ladies in kimonos' watching from windows in Bloomsbury, suggests that she assumed they were prostitutes. After the church service the cortège then carried on to Euston Station, where the coffin was placed on a train to travel north to Morpeth for burial in the Davison family plot.

SATURDAY, JUNE 14TH 1913 – FAKENHAM: QUEEN'S ROAD/BOURNE END: THE PLAT

[To London] John met me and we hurtled to Baker St on the underground which was filled to suffocation. I left my big luggage in the cloak room at Baker St station and, taking my bag and a small dress box with me, went with John to No 38 Upper Baker St – the Misses Raynes – where he is lodging. I had had a black coat and skirt sent there for Miss Davison's funeral procession and the landlady had given me permission to change in her room. They are dressmakers and let out rooms – but they do not usually let to ladies. However she seemed to like the look of me and offered me the best bedroom above the drawing room for 11/-. I said I would think about it. John had been hunting about and could find nothing cheap where they would take ladies and I am absolutely terrified of rooms in large Towns – one never knows what one might get into. So I ended by chancing the family displeasure and taking the room. I shall at least feel safe with John under the same roof. I tore into my black things then we tore off by tube to Piccadilly and had some lunch in Lyons. But the time was getting on – and the cortège was timed to start at 2 o'clock from Victora. So we got into a Victoria bus – but I thought I heard someone say the procession was in sight and so hopped out. No procession but lines of people. We dashed along and then the rumour went forward that the route had been altered – spread about by the police I suppose. People scattered and flew in all directions. We got another bus at Hyde Park Corner and did journey in that till Victoria when the procession had just started. We saw it splendidly at the start until we were driven away from our position and then could not see for the crowds and then we walked right down Buckingham Palace Rd and joined in the procession at the end. It was really most wonderful – the really organised part – groups of women in black with white lilies – in white and in purple – and lots of clergymen and special sort of pall bearers each side of the coffin. She gave her life publicly to make known to the public the demand of Votes for Women – it was only fitting she should be honoured publicly by the comrades. It must have been most imposing. The crowds were thinner in Piccadilly but the windows were filled but the people had all tramped north and later on the crowds were tremendous and oh, what a quality filled the windows and pavements in Bloomsbury. The ladies in the kimonos were a nightmare to me. The people who stood watching were mostly reverent and well behaved. We were with the rag tag and bobtail element but they were very earnest people. It was tiring. Sometimes we had long waits – sometimes the pace was tremendous. Most of the time we could hear a band playing the funeral march. Just before Kings Cross we came across Miss Forsyth – some of the NCS had been marching with the Tax Resisters. I had not seen them or should have joined in. I had a chat with her. Near Kings Cross the procession lost all semblance of a procession – one crowded process – everyone was moving. We lost our banner – we all got separated and our idea was to get away from the huge crowd of unwashed unhealthy creatures pressing us on all sides. We went down the Tube way.

But I did not feel like a Tube and went through to the other side finding ourselves in Kings Cross station. Saying we wanted tea we went on the platform and there was the train – the special carriage for the coffin – and, finding a seat, sank down and we did not move until the train left. Lots of the processionists were in the train, which was taking the body to Northumberland for internment – and another huge procession tomorrow. To think she had had to give her life because men will not listen to the claims of reason and of justice. I was so tired I felt completely done. We found our way to the refreshment room and there were several of the pall bearers having tea.

Monday, June 16th 1913 – Bourne End: The Plat/London: 38 Upper Baker Street

[To London] to 38 Upper Baker St and then Office. Miss Simeon has all the affairs of the fête in hand. Alexandra Wright came along and had a talk. I felt rather at sea, but suppose I shall pick the threads up as I go along. Then I went off to the [London] Pavilion and gave away notices outside the WSPU meeting. Just went inside for a few minutes – it was packed. Great indignation, of course, at the re-arrest of Mrs Pankhurst when she was starting off to join in the funeral procession. [To Upper Baker St] and I came to my room and had a thorough unpack and clean. Meant, of course, dusting out and papering drawers etc. The room is really filthy. But it has its points. [Dinner at Eustace Miles restaurant] and then sat down to writing and doing accounts of Fakenham and Dereham for Mrs Hartley and was writing until after 11. I was too tired to sleep and when I did the traffic woke me every five minutes for the greater part of the night and the bed was anything but bliss.

Tuesday, June 17th 1913 – London: 38 Upper Baker Street

At 6 am the steel constructed building operations just opposite started. Oh the banging – just the limit. Eliza [the maid] called me at 8 and brought up boiling water and an egg at 9. I reboiled the water and made my own cocoa but could hardly choke anything to eat down. Breakfasts in this sort of abodes are impossible – make one sick to think about. And poor Eliza has already become an obsession and makes me feel ill every time she comes near. So filthy, so mean, so little like a human being and she seems to like me and has quite long chats – but, oh, her presence and her hands !!! Ye gods!!!! Why was I made such a mass of sensitive feeling? To the Office.

Wednesday, June 18th 1913 – London; 38 Upper Baker Street

Felt so ill all day. Off to the Office getting there 10.30. Worked there all day. To lunch at the ABC with Gladys and Miss Burnaby the new assistant secretary, who seemed very nice but colourlesss. I tried to eat but, unusually for me, it has become most difficult and I can't be nourished on the small amount I get down. I feel so bad and have such a pain inside. Straight home by bus and lay down on the sofa in a state of collapse. John was in so I had to buck up and, as food was the next thing, he and I went off to a restaurant nearby. I ordered some tongue but could not fancy it so ate a salad and a roll. Home to bed. Shall never be able to go on till after next Wednesday. And it is such a shame. I had so counted on London. It is utterly spoilt for me and for John it would have been so ideal – we could have had such a fine time together. Oh why won't the gods let me enjoy myself?

FRIDAY, JUNE 20TH 1913 – LONDON: 38 UPPER BAKER STREET
Felt perfectly awful all day – dazed and strengthless. At work all day. Went to Harrods for lunch with Gladys and got down some macaroni and a roll. We sat on the Balcony and it was very nice only I can't appreciate any thing. Gladys later in the day left for Hythe. I was at those rotten sandwich boards again all day – more were wanted. Crawled home and, as usual, threw myself on the sofa. But John was waiting for me and I had to have food. We could not think where to go but I thought I could fancy food at the Popular – so we went. I had whitebait and olives – I have not eaten any meat since I came up to London. It could have been so jolly there, but it was all black black!!! Home straight in a bus – violently sick and awful pain – then some sort of sleep. I felt awful – was quite frightened.

SATURDAY, JUNE 21ST 1913 – LONDON: 38 UPPER BAKER STREET
Felt something awful. John saw me to the Office, where I had to pick up the sandwich boards – then as far as Baker St from the Tube. I went to Finchley Rd and to a flat in Netherhall Gardens where 5 of us got ready for the poster parade. Miss McGowan, Miss Mansell amongst them. I had quite meant not to go parading. I thought there would be a lot there, but felt I had to and walked as one in a daze. We walked from 11.30 to 1. A burst water main in Finchley Road was rather a counter attraction. Mrs Hartley was at the Flat when we got back. We had some lemonade and biscuits and then left. I came on top of a bus with Miss McGowan and Miss Mansell as far as my rooms – right off where the buses stop so that is most convenient. I went to see Dr Walter Sheldon at Cornwall Rd. He saw me at my very worst – I had no strength at all. He said I was 'absolutely done' and I ought to have 3 weeks complete rest and that I had better get off to Bourne End at once. I am sure he is right and no-one could be limper – I have no pulse. Back on a bus – meaning to pack up but I was so done I had not the strength. I couldn't do it. I lay down hoping to get up but it ended by John going out to buy Claret, galantine of chicken, rolls, butter, strawberries etc and I ate as much supper as I could and I crawled into bed as soon as I could.

SUNDAY, JUNE 22ND 1913 – LONDON: 38 UPPER BAKER STREET
What a day – enough to make the merriest sad. In that filthy room, waited upon by the filthiest of servants. Poor Eliza – the more I think of her the more sick I feel.

MONDAY, JUNE 23RD 1913 – LONDON: 38 UPPER BAKER STREET/BOURNE END: THE PLAT
I hoped I was better at first. I drank some cocoa and ate a piece of dry bread. I got ready and went out about 9.45. John went with me – I felt worse than ever once out. I took myself into Lyons and made myself eat a poached egg – and then to the Office. I told Miss Simeon I was 'done' and went to telephone to Alexandra but she was out. Just after, she walked in and was very good and quite calm about it – told me to go and that

if necessary I had better take all July. I finished off a few things and then quietly slipped out of the Office and by bus to Baker St. [Back to Bourne End] What a haven is a home and a nice clean bed-room.

TUESDAY, JUNE 24TH 1913 – BOURNE END: THE PLAT
In bed – hardly moved all day – felt very weak. But the medicine has done marvellous things with my appetite and I am eating again. Miss Simeon has written me a very nice letter – all seems going well. Poor John he is pretty miserable about it all.

THURSDAY, JUNE 26TH 1913 – BOURNE END: THE PLAT
In bed all day and felt rotten. I thought and thought and thought and worried and worried. The house and all the property up for sale to-day at the Mart.

SATURDAY, JUNE 28TH 1913 – BOURNE END: THE PLAT
Got up in the morning and felt less weak on my legs. We hear that the kitchen garden was sold but nothing else.

MONDAY, JUNE 30TH 1913 – BOURNE END: THE PLAT
Started my tonic Dr Walter sent. Felt rotten. Constance here for half an hour to tell us news, but, as usual, not at all interested in ours. She told us of the death of Mrs Willie Hucks at the birth of her eighth child. And no wonder – she has only been married about 10 years and was never a giant of strength. Poor thing – done to death – and what will those seven little mites do without her.

From Kate's Organiser's book: 'Wrote asking to be allowed to take July as holiday'.

THUSDAY, JULY 3RD 1913 – BOURNE END: THE PLAT
The Plat is let from 24th and no-one will decide where to go – so at supper time I suggested writing to Mrs Ainslie Hill about her house [at Folkestone].

Votes for Women, *4 July 1913 carried the advertisement: '2 sitting, 4 bedroom, bath, gas, electricity, garden, near links. 3 guineas including plate, linen. Maid could remain. Hill, 4 Salisbury Villas'.*

FRIDAY, JULY 4TH 1913 – BOURNE END: THE PLAT
Agnes brought in *Votes for Women* to me after breakfast and there, sure enough, was Mrs Hill's house advertised to be let for August. Very strange as, of course, I had no idea. We should just get in – Agnes would like it and it would be a change for Mother, save the expense of house hunting and, otherwise, it must be Gerrards Cross.

SATURDAY, JULY 5TH 1913 – BOURNE END: THE PLAT
Heard from Mrs Hill that she is willing to let us have the house for 3 gns weekly – 15gns for the 5 weeks. I wrote to Mrs Hill by return, taking the house – so that is well settled.

FRIDAY, JULY 18TH 1913 – BOURNE END: THE PLAT

To dress and try and look my best which I didn't though I had my new green satin dress on – with Mother and Daddie, much against my will, at 4.15 to Mrs Lehmann's garden party. Oh dear, I did hate it – worse than anything I have done for ages. I felt such a fool – and everyone seemed as if every human possibility had been sucked out of them by a Vacuum Cleaner. Crowds there – as well as all Bourne End. I spoke to very few – we sat at a tea table together and as Daddie began blustering at waiters – I refused to eat anything and, of course, I never do drink tea out like that – it was deadly strong. Later on there was a superior concert in the school room – a pretty girl singer and a pretty girl violinist – Miss Marjorie Howard. She was quite good – but the whole atmosphere was damning to Art. [Mrs Lehmann] was bustling about as busy as a bee – he [Rudolf Lehmann], as usual, was wandering about like a lost sheep but picking out the prettiest and most fashionable when he did speak to anyone at all. I always feel he is 'one of us' and, if one could get beneath the surface, one would find something strangely interesting.

In the ensuing few days Kate records much cleaning of the house ready for its summer let and, on 19 July, the Bourne End Regatta, which she found 'very different from the old festive times and there was a great sadness to feel so little of the place ours'.

THURSDAY, JULY 24TH 1913 – BOURNE END: THE PLAT/FOLKESTONE: 4 SALISBURY VILLAS

We started by the 1 o'clock train for Maidenhead, Reading and Folkestone, Daddie, Mother, Agnes and 2 cats, Mickie [Kate's dog], Cook and Ellen [the housemaid], eight small packages – two hampers having gone by luggage train. As Mrs Hill has left Plate and Linen it means much less packing.

FRIDAY, JULY 25TH 1913 – FOLKESTONE: 4 SALISBURY VILLAS

The others all went out – including the servants. They were out 3 to 9 to see the sea for the first time. Ellen was startled that it was so wide – she thought it would be more like Bourne End.

SATURDAY, JULY 26TH 1913 – FOLKESTONE: 4 SALISBURY VILLAS

The news has come to us that Thornbie [a neighbouring house to The Plat] has been sold for £1000. Bought by the Gilbeys who hold the £1000 mortgage on it – so it just means they have picked up the house as a bargain as the rent is £120. The Plat with £2000 Mortgage and our furniture mortgaged for another £1000 and living on a precarious £400 per year which must die with the old man. Oh the awful muddle – crass stupidity of it all – so unutterably sad and what on earth is before us. I doubt we shall ever be allowed to return to The Plat and, homeless and furnitureless, what shall we do? Can one feel good and peaceful with these happenings?

SUNDAY, JULY 27TH 1913 – FOLKESTONE: 4 SALISBURY VILLAS

At 2.45 with Agnes to Hythe – walked to the Sandgate Road and got the Motor. We walked through the hotel to the garden and just met the Wrights – Mrs and the two girls [Alexandra and Gladys] walking up. We were joined by Miss Lewis and Miss Cheffins and had tea on a Verandah. Somewhat constrained as these things are but it was a pleasure to meet Miss Cheffins, especially, again. They did not stay long as they have let the house and are busy and Mrs Wright went off with them so we four sat in the gardens and had one of those talks dear to the heart of Gladys.

The 'good lady' whom Kate refers to was the one she described as 'a most blatant woman' in the entry for 29 January 1913.

WEDNESDAY, JULY 30TH 1913 – FOLKESTONE: 4 SALISBURY VILLAS
Through the town down to the old part of the beach where we used to bathe – it is now like Margate – very common people. All the old-fashioned bathing machines are done away with. I sat there watching the people for some time. Then Agnes and I out down the High St and prowling about came in for an Anti Suffrage meeting, but the good lady was the one who was here to question the Rev. Llewellyn Smith at that afternoon meeting and she was most unpleasing.

SUNDAY, AUGUST 3RD 1913 – FOLKESTONE: 4 SALISBURY VILLAS
Tireder than ever – so spent the whole day in bed. Enjoyed reading *Woman and Labour* by Olive Schreiner. Mrs Hill has left us all her books – most good of her.

Kate spent the next couple of weeks enjoying the pleasures offered by Folkestone – aeroplane displays by Henri Salmet, a military tattoo, visits to the theatre, to Sanger's Circus, walking on the Leas and listening to the bands.

TUESDAY, AUGUST 19TH 1913 – FOLKESTONE: 4 SALISBURY VILLAS
To the station to meet the 2.50 train and the Misses Burkitt and their niece, Hilda Burkitt, the WSPU organiser who is staying with them. I had been dreading the afternoon as one's personal friends do not always 'do' at home, but I had drilled the family and all went off well.

[Evelyn] Hilda Burkitt (1876–1955) (later Mrs Mitchener) joined the WSPU in 1907 and in 1908 took charge of their Midlands campaign. She was imprisoned in Birmingham in 1909 after disrupting Asquith's visit, went on hunger strike and was the first there to be forcibly fed. In 1912 she was imprisoned for taking part in the London window-smashing campaign and again went on hunger strike. In November 1913 she was charged with attempting to set fire to a grandstand at Leeds Football Ground, imprisoned and went on hunger strike. May 1914 she was charged with arson at Felixstowe, held on remand, on hunger strike and forcibly fed until released in September after the WSPU amnesty.

FRIDAY, AUGUST 22ND 1913 – FOLKESTONE: 4 SALISBURY VILLAS
Daddie, Mother and I by the 2.5 train to Dover. Daddie went off to see the Cricket and Mother and I went first on the Admiralty Pier and then all round the Harbour. We were as far on the promenade as Mrs Wilson's house – just to show Mother – then by tram to Bridge St and to 26 Randolph Gardens and had tea with the Miss Burkitts, Hilda and Mrs Capell. Miss Burkitt, Hilda, Mother and I went to see the new purchase, No 7 Leyburne Terrace [Leyburne Road]. A wonderful house and extraordinary bargain £140 for 50 years. They are going to move in October.

'The Gilbeys' to whom Kate refers were the sons of her Aunt Agnes. It appears from her diary entry for 5 September that their sister, Kate's cousin Constance, knew nothing of their actions – 'she was very surprised. They don't like their womenkind to know of their doings'.

SUNDAY, AUGUST 24TH 1913 – FOLKESTONE: 4 SALISBURY VILLAS

After tea Agnes told me the news that had reached Mother and Daddie this morning in a letter from Mr Vernon. The Gilbeys have decided to sell us up for their £1000. Mr Vernon suggests that we shall not return to the Plat but that the inventory men shall go in at once. It was just like a blow upon the heart – though Agnes and I have been expecting it. The gay and reckless life is over indeed.

TUESDAY, AUGUST 26TH 1913 – FOLKESTONE: 4 SALISBURY VILLAS

Left at 9 for Central station, Mother and I, and by excursion special at 9.26 to Brighton. I had proposed househunting at Worthing. We shot from road to road – house to house. I did the business. Only one possible at £2-2-, which I think might come to 30/-. The £1-1- places were impossible and mostly so filthy that it did not do to think of them. It was an awful day. We were not in till 10.45.

THURSDAY, AUGUST 28TH 1913 – FOLKESTONE: 4 SALISBURY VILLAS/BOURNE END: THE PLAT

Off by the 11.20. Came via Redhill and changed at Reading and Maidenhead. We got home at 4.30. Everything in the house left beautifully. I shall begin peeling my room about at once – directly we have seen Mr Vernon and settled the date for getting out.

FRIDAY, AUGUST 29TH 1913 – BOURNE END: THE PLAT

Worked all day in my room – sorting out and throwing away. I am going to store my things – the things that are my very own. I don't know else what I could do. I have such quantities of books and all kinds of possessions and then my own furniture.

The mantelpiece in Kate's bedroom at The Plat, photographed by John Collins in 1909. Were these objects among the 'all sorts' that she took away in her 'large hamper'?

SATURDAY, AUGUST 30TH 1913 – BOURNE END: THE PLAT

A most awful day. I don't think I have ever gone through such a shame – and probably I never shall feel anything so acutely again. I dreaded seeing Mr Vernon more than I can say – the hours seemed as months dragging by till he came. Daddie took Agnes and I round the cases and cabinets and gave us out each a good many things to keep lest Mr Vernon should ask for the keys. He had asked for the Inventory so that anything missing he can see. Fortunately no end of my things are, as usual, packed away in the top cupboard – I never leave any of my own things for Lodgers which I can put away. He did not come till 4.30. Agnes and I took his tea into the Smoking –room and then sat down to hear what was to be heard. Probably we set the tone of calm dispassioned reasoning – though Daddie broke out a few times and nearly broke down when he said there would be nothing left for us – if 'Walden' [another Bourne End house], too, was sacrificed. Mr Vernon was as considerate as could be – but the man is a liar and a hypocrite and how Daddie could have trusted him and allowed him to muddle our affairs like this is past human comprehension. And now, of course, he is acting for himself first and then for Gilbeys. We have till the 15th to get out, but have promised to go before if possible.

The following days were spent in clearing out and packing up the possessions they could take with them. On 5 September Kate mentions coming across the stories and plays she had written when young. 'I am keeping such treasure with my diaries in the zinc lined chest. I wonder where or when if ever these treasures will see light again.'

SUNDAY, SEPTEMBER 7TH 1913 – BOURNE END: THE PLAT

I have written to Alexandra saying I shall be ready to return to work on Thursday week.

TUESDAY, SEPTEMBER 9TH 1913 – BOURNE END: THE PLAT

[Whiteleys' van came to take things to storage] I had taken my wardrobe, bureau, book case, wash-hand stand, table, bedside table, arm chair, a wooden arm chair, a chest of drawers, a plain chair, my little chair, John's Hamlet picture, my Madonna picture presented to me, bookshelves, all my books, china and glass for 3, a good bit of bedding, my large Hamper filled with all sorts, my wooden chest full of diaries, a crate filled with programmes and albums, a little red footstool and my Arundel Gardens carpet. I feel so delighted at saving my own.

WEDNESDAY, SEPTEMBER 10TH 1913 – BOURNE END; THE PLAT

Up to London. I hated the journey and felt very nervous at my office – which was the disposal of odds & ends – including false teeth cast off by Mother and Daddie, old Muffs, trinkets etc. So I spent all the morning in and out old clothes and bric a brac shops. It was really awful and I did wonder what I was coming to. Ended by leaving all my things and gaining 28/- but what a flattening experience. Of course I did not sell anything really good, but it is simply appalling what they offer one. But I found most of the people quite nice.

FRIDAY, SEPTEMBER 12TH 1913 – BOURNE END: THE PLAT/WORTHING: OCKHAM, PARK AVENUE

Years ago I have sat and wept picturing the moment when we should walk away from our home and our beautiful possessions. Mother went on early. I waited for Agnes and the cats, who Purcell wheeled to the station. Daddie walked out of the house after us. We left by the 10 o'clock train with 16 large packages and 16 small ones (some very precious). We have come away with a good deal. We all looked at The Plat and the river – such a gorgeous day – it did look so beautiful and then away. To Worthing. The house (by the way I must record the address) Ockham, Park Avenue, seemed very small crowded with furniture, but much cleaner than I had hoped. We have four bed-rooms and all fit in. Everyone kept good tempered. We even laughed. It didn't seem possible we were leaving The Plat for ever and always – and coming to Worthing. Why Worthing? – it's all so strange. Do I mind – or what makes me able to consider it all quite calmly? What is in store? No letter from John this morning or to greet me here. I did hope he would write. But he is careless and very busy. He does not think of these things. He always disappointed me.

TUESDAY, SEPTEMBER 10TH 1913 – WORTHING: OCKHAM, PARK AVENUE
A letter from Alexandra, appointing Monday for me to go to London.

MONDAY, SEPTEMBER 22ND 1913 – WORTHING/LONDON: 27 PEMBRIDGE CRESCENT
A quick train to London – a cab from Victoria to Pembridge Crescent. Alexandra in – tea in their beautiful airy and spacious drawing room – then unpacking – changed and sort out work till dinner.

The New Constitutional Society's autumn campaign in London centred on Whitechapel. The prime movers behind this idea may have been Mrs Barbara Kerr and her sister, Miss Raynesford Jackson, whose experience of the recent Whitechapel by-election had led them to conclude that it was not enough merely to make an appearance on such occasions but that constituencies had to be be worked beforehand to ensure the government candidate came bottom of the poll. An office had been opened at 136 Whitechapel Road and the plan, as set out in the 5 September issue of Votes for Women, *was to canvass the whole area with daily out-door meetings, culminating in a mass meeting with the Actresses' Franchise League, the Tax Resistance League and the Women Writers' Suffrage League on Tower Hill. The NCS were also holding Sunday meetings in Hyde Park, with Mrs Merivale Mayer as speaker.*

FRIDAY, SEPTEMBER 26TH 1913 – LONDON: 27 PEMBRIDGE CRESCENT
Off about 10.15 to Whitechapel. To the Committee rooms. Got my instructions from Miss Simeon and then out until about 2.45. Oh it was hot. Whitechapel is extraordinary. Miss McGowan had come down so I went off for her to Fleet St and fell in love with the editor and Advertisement Manager of the *Daily Herald*.

SATURDAY, SEPTEMBER 27TH 1913 – LONDON: 27 PEMBRIDGE CRESCENT
Another boiling day. [After lunch] on top of a bus to Whitechapel. It took longer than I expected and I was rather late. A meeting of women and girls who had been before – and a tea given them by Miss Raynsford Jackson who afterwards addressed them and could not be heard beyond the first row, I should say, and in any case was very tedious. However one girl ended by playing the piano and made a deafening row. Miss Mansell, Miss McGowan's nice friend, was there – she is a dear – she did all the tea. I chatted and handed round. The girls were so nice – nearly all Jewesses. The pitiful tales they tell of the sweated work is awful – and they are so intelligent – and quite well dressed. The Jews are an example to the gentile in that way.

MONDAY, SEPTEMBER 29TH 1913 – LONDON: 27 PEMBRIDGE CRESCENT

Off at 9.45 to Whitechapel. The train stuck ever so long in the tunnel and I was very frightened. I was about half an hour late. Canvassed the Hospital again and the shops and was walking about all day. The sights and sounds of Whitechapel are too awful – one begins to wonder what on earth will ever do the people any good. Back at 6.30 and scrambled into a bath.

WEDNESDAY, OCTOBER 1ST 1913 – LONDON: 27 PEMBRIDGE CRESCENT

Off about 12. Bus to Piccadilly Circus – lunch at [Eustace] Miles – by train from Charing Cross to St Mary's [the nearest railway station to the Committee room], getting there at 2 o'clock. I need not have hurried as we did not start out on our Poster Parade until 3 o'clock. Miss McGowan, Miss Simeon, Miss Goddard and myself, with Miss Mansell to help give out bills. It was a great success – the Whitechapel folks were very entertained and very few were rude and rough. We got back about 5 all very tired – it is tiring work, the pace is so slow and one has to be so keenly on the lookout for everything – and the mud and dirt in the gutter is so horrid. Then after tea I went off to Mark Lane again to give out bills. Had some sardines on toast at Lyons and to the Committee room 136 Whitechapel Rd at 7.45 where I was joined by Mrs M. Mayer and Mrs Kerr and we all went off to Mile End Waste for an open-air meeting at 8 o'clock. I gave out hand bills and chatted to the crowd. Some of our girl friends were there – they are so affectionate and nice. I was simply dead from standing and did not get home until 10.45. I was so tired I wept as I walked from the station.

THURSDAY, OCTOBER 2ND 1913 – LONDON: 27 PEMBRIDGE CRESCENT

To Whitechapel at 10.30. Miss Goddard was the only one who turned up till afternoon so she and I went off to the Docks to give out handbills. We had a funny morning, as I got arrested twice. The first time by a young and foolish Policeman for holding a Public Meeting where it was not allowed. 'Now then young woman come out of this' with a most savage pull at my arm, nearly knocking me over. It was so absurd – I was only talking to a Custom House official – a very jolly sort of man – and a few loafers had gathered round. The man was so very contrite for what he took upon himself to call his fault and we were both so polite and bowed so many times that the policeman stood silent and blushing and I had to go up to him in the end and say I was sure he only

ניו קאנסטיטושאנעל פטרייען
פאר פרויען רעכט.
136, וויטשעפעל רויד, איסט.

איהר גלויבט נ׳ט אין פרויען רעכט, אבער איהר
זייט איינשטימיג
צו הערען די אנדער זייט

קומט אין אונזער אפיס
פון 11 אוהר מארגענס, ביז 7־30 אבענדס,
און פרעגט זיך נאך
פאר וואס ?
פרויען ווילען רעכט

אויב איהר גלויבט אין פרויען
רעכט דען קומט און הערט ווי
איהר קענט זיי העלפען
קעמפפט פאר פרייהייט
אפען עהר מיטינגס יעדען אבענד

געדרוקט אין מ. וואסמאן׳ס איד׳שע און ענגלישע דרוקעריי, 90, ניו רויד, איסט.

Marjory Goddard was an organiser for the London Society for Women's Suffrage in 1913 and 1914.

Above: A New Constitutional Society leaflet written in Yiddish.

meant to do what he thought was his duty etc and he looked most shamefaced. Just shows what idiots these young men are and what a panic they are in. It was all most amusing, but I hate being touched. The other was more serious if equally funny. A severe and bearded official came savagely towards us – 'I shall have to trouble you to come with me'. I said 'Oh yes.' 'Who gave you permission to give out hand bills at the docks?' I said 'No-one' and that I did not know we needed permission and asked to whom I ought to apply. The question was treated with stony silence. So we walked majestically towards the police station – a crowd at our heels, of course. Finding his silence oppressive I handed the policeman a notice, saying 'have you seen one of these?' He took it, but the glance he gave me might have 'slain' me. He evidently had no sense of humour. Miss Goddard had to drop behind to stifle her laughter. When we got to the police station it all seemed to fall to pieces. I was very quiet but I was calculating every inch of the way. They did not ever take our names or addresses. And when, after a complete silence, I said 'Well is there anything more?' and they said 'No' we came away after a few minutes of more pleasant chat. Miss Goddard said she had never seen any one more completely self possessed than I was. I must say for the first few seconds I had turned very sick. I saw visions of dark cells with beetles – then I realised it could not be so bad and rested with the way I managed it and the only thing I said when I got there was that the offence was quite intentional and left them to take it or leave it as they pleased. Then we gave away the rest of our bills outside the Dock gates. Then back to Whitechapel where we waited till the others came and we poster paraded again. Miss Mansell came again to deliver handbills. We were not allowed to go through the City, but went all round the Tower Hill. We discarded our boards there and went back by train.

Friday, October 3rd 1913 – London: 27 Pembridge Crescent

I did not have to go to Whitechapel but wrote Dover letters all the morning. I went off at 1.45 to Princes Room at Hotel Cecil for the Actresses' Franchise League meeting – to give out notices for the Demonstration. Tried to rub it in all I could, but these are not the sort of people to go – the hall was packed with a large audience. Miss Nina Boucicault, the new Hon. Sec., took the chair. Dr Cobb spoke, but I only heard Miss Margaret Morrison and Mrs Pethick Lawrence. Dinner at Eustace Miles – bus to Kensington and to give away notices at the Town Hall at the Oxford Undergraduates MPU [Men's Political Union] meeting. Mr Harben in the Chair – Mr Nevinson [and] John Scurr.

Saturday, October 4th 1913 – London: 27 Pembridge Crescent

To Whitechapel, getting there soon after 1. We got the things ready and then Miss Goddard and I drove down in the cart seated on chairs and Miss Simeon and Miss McGowan in the Wagonette. We held up boards to advertise the meeting and created some excitement. It was an awful task getting the banners fixed up. We had 2 Platforms. Mrs M.[erivale] M.[eyer] took the Chair at one and had Mr Pethick Lawrence and Mrs Kineton Parkes and Miss McGowan at the other, with John Scurr, Mrs Nevinson and Miss Janette Steer. We had a good crowd but we ought to have had more. I only sold 7

Henry Harben (1874–1967) gave financial support to Sylvia Pankhurst's East London Federation of Suffragettes.

Henry Nevinson (1856–1941) journalist, supporter of women's suffrage and lover of several suffragettes.

John Scurr (1876–1932) London district chairman of the dockers' union. From 1913 Scurr supplied dockers as bodyguards for suffragette speakers in Hyde Park.

Margaret Kineton Parkes (c.1865–1920) secretary of the Women's Tax Resistance League.

Margaret Wynne Nevinson (1858–1932) wife of Henry Nevinson, member of WFL, Women's Tax Resistance League and the Women Writers' Suffrage League.

Votes and mostly to visitors coming from the Tower. I had some interesting chats with Americans. I was very glad when it was over – I didn't enjoy it. I rode back on the cart with Miss Goddard and left the banners etc.

With the conclusion of the Whitechapel campaign, Kate was sent once more to Dover. Miss Simeon was working similarly for the NCS in Bristol.

WEDNESDAY, OCTOBER 8TH 1913 – LONDON: 27 PEMBRIDGE CRESCENT/DOVER: 7 LEYBURNE ROAD

To Charing Cross and by the 7.15 train to Dover. To 7 Leyburne Road and the Burkitts' new house – they only moved Friday. A warm welcome.

THURSDAY, OCTOBER 9TH 1913 – DOVER: 7 LEYBURNE ROAD

Woke at 2 a.m. feeling ghastly and that my end had come, I felt like an inflated cylinder and most weird in the mind. It soon became apparent I was to be sick and I was, many times – until I could no more – with intervals of sitting on the edge of my bed and waiting. I was glad of the hot water bottle. Had my breakfast in bed and sat down to writing about 11. Had to stick at it as I had the difficult matter of the Dover Balance Sheet. Out after tea to see Mrs Buckland and Miss Chambers. Felt rotten all day.

FRIDAY, OCTOBER 10TH 1913 – DOVER: 7 LEYBURNE ROAD

Writing from 10.30 to 12 getting the Agenda ready for the evening. Miss White arrived about 4 o'clock. To the Annual General Meeting held at 11 Effingham Crescent. I had to preside but Mrs Buckland and Miss Falloon said a few words, as also Miss White, who I introduced as the new organiser. There were only 2 ordinary members there besides the Committee – simply dreadful. However the meeting went off very well and it was nice to see Mrs Wilson.

SATURDAY, OCTOBER 11TH 1913 – DOVER: 7 LEYBURNE ROAD

The Miss Burkitts are kind as ever but rather overdone with this huge house – no proper servant and that huge hulking boisterous Mr Dennis in the front room. I find the house very dirty and the meals very piggish.

Kate's stay in Dover was soon curtailed by her redeployment to Wantage, leaving Miss White from Winchelsea to continue with the Dover campaign. On 14, 15 and 16 October all the Fryes' furniture and effects were sold, on site, at The Plat.

WEDNESDAY, OCTOBER 15TH 1913 – DOVER: 7 LEYBURNE ROAD/WANTAGE: REDLANDS, ORMOND ROAD

By the 11.15 train to Reading. All yesterday I could not get it out of my mind – the Sale going on at the Plat. All our beautiful and cherished things being bought up and scattered to the winds. Miss Barnes was at the station very kindly and piloted me to Redlands and I had a very kind reception. Mr Fry, the curate, soon bounced forward and gave me a long greeting and we indulged in a wordy warfare.

THURSDAY, OCTOBER 16TH 1913 – WANTAGE: REDLANDS, ORMOND ROAD
I had some writing to do and then off to the town and to see Mrs Gurney Sheppard. She is far from well and cannot take any part in the work. Back to lunch. Out again to start my round of calling. First on the old members.

The complete contents of The Plat, everything from the 'Capital Electric Launches' – Loosestrife and Red Rattle – to '2 white sardine dishes and covers', had been sold. The South Bucks Press, *24 October, reported that 'many of the articles to be submitted for auction were of more than ordinary interest' and that dealers came 'not only from the immediate district, but also from London'. Among items singled out for special mention were a first edition of* David Copperfield, *a set of 20 original numbers in their paper covers, £7; a William and Mary longcase clock with fine seaweed marquetery, £45; a Chippendale kneehole writing table, £10 10s and a fine old 18th-century French rosewood secretaire, £25.*

SATURDAY, OCTOBER 18TH 1913 – WANTAGE: REDLANDS, ORMOND ROAD
Came in to find depressing letters from Mother and Agnes – all about the Sale. I couldn't stop my tears and had much ado to look decent for my lunch to be brought in. I wept a good deal in the afternoon and felt wretched. Mother, I hear, is very seedy and miserable – the truth of the sale has come home to her after a letter from Mr Vernon with some details – a large company 2 days made comfortable in a tent and chairs on the Lawn. I can just fancy I see them – Mr Tudor and all Wharf Lane enjoying the fun. The whole fetched well over £1000 – so Gilbeys will be paid.

Kate spent listless days making calls, canvassing and organising the next public meeting.

TUESDAY, OCT 28TH 1913 – WANTAGE: REDLANDS, ORMOND ROAD
A very busy day and feeling so weary. Out morning again after lunch to get hall ready. Out to hall at 7 – for the meeting at 8. Only 40 people present, but the night was awful. Miss Mary Fielden was the speaker and was very charming. Mrs Gurney Sheppard had sent to meet her and put her up. I had to take the Chair and did my best. Anyhow I got 4 members out of it.

WEDNESDAY, OCTOBER 29TH 1913 – WANTAGE: REDLANDS, ORMOND ROAD
Mrs Reeves lent me her room for the night as mine was wanted – so I had to move all my belongings early and worked in my pinafore – to Mr Fry's delight – 'a tamed and domesticated suffragette'.

Kate was now sent to nearby Reading where a by-election had been called, caused by Sir Rufus Isaacs' resignation of his parliamentary seat on being made lord chief justice. It was considered a crucial by-election for the Liberals, Isaacs having held it only by the narrowest of margins. The NCS's by-election policy followed that of the WSPU in campaigning against the government – that is the Liberal – candidate. The main topic of the campaign, however, was not women's suffrage, but Irish home rule.

Mary Fielden (1874–1961?) an experienced NUWSS organiser.

THURSDAY, OCTOBER 30TH 1913 – WANTAGE: REDLANDS, ORMOND ROAD/READING: 121 LONDON ROAD

Off by the 2.25 train from here to Reading. Miss McGowan met me. She has been here a week already for the by-election and Mrs Merivale Mayer joined her yesterday. My luggage was sent up and we came by tram to 121 London Rd (Mrs Chandler). Did what unpacking was necessary and then out to see if our Waggonette was placed where it should be at the Cemetery gates at 6.30. Finding all well I went for a walk till 7.30 – just to learn what I could of the streets and from the hoardings. I came across an open-air meeting with Butler, the Socialist candidate, himself speaking. [At the NCS meeting] The usual sort of mudslinging and with an excited gentleman in the crowd it became farcical. We couldn't get a crowd, we weren't in the right position. We all had a try, even I. I thought I was getting on when I had 2 men and a boy and one left saying 'hear hear' and 'That's quite right' – I was talking absolute tosh – too nervous and not yet in tune with a by-election. However, as I say, I thought I was getting on, but I got down to find one man had strolled away, the other appreciative, one dead drunk. So we moved our vehicle and eventually got a better crowd. It came on to rain in torrents. Then we were joined by Miss Mansell, who is here with Miss McGowan, and Miss Dorothy Pethick down here to sell *Votes* for the Fellowship – so, with Miss McGowan, we went off, leaving Mrs M.M. still talking. Miss Pethick is sleeping at my house so we walked back together in the soaking rain and she sat chatting while I had supper.

FRIDAY, OCTOBER 31ST 1913 – READING: 121 LONDON ROAD

Breakfast at 9 with Miss Pethick. She is very like her sister, Mrs P. Lawrence, and is very nice. Most compassionate, but not a kindred spirit. She went off dressed up to the nines to sell *Votes* in the Broadway. I went to Miss McGowan's, Queen Street, at 11. We had a talk and she explained things as she goes back tomorrow, leaving me in charge. Then together to the Committee room she has taken 69 London Rd. A dear little place. Miss Mansell was already there fixing it up. We got it beautifully done – most swanky. Miss McGowan went off early and Miss Mansell – I joined her at the dinner-hour meeting place at 1.30. No Mrs M.M. so we did not hold the meeting but went and supported the WSPU speaker who had no crowd. It is war to the knife with the two [Mrs M.M. and Miss McG.] here. It is a good thing one is going. Miss McGowan wept when she spoke of her trials [with Mrs M.M.]. I mean to take her lightly. Off to Committee room – to have it open at 3.30 and alone there till 5. I have put up the Office Hours 11.30 to 1 3.30 to 5. I took some bunting and things I have down with me and worked at it all the afternoon. No-one came near. Back to tea and then down there to get *Votes* and leaflets and to the Abbey Rd at 7 for meeting at 7.30. But it was a very bad pitch. I had another try and talked longer but awful drivil. Eventually about 8.30 we moved to the Butts. What a pandemonium. I never saw such a sight – a dozen or so meetings going on – the WSPU with a splendid crowd – everyone shouting everyone down – a contest in lung power – oh it was too funny. I wandered around selling *Votes*, when we got an opportunity. Mrs M.M. wasn't there – so we did not hold a second meeting. I must certainly fix things up better than this. Mrs M.M. and I came by tram together as she is staying next door to me. [Of Kate's digs] A very nice landlady who boards me for £1-1 per week – a variety of food but of a coarse kind.

Dorothy Pethick (1881–1970) sister of Emmeline Pethick-Lawrence, left the WSPU after the dismissal of her sister and brother-in-law. Kate's mention of 'to sell *Votes* for the Fellowship' refers to the 'Votes for Women Fellowship' which was the Pethick-Lawrences' main campaign, centred on *Votes for Women*, the paper they took with them from the WSPU. In 1913 Pethick went on a lecture tour of the US with Miss Margaret Hodge.

The WSPU campaign was organised by Elizabeth Grew from an office at 49 Market Place. The WSPU resources were very much greater than those of the NCS, with an army of canvassers and a motor car at their disposal. WSPU speakers concentrated on the iniquities of the 'Cat and Mouse Act' and of forcible feeding.

SATURDAY, NOVEMBER 1ST 1913 – READING: 121 LONDON ROAD

I met Miss Gwen Richard, a WSPU speaker, who was holding the people so splendidly last night in the Butts. Back again to office at 3.30 – and Miss McGowan came in about 4 and we had a long talk about arrangements. We shut up at 5 and, just as we were coming away, met Mrs Graham so all went and tea together. She is a most hysterical woman, but so kind I always get on well with her. Then to the Butts at 7 to see if our Waggonette was alright. Mrs M.M. turned up about 7.30 and the meetings began all around us. However there was so much feeling and friction between my two speakers as to who should begin. It was Mrs M.M.'s turn but she said she was not sent down to Chair and would not – she was sick of the NCS, she shouted out. Both she and Miss McGowan shed tears of rage, were violently rude to one another and walked away. I tried to smooth over matters to Mrs Graham feeling very blue – and also very disgusted when Mrs M.M. asked me if I would take the Chair and I said I would and would do my best. So I spoke for about 10 minutes and got somewhat of a crowd, then introduced Mrs Merivale Mayer. But there was so much noise and racket she could not be heard – I don't think she tried and she soon sat down. She had another little try and then gave it up, it did look a bad lookout for next week. Then I asked Miss McGowan, who made a heroic effort, but she was so hoarse and the Free Cinematograph display by the *Daily Mail* started its funny series of pictures. The crowd was dense but all turned to the pictures and we were the worst placed for the noise of the children. I turned my back on it I was so disgusted and Miss McGowan gave it up. However she made another start and got a fine crowd round her for about half an hour. She and Mrs M.M. both went off to London on the 9.44 train – such a relief to get them both out of Reading.

SUNDAY, NOVEMBER 2ND 1913 – READING: 121 LONDON ROAD

[Recently arrived to stay in the house] Miss Janet Payne of the NU – a very young fair conceited little NU organiser in training. She naturally wanted a fire – so as I did not want to have to ask her up in my room – I lit the sitting room one for her – fetched her coal, made it burn, let her have milk and did what I could for her. She has the typical NU outlook. Almost as bad as the Antis.

Janet Eleanor Payne (1889–1974) member of a Hertfordshire Quaker family, in 1914 was an active member of the Friends' League for Women's Suffrage. Under her married name, Janet Whitney, she wrote novels and biographies of Quaker worthies.

MONDAY, NOVEMBER 3RD 1913 – READING: 121 LONDON ROAD

Woke with rather an oppression upon me, wondering how I was going to conduct the campaign successfully. Mrs M.M. had been pretty rude when I had talked to her, and said I must leave the responsibility of the open-air meetings to her 'she wasn't there to organise' etc. However I determined to take it lightly. To the Office. All the afternoon standing outside trying to sell *Votes* or advertising the two meetings I have determined to hold in the office. I had arranged for an oil heating stove as I was perished and found it very successful. I had a good walk round to find some dinner-hour pitches – so was not in till 2.30. At 5.30 went to keep our pitch in the Butts and then to tea at a Café. Back at 7. Mrs M.M. joined me at 7.45 and we then proceeded to move the Waggonette to where she thought. About 8 she climbed up like a lamb and began and kept on until past 9 and we had quite a good little meeting. Of course the noise and excitement was tremendous again. And at one time the Salvation Army band. What a world.

This was the first by-election contested by what Kate refers to as 'the different League' – the newly-formed National League for Clean Government, whose laudable aim – the elimination of corruption in government – masked strong anti-semitic sentiments. As Kate notes on 6 November, the brothers Cecil and G. K. Chesterton were among the League's leading campaigners. After his defeat G.P. Gooch, the Liberal candidate, rejected active politics, becoming an eminent historian.

TUESDAY, NOVEMBER 4TH 1913 – READING: 121 LONDON ROAD

Breakfast at 9 with Miss Payne, who is a right clever little thing, but very conceited. Perhaps she will improve with age – or perhaps grow worse. I have an idea she would not know if anyone was 'pulling her leg'. Office 11.30 to 1 – when Mrs M.M. joined me and I piloted her to the Caversham Road – first going into the Co-op Stores and borrowing a stool, which we carried to our pitch and had a most excellent meeting of the men who went in to work at 2 o'clock. An Anti Socialist of vile and awful mien tried to shout us down but Mrs M.M. got the crowd by talking Socialism, hardly a word of suffrage. However she was very heated and excited and, though it wasn't quite what we were there for, they were all working men and it went down. The others had to shut down. There are the wickedest looking set of villains I have ever in my life beheld here – whether they be for either candidate or for the different League – never could one behold worse countenances. I begin to feel to look quite as bad – in a soft slouch hat and blanket coat under ordinary conditions I should be well dressed for the country – here I feel eccentric. Mrs M.M.'s face I have never admired. Someone came up and looked curiously at me – raised his hat and smiled – certainly I did not recognise him till he spoke but 'You are Miss Frye are you not?' and then I remembered – Mr Campbell Joseph who I met at Ashford – my friend and gossip. It was clever of him to remember me. How it brought it all back. He is speaking here for Mr Gooch – one of the party men but I believe he has at heart something better in him than mere party. I was quite pleased to see him and he was excited. I told him I thought we all looked an unutterable set of villains and he laughed. We had quite a chat. A great rush to get back to the shop at 3.30, where I waited till 5.30. Had one or two people in. Back to tea at 6 – off at 7 for the Queen's statue outside the Town Hall, where we held a meeting. Quite a nice crowd – 8 to 9. Then we both went in to the Town Hall to hear what we could of the NU meeting. It was deadly – awful speakers, like being back 10 years. Mrs M.M. did not stay long, but I stayed as I want to learn about things in Reading. It was so dull I could have cried. In 10.30 to supper and was joined by Miss Payne and we stayed up some time talking.

WEDNESDAY, NOVEMBER 5TH 1913 – READING: 121 LONDON ROAD

Office 11.30 to 1. Outside most of the time trying to get people to talk to me. Back at 3.

Mrs M.M. turned up at 3.15 and – at 3.30 – not a soul. However 7 people turned up and we held a nice little meeting and made one member – a nice girl at the college. At 7.30 to Cork St, where we had ordered the Waggonette but there was no space for us. So I stood and sold *Votes* until Mrs M.M. came, then we moved to the Butts and got a good pitch and had a splendid little meeting. But, oh, it was so rowdy – the Hooligans with squibs and crackers and tin trumpets and rattles – oh, it was a noise. The WSPU had a good crowd but the boys were so awful and put fireworks underneath the Waggonette – so eventually a policeman came up and they stopped – so we got their crowd. My friend and gossip suddenly appeared on the scene. Mrs M.M. had just started and I was standing beside the vehicle so we two, talking, collected the crowd – people came out of curiosity. He was so obviously interested and moved. How the atmosphere of the Fernley Hotel came back. We had as long a talk as he dared say [sic] and asked all sorts of questions of the work – where I had been. Told me he has two sisters living in Reading and that he himself lives near Dover. I did see an expression in the tail of his eye when I told him I had been there 3 months this year. It does seem strange that fate decided we should not meet in Dover but in Reading. He was at the meeting Masterman [the Liberal MP] was speaking at here and he said it made him feel sick to see the Women thrown out. He was most impressed that my enthusiasm was in no way abated – said women were wonderful the way they were able to concentrate. But I said, no, it was only that something had to be done and the Vote was the best way I could see of getting that something done. He even asked after my acting – he had not forgotten much. His nice brown eyes were gleaming (but he has black teeth). I thought he looked smartened up since yesterday, better brushed and put on. It was the same thing over again – and yet it struck me that he had got married since I met him – there was a something. I wonder what he does for a livelihood besides talking about the Insurance Act. What is it that attracts one person to another? I shall never forget that firework night. I did have a task with the boys but managed them fairly well, made one or two buy *Votes*. I had a horrid wad of something soft and squashy strike me on the mouth, but I just took my handkerchief and wiped it off and I could see the crowd was with me. The boys however never got a squib under my skirts – I walked away in time. Well, it was exciting.

THURSDAY, NOVEMBER 6TH 1913 – READING: 121 LONDON ROAD

Expected Mrs M.M. for a dinner-hour meeting but she did not turn up. Back at 3 for the second of our meetings. Mrs Spikes and a friend of hers turned up – and our new member and a friend I got to come in and then 2 young men students – very self conscious but brave and I collected 3 other people also from the street. Making 9. I let the students out before they got too fed up, but I think they enjoyed the experience. Mrs M.M. went off at 5. I had to wait to clear up – then into my tram got one of the students and sat opposite. Quite a decent boy – has been studying in France and Persia for 2 years but he was very shy. However we chatted until I had to get out. He must have been hanging about some time. We were to have held a meeting in the Butts but it came on a deluge of rain so we made for the Corn Exchange and went to the Clean Government League Meeting. Cecil and G.K. Chesterton speaking. A bigger or more horrible look-

Annie Spikes (1861–1949) wife of an education inspector. 47 Alexandra Road, Reading.

ing man than G.K. I never saw – I am glad he is an Anti – imagine being his wife!!! And Cecil looks as great a villain – they had got a frantic humpbacked man and several other terrible specimens. The pot calling the kettle black – but their revelations were appalling. Mrs M.M. got completely carried away, shouted out 'hear hear' etc and, as everyone had their eye on us, I didn't like it – and their attitude on the woman's question would have prevented me agreeing with anything they said – and I told her so and quieted her.

FRIDAY, NOVEMBER 7TH 1913 – READING: 121 LONDON ROAD

Mrs M.M. joined me and we had a dinner-hour meeting in the Caversham Rd 1.15 to 1.30 and then went and supported the WSPU at our old pitch 1.30 till 2. They had a fine meeting and a working-woman speaker. To the Butts 7.30 and we had our good pitch again opposite the Anti-Suffrage shop and Mrs M.M. spoke from 8 to 9. Then she went off and caught the 9.40 train to London. We have got on quite well during the week but I was thankful to see her go. As the spirit of unrest has entered in I strolled about selling *Votes* – went into the Market Place where everything was at its wildest. I nearly got knocked down – one youth struck me a savage blow but I kept on selling *Votes* and had a magnificent sale. Saw Francesca Graham who had just been chucked out of a Liberal meeting. She was alright but had a strained unnatural expression. Saw the torch-light procession and Capt. Wilson in his Motor Car. Saw my friend and gossip standing at the Committee room door in the Market Place with a lot of others and avoided him like poison. I felt so unchaperoned. I hope he did not see me – it wasn't that I wanted to cut him, but it wasn't the moment for us to meet.

SATURDAY, NOVEMBER 8TH 1913 – READING: 121 LONDON ROAD

Polling day. My work over. I went to the Committee room 11 and was till 1.30 packing up – paying bills etc. [Afternoon to the Town Hall] sold several *Votes* outside. Then to sell them in Broad St. Tea at 5.30 with only 1 copy left. It took me sometime to get rid of that one, but at last two college boys came up for a rag and when, at last, they produced a penny and I handed over the paper I thanked them for buying my last copy and said I was now free to go home. I had a good walk round – and enjoyed the excitement but felt it wisest not to think of venturing out later. The shops were being boarded and barricaded as if for a siege. So I got a Library Book and got back at 8. Sat reading till 10.45 when I heard cheering – so I rushed out and a man passing in a motor called out – 'Wilson majority'. I had had a letter from Gladys asking me to try and get speech of Wilson or his Agent. I knew it was impossible but I got ready and went out at 11 and went to the Salisbury Club. Got permission to stand inside by making myself agreeable and talkative and stuck it till 1am and kept a place in the front row, though it was all most horrible. Capt. Wilson's people getting drunker and drunker every minute. It was disgusting. And when he [Capt. Wilson] did arrive he was carried shoulder high and was rushed past me. I just caught his expression as he was hoisted and knew how he was hating that actual moment and then I bolted and forced my way out through the cheering crowds. Well, I am glad we have 'Kept the Liberal Out' – but what next?

Francesca Graham (1887–1973) educated at Queen's College, Harley Street, 1897–1906. Probably the daughter of the Mrs Graham who presented the NCS with its banner and whom Kate termed 'hysterical' but 'kind'.

Kate returned to Wantage on 13 November, lodging with Mrs Barnes as she continued to canvass. This is the final entry in the thick and heavy volume that she had begun on 29 January 1912.

SUNDAY, NOVEMBER 16TH 1913 – WANTAGE: REDLANDS, ORMOND ROAD
To tea with Mrs Colquhoun at 4.30 to meet her daughter who helps us at the NCS sometimes. He was also there. They are frightfully bigoted Unionists – absolutely party mad, but have a charming house. And so I have come to the end of this volume with no book to go. It would be more sensible to leave off writing a diary at any rate such an extensive one – but more lonely.

MONDAY, NOVEMBER 17TH 1913 – WANTAGE: REDLANDS, ORMOND ROAD
It has taken me some time to decide whether or no I will continue to write a daily diary. It becomes a tax upon time, and a bulky volume such as this – a tax also to my Trunk. And I seem destined now to live a roving life. I have no home, my goods are stored and who can tell when I shall them to hand again – and in this case I can face a more comfortable life without the extra encumberance of diary writing – and diaries to keep. But how I should miss having no record of time, places, names and addresses to refer to. But beyond everything is the feeling that I don't want to give up my diary. It is such an old friend. I cannot be sure it is right at this moment to cut myself off from self expression when so many friends have been taken perforce from me. So this is to be a compromise. At first I made up my mind to buy a regular servicable book printed for diary writers and just put bare facts – but what was I to do from now until January 1st and that would not really answer the purpose and be an outlet and safety valve. So I have decided to fill at least one more of the old sort of books, as, after great storm and stress, I have secured one from Whiteleys at the old price – 2/9 – though they vow never again – and I shall put just the main facts of existence, except when I feel inclined to let out and it will be more a Journal than a diary, and I shall feel that it will fill both wants – a book of reference – and an old friend. So here goes. Out canvassing after writing in the morning. To meet Mrs Merivale Mayer. Took her to her rooms at 4pm. Then a car came for me and I called for Mrs M.M. and we drove to East Challow for a meeting in the Reading Room there – and I spoke a few words. The hall was packed and it was a most extraordinary and orderly meeting.

WEDNESDAY, NOVEMBER 19TH 1913 – WANTAGE: REDLANDS, ORMOND ROAD
Call from Mrs M.M. as I was going to see Mrs Sheppard. I had to take her along. To Childrey for meeting in the evening. Drove in car. Picked up Mrs M.M., who was very rude about going early – and Mrs Deare who is always a balm to a sore spirit. I had to take the Chair. We had a most splendid meeting. Dr Macran was there – looking as mad as a hatter.

FRIDAY, NOVEMBER 21ST 1913 – WANTAGE: REDLANDS, ORMOND ROAD/READING: 121 LONDON ROAD
Left by 2.30 train for Reading and up by tram to 121 London Road – my old rooms. Always a relief to be away from Wantage.

SATURDAY, NOVEMBER 22ND 1913 – READING: 121 LONDON ROAD
Out to the town i.e. to Broad St, to Town Hall, WSPU offices. Bought a second-hand Walt Whitman for 6d. This is delicious stuff.

MONDAY, NOVEMBER 24TH 1913 – READING: 121 LONDON ROAD
To see Miss Cobb – WSPU offices. Out [at] 3 to see Hon Treasurer NU. Fearful person – as bad as an Anti. Called on 3 Vicars – out till 7.

TUESDAY, NOVEMBER 26TH 1913 – READING: 121 LONDON ROAD
Report. Out to see Miss Cobb. Out till 7 calling – 4 Vicars. Came in very depressed – they are an awful lot.

SATURDAY, NOVEMBER 29TH 1913 – READING: 121 LONDON ROAD
Out at 11 to deliver tickets and notices to order. Ordered second lot of printing now I have the Chairman's name for Dec 11th. Gave away bills in the Broadway 12 to 1. Had a long conversation with my young Student boy. I am always running across him. Canvassed 3 to 5 again 6 to 8.

MONDAY, DECEMBER 1ST 1913 – READING: 121 LONDON ROAD/LONDON: 27 PEMBRIDGE CRESCENT
To town to see Miss Cobb. Second lot of printing arrived. 5 thousand hand bills. Packed up after dinner. Up to London by the 5.5 non stop train to Paddington. Taxi to Pembridge Crescent.

TUESDAY, DECEMBER 2ND 1913 – LONDON: 27 PEMBRIDGE CRESCENT
I wrote an article for the Reading paper and got the advertisement ready. Then after lunch to Park Mansions Arcade for the NCS Bazaar. Opened at 3 by Lady Brassey and a great crowd of people present. Held in the new room. Then I took up my post in the Office and Palmisted 3.30 to 6. Then we 3 [Kate, Alexandra & Gladys] came home by bus – had dinner and went back again 8 to 10. And I did some more Palmistry – made £1-1.

WEDNESDAY, DECEMBER 3RD 1913 – LONDON: 27 PEMBRIDGE CRESCENT
Back to Office at 3 for second day of Bazaar. Lena Ashwell was to have opened it but did not come, so Mrs Chapman did. I kept hard at work Palmisting 3.30 till about 6.30. Made another £1-1 and one lady asked me professionally to a party next week. I had my portrait sketched by an artist there – quite clever I think.

THURSDAY, DECEMBER 4TH 1913 – LONDON: 27 PEMBRIDGE CRESCENT/READING: 121 LONDON ROAD
By 10.50 train to Reading. The first object I saw here was my Student but I hid. I wonder if he went to meet every train during the morning. I expect I told him I was returning to-day. But I felt so plain. Got rather wet getting to the GW Hotel for the WSPU meeting. Miss Margesson was speaking and a good number were present. I gave my

Octavia Lewin Cobb (1858–1949) WSPU organiser, working from the WSPU office at 49 Market Place. In 1911 she had been recorded as 'suffragette' on the census return of a boarding house in Church Stretton, Shropshire. Her late father had been a banker and one-time mayor of Banbury and she now lived at 40 Redlands Road with her elderly mother, Mrs Octavia Cobb, and her sisters, Edith and Emily. The latter was a librarian at University College, Reading.

Catherine Margesson, daughter of Lady Isabel Margesson, who was sister to the Earl of Buckingham. Both mother and daughter were active supporters of the WSPU.

notices away and talked to the people. Got some promises of help but not much. Then out canvassing until 7.30. I am glad to be back as I am very anxious about my meeting.

Marjory Goddard came from London to help Kate.

SATURDAY, DECEMBER 6TH 1913 – READING: 121 LONDON ROAD
Miss Goddard and I both out canvassing. I purchased Boards and all the ingredients for making sandwich boards.

SUNDAY, DECEMBER 7TH 1913 – READING: 121 LONDON ROAD
Started sandwich boards as soon as I was down and we both worked from 2 until 8 with interval for tea. It really was a work.

The National Service League was a pressure group formed in 1902 to warn against the inadequacies of the British Army and to advocate a scheme of national service.

MONDAY, DECEMBER 8TH 1913 – READING: 121 LONDON ROAD
A day of canvassing and calling. In the morning we both went to the Caversham Road and gave notices to the working men there. Saw my Student – and somehow he followed us and got in the same tram and had a chat. I gave away at the Town Hall at a National Service League meeting at 8 o'clock.

TUESDAY, DECEMBER 9TH 1913 – READING: 121 LONDON ROAD
Breakfast in bed as I felt so queer on waking. But had to be braced up for the Poster Parade at 11.30. Mrs Stansfield and Mrs Dick and our two selves. We were not in until 1.15 and did the Town thoroughly.

Huntley and Palmers was the largest biscuit maker in the world. Kate's comment about the girls' suitability for motherhood reflects the prevailing concern with eugenics.

WEDNESDAY, DECEMBER 10TH 1913 – READING: 121 LONDON ROAD
Canvassing. Outside Huntley and Palmers at 12.30 to give bills to girls coming out and at 1 for the men. Seven thousand work there and it is a sight to seem them dash out as the Hooter goes at the hour. The girls are not as wild as many factory girls, but they don't look suitable mothers-to-be of the coming generation – very anaemic – and – as for the men – most of them look horribly ill. I suppose it is the heat of the fires in there, but it is pathetic. Canvassing in the evening. To concert at the Town Hall at 8 to give away bills. I know the meeting is going to be a failure.

Martha Louisa Stansfield (1867–1933) wife of the educational secretary of a religious society. 29 Upper Redlands Road, Reading.

THURSDAY, DECEMBER 11TH 1913 – READING: 121 LONDON ROAD
Felt depressed all day. Met [Miss Goddard] at Sutton's, the seed people, and there got rid of the rest of our hand bills in the Broadway until 2. Writing all afternoon – Agenda and arrangements for Stewards etc. Both to the hall. A dancing class going on – so could not begin to get fixed up. I had to leave Miss G. to it while I went to meet Mrs Pertwee

at the station at 7. Took her to the Hotel for dinner. Back to hall – a few people came early but the rest dribbled in and it was awful. I could have sunk through the floor and my face was burning with the agitation – only about 150 people in all. I have never had a failure here. What is it? Have I not done enough canvassing or advertising or what? I was miserable and it was a beautiful meeting. Dr Frank Moxon spoke after Mrs Pertwee in the Chair. I did not hear much but he described the whole process technically – of forcible feeding from the medical point of view. I had to wait about for the Rev. Lewis Donaldson, who came from Leicester and he did not get to the Hall until about 8.30. My heart went out to him at once – we loved one another – one can always tell. What a man – why are there not a few more as exciting and exhilarating? Of course he is mad – then so am I really – though I try and appear calm – but how much nicer. He spoke magnificently – never have I heard anything more beautiful – and those who heard him must have been impressed from his fervour – what a gift to speak to people like that. He took hold of me as he came from the platform. 'Let me speak for you again. I should like to.' It took away all my disappointment. He had not been disgusted with the badly filled room. I tried to be nice to Dr Moxon and I liked his nice brown honest eyes – but he was not thrilling. He and Mrs Pertwee – who had made a very bad Chair I thought – no appeal at all – went off to catch the train and I had a little talk to the dear thing. It is a little like the Rev. Hugh – only much more robust and more 'jolly' – a younger man too. Home to supper after packing up, thanking Stewards etc. Both [Kate and Miss Goddard] very disappointed. Oh dear how I hate a failure – it does not do me any good.

FRIDAY, DECEMBER 12TH 1913 – READING: 121 LONDON ROAD

Went to see Miss Goddard off at 11. Why is it I am always so pleased to get rid of people? I only live for the time to be alone again. And Miss G. has been so good and enjoyed it all so much. But of course she is not really companionable to me – how could she be? – and then who is? – and before those simple adoring people I talk too much and brag and exaggerate and tell too much of the truth too – and they always remember it and ask one awkward questions too. One does it to seem clever at the moment, I suppose. After to see Miss Cobb and pretend I wasn't disappointed. Then a round of the newspaper offices to see reporters. I did them no good – they had got it all there and would not add any. I wasted a lot of breath. I seemed to impress some of the young men, some of Mr Donaldson's magnetism remaining over. I saw Mrs Stansfield and she is so pleased she has promised me £2 as a donation.

SATURDAY, DECEMBER 13TH 1913 – READING: 121 LONDON ROAD/WANTAGE: REDLANDS, ORMOND ROAD

12.42 train to Wantage. Rushed to Ormond Road, where I was greeted very kindly by Miss Barnes. I snatched some lunch and rushed off to The Ham for meeting of members at 3 o'clock. And we started the Wantage branch of the NCS. Mrs Gurney Sheppard gave us a delightful tea.

TUESDAY, DECEMBER 16TH 1913 – WANTAGE: REDLANDS, ORMOND ROAD

Out canvassing and again out 3 to 4.30 for my meeting. Met the Vicar in the morning

Dr Frank Moxon had been monitoring the physical condition of suffragettes after their release from hunger striking.

Rev. F. Lewis Donaldson (1860–1953) vicar of St Mark's, Leicester, was a Christian socialist and a supporter of women's suffrage. He had a reputation as an excellent speaker. His wife was a vice president of the Church League for Women's Suffrage.

and Mr Fry in the afternoon – actually in the same house urging people to go to their service. They purposely fixed it on the night of our meeting when that particular service is usually much nearer Christmas. Pigs!!! Yes they are. Had my tea – changed – then to the hall at 6.30 to see all in order as I had not been earlier. Mrs G. Sheppard put Mrs Pertwee up but she herself was away. A Miss Grace Hadow, such a nice women, came to take the Chair and Mrs Pertwee gave a delightful address – but we were only 18 people in all. I could have fainted. Miss Hadow was just charming about it. Mrs Pertwee just a bit ruffled – and I don't wonder. 'Why I had 100 people in a drawing-room on such and such a day' etc. However we made 1 member and, as usual, my good friend, Mr Overton, was there to cheer. Why is it that I appreciate a man around me? I don't really admire them and Mr O is exceedingly quaint, but there it is.

On 17 December, meeting up with John on the way, Kate travelled to Worthing, where the family was now living. Agnes had been ill.

MONDAY, DECEMBER 22ND 1913 – WORTHING: OCKHAM, PARK AVENUE

[A day shopping in Brighton] Brighton and the same old people – the very same old people – fatter, older, vulgarer (if possible), the same type of racing man and woman, the same hotels. I suppose the same sea, but one could not see it for the mist – it took me back in thoughts of bygone days. Our old triumphs at the Metropole in our clothes and expensive furs – doing the smart. I remember a pink evening dress and a young man following me about and gazing at me. Why did he do it? I thought through admiration. Well, perhaps it was. I believe I was very pretty and very unusual in those days. I always feel given nice clothes and etc now I could look nice and attractive. I hate being shabby. It is bad enough to grow old, but to grow dowdy with it, but what can one do without money and lots of it. I do seem to grumble. I seem to forget I am aiming for 'goodness' in an advanced and suffrage meaning, and that really any other state is very petty.

As ever, Kate was in tune with the times. Christabel Pankhurst's book, The Great Scourge and How to End It, *promoting 'Votes for women and chastity for men', had recently been published and was being promoted very vigorously by the suffragette press. 'The Great Scourge' was syphilis.*

WEDNESDAY, DECEMBER 24TH 1913 – WORTHING: OCKHAM, PARK AVENUE

We had had an agitating day. John and I coming near a scene – how is it in a moment a thing may happen to fill one with enough violent emotion to wreck a life? Everyone is telling of Christabel Pankhurst's book and certain Diseases. When we just went out either he or I mentioned the question it involves. Strangely enough I had never thought of John being different in such a way to what I should approve of, how shall I express it – it is so difficult – well, guilty of immoral relations with woman for his health and convenience. A question of love and passion would be a different matter. And then the remembrance of the statistics – the number of men who must use women – sent me reeling over – just as if I had had a blow in the face – why should I think John different to the rest – how should he be? I asked him as point blank as I could – in the crowded

Grace Hadow (1875–1940) lecturer at Lady Margaret Hall, Oxford and secretary of the Cirencester branches of the NUWSS and of the Conservative and Unionist Women's Franchise Association.

thoroughfare. He didn't answer readily enough or straight enough and so I knew. I did not know what to do. I wanted to lose him then and there. I never wanted to look at him or speak to him again. The question was – how I could end it between us? I was struck dumb – I couldn't speak to him – my hair was on fire – I could hardly keep the tears out of my eyes. I carried Mickie in my arms and went on with my shopping. John, of course, knew something had happened – I don't suppose he realised the situation and we had to get our Christmas presents. I tried to help him – to be kind – but I was already facing the future. I felt it might be unjust but that it was a physical impossibility to do anything else than to end it all as soon as possible. What excuse should I give everyone? On the Parade he became wrought up to a fearful pitch – I suppose I said things – 'I was cruel' – 'Never, never, never' etc. I told him I could not believe him. 'Why this all suddenly?' etc. It had only just occurred to me. 'I was unjust' 'This was a nice Christmas' etc 'What was going to happen?' Well it did seem a NICE Christmas eve I must say. I was absolutely stricken. We had it all out again on the way home and he swore 'never had it been so with him – or with his father or uncles – none of his people – he knew lots of men – couldn't understand them – thought they must be mad.' Etc etc. I had to believe – how cruel not to – besides I did believe – if it had been otherwise with such a transparent person and with my senses I must have known. I have always put him clean outside any suspicions of that sort. But he had not seemed to mind my question – perhaps he did not realise what I meant. Certainly his answer was not conclusive – and in a mad bound my brain had seized upon the belief in the worst. We had it at intervals all day – I grew comforted, but it was very awful. He did not realise in the least. A man, any sort of man, would not. I suppose my warning would only sound like a threat that if ever such did happen – that he should lay a finger on a woman to help on with the evil of the world – that never, never would I have anything to do with him again. But is anything worth all this? Is any man possible if the physical relations have been made so repulsive and dangerous between man and woman – and if no-one is delicate and decent about them? I never wanted to marry, though I did not know why, and now the whole idea is repulsive to me. And yet I suppose I am in love. I suppose it will have to be faced one day.

On 8 January Kate returned to Reading and the NCS campaign.

FRIDAY, JANUARY 9TH 1914 – READING: 121 LONDON ROAD

My birthday and I am 36. What an age – quite done for – yes, a woman is done for after 35 – especially if she can't afford to dress well or look smart. I have wept a good deal during the day – everything seems so hopeless and I hate to be back at work again – and I hate to have leave them at Worthing in that filthy house. Out 5 to 6.30 to see Miss Cobb etc. Wrote till 8 – supper – wept again and then to bed.

In 1913 Wessex Hall was newly opened in Redlands Road as the third hall for women at University College Reading.

FRIDAY, JANUARY 16TH 1914 – READING: 121 LONDON ROAD

To call on a certain Mrs Gilford and investigate the Wokingham Road in the morning. Went quite in the country. Earley it is called. To tea with a Miss Sharps [?] at 4 o'clock, she is warden of Wessex Hall and seems a nice girl – afterwards to see Mrs Wild and Mrs Stallard, old London St friends.

THURSDAY, JANUARY 20TH 1914 – READING: 121 LONDON ROAD

The printing arrived at 12.30. Wrote all the morning and started canvassing in the afternoon. Did Craven Road, but it was an awful business. [After tea] to the [Women's] Freedom League Meeting at Palmer Hall. Miss Anna Munro was the speaker – they have just started a branch down here.

THURSDAY, JANUARY 29TH 1914 – READING: 121 LONDON ROAD

Out 7.30 to hear Dr Saleeby lecture on 'Patriotism and Parenthood'. The hall was not nearly full and more than half the audience women. Sat next to Miss Osmond of the Theosophical Society. Met Miss Smith of the [Women's] Freedom League coming out and we all walked up here together.

TUESDAY, FEBRUARY 3RD 1914 – READING: 121 LONDON ROAD

Out 3.30 to 7 up Wokingham Rd way to see Miss Cobb's people [i.e. WSPU members] in that district. All too poor to help.

SATURDAY, FEBRUARY 7TH 1914 – READING: 121 LONDON ROAD

Canvassed the London Road 11.30 to 1.30 for School meeting. Out at 6 to the Library – a pouring wet night. I changed my book – or rather renewed it – and sat in the Reading Room until 8 o'clock. I saw my Student out of the tail of my eye but as one could not talk there I did not want to see him. However as I came out he was standing in the hall. I spoke a word and he followed me out, leaving his friend, and saw me in to the tram. 'Would I have coffee?' – blushing a fine purple – I was quite as upset myself. I should have liked to have a talk to him – but one does not know – and of course one always refuses without giving oneself time to reason. Why should not I have gone? – I am nearly old enough to be his Mother – we should both have enjoyed – perhaps I should have made some real difference to him for the rest of his life, but one does not do these things because, forsooth, 'common' girls do and because one is different. So silly but there it is – as I say, one does not reason about it, it is just instinct. So I came home and no-one to talk to.

Marie Bashkirtseff (1858–1884) Russian diarist, painter and sculptor studied art in Paris. From the age of 13 she kept a journal, later published and still in print today, recounting her struggle as a woman and as an artist.

SUNDAY, FEBRUARY 8TH 1914 – READING: 121 LONDON ROAD

I am reading *The Journal of Marie Bashkirtseff*. It is too absolutely interesting for words – and yet all so natural. Take the Russian out of her that goes in someways more and in

Alice Gilford (c 40) wife of a doctor. 60 London Road, Reading.

Henrietta Wild (1857–1922) shopkeeper. 71 London Road, Reading.

Anna Munro (1881–1962) a Scotswoman, in April 1913 had married Sidney Ashman, a Berkshire supporter of the Men's League for Women's Suffrage. Anna Munro's sister-in-law was secretary of the Newbury and Thatcham branch of the WFL.

Dr C. W. Saleeby (1878 -1940) popular lecturer and writer, a Fabian and an espouser of eugenics, rational recreation and dress reform.

some ways not so far – it isn't far off me in the inmost soul. Only in performance she was a genius – she could do – I can only dream what I could and do – accomplish. It made me want to read my old Journals but how tame after Marie's. I was always for putting time and place and leaving out the really interesting bits in consequence – though I sometimes think I catch atmosphere. That is the disadvantages of writing a diary instead of a Journal – one only ought to write when one is inspired and at the moment the feeling or idea strikes one – but with a diary the date and correctness is the thing. If I can't write up to the date I at least make notes so as not to get the dates wrong.

WEDNESDAY, FEBRUARY 11TH 1914 – READING: 121 LONDON ROAD

At last – the day of my meeting and it just poured all day long. I could not attempt to go out in the morning but made my preparations. Changed my dress – lunch at 1 and off at 1.45 to the Great Western Hotel where we held the meeting. Just saw it ready then to meet Mrs Chapman and Alexandra at 2.27 and bring them across. Miss Cobb and Mrs Julius arrived early to Steward. I was in a terrible state lest no-one should come but the room was practically full, though none of the people I most wanted and expected turned up. I feel I might just as well not have been here these last three weeks working for it – only a few outsiders came. Alexandra took the Chair. She said a good deal and her voice did not sound quite as clenched as of old – but it was a good bit squeezed – and I did not feel she was holding the people. Mrs Chapman spoke well and was very charming. As usual at these times I feel dazed – only semi-conscious. I might do or say anything mad. We had a hurried tea and Alexandra and I saw Mrs Chapman to the train for the 5.5 and went back and finished our tea. Mrs Graham then went off – she had been very trying – then Miss Cobb left – and Alexandra and I had a chat and I saw her off at 6.10. I went back to Hotel – packed and settled up.

SATURDAY, FEBRUARY 14TH 1914 – READING: 121 LONDON ROAD

Out 11 to 1.15. Canvassed Grange Avenue – it took for ever and then I only did part of one side. There seems a lot of sickness about and I just escaped a house with fever. Out at 7 to the Library and then at 8 to a Theosophical Lecture on 'Life after Death'. I much enjoyed it and had a chat with the speaker afterwards – a large pale man – who said that we might possibly meet during the night on the Astral Plain.

SUNDAY, FEBRUARY 15TH 1914 – READING: 121 LONDON ROAD

Read all the afternoon – a book of Turgenev. In a letter to John I told him if there should be a vacancy in his co[mpany] at the Summer Tour I would apply and join. It came to me yesterday I must do this. Friday I had as little idea of it as the man in the moon – probably less. I don't suppose anything will come of it, but I should like the chance of trying the stage once more. As for this work I am completely fed up with it. It is people's own loss if they are not Suffrage, but I seem to have lost the knack of converting them. Personally I am keener than ever but I feel I loathe and detest the work of it.

MONDAY, FEBRUARY 16TH 1914 – READING: 121 LONDON ROAD

Canvassed Caversham Road in the morning and bawled at people in their doorways as the Trams clanged past.

TUESDAY, FEBRUARY 17TH 1914 – READING: 121 LONDON ROAD

Out giving away handbills. At 7 o'clock to the Wokingham Road Schools for the meeting at 8. I had to take the Chair and Mrs Merivale Mayer came down from London to speak. It was most awful – only 18 people turned up – and after all those promises. We made 1 member.

MONDAY, FEBRUARY 23RD 1914 – READING: 121 LONDON ROAD

I went at 4 o'clock to tea at the Cobbs – saw Mother aged 89 and the 3 maiden daughters. Came back and had a rest and then to the National Union [for Women's Suffrage Societies] meeting at the Town Hall. A Councillor in the Chair and Mrs Philip Snowden and Mrs Rackham as speakers. The hall was fairly full. I disliked Mrs Snowden's attitude very much but she went down with the multitude and she is a magnificent speaker. All the Suffrage people I knew seemed to be there and there was only one hand held up against the resolution.

Kate's Organiser's book reveals that Mrs Merivale Mayer addressed this meeting on the subject of 'Woman's Place in the Citizen Life' and that the collection came to 6d and sales of Literature 7d.

TUESDAY, FEBRUARY 24TH 1914 – READING: 121 LONDON ROAD

Out canvassing 11 to 1 in the Caversham Road. Dozens of people have promised to come but I never knew a place like Reading for broken promises. Off at 7 for the Swansea Road School. Mrs Merivale Mayer speaker – self in the Chair and a more miserable meeting I have never known. Only 16 persons – made only 1 member – it really is too awful. It is no use minding, but I must say it is depressing and I might just as well never have come to Reading.

WEDNESDAY, FEBRUARY 25TH 1914 – READING: 121 LONDON ROAD

Had to go to the Swansea Road Schools for a cloak left by Mrs M.M. Who should I chance upon but the Student. I told him I was about to leave Reading and I think he was sorry – though only twice have we spoken this year. I think he must be a nice child though a quaint one. He owned to being 'sentimental'. We shook hands at parting. I don't know his name. Changed, had an early tea. I expected a meeting of members. Only Mrs Stansfield, Miss Cobb and Mrs Julius turned up. Consequently Mrs Stansfield put her foot down and the Branch was not set going. I am beyond disappointment over Reading – nothing goes right here.

Ethel Snowden (1880–1951) wife of the ILP politician, Philip Snowden. At this time Ethel Snowden was a member of the NUWSS's Election Fighting Fund Committee, formed to support Labour party candidates. That may have been the aspect of Ethel Snowden to which Kate took exception.

THURSDAY, FEBRUARY 26TH 1914 – READING: 121 LONDON ROAD/WORTHING: OCKHAM, PARK AVENUE

Lugged my bag to the station and left it in the cloak room. Left my library book, then took a tram and got to Miss Cobb's just before 4 for a tea and meeting after to discuss the possibility of starting a Suffrage Shop and Library and Club for the 5 societies now in Reading. I only spoke once – Dr Armitage was in the Chair. Nothing much was arrived at and when Dr Armitage left I also crept out, with a quiet handshake all round, and flew down the road and reached the station in time for the 6.10 train to London. From Paddington I had to get my trunks taken to Liverpool St and put them in the cloak room. Then on the underground again to Victoria with my bag, case and book and by the 8.35 train to Worthing

Kate spent a few days with her family in Worthing before continuing the NCS campaign in Norfolk.

TUESDAY, MARCH 3RD 1914 – WORTHING: OCKHAM, PARK AVENUE/FAKENHAM: QUEEN'S ROAD

[To Fakenham] to Mrs Rush's, Queen's Road, my old rooms and found things very nice.

WEDNESDAY, MARCH 4TH 1914 – FAKENHAM: QUEEN'S ROAD

Had to go out and order the Printing and to the post. Norfolk seems much nicer than Reading, and the air, although wet, so much more invigorating.

MONDAY, MARCH 9TH 1914 – FAKENHAM: QUEEN'S ROAD

At 4.30 to tea with Mrs Johnson. Her daughter is just up after a poisoned throat. We did not have tea until about 5.30 or 6 – and I was made to remove my hat etc – then when the meal came we all sat round and ate boiled eggs. Everything was quite nice really, but it all tasted as if it had been cooked on a houseboat and I wanted badly to be sick. Then the lunatic son sat opposite and he had different food to ours and scraped some stuff out of a tin to put on his bread and grinned at me. Oh it was awful. I did not get away till nearly 8 o'clock

Eleanor Johnson (1851–1925) a committee member of the local NCS branch, was the wife of an electrician and ran a registry for domestic servants. Her daughter, Florence, was the head teacher of a county council school. When filling in the 1911 census form her husband noted that she had borne nine children, of whom four had died, and in the 'Infirmity' column, against the entry for their son, Ernest, wrote 'From 6 months feeble minded'. Oak Street, Fakenham.

TUESDAY, MARCH 10TH 1914 – FAKENHAM: QUEEN'S ROAD/EAST DEREHAM: 3 ELVIN ROAD

To Dereham. Mrs Teanby met me and we drove to Elvin Lodge in the bus. She is having me as a P[aying] G[uest]. I don't think Mr Teanby approves but was very civil to me. We had tea – all sorts of things – hot cakes – then I unpacked and at 6 we had another tea – fish etc – and Miss Cory attended that meal. Then just before 8 we three went off to the YMCA Lecture room for a Members' meeting. Only 9 turned up so it was very informal. I was supposed to speak – but we just talked. Then got back and were invited to partake of another meal. I ate ginger biscuits then about 11 o'clock to bed. Everything spotless – crochet work on everything – and everything very nice.

On 10 March a WSPU member, Mary Richardson, attacked the Velasquez painting, 'Venus with a Mirror', hanging in the National Gallery, in order to draw attention to what she saw as the slow destruction of Mrs Pankhurst, who had, on 9 March, yet again been arrested.

WEDNESDAY, MARCH 11TH 1914 – EAST DEREHAM: 3 ELVIN ROAD

Miss Cory here at 10.30 and we went through the people I am to call upon. Out 12 to 1. To see Miss Shellabear. Very off, of course, the latest – the Rokeby Velasquez – is upsetting everyone now. Out 2.45 to 6.15. Calls. Happened on the new people at Quebec Hall who are keen WSPU. Had tea with Miss Louisa Gay who has done 8 months – a very jolly girl – she means to do some waking up if she can. Then to see Mr and Mrs Hewitt – I do like them so. Miss Cory and Mrs Goddard here 8 to 10. Talking. Talking. Talking.

MONDAY, MARCH 16TH 1914 – FAKENHAM: QUEEN'S ROAD

To meet Miss Hodge [the speaker] who arrived safely. I took her to Mrs Stimpson who put her up, then to arrange the hall for the meeting at 8. We had a fair number of people and it went off very well. I took the Chair myself and felt an awful ass. Miss Hodge was quite good.

The 'usual question' addressed by Miss Hodge was doubtless that of prostitution and the white slave trade.

TUESDAY, MARCH 17TH 1914 – FAKENHAM: QUEEN'S ROAD/EAST DEREHAM: 3 ELVIN ROAD

Both [Kate and Miss Hodge] by 3.47 Dereham. Sent our things to Mrs Teanby's and Mrs Hewitt's respectively – walked to the Masonic Hall where the Committee were at work – then to Quebec Road – then with Mrs Teanby. To the Hall at 7 for the Social At Home at 7.30. A huge success. 70 people. I quite enjoyed myself – principally because I looked right and because I spoke well – the best I have done. I had to take the Chair for Miss Hodge, the Rev. Anthony Fenn being ill with flu and, as she spoke principally upon the usual question, it took some toning down.

Louisa Gay, a teacher from South Croydon, had been sentenced to eight months' imprisonment in January 1913 for pouring black dye into a post box at Tanners Hill, Deptford, and damaging its contents.

Margaret Hodge had lived for 12 years in Australia and was a member of the executive committee of the Australian and New Zealand Women Voters' Committee (London). She had been a member of the WSPU, but had moved over to the NCS. Shortly after this meeting she travelled, with Dorothy Pethick, to New York, to lecture there before moving on to Chicago and Toronto. See also entry for 16 March 1915.

THURSDAY, MARCH 19TH 1914 – EAST DEREHAM: 3 ELVIN ROAD

Telegram from Agnes – grave news telling me that Daddie had been taken ill and an operation was talked of. [Another telegram] Operation over – doctors hopeful.

SATURDAY, MARCH 21ST 1914 – EAST DEREHAM: 3 ELVIN ROAD/WORTHING: OCKHAM, PARK AVENUE

[Back to Worthing]– was met at the station by Agnes and Mother. Daddie passed away peacefully at 10.30 last evening at a nursing home.

It now fell to Kate to take charge of the family finances. She was summoned by her cousin, Newman Gilbey, to an interview at the imposing Gilbey headquarters in the Pantheon in Oxford Street. Newman explained how incompetent Frederick Frye's business dealings had been and how Gilbeys had lost a considerable amount of money on their investment in Leverett and Frye. In the circumstances they were only able to make Kate's mother an annual allowance of £150 for five years. Newman Gilbey suggested that Agnes should find work; Kate refused to discuss her own affairs. As she wrote, 'I ought to be proud to be independent, but the idea just terrifies me'. In the event

Newman's mother – Kate's Aunt Agnes – doubled their income by giving her sister, Mrs Frye, an additional allowance of £150 a year and let Kate and Agnes know that in her will she had left them an annual allowance of £50 a year each for life. After a month in Worthing Kate returned to London and the NCS office. This marked the end of her campaigning in the country. From now on she was to be deployed in London's outer suburbs.

MONDAY, APRIL 20TH 1914 – WORTHING: OCKHAM, PARK AVENUE/LONDON: 49 CLAVERTON STREET

[To London] I got a four wheeler and drove to Claverton St – to my old rooms. It must be 3 years and more since I was in it. Miss Heffer and her sister look just the same – if anything more prosperous. Oh the room felt hot and oh the colour of the sheets. However I would not let myself dwell on things and set to work to re-paper and dust all drawers and cupboards with raising as little dust as possible. At least I felt I could put a few things away, and the food cupboard I made nice. A summer night. I lay and thought about things and felt wonderfully calm and so extremely thankful for the wonderful peace that has come to my soul.

This performance of Ibsen's Ghosts, *in which Bessie Hatton played Mrs Aveling, was staged by J.T. Grein for the benefit of the New Constitutional Society. The play received its first British public licensed performance on 14 July, after the Lord Chamberlain had lifted his censorship ban.*

SUNDAY, APRIL 26TH 1914 – LONDON: 49 CLAVERTON STREET

To the Chapel Royal – and with beating heart entered. I don't know why I feel guilty but I did not want to be seen. I loved the service, it was so nice. Mr Cecil Chapman read the lessons, and the Rev. Hugh preached – very nice but not one of his best, I should think, but he told us not to be afraid of receiving friendliness and help – or it would be too late to let people love us. I liked him immensely in the church – so dignified. It was very full, just the people I should have expected. I have not set eye on him for 3 years – what a strange world – the last words he said were 'I shall come back and see you next week'. To the Court Theatre at 7 o'clock – to take charge of the Box Office at 7.30 for the performance of 'Ghosts' at 8pm. My word it was a game. A perfect scramble. I had no idea it would be like that – I don't know how I kept my head. The people outside just stampeded. One could not take any money as we should have broken the law so I just had to do it on my own responsibility and take names and addresses. I did not do it well but I did it somehow. [The play was] very well done – especially Leon Quartermain – Miss Bessie Hatton I did not care so much about – too much like the old-fashioned idea of Ibsen – Grein has arranged the performance for the NC Society and they have organised and done it. The theatre was very full – and quite an interesting audience. I had a talk to Mrs Chapman –also Mr Chapman. I did not mind being gazed at as I had my new frock on and if I did look very pale and tired I looked at any rate interesting.

MONDAY, APRIL 27TH 1914 – LONDON: 49 CLAVERTON STREET/27 PEMBRIDGE CRESCENT

Packed up. Oh I am so sick of packing, and had unpacked so completely and comfortably. I hated leaving my little dirty room. Left my things to come by Carter Paterson and took my bag to the Office. Met Miss McGowan and Alexandra and we had a talk about my work. I don't believe she half likes handing over any part to me. To Pembridge Crescent – I found my luggage had arrived but was not upstairs so had to unpack in the hall and then the maids got it up.

TUESDAY, APRIL 28TH 1914 – LONDON: 27 PEMBRIDGE CRESCENT

I went off to Peckham at 10.30 to begin to find out something about the place and call on some of the local members. I longed to go to the At Home at 3 to hear the Rev. Hugh Chapman but I had been as good as told I was not expected to appear, naturally they don't want the organisers there every Tuesday, wasting their time, and I couldn't ask for an exception to be made in my case, but I was told to be there after to rope people in and I did hope I might see him. I got there at 4, but he had spoken and gone. I was fearfully disappointed, but somehow glad.

WEDNESDAY, APRIL 29TH 1914 – LONDON: 27 PEMBRIDGE CRESCENT

Off to Twickenham. Made a call at Teddington. Lunch at Richmond. Train to Sloane Square and arrived at the N[ew] C[onstitution] Hall in time for the speakers' class at 3. I was horribly frightened. Mrs Pertwee pounced on me to take the Chair. This is Alexandra's idea. Miss Simeon has been attending it, but it's too awful the agony I suffer. Lots of the pupils speak really well.

SATURDAY, MARY 2ND 1914 – LONDON: 27 PEMBRIDGE CRESCENT

To Hounslow. Called on a quantity of Vicars – spent over an hour at one place.

SUNDAY, MAY 3RD 1914 – LONDON: 27 PEMBRIDGE CRESCENT

Gladys and I went off by bus and train to Harlesden to have tea with Miss Wiskemann and family, which we had in the garden, so I was glad I had my fur coat on. The Austrian gentleman who frequents the NCS At Homes was there and Miss Wiskemann only met him on Tuesday. She is a most peculiar young woman. I am sure in the meantime they have met. I could not do with her myself. She is not ladylike or nice in her methods but Gladys, though she complains, seems rather envious, I think. Well, they are both a lot younger than I am – perhaps I don't understand – but I was never like that with all my wickedness.

WEDNESDAY, MAY 6TH 1914 – LONDON:27 PEMBRIDGE CRESCENT

To Office. Lunched alone and studied *The Times* for my speech. Then to the speakers' class. I was in worse agony than before, but Mrs Palmer has told them I must be made to speak – that I can speak. I spoke on the Political Situation. There is now a rumour that I am to speak at one of the big At Homes. Most of them are very dull but quite good.

THURSDAY, MAY 7TH 1914 – LONDON: 27 PEMBRIDGE CRESCENT

To Hounslow. Calls. Came in for quite a bad thunderstorm and as it was still pouring went on the Tube under the river [from Waterloo] to Piccadilly and to the Aquascutum shop and ordered a new coat. I have had my old one 10 years this summer.

WEDNESDAY, MAY 13TH 1914 – LONDON: 27 PEMBRIDGE CRESCENT
To Office. Lunch alone in agony trying to think out my speech 'What is the Womanly Woman' – then to the speakers' class at 2.30. As usual I got a lot of applause and encouragement.

SATURDAY, MAY 16TH 1914 – LONDON: 27 PEMBRIDGE CRESCENT
[Afternoon] to Peckham by bus. Had a most tiring afternoon going all over the place – Dulwich, Herne Hill, looking for a speaker. There had been a special Committee called to consider the Ipswich election and a great row at it according to A[lexandra] & G[ladys]. Miss McGowan is to go off Monday – and she wanted to take Miss Simeon and G. would not spare Miss Simeon. They wanted Miss McG. to have me but she refused me at any price – and I gather must have said some very disparaging things. I have somehow guessed that there is some sort of feeling – I believe Miss McG. is jealous. I can't see any other reason. I am jolly glad – I should have hated to go, but A. seems to imply that if I don't speak up for myself at Committee that I shan't be much thought of. I think it is all beastly. Goodness alone knows what they want. I get so worked up sometimes I feel I must send in my resignation. If they could say straight out instead of implying that something is wrong. I as good as told A. if they did not like me I would leave – that I would not wait for them to discuss me, as they have Miss Goddard at Miss McGowan's recommendation. This seems to have been a most unpleasant week. Naturally it has taken me some time to get the things going in London but no one could do much more than I do.

MONDAY, MAY 18TH 1914 – LONDON: 27 PEMBRIDGE CRESCENT
Had to move some of my things upstairs after breakfast as Mrs Pertwee is coming. I told Alexandra it was an opportunity to get rid of me, but they asked me to stay on until Whitsuntide, so I am sleeping in a tiny room upstairs. To Hounslow calling and canvassing [until] 4.30. A train to Peckham for the open-air meeting. One Mrs Bostock turned up to take the Chair, and one Mr McKillop from the Men's League was the speaker. But he was in rather a 'mood' – a queer being – and he did not handle the men and had to give up to Mr Bostock. He came up to me and told me I ought to speak once in such a manner that I said 'very will I will' – so when Mr Bostock had a huge crowd but rather turbulent up I got – and I really did do it well. I did not speak for more than 10 minutes or so but I absolutely got the crowd round and held them. It was lovely speaking to a big crowd. I have never seen such a big one and they were so quiet and applauded when I got down. I could see Mr McKillop was impressed – he was quite different and told me I spoke alright. I was very bucked. We walked as far as the tram together. He has only one arm.

John McKillop (b. 1862) had been the first librarian at the London School of Economics but by 1911 was secretary to an MP. His wife, Margaret (1864–1929), was a lecturer in chemistry in King's College, London, Woman's Department.

WEDNESDAY, MAY 20TH 1914 – LONDON: 27 PEMBRIDGE CRESCENT
To Office – a morning's work – bought an orange and went and sat in the park and ate

it and tried to make up my mind what I was going to speak about. To the class at 2.30 – the last of the season –I am so glad – they do frighten me. Mrs Pertwee told me last night that a week ago a lady came to hear the class and make arrangements with her for private lessons and, after asking who I was, said she wished to be taught to speak just like me – my manner, my voice and my way was quite charming and she wished to take me as her model. I wonder if Mrs Pertwee will be able to manage it all. But of course it does sound encouraging. Well, I spoke on 'What it is we are really asking for?' and, having done a little cramming, did alright – at any rate the class was loud in its praise.

While the NCS still put its faith in the ability of its speakers to persuade the masses of the rightness of their cause, the WSPU, having failed to influence the government, decided to appeal directly to the King. Of the hundreds who took part in the melee on 21 May, only 66 were arrested. During the following day's court proceedings the prisoners defiantly subverted the solemnity of the occasion.

THURSDAY, MAY 21ST 1914 – LONDON: 27 PEMBRIDGE CRESCENT

To Office. Then in the afternoon I went to Buckingham Palace to see the Women's deputation – led by Mrs Pankhurst which went to try and see the King. It was simply awful – oh! those poor pathetic women – dresses half torn off – hair down, hats off, covered with mud and paint and some dragged along looking in the greatest agony. But the wonderful courage of it all. One man led along – collar torn off – face streaming with blood – he had gone to protect them. Fancy not arresting them until they got into that state. It is the most wicked and futile persecution because they know we have got to have 'Votes' – and to think they have got us to this state – some women thinking it necessary and right to do the most awful burnings etc in order to bring the question forward. Oh what a pass to come to in a so-called civilised country. I shall never forget those poor dear women. The attitude of the crowd was detestable – cheering the police and only out to see the sport. Just groups of women here and there sympathising, as I was. I saw Mrs Merivale Mayer, Miss Bessie Hatton and a good many women I knew by sight. I stayed until there was nothing more to be seen. The crowds were kept moving principally by the aid of a homely water cart. It was very awful. Mrs Pankhurst herself was arrested at the gates of the Palace. I did not see her but she must have passed quite close to me. I went to Victoria and had some tea and tried to get cool, but I felt very sick. The King could have done something to prevent it all being so horrible – he isn't much of a man. Back by bus. They [the Wrights] wanted to hear about it, but they don't take quite the same view of it that I do. They seem so 'material' in all their deductions – it's all so tremendously more than that.

FRIDAY, MAY 22ND 1914 – LONDON: 27 PEMBRIDGE CRESCENT

Most fearfully hot. To Hounslow – canvassed Bath Road and an irate gentleman created a fearful scene – said all sorts of militant things – amongst others that he hoped I would burn in hell and that he should be able to watch it. It created so much excitement I had to hold a little open-air meeting for the benefit of some gentlemen mending drainpipes. Oh it was a scorching day. [Later] to the Holborn Hall for the Women Clerks and Civil Servants Suffrage meeting. Miss Gore Booth in the Chair.

TUESDAY, MAY 26TH 1914 – LONDON: 27 PEMBRIDGE CRESCENT
[Kate had been ill.] Felt better, but pretty rotten legs and a busy day. Off at 5.45 to Hounslow by train from N[otting] H[ill] G[ate]. To the Council Hall for the meeting. Miss Kate Hessel was the speaker. It was really quite nice and successful – we made 3 members and 4 sympathisers and the room was full. Not the result of my canvass however.

THURSDAY, MAY 28TH 1914 – LONDON: 27 PEMBRIDGE CRESCENT
To Office. Letters to 12.15 and then afterwards the Committee – with such a long list of things arranged and done that I think I startled them. I could not be expected to get the grip of things all at once in London, but I seem to have got it now right enough. Several people have told me how much they would rather have me to organise than Miss McGowan. She is most awfully jealous – it's absurd – she is better at her job – fine at it, a magnificent speaker, but each person does some job better than another. Everyone is quarrelling and I hate it. Then a report of Tuesday's meeting for the *Middlesex Chronicle*.

FRIDAY, MAY 29TH 1914 – LONDON: 27 PEMBRIDGE CRESCENT
Took my dress box first to N[otting] H[ill] G[ate] and ordered Carter Paterson for the 3 big boxes to come on Tuesday and take them to Claverton St as, I am happy to say, I can go back there. I departed with my hand bag [to Worthing].

TUESDAY, JUNE 2ND 1914 – LONDON: 27 PEMBRIDGE CRESCENT/49 CLAVERTON STREET
To Office. Then to 49 Claverton St. Not my old room – it is let – but the large one at the top in the front – large and airy and very nice and which I am to have for the same rent as the more or less permanent lodger has gone off on tour – and Miss Heffer said she would rather I had it than anyone.

At this late stage in the campaign, Kate made her first formal suffrage speech. The 'Byron fête' was an NCS fund-raising event to be held in Lady Byron's Hampstead house and garden on 25 June.

TUESDAY, JUNE 9TH 1914 – LONDON: 49 CLAVERTON STREET
Tried to think collectedly about my speech and failed. Then dressed carefully in my best. At 3 to the N.C. Hall to make my Debut as a speaker. Mrs Cavendish Bentick was in the Chair and Miss Perkins spoke at length, and I thought very badly, about barmaids and then Miss Simeon made a long appeal for the Byron fête – then the collection – then me. I don't know how I felt – not nervous – I suppose it was hyper nervousness, but I know I appeared utterly unmoved. I started badly but didn't seem to mind. Then I got into the swing, and said something of what I wished to say – the audience was most patient and the room was very full. I could feel they were interested, though why I cannot imagine. The comments were most amusing. Strangers came up and wrung my hand and thanked me. Baroness de Knoop, in particular, I remember making a great fuss – they flocked round for cards for Mrs Innes' At Home (but they won't come).

Baroness de Knoop, [Freda] (1854–1932).

Mrs Hartley was very nice 'Why haven't we had you to speak to us before? You must speak often'. Miss Forsyth said it was a 'Very thoughtful speech' – Mrs Pertwee was delighted – she felt she had done it all, not a scrap of it really. I was strung up and out it came, that's all – and with all the art that years ago I trained for on the stage – only they don't recognise the 'Art'. Gladys was most complimentary. Alexandra delighted. She says I am so extraordinarily fluent and that I charm people. She said Mrs C.B.'s face was a study – that I quite fascinated her. I knew Mrs C.B. was very irritated at the idea of my speaking – I could feel it in my bones – and it wasn't a cheerful feeling. I so enjoyed meeting Miss Blomfield, since she spoke to the King at the Court and said 'Your Majesty in God's name stop forcible feeding'. What pluck – and she is so sweet to look upon.

Mary Blomfield (1888–1950). Presented to the King at Court on 4 June, dropped to her knees before him crying 'For God's sake, your Majesty, put a stop to forcible feeding.' From 1912 was honorary secretary of the Chelsea, Westminster and St George local committee of the NCS. 97 Cadogan Gardens, Chelsea.

MONDAY, JUNE 22ND 1914 – LONDON: 49 CLAVERTON STREET

[At 7pm] had to start for the open air meeting at the Triangle [Peckham]. Miss Dransfield turned up but Miss Winsor (from Penn USA) was so late that I had given her up and, though it was a great effort to speak – I got up and held forth until she turned up and then I introduced Miss Dransfield. Miss Winsor delighted the people but these last few weeks it has been a difficult audience and when we walked down the Lane we had a mob again behind us to see us into the train. The surprised faces of the people coming up the Lane and the people getting off the train is really amusing.

Mary Winsor (b. 1873) from Haverford, Pennsylvania, State congressional chairman of the National American Woman Suffrage Association, reported on the English suffrage movement to the American Academy of Political and Social Science.

THURSDAY, JUNE 25TH 1914 – LONDON: 49 CLAVERTON STREET

Tube to Hampstead and walked from there to 'Byron Cottage'. [At the fête] had the task of looking after the Literature – grilling in the sunshine and working the cash register which for a wonder came out quite correct. I think it was a great success – crowds of people and it all seemed to go well.

Miss McGowan was living just over the road from Kate, at 78 Claverton Street. The lateness of Miss Mansell's visit this Friday evening might indicate that she, too, was living close by, probably with Miss McGowan.

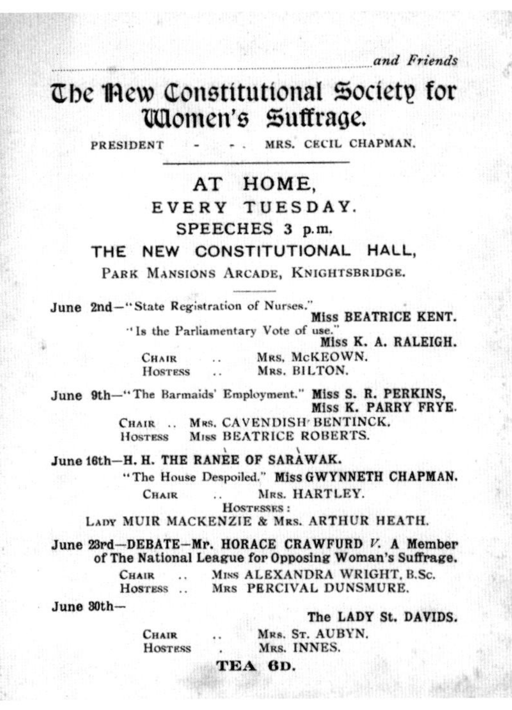

.... *and Friends*

The New Constitutional Society for Women's Suffrage.

PRESIDENT - - . MRS. CECIL CHAPMAN.

AT HOME,
EVERY TUESDAY.
SPEECHES 3 p.m.
THE NEW CONSTITUTIONAL HALL,
PARK MANSIONS ARCADE, KNIGHTSBRIDGE.

June 2nd—"State Registration of Nurses." **Miss BEATRICE KENT.**
"Is the Parliamentary Vote of use." **Miss K. A. RALEIGH.**
CHAIR .. MRS. McKEOWN.
HOSTESS .. MRS. BILTON.

June 9th—"The Barmaids' Employment." **Miss S. R. PERKINS, Miss K. PARRY FRYE.**
CHAIR .. MRS. CAVENDISH BENTINCK.
HOSTESS MISS BEATRICE ROBERTS.

June 16th—H. H. THE RANEE OF SARAWAK.
"The House Despoiled." **Miss GWYNNETH CHAPMAN.**
CHAIR .. MRS. HARTLEY.
HOSTESSES:
LADY MUIR MACKENZIE & MRS. ARTHUR HEATH.

June 23rd—DEBATE—Mr. HORACE CRAWFURD *V.* A Member of The National League for Opposing Woman's Suffrage.
CHAIR .. MISS ALEXANDRA WRIGHT, B.Sc.
HOSTESS .. MRS PERCIVAL DUNSMURE.

June 30th—
The LADY St. DAVIDS.
CHAIR .. MRS. ST. AUBYN.
HOSTESS . MRS. INNES.

TEA 6D.

The New Constitutional Society 'At Home' calendar, June 1914. Kate preserved this evidence of her first formal appearance as a 'suffrage speaker'.

FRIDAY, JUNE 26TH 1914 – LONDON: 49 CLAVERTON STREET

To the Committee. Rushed off and went to Mrs Kerr's house to help her over a meeting of the Leaflet League and did not get away till 6.30. Mrs Chapman and Mrs Cavendish Bentinck spoke. Bought my food and had supper indoors. A visit from Miss Mansell from 9 to 11.30 to let out to me how utterly miserable she is and what a fearful life Miss McGowan leads her. It was really awful – I did what I could to comfort her but I hate scenes, and she was dreadfully overwrought. I told her of my woes and that seemed to comfort her, but I feel sometimes I haven't any more patience with these made up miseries of tempers and temperaments. I know they cause most of the tragedies of the world but they seem so futile.

MONDAY, JUNE 29TH 1914 – LONDON :49 CLAVERTON STREET

To meet Mrs Chapman at 3.15 – she was 15 minutes late and by train to Peckham where we started our canvass. It was really very amusing – she is so imperious, but we got on very well. She went off by train. I did a little more canvassing and then to our meeting place soon after 7.30 and Mrs Merivale Mayer appeared at 8. I just took the Chair for her and she held on at great length. She had a huge crowd round her all the time.

TUESDAY, JULY 7TH 1914 LONDON: 49 CLAVERTON STREET

[John] is as absolutely devoted as ever – seems to care for nothing or nobody but me – it's extraordinary and has now been going on eleven years with undiminished fervour. Poor dear, I wish I could make him happy. After lunch we [John was accompanying her] proceeded to Isleworth but quite lost ourselves as we went by train from Victoria to Spring Grove then walked a long way to the Main Road and there had to take a bus. Then I had to visit the Police about the meeting and get a Lorry which took about 2 hours and found Mr Rix had got the wrong information – that there is no Green but the meeting must be held in the Upper Square and the thousand hand bills will have to be altered. John says that organising is far harder work than the Stage.

THURSDAY, JULY 9TH 1914 – LONDON: 49 CLAVERTON STREET

[After lunch] went off to Hounslow by train and canvassed all up and down both sides of the high street and all over the place, and at o'clock to Parke Davis Dye Works as the people came out.

FRIDAY, JULY 10TH 1914 – LONDON: 49 CLAVERTON STREET

[With John] to Office for the Banners and Leaflets. By bus to Hammersmith and train to Hounslow, where we got rid of the rest of the thousand handbills. To Broadway at 7.15 and the Lorry arrived at 7.30 and we decorated it, getting an enormous crowd of children round. Then the speakers, Mrs Kerr and Mr McKillop, arrived and Mr Fox in the Chair. Miss Raynsford Jackson and Miss Arber came down to help with giving out notices. We had a huge crowd, and ours was the first open-air meeting ever held in Hounslow. The people were a bit troublesome at first but came round wonderfully. We had a little passing trouble with the trumpets and a gramophone but I managed to quell it and we really had a magnificent meeting.

Kate refers in this entry to the pitch of aggression that now marked relations between the WSPU and the government. Mrs Pankhurst had been arrested, yet again, a few days previously. She had immediately undergone a hunger and thirst strike and was released on a four-day licence, under the terms of the 'Cat and Mouse' Act. She was rearrested on 16 July. Other leading members of the WSPU, such as Flora Drummond, Annie Kenney and Norah Dacre Fox, were also under constant threat of rearrest after failing to comply with the terms of their licence. In May and June the number of arson and bomb attacks had escalated throughout the country and already in July there had been explosions at Roslyn Chapel in Edinburgh and, on the day previous to this entry, at St John's Westminster.

MONDAY, JULY 13TH 1914 – LONDON: 49 CLAVERTON STREET

[After lunch] I met Mrs Chapman and we went together to Peckham and canvassed. To the Triangle at 7.30. Had to take the Chair and as Miss Fedden had not turned up at 8.15 I went on as long as I could as Miss D'Oyly was the only other speaker. But Miss Fedden arrived and held the crowd for a long time. [Miss Fedden] is a nice woman but overwrought with militancy. The things that are going on are too awful. It is enough to wring anyone's heart and mind.

As the WSPU struggled to survive, Kate – and the New Constitutional Society – continued to 'palm'.

TUESDAY, JULY 14TH 1914 – LONDON: 49 CLAVERTON STREET

To the Summer Sale and Tea at the N[ew] C[onstitutional Society] hall. The Palmist failed and I had to Palm – I hated it, but I really had quite a good time. Miss Lena Ashwell opened the Sale – and though there did not seem many people we made quite a lot of money. Mr Grein came straight from the Haymarket Theatre and the first public Perfomance of 'Ghosts' as it has now been licensed and had his hand read. But it was really very funny as he seemed to want to talk more about me – told me to go and see him – gave me his card, and said he liked my 'eye'.

[Constance] Marguerite Fedden (1879–1962) member of a wealthy Bristol family, at this time was principal of a College of Housecraft and Domestic Science, 4 Chichester Street, Pimlico. During the First World War she worked as a VAD nurse at Salonika.

Eliza Melling (b. 1860 in India) wife of a retired employee of the Bombay Port Trust and mother of two art student daughters. 75 Overhill Road, East Dulwich.

WEDNESDAY, JULY 15TH 1914 – LONDON: 49 CLAVERTON STREET

[Set off from] Victoria for Lordship Lane – and though we asked 2 officials the train crashed through to Crystal Palace. I was mad. Had to wait some time to get back – then a long walk to find Mrs Melling 75 Overhill Road and the meeting was half over. Miss McGowan had organised it and I had asked some of my new Peckham People and wanted to go to see them and because the Rev. Hugh was down to speak – but I felt I was not going to meet him and he was not there. Miss McG. was in the Chair, Mrs Chapman speaking. A very fine meeting, about 50 people there, but very few would join. [With John] to St James's Theatre to see 'An Ideal Husband'. I could hardly sit it out – such Anti suffrage old-fashioned twaddle – as for the end of the last act – tosh – I rose up and stormed out before the curtain fell. We were simply prancing with disgust. I never did like Oscar Wild [sic], but the play is the limit.

THURSDAY, JULY 16TH 1914 – LONDON: 49 CLAVERTON STREET

[After lunch] We [John & Kate] went to Hammersmith and then train to Isleworth and we bill distributed until 6. It was very hot. John was quite exhausted – says he couldn't do my work. We got the Townsfolk, the Brewery people and the Pears soap people so did it thoroughly – 1000 handbills.

The office of the Men's League for Women's Suffrage was at 136 St Stephen's House, Westminster. One of its main functions was to supply speakers for other societies.

FRIDAY, JULY 17TH 1914 – LONDON: 49 CLAVERTON STREET

I had received letter from Mr Dingle saying he could not speak – so, as soon as as I was up, I went off to the Men's League at Westminster and saw someone there who called Mr McKillop in from an office next door and he, like a lamb, said he would come to Isleworth in Mr Dingle's place. I expected to have to rush round London. Train to Isleworth arriving at 7.15 – at the Upper Square. There were hundreds of children ready to greet us. I got a friendly feeling and they were very good but a great nuisance. John went off to find the Lorry as it was not punctual, but he missed it and it arrived alright and I got it fixed up. By the time the speakers – Mrs Dransfield in the Chair, Mrs Merivale Mayer and Mr McKillop and Miss Fraser to help had arrived we were absolutely mobbed – and we got a huge gathering. The first Suffrage meeting of any kind which has been held in Isleworth. Mrs Mayer as usual was very disagreeable when she arrived, but it was really such a magnificent meeting she was quite pleased at the end, and as usual she spoke splendidly and we quite got the people round.

THURSDAY, JULY 23RD 1914 – LONDON: 49 CLAVERTON STREET

To Office to attend the Committee for the last time as we break up next week. It was simply awful – Alexandra Wright lost her temper before everyone and made a scene – and then Miss McGowan lost hers and was frantic and Gladys was very rude to her. I felt like walking downstairs and away, but I made myself go back and gripped Ailie [Alexandra] by the arm and did what I could to soothe her. Everyone left but Mrs Hartley. She is very good with everyone and we four went out to lunch at Harrods together. But it was all most sickening.

On this day, although Kate took no part, a deputation of men from Ashford called on the prime minister to lobby in favour of women's suffrage. Asquith was not at home. The deputation was afterwards entertained by Mrs Chapman and other members of the New Constitutional Society, suggesting that the project was the result of the campaign the society had conducted in that area of Kent.

SATURDAY, JULY 25TH 1914 – LONDON: 49 CLAVERTON STREET/WOOBURN: THE KENNELS

[Went to Wooburn by train] I felt so awful going to the old place – I just glued my eyes to the window. I couldn't help it when we came to Winter Hill and Cock Marsh and the river and then the train stopped on the Bridge and I saw the dear old 'Plat'. It was a gorgeous day, but a very high wind and the river was lashing about and the trees swaying and there stood the house. It really seems utterly grotesque that it should be all as it is –

that the others live in poky lodgings and I exist on £2 per week in a dreary London bed-sitting room – sometimes it seems it cannot be. [To the Kennels – one of the Gilbey houses on the Wooburn estate] and then a chat to Constance. She seems less narrow than she did. Of course I could not speak of my work – that is taboo – but I mentioned one or two facts concerning it – that if, as seems possible, we are in for a General Election I shall not get off next week for my holiday etc, and there didn't seem quite such a stiffening. But perhaps someone she respects has come out for Suffrage – or is it the Bishop of Kensington? I suppose if an election comes I shall go through with it but I shall much fear a collapse – and, fought on the Irish question, we shan't get a look in – shan't be listened to. Now there seem such European complications – Austria and Servia – perhaps our domestic parliamentary quarrels will have to take a second place. The papers seem full of rumours of trouble here and elsewhere.

MONDAY, JULY 27TH 1914 – WOOBURN: THE KENNELS/LONDON: 49 CLAVERTON STREET

[Back to London on train] I was very absorbed in the paper. Great and serious news – a terrible conflict between the Nationalist Volunteers in Dublin and the Police – 3 shot dead and many wounded. Will this mean an Election – things seems really serious in Ireland – and then the even more serious continental news. We [Kate and Mrs Chapman] went to Peckham together canvassing. We kept on until about 5.30 – having the usual sort of experiences – then tea together in the ABC and I saw Mrs Chapman off. I did some more canvassing then bought an evening paper and went into a Lyons and ate a macaroni and read it. There is going to be serious war and Russia and Germany are beginning to fall out now. Oh dear. To the Triangle at 7.45 – and our meeting at 8. I took the Chair and Miss Hawley and Miss D'Oyly were the speakers. I got the names of 10 sympathisers and we had a nice meeting and did not keep it going so long as usual.

WEDNESDAY, JULY 29TH 1914 – LONDON: 49 CLAVERTON STREET

[Office] Gladys was there – very important and bad tempered. How she snapped at me. Mrs Chapman came in and she was discussing the grave crisis of the War, the area is spreading. Said good-bye to Miss Burnaby who is leaving the staff as she has a very good appointment elsewhere – and goodbye also to Miss Simeon and Gladys. It seems so final somehow. I could wish I wasn't going back. I have grown so sick of the work. In saying good-bye to Gladys she said to me 'Please don't make a speech' in such a rude aggressive manner I tried to turn it off by saying if I were doing so it was because I had had so much practice lately, and she said 'Oh! Yes, Mr McKillop has been in today singing your praises – saying how well you speak that you ought to be made to speak, and what a splendid organiser you are, and what a wonderful person altogether'. So I suppose that was the trouble. I got my Salary and holiday cheque and made off.

Kate's mother and sister had moved house in Worthing, closer to the sea.

THURSDAY, JULY 30TH 1914 – LONDON: 49 CLAVERTON STREET/WORTHING: 10 MILTON STREET

[To Worthing] At Victoria it was a pandemonium. I don't know what was the matter with the station – it couldn't be all the holiday traffic, but I had to fight to get a Porter and to get my luggage put in the train. The journey seemed short as I had bought no end of papers to read of the Crises – it is becoming too awfully serious for words. Home politics are clean out of it at this moment – everyone's interest is fixed further afield. Fancy a European War at this period of our so called civilisation.

TUESDAY, AUGUST 4TH 1914 – WORTHING: 10 MILTON STREET

Well it is settled – England is to go in with France to protect her and Belgium. What a slap in the face for Germany!!! Germany expects to be allowed to walk over anywhere just as she pleases. What a brutal country – and what a Kaiser.

At the outbreak of war all the suffrage societies suspended their direct campaigning for the vote and put their energies into supporting the patriotic cause. At the end of her summer holiday Kate returned to work for the NCS whose contribution to the war effort was to open a workroom on their premises, employing dressmakers who had been laid off by traditional garment manufacturers.

THURSDAY, AUGUST 27TH 1914 – WORTHING: 10 MILTON STREET/LONDON: 49 CLAVERTON STREET

To 49 Claverton Street and the back ground-floor bedroom. Miss Heffer is going to let me go upstairs later when the room is cleaned, I couldn't stand this – most dismal – a dark red paper – no proper table – only 2 broken-seated cane chairs – no cupboard for stores and an ordinary gas burner, had to light 2 candles for supper and to read the latest War news in a *Star* I rushed out to buy. Oh what a dismal room. How can one bear this sort of thing. But it is peaceful.

Margaret Simeon's sister, Catherine, a gymnastics teacher at Bedales School, had very recently married Alfred Marshall.

FRIDAY, 28TH AUGUST 1914 – LONDON: 49 CLAVERTON STREET

To the Office. Miss Simeon just back from her holiday. Her sister was married just a week when her husband, who was a reserve R[oyal] E[ngineer], went off to the Front. Those things are tragic. Miss McGowan and Gladys turned up and later Alexandra turned up and explained all the new scheme to us. I am to take Miss McG.'s place and run the Workroom and Miss Simeon is to run the Office. I tried to take it calmly but my brain reeled a bit. There is a splendid forewoman and 11 girls in the Hall hard at work. All have been deserted owing to the War. Miss McGowan showed me the books etc and again I tried to keep calm. I left about 6. The news of the appalling losses to the British was so disturbing – I bought a paper and walked on reading it and ended by walking as far as Slaters in Victoria Then I dined at 7.30 and walked all the way to Claverton St.

John Collins, who had fought in the Boer War, had long been an enthusiastic member of the Territorial Army. Now, in August 1914, an officer, he was stationed at Shoeburyness with the Essex and Suffolk Royal Garrison Artillery.

VOTES FOR WOMEN.

The Women's Social and Political Union.

OFFICES: LINCOLN'S INN HOUSE,
KINGSWAY, W.C.

Mrs. Pankhurst, Hon. Treasurer.
Mrs. Mabel Tuke, Hon. Sec.

All Communications, unless marked "private" will be opened by the Hon. Secretary.

Auditors: Messrs. Frank ...
... Mansion House Chambers, ... Bucklersbury, E.C.
Telegraphic Address—WOSPOLU, LONDON.
Telephone 2724 Holborn (three lines).

August 13th, 1914.

Dear Friend,

Even the outbreak of war could not affect the action of the W.S.P.U. so long as our comrades were in prison and under torture.

Since their release it has been possible to consider what should be the course adopted by the W.S.P.U. in view of the war crisis.

It is obvious that even the most vigorous militancy of the W.S.P.U. is for the time being rendered less effective by contrast with the infinitely greater violence done in the present war not to mere property and economic prosperity alone, but to human life.

As for work for the vote on the lines of peaceful argument, such work is we know futile even under ordinary conditions,

SUNDAY, AUGUST 30TH 1914 – LONDON: 49 CLAVERTON STREET

Great meetings are being organised to help inspire the men of the country. The Women are being implored to send their men forth. Well all I possess is doing his duty – if he was sent to the Front – terrible as it would be – I could only say 'go'. How the men can hesitate I don't know. A walk to the Chapel Royal for service at 6.30. A truly wonderful sermon telling us we must all be prepared to give our only son – and when God asks for him say 'Rather'. He [Hugh Chapman] really is quaint at times, but apart from that it was one of his inspired sermons. The poor dear looks 20 years older – so thin and stringy. The Chapel was packed. I walked up the Strand – a fresh set of posters and paper boys yelling all different news and no end of people – all very quiet – a hushed feeling every where. People just looking into one another's faces anxiously.

MONDAY, AUGUST 31ST 1914 – LONDON: 49 CLAVERTON STREET

A tremendous day of work at the Office. My hair nearly stood on end. Miss Green there most of the day – and Mrs Kerr a long while. I only dashed out to lunch at 1.30 back at 2. Swallowed a cup of tea and then worked on until 8. I was so glad when the Office was quiet and all had gone and I settled down to jobs I had put aside for that time. If only I were efficient. Miss Simeon is so trained and capable. I took a bus to Victoria but there found such crowds of people at the station expecting the Wounded to arrive back that, tired as I was, I stood. No wounded, but hundreds of foreigners from a continental train.

On the outbreak of war the WSPU 'decided to economise the Union's energies and financial resources by a temporary suspension of activities'.

TUESDAY, SEPTEMBER 1ST 1914 – LONDON: 49 CLAVERTON STREET

A fearful day in the Office – Flora Annie Steele and several visitors with schemes before the Committee at 11.30. I played the Sec.'s part and it was awful. Hard at it until 7. Miss Simeon stayed on until 6 – I didn't finish my work but I felt tired and it was wisest to stop. It surely can't be like this every day. Not only the office work but the Workroom.

Wednesday, September 2nd 1914 – London: 49 Claverton Street

I was at it all day at the Office – and as Miss Green came in after tea I was delayed again and did not get away until 6.30. However not a day like yesterday and I was thankful for it. A good many visitors though and orders – and a good list of things held over for the morrow. In at 7.30 to find I was partially moved up to my old quarters – which have been spring-cleaned. It was quite thrilling and exciting – like coming home. I did enjoy it. Started a little extra dusting and putting straight – had supper – half a bottle of claret I brought with me from Worthing and really felt quite drunk but, an effort of mind over matter, got up and finished my jobs – then some writing. The light in Big Ben is not lit at night now. I am near there if Bombs are dropped. Oh dear.

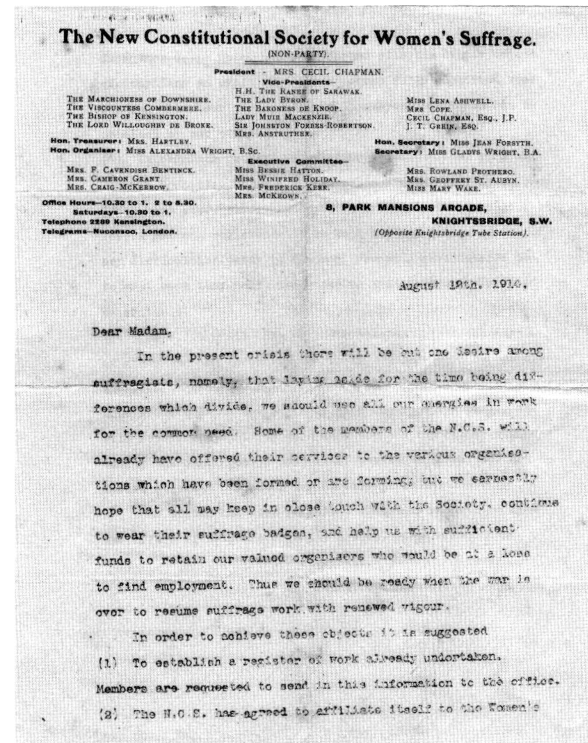

The New Constitutional Society for Women's Suffrage.

(NON-PARTY).

President - MRS. CECIL CHAPMAN.

Vice-Presidents—

The Marchioness of Downshire.
The Viscountess Combermere.
The Bishop of Kensington.
The Lord Willoughby de Broke.
H.H. The Ranee of Sarawak.
The Lady Byron.
The Baroness de Knoop.
Lady Muir Mackenzie.
Sir Johnston Forbes-Robertson.
Mrs. Anstruther.
Miss Lena Ashwell.
Mrs Cope.
Cecil Chapman, Esq., J.P.
J. T. Grein, Esq.

Hon. Treasurer: Mrs. Hartley.
Hon. Organiser: Miss Alexandra Wright, B.Sc.
Hon. Secretary: Miss Jean Forsyth.
Secretary: Miss Gladys Wright, B.A.

Executive Committee—

Mrs. F. Cavendish Bentinck.
Mrs. Cameron Grant.
Mrs. Craig-McKerrow.
Miss Bessie Hatton.
Miss Winifred Holiday.
Mrs. Frederick Kerr.
Mrs. McKeown.
Mrs. Rowland Prothero.
Mrs. Geoffrey St. Aubyn.
Miss Mary Wake.

Office Hours—10.30 to 1. 2 to 5.30.
Saturdays—10.30 to 1.
Telephone 2289 Kensington.
Telegrams—Nuconsoc, London.

8, PARK MANSIONS ARCADE,
KNIGHTSBRIDGE, S.W.
(Opposite Knightsbridge Tube Station).

August 18th. 1914.

Dear Madam,

In the present crisis there will be but one desire among suffragists, namely, that laying aside for the time being differences which divide, we should use all our energies in work for the common need. Some of the members of the N.C.S. will already have offered their services to the various organisations which have been formed or are forming; but we earnestly hope that all may keep in close touch with the Society, continue to wear their suffrage badges, and help us with sufficient funds to retain our valued organisers who would be at a loss to find employment. Thus we should be ready when the war is over to resume suffrage work with renewed vigour.

In order to achieve these objects it is suggested

(1) To establish a register of work already undertaken. Members are requested to send in this information to the office.

(2) The N.C.S. has agreed to affiliate itself to the Women's

The New Constitutional Society suspended the suffrage campaign in order 'to use all our energies in work for the common good'.

Saturday, September 5th 1914 – London: 49 Claverton Street

A good rush over the orders but I cleared up fairly well. Did not leave until 4.30. Then a bus to Victoria – did my shopping and walked down. Went down beside the LCC Dock Station and saw the Belgian Refugees camp in Hudson's furniture Depository [in Wilton Road, Pimlico]. Poor souls they do look miserable – boy scouts on guard and ladies and officials in and out. Lots of company of soldiers about everywhere – bands playing, bayonets gleaming but what I like seeing here is the companies of new recruits in civilian dress. Several mornings from my bus I have seen them marching – well-dressed young men all a bit pale and anxious, but marching with a good swing. It made tears come to my eyes the first time I saw them.

Monday, September 7th 1914 – London: 49 Claverton Street

To the Office and the usual busy day – something or someone to interrupt just when one was getting on. A photographer from the *Daily Mirror* in the middle of the afternoon and Mrs Kerr and Miss Green both in.

Tuesday, September 8th 1914 – London : 49 Claverton Street

To the Office just after 10. The *Daily Graphic* sent to photograph the Workroom. I made a great effort to begin cleaning up but at six o'clock an interviewer came from the *Women's Dreadnought* – then Miss Gray the forewoman who told her life's story. She is a

Love from us all. For heavens sake don't any of you make anything for the war! Send me a line as to how you are all getting on.

TELEPHONE, 1107 PUTNEY.

Aug: 16th 1914.

THE COTTAGE,
ROEHAMPTON. S. W.

Yrs Alexandra Wright

Dear Kate.

I have written so many letters that I can't write you a long one. You will already have had the official letter with the first indication of what we are doing. I came up on Monday & have been busy ever since. The hall will be opened as a work-room on Monday, where it will all end I don't know –!! Gladys is coming up next week & we shall partly open Pemb: Gard: Mrs Chapman wouldn't trust any one else to start things – her idea is for us to get things going – then to call you & Miss Simeon back at beginning of Sept: & go for our own holiday, but I shall be able to tell you more definitely when I have seen Gladys.

There will be a good deal of distress, but one imagines – nothing like what there will be in Germany, as long as we command the sea – which we seem to be doing

charming girl really and if a lady would be really delightful. Like all those girls she is touchy. Yesterday she was on the point of leaving us then and there. She isn't strong and gets overdone and really it is a rush.

Friday, September 11th 1914 – London: 49 Claverton Street

[John in London] So at 1 o'clock he came along looking very splendid in khaki and we went out together to lunch in Harrods. Miss Green in soon after 4. Miss Gray down to see her – then Mrs Foster and Mrs Harvey from Dover turned up and I tried to divide myself. Off at 5.40 and went with John by Tubes and train to Fenchurch St and saw him off at 6.26 to Shoeburyness. It was fearfully exciting. Everyone stares at an officer and he looks an important one with his little strip of colour.

Saturday, September 12th 1914 – London: 49 Claverton Street

I thought at first the work would be normal but it became overwhelming – interruptions every few minutes and a telegram from Aldershot about 500 shirts. Worked till 7.30 like a steam engine – and then there was lots more I could have done. I had no end of letters and then all the books to do. Miss Green had got all the wages wrong – so it was an awful muddle

The 'rescue party' to which Kate refers was a group of women doctors, nurses and orderlies, led by the redoubtable Mrs St Clair Stobart of the Women's National Service League, that sailed for Antwerp on 22 September.

Alexandra Wright puts Kate in the picture. Mrs Chapman trusts only the Wright sisters to plan the NCS war work; Kate and Miss Simeon are then to put it into operation.

Tuesday, September 15th 1914 – London: 49 Claverton Street

Got to Office at 10 o'clock. Mrs Foster from Dover was in helping all the afternoon. I stayed on a bit to finish up and did not leave until just upon 7. Miss Simeon went off in good time as she was going to see her sister who is going to Belgium on Monday with some sort of rescue party. She was only married a week when her husband was called to the Front. In a letter from Mrs Chapman today she says her grand-daughter has heard that her husband is wounded and missing. It's perfectly awful for people.

Saturday, September 19th 1914 – London: 49 Claverton Street

Another terrible day of work. Mrs Kerr and Miss Green both there and helping to cut out – for our Aldershot order of 500 shirts. Tables arriving. Telephoning for machines – more girls etc – paying out money for wages – paying money in the Bank – and lots of

The NCS War Relief Work Room – with the Society's banner in the background.

people in and out. Miss Gray and Miss Green were cutting out until 4 o'clock. I cleared up – did the accounts and finished up the week's work and left everything straight for Monday.

Lilian Rose Gray (b.c.1882 in India) in 1911 was a dressmaker, living in Wandsworth at the home of her cousin, a bookseller.

WEDNESDAY, SEPTEMBER 23RD 1914 – LONDON: 49 CLAVERTON STREET

Had a very busy day – a huge pile of letters – orders etc which always complicates matters – people in and out all day – discussions with Mrs Kerr, Mrs Hartley, Mrs Cavendish Bentinck – a man from the Westminster Committee etc and the work going badly in the Workroom. So it ended by my staying until 8.30. It [Claverton Street] is a gloomy street – worse than ever. Some of the lamps not lit at all and all the others smeared with red-brown paint all over the top. The search light very busy.

Kate's anti-Semitic thoughtlessness was very much of its time.

SATURDAY, SEPTEMBER 26TH 1914 – LONDON: 49 CLAVERTON STREET

After lunch I strolled through the Park – listened to a recruiting speech for some time – a most unattractive Jew – a huge crowd round but the most awful set of people imaginable – it looks as if all the decent men have joined by now. Down Regent St across Leicester Square where the usual appalling crowd had congregated. Such awful looking men and women – it does make one feel proud that the man who belongs to one is clean and upright and a soldier.

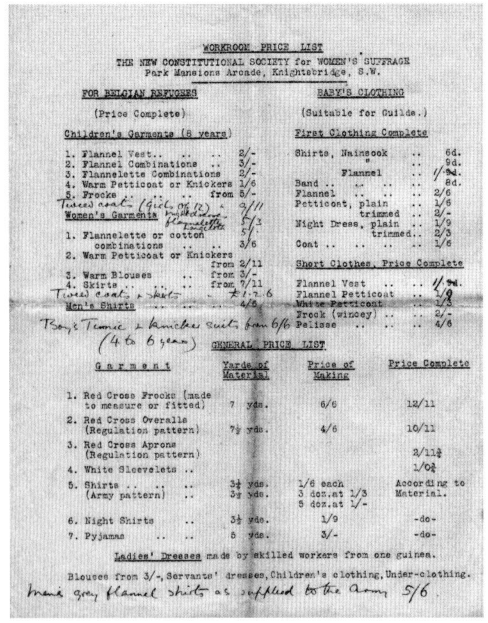

WORKROOM PRICE LIST
THE NEW CONSTITUTIONAL SOCIETY for WOMEN'S SUFFRAGE
Park Mansions Arcade, Knightsbridge, S.W.

FOR BELGIAN REFUGEES
(Price Complete)

Children's Garments (8 years)

1. Flannel Vest.. .. .. 2/-
2. Flannel Combinations .. 3/-
3. Flannelette Combinations 2/-
4. Warm Petticoat or Knickers 1/6
5. Frocks .. .. .. from 5/-

Tweed coats (Girls of 12) 9/11

Women's Garments

1. Flannelette or cotton combinations 3/6
2. Warm Petticoat or Knickers from 2/11
3. Warm Blouses .. from 3/-
4. Skirts .. .. .. from 7/11

Tweed coats & skirts £1.2.6

Men's Shirts 4/6

Boy's Tunic & knicker suits from 6/6 (4 to 6 years)

BABY'S CLOTHING
(Suitable for Guilds.)

First Clothing Complete

Shirts, Nainsook .. 6d.
" .. 9d.
Flannel .. 1/-
Band .. .. 8d.
Flannel 2/6
Petticoat, plain .. 1/6
trimmed .. 2/-
Night Dress, plain .. 1/9
trimmed.. 2/3
Coat 1/6

Short Clothes, Price Complete

Flannel Vest 1/-
Flannel Petticoat .. 1/9
White Petticoat .. 1/3
Frock (wincey) 2/-
Pelisse 4/6

GENERAL PRICE LIST

Garment	Yards of Material	Price of Making	Price Complete
1. Red Cross Frocks (made to measure or fitted)	7 yds.	6/6	12/11
2. Red Cross Overalls (Regulation pattern)	7½ yds.	4/6	10/11
3. Red Cross Aprons (Regulation pattern)			2/11¾
4. White Sleevelets ..			1/0¾
5. Shirts .. .. .. (Army pattern) ..	3¼ yds. 3½ yds.	1/6 each 3 doz.at 1/3 5 doz.at 1/-	According to Material.
6. Night Shirts ..	3½ yds.	1/9	-do-
7. Pyjamas	5 yds.	3/-	-do-

Ladies' Dresses made by skilled workers from one guinea.

Blouses from 3/-, Servants' dresses, Children's clothing, Under-clothing.

Men's grey flannel shirts as supplied to the army 5/6

MONDAY, SEPTEMBER 28TH 1914 – LONDON: 49 CLAVERTON STREET

To the Office getting there soon after 10 – to see to things before the Committee. It was not over till past one. An afternoon of interruptions and work. Some fearsome people came into the Office. One like a nightmare, only fit for the scrap heap – another quite drunken made an awful scene.

The Women's Emergency Corps had been formed in August at the instigation of Evelina Haverfield and Eva and Decima Moore to train women as uniform-wearing signallers, dispatch riders, and telegraphists.

THURSDAY, OCTOBER 1ST 1914 – LONDON: 49 CLAVERTON STREET

[After work] to the Kingsway Hall for a meeting of the Women's Emergency Corps. Miss Simeon and her sister were there so I sat with them. Miss Simeon is of course a dear but she does take life seriously. I didn't think much of the meeting – very full and over £500 collected. Duchess of Marlborough in the Chair. Miss Elizabeth Robins – Mrs Pethick Lawrence, Miss Constance Collier and Miss Lind-af-Hageby (the last named I really went to hear) was simply splendid – she can speak. The others were fearfully tame.

MONDAY, OCTOBER 5TH 1914 – LONDON: 49 CLAVERTON STREET

The usual busy day at the Office. Miss Wiskemann came in and wanted someone to help her sell Literature at the Court Theatre so in a weak moment I promised and it made a great scramble getting things done. To the Court Theatre. Miss Wiskemann and 3 other helpers besides myself and not one of us really wanted at all – no one came to see the play 'The Sphinx' and no one wanted books and 'The League of Isis'.

THURSDAY, OCTOBER 8TH 1914 – LONDON: 49 CLAVERTON STREET

Left soon after 9 o'clock and got a fitting of my dress in the Workroom before going to the Office. A very heavy day. The executive met at 11 o'clock. I was not present but sitting in the same room was disturbing – and I was like a jack-in-the-box all morning. [Afternoon] a constant stream of people for orders etc and Alexandra and Gladys there all the time. Walked all the way home – via Hyde Park Corner. The search lights on the top of the Arch are most fascinating to watch. But the neighbourhood itself is dark as a bag – I was amused to see the news vendor at the Corner lighting up his posters stuck on the railings at St George's Hospital with a small pocket electric light. Bought a hat in the Buckingham Palace Rd for 7s 11¾ and brought it home in a paper bag – along with a cutlet, tomatoes and fish for breakfast.

Consuelo, Duchess of Marlborough (1877–1964) neé Vanderbilt, American heiress, promoted women's suffrage and prison reform.

Constance Collier (1878–1955) renowned actress.

Louise Lind-af-Hageby (1878–1963) Swedish feminist and anti-vivisection campaigner.

Above: War Work price list

TUESDAY, OCTOBER 13TH 1914 – LONDON: 49 CLAVERTON STREET

The [NCS] meeting was at 3 – but so many people came it was suddenly arranged to move it to the Knightsbridge Palace Hotel. I stood in the Arcade from 3 to 4.15 directing people and then ran in the Hotel and heard Mrs St Clair Stobart giving some of her experiences. She has just come back from Antwerp – before that she was in Brussels with her Ambulance Corps and was sent home from there. Twice she has lost the whole of her outfit, was arrested as a spy and given 24 hours before being shot – but somehow she got free. She says the majority of the Germans are like mad dogs against the English – and that the Officers say it is a war of Annihilation. She spoke very beautifully about it all. A lot of money was raised for her – almost £30 – and she got the promise of a Motor Ambulance. Lots of the folk came back to tea and to see the Workrooms.

Kate's mother and sister had moved from Worthing to 58 Portland Road, Hove. Rooms were found for the weekend for John and Kate in a neighbouring guest house.

SATURDAY, OCTOBER 17TH 1914 – LONDON: 49 CLAVERTON STREET/HOVE: 42 PORTLAND ROAD

[John] came along [to Office] at 1 o'clock and helped me to balance accounts and run messages and generally excite the office – and we got off about 1.30. He has got leave till tomorrow – and had to come to London to get a Sam Brown – this and his sword was stolen from the Mess after Church Parade last Sunday. No sign of it – a real bare-faced robbery – and it was his Father's – I think it is too awful. [Took] the 4.30 to Hove. Had a carriage to ourselves as far as Brighton – and I suggested we should get married at Christmas and share a Flat. I have been so miserable all the week – tears trickling into my boiled egg at supper – that I feel something must happen. Of course it's a very rash suggestion – but John was pleased at the idea. It would be very peculiar – but I don't see I could be much more miserable married – and if we don't make some sort of effort it will never happen.

SUNDAY, OCTOBER 18TH 1914 – HOVE: 42 PORTLAND ROAD

Walked right along the Front as far as the Metropole – the same old crowd – but plenty of khaki. Agnes and Mother were very impressed by the saluting of John that went on – he did look nice – much nicer than any of the other officers. We stood at the corner where eleven years ago all but a few days he proposed to me. I was fearfully indignant. I thought he oughtn't to have done anything of the kind, but I suppose he couldn't help himself and he doesn't seem to have thought of a single creature other than myself ever since. It's a good long slice out of life – 11 years. [After seeing John off] we three sat round the fire and I told them the conclusion John and I had come to. Of course Mother was a bit shocked but I have known her take things worse. Agnes was very sympathetic and she thinks we should be doing quite right if we really want to. Mother rather startled me by saying she did not think Aunt Agnes' £50 would come to me if I married. In that case it's all off as I should want to feel I had something at the back of me. The only thing will be to consult Constance.

Mabel St Clair Stobart (1862–1954) had organised an all-women medical unit during the First Balkan War, 1912, and immediately on the outbreak of war in August 1914 had formed the Women's National Service League. During the course of the First World War she took groups of women relief workers to Belgium, France and Serbia, setting up tented hospitals and emergency dispensaries.

TUESDAY, OCTOBER 27TH 1914 – LONDON: 49 CLAVERTON STREET

The usual Tuesday morning scramble and turn out. The At Home in the afternoon. Miss Walsh spoke on the condition of the Belgian refugees in Holland. It's perfectly awful. Not many people so our Workroom did not benefit much. Cleared away and then got ready for the Workroom tea at 6. The girls all came and were as happy as crickets – not a bit shy. Mrs Chapman was there – Mrs Tite, Miss Green, Mrs Evans, Miss Wake, Baroness de Knoop and several others and Mrs Kerr, of course, who had provided the tea. Afterwards she spoke to them and a Mrs Francis and Mrs Chapman then we sang 'God Save the King' and had three cheers for everyone including 'Miss Frye' – and all parted in good spirits.

WEDNESDAY, OCTOBER 28TH 1914 – LONDON: 49 CLAVERTON STREET

Mother seems very much against the scheme [marriage]. If people are going to argue and be cross about it we shall have to give it up. I suppose it won't matter. I don't suppose the NCS Committee will approve. If only people needn't know. Why should these matters have to be discussed and pulled about? Of course if Miss Emma doesn't help and if Aunt Agnes' £50 per year doesn't come to me if I marry it's bound to be all off. The NCS is so uncertain I shan't dare embark upon a Flat. Mr Nevinson the War Correspondent was in the office today. He is going out again tomorrow – only arrived here on Sunday. He says the papers are not allowed to print the truth.

TUESDAY, NOVEMBER 10TH 1914 – LONDON: 49 CLAVERTON STREET

In a fearful state of excitement. New dress made in the Workroom much admired by everyone – new coat – new hat. [In afternoon] I was deputed to look after Professor l'Abbé from Louvain who was to speak. Such a plain person but everyone seemed captivated and he was certainly very pleasant. Then Mrs Chapman, Mrs Hartley and some people and then about 10 minutes to 3 – the Rev. Hugh – eyes on the stars in a mist – towed along by 2 ladies and another man – some miserable MP. I didn't take any notice of the Rev. one. He looked at me perfectly blankly and I took it that he did not know me, and I wasn't going to introduce myself. I certainly felt damped – not to say disgusted. Whether or not he did know me, I don't know but I suggested getting them all to see the Workroom and got them there, where they stood about talking of other things. Seeing that was no good from my point of view – I slowly attacked Mr Chapman – who with a grin said 'Well and how are you getting on, and what are you doing now-a-days?' or words to that effect. I was so startled – the only thing I could have said 'You do know me then?' but of course I didn't. So I stared at him and said I didn't know what I was doing – then pulling myself together I told him about the Workroom and told him how necessary it was we should have money, but when he asked for facts and figures, I couldn't tell him anything – only that the wages came to £25 odd. The meeting was held in the Knightsbridge Palace Hotel and we were crowded out – a hundred or more had to be turned away, but I insisted upon those who had got downstairs as far as the door being let in. I fought Alexandra over it and got my way. She sounded quite overwrought, but I knew we should offend people terribly if we were not tactful. Then I got on the door where I remained opening and shutting and making myself generally useful. Getting money from those who left early and when the people came out giving them all a notice of the Workroom and talking to people about it. I was really excited. When I heard 'hullo' and someone clutched hold of my dress 'I did my very best for you'. Said I, 'I am sure you did'. I hadn't heard him, but several people said he had never spoken so beautifully before. 'Do you come to the Savoy?' I hesitated, hating in a way to say I did – wanting to say 'Well you ought to know'. So I said 'Yes' – very reluctantly. 'Where are you living now?' With a surging mass of people about us I could hardly say Pimlico and I really hadn't the face to say 'Belgravia' – I should have yelled – so I said casually 'oh roundabout – in diggins'. 'Write to me – you must come and have tea with me at the Savoy' (oh that old tea and 'write to me'). So I said I should do no such thing. 'Yes, write to me' as he went upstairs. I laughed and said I couldn't dream of doing anything of the sort.' 'Write to me' and as he vanished I still heard 'Write to me'. Of course he is quite mad – but I do love him. [Back to Claverton Street] I got in and sat and wept. Found a letter from Constance. Before I opened it I said 'I don't care – £50 or no £50 I will marry John'. I don't know if I meant it but anyway it does not seem as if I am to be put to the test – as far as I can make out the £50 per annum comes to me married or unmarried.

THURSDAY, NOVEMBER 12TH 1914 – LONDON: 49 CLAVERTON STREET

A fearful day. Committee 10.15 to 11.45 – then people, people, people to see me. Then by tube to Belsize Park and to 80 Antrim Mansions, Haverstock Hill to speak at a Drawing-room meeting. I was so miserable I don't know how I got through at all, but when I started I got wound up and went rambling on for about half an hour. There were only about 12 people present, and a Miss Wilson took the Chair, and Mrs Lynch was the hostess.

Mrs Arthur Lynch, wife of an Australian doctor.

The 'sliding stairway' to which Kate refers was the escalator introduced in April 1914 at Embankment station, which she used after travelling back on the Northern Line from Hampstead.

WEDNESDAY, NOVEMBER 18TH 1914 – LONDON: 49 CLAVERTON STREET

[After lunch] I went by Tube to Hampstead and to Miss Holiday's At Home – Oak Tree House, Branch Hill at 3 o'clock. Only about 20 people there, but the Studio was ever so nice and I loved it. I was awfully frightened for about 10 minutes before I began to speak, then it all suddenly went away. Mrs Chapman took the Chair. Mrs Kerr spoke next and then I did and then the collection was taken. Miss Holiday later on introducing me to her father said 'This is Miss Frye who is a great dear and who we all love' and she kissed me at parting – so I suppose I was a success. I came by Tube and the sliding stairway back.

Winifred Holiday (1866–1949) violinist, daughter of Henry Holiday, painter, stained glass designer, illustrator and sculptor. By 1912 she was a member of the executive committee of the NCS, which in 1914 published her pamphlet *Woman Under a Liberal Government, 1906–14*, subtitled 'an account of the manner in which Liberal Principles are applied to the "protected Sex"'. In her summation 'The Liberal government has drifted into Government by Anarchy … and since it governs by anarchy, so it has created anarchists who reply to it with fire and bomb'. This was very much the attitude of the NCS.

FRIDAY, DECEMBER 4TH 1914 – LONDON: 49 CLAVERTON STREET

To Office and hurtled through my work. First a Telephone wail from John. He couldn't get the Licence because he didn't know the name of the Church. I did, but I could not send it through the Telephone with Gladys and Miss Simeon listening. Then just before 12 he turned up and we went off together. Walked to Hyde Park Corner though the rain had started. It didn't damp our ardour and we were in holiday mood. First to the A[rmy] & N[avy] Stores – and to buy the wedding ring. I asked in a most careless tone as if I was in the habit of buying them daily. We got one at length – 26/- – off a dignified gentleman who grew very friendly under our influence.Then we decided to have lunch and decided on the 2/- menu but our Waiter took such a fancy to us he gave us all sorts of extras and we laughed till we cried. The store was packed with officers – it was most exciting. Then to Ludgate Circus and to Creed Lane in the shadow of St Pauls to an office that has been in that locality for 300 years and we bought the Licence. It was most thrilling like a scene out of Dickens – a musty old-world place – no telephone, no typewriters or central heating and 2 old gentlemen who wrote everything in the most perfect handwriting.

TUESDAY, DECEMBER 8TH 1914 – LONDON: 49 CLAVERTON STREET

A hitch in the order for a thousand shirts – so I was most of the day trying to unhitch it. Left the meeting just started in the office and then went off by bus to the Strand and to call on Mrs Lade at the Royal Savoy Chapel Schools as she has the matter in hand. She kindly gave me tea then I went off to the Hotel Cecil to see a Mrs Cunliffe Owen who is arranging the shirts for the Sports Battalion. But I waited a long time and then she wouldn't see me – but it was quite interesting there. Back to let Mrs Lade know.

THURSDAY, DECEMBER 10TH 1914 – LONDON: 49 CLAVERTON STREET

Committee at 10.15 – and the executive after – so the usual rush. Heard from Mrs Lade that it is alright about the order – so when I could get through my work off I went to the Strand and to see her at the Choir Schools – only to find that the order is off again although the flannel has actually been ordered. That Mrs Cunliffe Owen is a dreadful woman. [Later] to 14 Warwick Crescent and a party given by Miss Green and Miss Holding to the Work girls. It was a great success – the girls were as happy as possible. Miss Simeon, Miss Gray – Alexandra and Gladys and these besides. The entertainment delighted all – it was really good – Margaret Balfour to sing and lots of other real singers. Of course they sang tosh – including 'Tipperary' and we all joined in the Chorus – and there was a splendid conjurer who afterwards did ventiloquism with the loveliest doll who moved all over and even wept – squirted a stream of water out of one eye.

MRS. HENRY HOLIDAY
At Home
WEDNESDAY, November 18th, at 3 o'clock,
IN
THE STUDIO, OAK TREE HOUSE,
BRANCH HILL, HAMPSTEAD,
(kindly lent by Mr. Henry Holiday)
IN AID OF
The New Constitutional Society for Women's Suffrage War Relief Workroom.
Samples of the Work will be on view.
Chair: MRS. CECIL CHAPMAN. *Speakers:* MRS. KERR. MISS PARRY FRYE.
Speeches 3 o'clock.
Tea 4-30.
R.S.V.P.

Kate was now an official NCS speaker, her name printed on this invitation

MONDAY, DECEMBER 21ST 1914 – LONDON: 49 CLAVERTON STREET

[Afternoon shopping] It seems a selfish Christmas – I have only bought such little things for everyone and such lots of things for myself – simply throwing about money. I do feel reckless. New vest, knickers, a nightdress – bodice material to make a rest gown and under clothes – all sorts of things. But though I started out with the idea I wouldn't get anything – like everything it has grown and grown. I should like some nice frocks and things too. I do see it would[n't] really make any difference to John's happiness but it would make me feel nicer and daintier. But I don't want to seem unthankful and am feeling fearfully happy as things are. I do hope it will be a success. It rests with him – if he doesn't prove disappointing and take too much for granted. He is a dear but a little careless. I expect we shall have some wild moments of miserable unhappiness when we shall say or feel 'Oh how could you' – but I hope such feelings won't last. I have got such a queer horrid nature – I don't easily shake things off – I can't forget – and for that reason – I pray God he is careful. And I want to be awfully nice to him too – and I want him to be able to see and appreciate what is really nice. Oh I hope we shan't spoil it all. Starting out in a mood of doubt is disastrous – and foolish.

TUESDAY, DECEMBER 22ND 1914 – LONDON: 49 CLAVERTON STREET

Miss Green and I lunched together and I told her about the 9th Jan – and she is such a dear and she was awfully nice about it and beamed and told me I was to be sure and tell John he was a very lucky man. We got to the Westminster Palace Hotel about 2.30. Sir Robert Baden Powell was the speaker on 'Girl Guides' but as he spoke principally upon 'Boy Scouts' I didn't seem to learn much. The room was pretty full – entrance 1/- – but as we were not allowed to have a collection we only just cleared expenses. I talked to as many as I could about the Workroom. I also had a long chat with the dear old Rev. one. Of course I love him dearly but he always strikes me as being the quaintest thing I have ever met – and such an absolute child.

WEDNESDAY, DECEMBER 23RD 1914 – LONDON: 49 CLAVERTON STREET

Had quite a surprise first thing by a presentation of an Ink Pot from all the girls – so really nice of them. They had given Miss Gray a flower stand. I told Miss Gray later on that I was going to get married and she was very interested and full of good wishes. The girls were crazy with excitement all day. I had a thorough clear out and tidy up of everything – then locked up – at 8 o'clock. Had such a queer feeling as I came away – like locking my old self within – because probably my old self never will return – if I am married by then it will be so different.

Kate spent the holiday at Hove.

FRIDAY, JANUARY 8TH 1915 – HOVE: 58 PORTLAND ROAD

When next I write I shall be back at Claverton St I suppose and if our plans do not go astray shall no longer be Kate Frye, but Mrs J.R. Collins. It seems rather fitting I should be penning a few lines in my old friend the diary at such a moment though it is very difficult to know what to say. One might be sensational – or romantic – a hundred moods would make a hundred different atmospheres – but I am too old to want to write from a dramatic point of view at this moment – and all I can say is – I feel I am craving and praying that my marriage shall be a success and shall bring happiness to us both and to others. The only fear I have tugging at me is that I may regret my freedom and find John a careless husband. I know I want too much of an 'understanding' in my friends but I do hope he will try to understand and will become larger minded. I know I want too much altogether – but if we only get a happy companionship we must be content – and now I must leave it until I know – for I shall know a little by Monday.

SATURDAY, JANUARY 9TH 1915 – HOVE: 58 PORTLAND ROAD

My Wedding Day and my Birthday. 37. Wore my best black frock – new boots, my silk hat which is quite pretty – squirrel coat and muff. Agnes' present [a gold watch and bracelet] has blue stones in it and I borrowed a handkerchief from Mother. I was wearing a mixture of old and new. Then just after 12.30 Mother, Agnes and I left in the taxi for All Saints Church, Hove. We walked up the Church – Mother and I together and she and Agnes went into a seat. Then I saw John coming from the Vestry. I was only conscious that he looked alright and not nervous. I spoke very, very slowly I noticed, as if I were weighing every word – and I said 'obey' most deliberately and carefully. I would have rather had it left out altogether – but had come to the conclusion that if I had the Church of England marriage service at all there wasn't much more objection to that one word than to much of the other. That I still object fundamentally to unequal vows is one thing very sure – but it has been so restful not to have to go and argue with the Vicar beforehand which I meant to do and should have done if I had not been so tied to the house. He would not have altered it I am sure and it would have spoilt all the joy of the good feeling. It probably sounds lazy – one ought to battle for one's conviction. Brighton was all en fête as the King and Queen had come to visit the wounded – and as chance would have it when we were turning off the front we saw a little group of people and finding the King was expected we waited for about 10 minutes. Then past they came – the King quite deliberately turning to John and returning his salute – it was exciting – and on my Wedding day too. I wanted to stop them and tell them all about it. Then back to 58 Portland Road. I just took off my hat and coat and John came upstairs. And John kept kissing me and I said 'someone's coming' in the old way, forgetting it wouldn't matter. [Lunch] John looked at the presents. He had brought me a cheque for £50. [Tea] We had a wee cake covered with white sugar and I cut it with John's sword. [At Brighton] caught the 4.40 train. It proved slow – but it didn't seem to matter – we just sat and hugged each other – Government compels us now-a-days to travel with the blinds down so it was alright. [At Victoria] Taxi to the Great Central Hotel. I suggested we had better not pay too much, but it was really rather nice on our arrival not to be consulted and just taken to the first floor – No 123. I suggested to John – my husband – that he could go on down while I changed but he flatly refused so he sat and watched me do my hair and then did my dress up for me. We went straight into dinner about 8.15 and had 9 rather bad courses – very few people there and the room gradually emptied till we were the last. I was hungry and ate quite a lot. Then we strolled round the palm court where a band was playing but we didn't seem to want people so we went in the Drawing-room. Then we both said we were tired so I said I thought I had better go to bed – it was then 10. John said he would come – but I told him not for 20 minutes.

He didn't like it but gave in and I went and got the key and went up alone. I was so excited – who isn't at such a moment – I undressed all backwards and was only just done when John arrived. Ours was a gorgeous room the bed in an alcove. We had meant to have a fire – it would have been nice but really the room was so warm we didn't need it. I laughed at first. Later I shed a tear or two and John would turn up the light to look at me – then he saw my tears and wept himself. We did try to go to sleep – but I don't think John had more than 2 hours and I had considerably less. But we were very very happy.

John departed early in the morning to Shoeburyness and Kate returned to the office. The business of the NCS continued much as before until, at the end of March, the Workroom closed due to a resurgence in the garment trade, for which Kate thought the new style for fuller skirts was responsible. Then, in April, seeds of dissension were sown when it was announced that an International Congress of Women would convene at The Hague. Around 1200 delegates from 12 countries attended the Congress hoping that the women of the warring countries could be organised to exert a moral force for peace. The British government, however, prevented interested British women from attending by refusing them passports and suspending the ferry service across the Channel. The Peace Conference led to the founding of the Women's International League for Peace and Freedom but, as Kate relates, the issue divided suffragists.

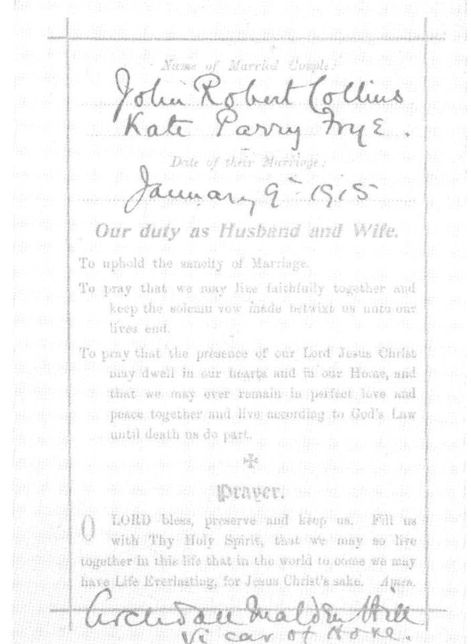

Name of Married Couple:

John Robert Collins
Kate Parry Frye.

Date of their Marriage:

January 9th 1915

Our duty as Husband and Wife.

To uphold the sanctity of Marriage.

To pray that we may live faithfully together and keep the solemn vow made betwixt us unto our lives end.

To pray that the presence of our Lord Jesus Christ may dwell in our hearts and in our Home, and that we may ever remain in perfect love and peace together and live according to God's Law until death us do part.

✠

Prayer.

O LORD bless, preserve and keep us. Fill us with Thy Holy Spirit, that we may so live together in this life that in the world to come we may have Life Everlasting, for Jesus Christ's sake. *Amen.*

TUESDAY, APRIL 20TH 1915 – LONDON: 49 CLAVERTON STREET

Some office work then to finish off the Hall – put things out for Sale etc. I arranged a stall of Workroom things – haberdashery etc. Meeting at 3 o'clock. Afterwards there was a great disturbance. Mrs Cecil Chapman from the Chair condemned the Peace Conference which is to take place at The Hague. I agree with her. How can English Women at the moment go and prattle with German Women of peace when there will and can be no peace until Germany has withdrawn her hosts from Belgium, France and

Kate laid the photographs of John and herself, together with their 'Marriage Card', between the pages of the wedding day diary entry.

Poland? At the moment when thousands are laying down their lives for women to talk like that is to my mind showing a tremendous lack of nationalism. We didn't want to fight – we were totally unprepared – the more credit in one way to us – and if German women want peace let them begin to preach it in Germany. I very much suspect this talk. However to go back. Miss Wiskemann, who is half German, didn't like it – and, instead of publicly protesting, she was heard saying things to people by several of our members who are most fiery the other way and told Mrs Hartley we had a traitor in our midst, and Mrs Hartley, never too cool in an emergency, went for Gladys, whose friend Miss W. is – and I'm not sure didn't go for Miss W. herself. Anyhow Miss W. is not coming amongst us again but going over heart and soul to the United Suffragists who I think are utterly mad and will do our cause much harm by pressing the question of 'Votes' at this minute. How can they – in this life and death struggle? If the NCS took that line I should have to leave them. I couldn't bear it – it's wicked and selfish and small – nothing matters except we beat Germany – but people are leaving us because we do not press Votes. It is a mad world.

WEDNESDAY, APRIL 21ST 1915 – LONDON: 49 CLAVERTON STREET

To Office. To find Miss Simeon in a flame and that she had sent Mrs Chapman her resignation on account of Mrs Chapman's words about the peace conference. Gladys came in in the midst of it and we all talked until 11. Gladys, as usual, argued in a very logical and business like way – Miss Simeon from an utterly unreal unpractical and idealistic point of view. I think ideals are splendid but why not ideals about England and her love of freedom and fair play. So Miss Simeon is leaving us. Christian Science has come in and is the excuse for not working for Suffrage but in any case she would have been unable to work for it much longer I believe. And a year ago she was a violent Militant!!!

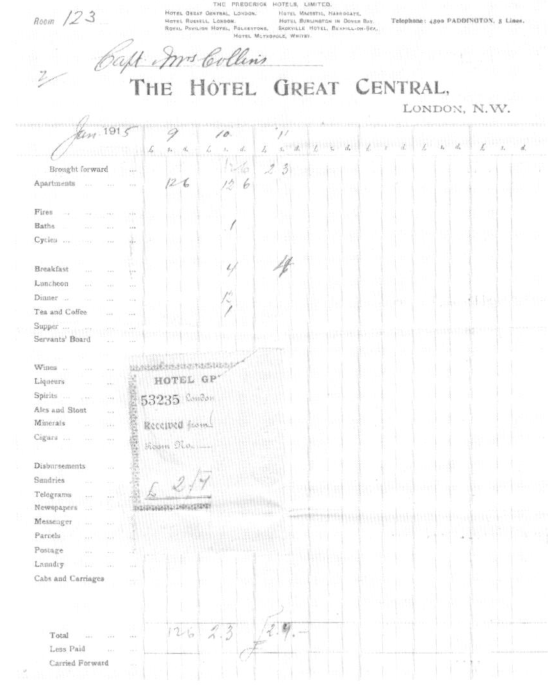

Room 123

Capt & Mrs Collins

THE HÔTEL GREAT CENTRAL,
LONDON, N.W.

Jan 1915	9	10	11
Brought forward		12 6	2 3
Apartments	12 6	12 6	
Fires			
Baths		1	
Cycles			
Breakfast		4	4
Luncheon			
Dinner		12	
Tea and Coffee		1	
Supper			
Servants' Board			
Wines			
Liqueurs			
Spirits			
Ales and Stout			
Minerals			
Cigars			
Disbursements			
Sundries			
Telegrams			
Newspapers			
Messenger			
Parcels			
Postage			
Laundry			
Cabs and Carriages			
Total	12 6	2 3	£2 4 –
Less Paid			
Carried Forward			

HOTEL GR[illegible]
53235 London
Received from
Room No.
£ 2/4

Kate carefully preserved these mementoes of her wedding night.

When Kate returned in mid-May from a three-week holiday it was to find that Mrs Chapman had offered the services of the NCS to help run a canteen set up at the Enfield Lock Small Arms' Factory under the auspices of Lady Lawrence's Munition Makers Canteen scheme. The managing – or mismanaging – of the canteen was to be a source of endless squabbling involving the Wright sisters and numerous, doubtless well-meaning, volunteers. As Kate wrote on 4 June 'No peace at all. Nothing but rows over the Canteen People coming in to complain of muddles even at 10.15 before I had my hat off.' Otherwise Kate helped the NCS with what might be termed its educational work – holding weekly meetings in Knightsbridge addressed by speakers on issues of topical, rather than specifically suffrage, interest.

She makes little mention of other erstwhile suffrage societies until on 17 July she took part as a marshall in 'The Right to Serve' March – or 'Great Procession of Women' – organised by Emmeline and Christabel Pankhurst, at Lloyd George's suggestion and with the government's financial support, with the aim of encouraging women to take up war work in munitions factories.

SATURDAY, JULY 17TH 1915 – LONDON: 49 CLAVERTON STREET

A very dull morning and it just started to rain as I went out. I was prepared for wild weather as the wind too was very fierce – a short grey linen dress – a woollen coat to keep me warm – Aquascutum – boots and rubbers – a small cap tied on – and an umbrella. It was fortunate I was so prepared as it turned out a wicked day and rained till 4 o'clock. I went by bus to Westminster and walked along the Embankment to see if there were any signs of preparation but it was pouring by then so there was nothing. I went to Slaters in the Strand and had some lunch and back on the Embankment by one. There from the paving stones sprang up marshalls and assistant marshalls (I was a marshall with a broad red sash) all like me hurrying to posts. Mine was 101 and only 100 were given out – so I claimed mine and stood behind the last soldier with 101 until nearly 3.30. But the rain kept the people away who would have filled the last of the 125 sections and we marshalls and assistant marshalls had very little to do. Our section commander never came along at all so we had to organise ourselves. Miss Barnes of the Knitting Dept came along to be in my section. She is a thoroughly good sort. Just before 3.30 we discovered if we were to march we must arrange ourselves – so a few people did one thing – a few another. I ran down the line telling people to come along and so we caught up with the front. Banners and bannerettes were hastily pulled out of carts and we were off. I went up and down giving directions and making us as trim as possible. We were a motley crew but we had some fine banner bearers and the greater number of us looked very neat in rainproof coats. And so off again on the great Women's Patriotic Procession organised by Mrs Pankhurst and led by her. Mr Lloyd George received a deputation of women concerning Munitions. Mrs Chapman walked all the way in the first section and went in with the deputation. It was a long and interesting procession but would have been longer had the weather been better. But the rain stopped about 4 o'clock and actually just as I got back to the Embankment at 6 o'clock the sun came out. The procession started off at 3.30 sharp. There were no end of Bands and they helped one tremendously. The route was long – Embankment, Whitehall, Cockspur St, Pall Mall, St James, Piccadilly, Park Lane, Oxford St, Regent's St, Haymarket, Northumberland Avenue on to the Embankment again when we gave up banners and those who could went along on to hear Mr Lloyd George speak from a balcony looking over the Embankment. I saw him watching the whole thing from there as we went along. Such a crowd to watch us all along the route and the Clubs packed with people. At intervals tables with ladies taking signatures of women ready to do munition work. It was very inspiring and invigorating and though I felt very tired and seedy before I think the walk did me good. I was a bit stiff and glad to sit down. I made my way to the Strand and had some tea.

As Kate's involvement in the suffrage campaign had begun with one procession, the 1907 'Mud March', so, in effect, it had now ended with another. The 'Right to Serve March' was the last formal suffrage-related event in which Kate took an official part. At the end of July she went on holiday, first to Hove and then, in August, to Shoeburyness – with John – staying in digs, and then on to his hometown of Knaresborough. There Kate appears to have had a complete collapse of health, although it is not at all clear where the problem lay. However she found a doctor who pleased her immensely, who was most solicitous and who was keen to offer a succession of remedies and treatment – all, it would appear, to little effect. Agnes and her mother came north to look after her and they all remained until autumn 1916 at 'Thorncroft', the house that had belonged to John's aunt, Emma Collins.

On 30 April 1916 Kate tendered her official resignation to the NCS, although she did maintain contact. On 4 December when she was in London with John, who was about to go to the Front, she wrote in her diary that they went, 'to Knightsbridge and to the NCS Offices – Park Mansions Arcade. There I found Miss McGowan, Miss Abbott and Miss Perceval Clark and had such a nice greeting from all and paid my sub. – long overdue. Ran up just to see the Workroom which is now used as a Hospital equipment workroom for voluntary workers. We did not stay long.'

With her mother and Agnes, Kate spent the last two years of the war in a house at Berghers Hill, a remote hamlet above Wooburn. 'The Heights' was lent to them by Kate's aunt, Agnes Gilbey, having previously been the home of another of her sisters, Anne Crosbie. John came unscathed through the war, having been, rather to his surprise and to Kate's pleasure, awarded the Military Cross. As Kate wrote in her diary on 27 July 1917, 'A letter from John telling me somewhat of why he has been decorated. It was at the Battle of Arras – he crossed 200 yds of No Man's Land, laid a telephone, located the barbed wire and smashed

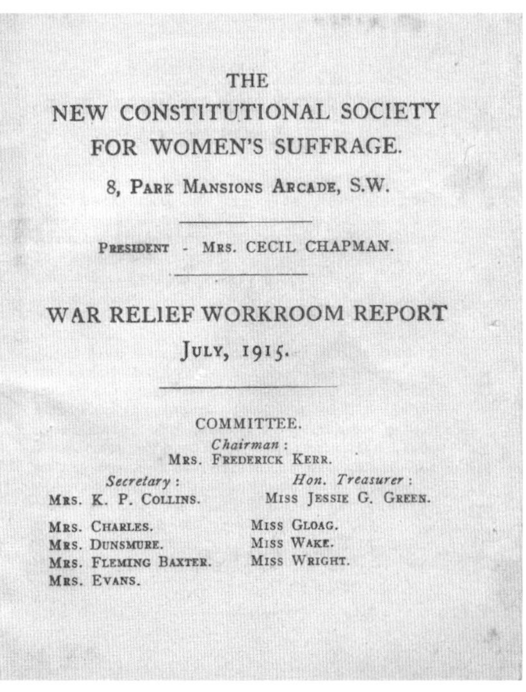
THE
NEW CONSTITUTIONAL SOCIETY
FOR WOMEN'S SUFFRAGE.
8, PARK MANSIONS ARCADE, S.W.

PRESIDENT - MRS. CECIL CHAPMAN.

WAR RELIEF WORKROOM REPORT
JULY, 1915.

COMMITTEE.
Chairman :
MRS. FREDERICK KERR.

Secretary :	*Hon. Treasurer* :
MRS. K. P. COLLINS.	MISS JESSIE G. GREEN.
MRS. CHARLES.	MISS GLOAG.
MRS. DUNSMURE.	MISS WAKE.
MRS. FLEMING BAXTER.	MISS WRIGHT.
MRS. EVANS.	

Kate was still secretary of the New Constitutional Society when its 1915 Annual Report was published.

it up with his guns.'

Although Kate makes no mention of the labours of her former colleagues, from 1916 the NCS contributed more to the suffrage cause than merely the holding of uplifting meetings. Represented by Mrs Chapman and Miss McGowan it was one of the groups that comprised the Consultative Committee of the Women's Constitutional Suffrage Societies, formed in response to the government's proposal to make changes to the electoral register at the end of the war. The Consultative Committee's aim – to ensure that women were included in the revised electorate – was successfully realised in the 1918 Representation of the People Act that gave the vote to women over the age of 30.

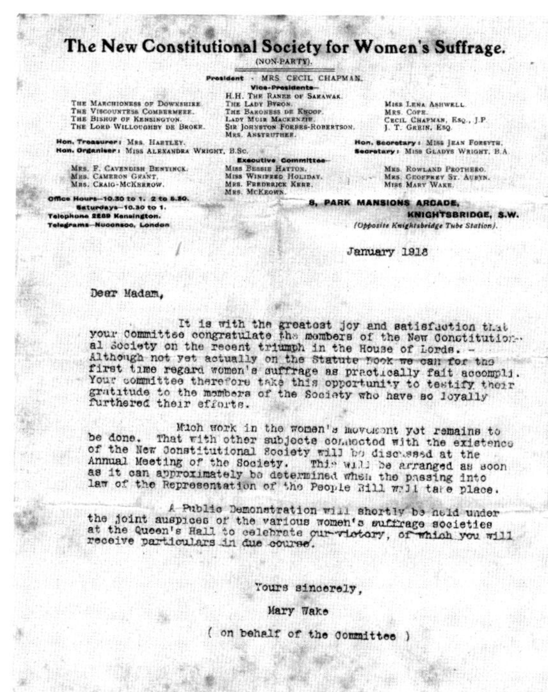

The New Constitutional Society for Women's Suffrage.
(NON-PARTY).

President - MRS CECIL CHAPMAN.

Vice-Presidents—
H.H. The Ranee of Sarawak.
The Marchioness of Downshire. The Lady Byron. Miss Lena Ashwell.
The Viscountess Combermere. The Baroness de Knoop. Mrs. Cope.
The Bishop of Kensington. Lady Muir Mackenzie. Cecil Chapman, Esq., J.P.
The Lord Willoughby de Broke. Sir Johnston Forbes-Robertson. J. T. Grein, Esq.
Mrs. Anstruther.

Hon. Treasurer: Mrs. Hartley. **Hon. Secretary:** Miss Jean Forsyth.
Hon. Organiser: Miss Alexandra Wright, B.Sc. **Secretary:** Miss Gladys Wright, B.A.

Executive Committee—
Mrs. F. Cavendish Bentinck. Miss Bessie Hatton. Mrs. Rowland Prothero.
Mrs. Cameron Grant. Miss Winifred Holiday. Mrs. Geoffrey St. Aubyn.
Mrs. Craig-McKerrow. Mrs. Frederick Kerr. Miss Mary Wake.
Mrs. McKeown.

Office Hours—10.30 to 1. 2 to 5.30.
Saturdays—10.30 to 1.
Telephone 2289 Kensington.
Telegrams—Nuconsoc, London

8, PARK MANSIONS ARCADE,
KNIGHTSBRIDGE, S.W.
(Opposite Knightsbridge Tube Station).

January 1918

Dear Madam,

It is with the greatest joy and satisfaction that your Committee congratulate the members of the New Constitutional Society on the recent triumph in the House of Lords. - Although not yet actually on the Statute Book we can for the first time regard women's suffrage as practically fait accompli. Your committee therefore take this opportunity to testify their gratitude to the members of the Society who have so loyally furthered their efforts.

Much work in the women's movement yet remains to be done. That with other subjects connected with the existence of the New Constitutional Society will be discussed at the Annual Meeting of the Society. This will be arranged as soon as it can approximately be determined when the passing into law of the Representation of the People Bill will take place.

A Public Demonstration will shortly be held under the joint auspices of the various women's suffrage societies at the Queen's Hall to celebrate our victory, of which you will receive particulars in due course.

Yours sincerely,

Mary Wake

(on behalf of the Committee)

Wednesday, February 7th 1918 – Berghers Hill: The Heights

A day of excitement. It felt like someone's birthday, a personal affair – but in truth it was the birthday of a great new era. The *Daily Telegraph* unusually early, with the announcement of the passing into law of the Franchise Bill and 'Votes for Women'. I had to do something to celebrate so I wrote as gracefully as I could to Mrs Cecil Chapman acknowledging her share in the movement and her leadership of the NCS. Also to Alexandra.

Sunday, February 10th 1918 – Berghers Hill: The Heights

One of my afternoon letters was to Gladys Simmons [née Wright] in commemoration of the passing of the Franchise Bill. Haven't had a single letter from anyone concerning it – I said I wouldn't but it seems very strange – that someone hasn't though of me in connection with the work.

Wednesday, June 5th 1918 – Berghers Hill: The Heights/London: 27 Pembridge Crescent

We [Kate and Alexandra Wright] started for the meeting about 3 – Mrs Kerr's, 27 Hereford Square – the NCS for WS last meeting to meet Mrs Cecil Chapman and disband the Society. It all seemed rather sad but I saw nothing else for it, especially as Mrs Chapman was not willing to continue as the head if the society was reformed on other lines. We have got the Vote – the work of the society is done. It was very interesting seeing and talking to old friends – Mrs Chapman, Mrs Hartley, Miss Green, Mrs Hele Shaw, who I did enjoy seeing again, also to my great joy Mrs Wilson of Dover. Everyone was so nice and had quite a welcome for me. We were almost the last to leave.

The first election at which newly enfranchised women – and men – were eligible to vote was held in December 1918. It is known as the 'Coupon Election' because a 'coupon' – an endorsement – was given by the Lloyd George and Bonar Law Liberal/Conservative coalition government to candidates from both parties who had their approval. The majority of those Liberals who continued to support Asquith did not receive the 'coupon' and were routed. The MP for Berghers Hill, a Coalition Conservative, was not opposed.

SATURDAY, 14 DECEMBER 1918 – BERGHERS HILL: THE HEIGHTS

The General Election and women for the first time going to the Polls. Such a sell – no Contest here.

SUNDAY, 29TH DECEMBER 1918 – BERGHERS HILL: THE HEIGHTS

It is simply wonderful a majority of 248 for the Coalition Government – and Asquith and practically all his wretched set of followers out. And Ramsay Macdonald, Philip Snowden and company equally routed and magnificent majorities over them. It was good reading.

Kate was delighted when, at the 1924 general election, she was at last able to cast a vote. As, at this time, she and John were still able to maintain a flat in London, she voted in North Kensington. Percy Gates, the Conservative candidate, was elected MP to the seat once held, as a Liberal, by Kate's father.

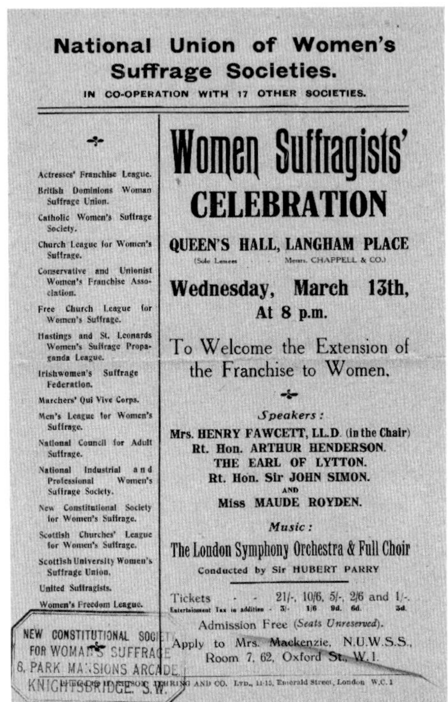

National Union of Women's Suffrage Societies.

IN CO-OPERATION WITH 17 OTHER SOCIETIES.

Actresses' Franchise League.
British Dominions Woman Suffrage Union.
Catholic Women's Suffrage Society.
Church League for Women's Suffrage.
Conservative and Unionist Women's Franchise Association.
Free Church League for Women's Suffrage.
Hastings and St. Leonards Women's Suffrage Propaganda League.
Irishwomen's Suffrage Federation.
Marchers' Qui Vive Corps.
Men's League for Women's Suffrage.
National Council for Adult Suffrage.
National Industrial and Professional Women's Suffrage Society.
New Constitutional Society for Women's Suffrage.
Scottish Churches' League for Women's Suffrage.
Scottish University Women's Suffrage Union.
United Suffragists.
Women's Freedom League.

Women Suffragists' CELEBRATION

QUEEN'S HALL, LANGHAM PLACE
(Sole Lessees - - Messrs. CHAPPELL & CO.)

Wednesday, March 13th, At 8 p.m.

To Welcome the Extension of the Franchise to Women.

Speakers:
Mrs. HENRY FAWCETT, LL.D. (in the Chair)
Rt. Hon. ARTHUR HENDERSON.
THE EARL OF LYTTON.
Rt. Hon. Sir JOHN SIMON.
AND
Miss MAUDE ROYDEN.

Music:
The London Symphony Orchestra & Full Choir
Conducted by Sir HUBERT PARRY

Tickets - - 21/-, 10/6, 5/-, 2/6 and 1/-.
Entertainment Tax in addition - 3/- 1/6 9d. 6d. 3d.

Admission Free (*Seats Unreserved*).

Apply to Mrs. Mackenzie, N.U.W.S.S., Room 7, 62, Oxford St., W.1.

NEW CONSTITUTIONAL SOCIETY FOR WOMAN'S SUFFRAGE
6, PARK MANSIONS ARCADE.
KNIGHTSBRIDGE. S.W.

... AND CO. LTD., 11-15, Emerald Street, London W.C.1

Top: Although she kept this flyer, Kate did not attend the 13 March celebration

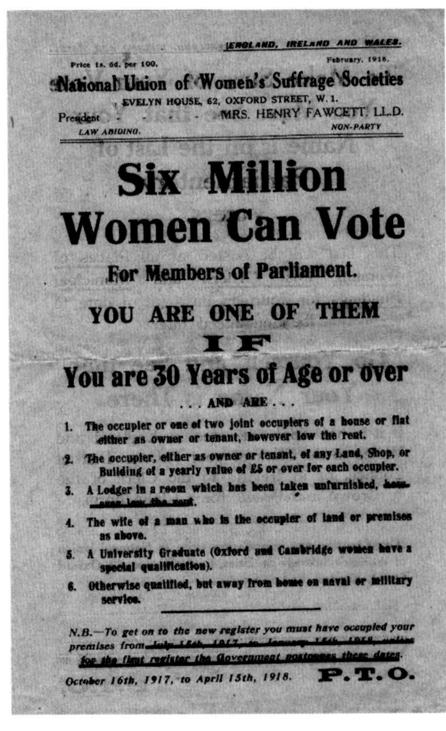

ENGLAND, IRELAND AND WALES.

Price 1s. 6d. per 100. February, 1918.

National Union of Women's Suffrage Societies

EVELYN HOUSE, 62, OXFORD STREET, W.1.

President - - - - MRS. HENRY FAWCETT, LL.D.

LAW ABIDING. NON-PARTY

Six Million Women Can Vote

For Members of Parliament.

YOU ARE ONE OF THEM

IF

You are 30 Years of Age or over

... AND ARE ...

1. The occupier or one of two joint occupiers of a house or flat either as owner or tenant, however low the rent.
2. The occupier, either as owner or tenant, of any Land, Shop, or Building of a yearly value of £5 or over for each occupier.
3. A Lodger in a room which has been taken unfurnished, ~~however low the rent~~.
4. The wife of a man who is the occupier of land or premises as above.
5. A University Graduate (Oxford and Cambridge women have a special qualification).
6. Otherwise qualified, but away from home on naval or military service.

N.B.—To get on to the new register you must have occupied your premises from ~~July 15th, 1917, to January 15th, 1918, unless for the first register the Government postpones these dates~~.

October 16th, 1917, to April 15th, 1918. **P.T.O.**

Bottom: Although the vote had been won, the struggle continued – to ensure that it was used.

Top: The Equal Rights March in Hyde Park, 3 July 1926, snapped by John Collins.

Bottom: Mrs Pankhurst addressing the Equal Rights Demonstration from the Six Point Group platform.

WEDNESDAY, 29 OCTOBER 1924 – LONDON: FLAT F, 13 COLVILLE SQUARE

Polling day. I was thankful to have something definite to go out for. Elections seem somehow in my blood – I don't feel at all comfortable while they are going on. I was not up very early but did some sewing on my fur coat before having some Bovril at 1 o'clock and at 1.30 off to the Free Library in Ladbroke Grove to vote for Mr Percy Gates. Much relish in voting – but little in recording a vote for Mr Gates. It is a straight fight this year – Conservative & Labour.

Two years later Kate and John watched – but did not take part in – one last suffrage procession. Named the 'Equal Rights Procession', it was an element in the campaign to persuade the government to give votes to women at 21 – and for peeresses in their own right to be given a seat, voice and vote in the House of Lords.

SATURDAY, JULY 3RD 1926 – LONDON: FLAT C, 57 LEINSTER SQUARE

[After lunch] changed, off with J[ohn] – bus to Marble Arch and walked to Hyde Park Corner. Sat a little then saw the procession of women for Equal franchise rights and to the various meetings and groups. Heard Mrs Pankhurst and she was quite delightful. Also saw Ada Moore – getting very old. Saw Mrs Despard 82 and walked all the way. And the Actresses' Franchise League.

Kate's involvement with the women's suffrage campaign ended, perhaps fittingly, with her attendance at the funeral of the woman who had done so much to publicise it.

FRIDAY, JUNE 15TH 1928 – LONDON: FLAT C, 57 LEINSTER SQUARE

Mrs Pankhurst is dead – she died yesterday in London – for several days there have been bulletins. I am very grieved she is no more. I feel I should like to be present at her funeral.

MONDAY, JUNE 18TH 1928 – LONDON: FLAT C, 57 LEINSTER SQUARE

Cloudy and a cold wind but the rain kept off. Two buses to Westminster and to St John's Church Smith Square. Had no ticket but being very early before 10 – I was let in up in the Gallery of the Church and sat over the Chancel and in front of Mrs Pankhurst's Coffin. The flowers were marvellous – most beautiful. A wonderful service but very sad – sad in itself and to see & feel us all so old and grey and ill. A bus to

Brompton Cemetery an enormous crowd there. Followed the Coffin and saw the end – then got away.

Kate made no mention in her diary of the passing, on 2 July, of the Representation of the People (Equal Franchise) Act by which votes were finally given to women on the same terms as men. A chapter in her life had closed.

Notes

1. See, for instance, the manuscript prison diaries of Mary Anne Rawle, Elsie Duval and Katie Gliddon (Women's Library); that of Olive Walton and Florence Haig (Museum of London); that of Olive Wharry (British Library) and that of Anne Cobden Sanderson (London School of Economics). Other manuscript diaries recording their authors' involvement with the suffrage movement include: those of the Blathwayt family – mother, father and daughter (held in the Gloucestershire Record Office); that of the Women's Freedom League speaker Eunice Murray (held in the Women's Library, together with a bound copy of the Diary of Eunice Guthrie Murray, transcribed by Frances Sylvia Martin); that of Dr Alice Ker (held in a private collection); that kept by Margery Lees during the 1913 NUWSS Pilgrimage (Women's Library) and that of Elizabeth Robins, the actress (held in the Fales Library, New York). Diaries and letters of Ruth Slate and Eva Slawson, edited by T. Thompson as *Dear Girl: the diaries and letters of two working women* (1897–1917), Women's Press, 1987, give a flavour of life in the Women's Freedom League.
2. The suffrage element in Kate's diary is paralleled by another item from her surviving archive, the formal 'Organiser's Report Book' that she kept between 25 April 1912 and 28 July 1914. In this she gives full details of her daily work – the halls she inspected and the cost of hiring them, the methods she used to obtain names for canvassing, the areas covered, the letters she wrote, the printers she visited and the cost of posters and flyers, the chairmen she sought, and the members she made for the NCS. The Women's Library holds only the NCS's first three Annual Reports and a couple of flyers. There is no record of any other material relating to the NCS in any other British archive. It would appear that all the society's records were destroyed when it disbanded in June 1918.
3. F. Thurber, *Coffee: from plantation to cup*, American Grocer Publishing Co., 1881, pp 408–11 gives a brilliant and exhaustive description of a Leverett and Frye shop – that at 119 Gloucester Road, Regent's Park, London. Thurber mentions the 'most tastefully dressed' window displays, one of which was devoted to the 'bottled wines of Messrs. W. and A. Gilbey', and describes in detail the firm's method of business. After the demise of the English business, Leverett and Frye continued to operate a chain of stores in Ireland, of which, in the 1950s, Terry Wogan's father was general manager.
4. A Waugh, *Merchants of Wine: being a centenary account of the fortunes of the House of Gilbey*, Cassell & Co., 1957, p. 23.
5. The fate of Leverett and Frye Ltd may be traced through the papers held in the National Archives (BT 31/15406/41658). When founded in 1894 most of the 29 shareholders were the grocers who managed Leverett & Frye shops, although W. & A. Gilbey held the majority of the shares. In 1894 Leverett & Frye, described in the article of incorporation as 'retail grocer, provision merchant, tea dealer and wine and spirit merchant', had 24 premises in London, 4 in Hampshire and 9 in (southern) Ireland.
6. It may have been that this branch of the Gilbey family was undergoing some financial crisis of its own. Although Kate makes no mention of it, the whole Wooburn House Estate had been put up for sale, to be auctioned by Hampton and Sons on 30 July 1912 (see advertisements in *The Times*, 6, 13 & 20 July 1912). It would appear that only one small freehold, worth £150, was sold. A couple of weeks previously, on 13 July 1912, The Plat, together with two adjoining properties, for both of which Frye appears to have held the leases, was offered for auction at a 'Peremptory Sale'. Again, on this occasion only a small plot of land was sold. The Plat was finally sold at auction a year later, on 26 June 1913.
7. Katharine Parry and John R. Collins, *Cease Fire*, French's Acting Editions, 1921. Many of the typescripts of the unpublished plays survive in Kate's archive.
8. Actor manager Ben Greet had founded this, the first acting academy, in Bedford Street, Covent Garden, in 1896.
9. Diary entry for 20 September 1904. The play was *Thoroughbred* by Ralph Lumley, produced by John Collins and Edward Coventry, which toured, at a loss, throughout England, Ireland and Scotland.
10. A tour organised by Archie Parnell and Alfred Zeitlin Ltd.
11. Agnes and her mother lived at The Old Cottage. Kate and John lived for a time at The Heights, a house owned by the Gilbeys, and then at Hilltop.

12. Kate gives this description of the bookcase on the day she acquired it, 8 October 1908.
13. Entry for 18 September 1913.
14. Mary Lowndes' design for the North Kensington banner can be viewed at the Women's Library (2ASL/11/77).
15. Notice of the formation of the NCS. The Women's Library (2LSW/E/15/02/11).
16. See E. Crawford, *The Women's Suffrage Movement: a reference guide*, Routledge, 1999, p.478.
17. For instance on the copy of the programme held in the Women's Library (2LSW/E/15/02/11).

Sources and bibliography

Websites

www.ancestry.co.uk

www.findmypast.co.uk

www.historicaldirectories.org

Oxford Dictionary of National Biography – accessed through the London Library

www.visionofbritain.org.uk

Who Was Who Online – accessed through the London Library

Archives

Buckinghamshire Archives

Colindale Newspaper Library

Kensington and Chelsea Local Studies Collection

London Metropolitan Archives

National Archives

The Women's Library

Westminster Archives

Newspapers

Bucks Free Press, Eastern Daily Press, The Common Cause, The Daily Mirror, The Suffragette, The Times, The Vote, Votes for Women

Bibliography

Adams, E. (ed), *Westbourne Grove in wealth, work and welfare*, Gloucester Court Reminiscence Group, 2000

A.J.R. (ed), *The Suffrage Annual and Women's Who's Who*, Stanley Paul, 1913

Bunkers, S. and Huff, C., *Inscribing the Daily: critical essays on women's diaries*, University of Massachusetts Press, 1996

Cockin, K., *Edith Craig (1869–1947): dramatic lives*, Cassell, 1998

Cowman, K., *Women of the Right Spirit – paid organisers of the Women's Social and Political Union (WSPU)*, Manchester University Press, 2007

Crawford, E., *The Women's Suffrage Movement: a reference guide*, Routledge, 1999

Crawford, E., *The Women's Suffrage Movement: a regional survey*, Routledge, 2002

Davis, T., *Economics of the British Stage*, Cambridge University Press, 2000

Easedown, M. and Sage, L., *Hythe: a history*, Phillimore, 2004

Eustance, C., Ryan, J., and Ugolini, L. (eds) *A Suffrage Reader: charting directions in British Suffrage History*, Leicester University Press, 2000

John, A., *Elizabeth Robins: staging a life*, Routledge, 1995

John, A., *Evelyn Sharp: rebel woman*, Manchester University Press, 2009

Kidd, J., *Gilbeys, Wine and Horses*, Lutterworth, 1997

Moore, E., *Exits and Entrances*, Chapman and Hall, 1923

Nevill, A., *The Story of Folkestone*, Antony Rowe, 2009

Norton, B., *The Story of East Dereham*, Phillimore, 1994

Stratman, L., *Whiteley's Folly: the life and death of a salesman*, Sutton, 2004

Thompson, T., (ed), *Dear Girl: the diaries and letters of two working women (1897–1917)*, Women's Press, 1987

Thurber, F., *Coffee: from plantation to cup. A brief history of coffee production and consumption*, American Grocer Publishing Co., 1881

Waugh, A., *Merchants of Wine: being a centenary account of the fortunes of the House of Gilbey*, Cassell & Co., 1957

Wheals, B.B., *Theirs Were but Human Hearts: a local history of three Thameside parishes – Wooburn, Little Marlow and Hedsor*, H.S. Pub., 1984

Index